Max-Planck-Institut für ausländisches
öffentliches Recht und Völkerrecht

Beiträge zum ausländischen öffentlichen Recht und Völkerrecht

Begründet von Viktor Bruns

Herausgegeben von
Armin von Bogdandy · Rüdiger Wolfrum

Band 194

Rüdiger Wolfrum · Volker Röben (eds.)

Legitimacy in International Law

Springer
the language of science

ISBN 978-3-540-77763-2 Springer Berlin · Heidelberg · New York

e-ISBN 978-3-540-77764-9 DOI 10.1007/978-3-540-77764-9

Beiträge zum ausländischen öffentlichen Recht und Völkerrecht ISSN 0172-4770

Bibliografische Information der Deutschen Nationalbibliothek
Die Deutsche Nationalbibliothek verzeichnet diese Publikation in der Deutschen Nationalbibliografie; detaillierte bibliografische Daten sind im Internet über http://dnb.d-nb.de abrufbar.

Herstellung: LE-TEX Jelonek, Schmidt & Vöckler GbR, Leipzig
Einbandgestaltung: WMX Design GmbH, Heidelberg

Gedruckt auf säurefreiem Papier

9 8 7 6 5 4 3 2 1

springer.com

Table of Contents

* The reports by Hanspeter Neuhold, Volker Röben and Kong Qingjiang were submitted after the symposium took place and thus did not form part of the discussion.

Legitimacy of International Law from a Legal Perspective: Some Introductory Considerations

Rüdiger Wolfrum

I. Introduction – on Legitimacy in International Law in General

This Seminar is and is meant to be a continuation of the Conference in November 2003 on Developments of International Law in Treaty Making.[1] The issue of the legitimacy of new forms of international law-making was touched upon, but it was not in the focus either of the Conference or of the individual contributions. This Seminar should equally be seen as a continuation of the "American-European Dialogue: Different Perceptions of International Law"[2] Workshop since it is the question of the legitimacy of international law which is at the roots of such different perceptions.[3]

Before we deal with the legitimacy of particular international law measures as envisaged in the programme of this Seminar it is advisable for this Introduction to put the issue in a broader context, or in other

---

1 R. Wolfrum/V. Röben (eds.), *Developments of International Law in Treaty Making*, 2005.

2 See the publication of the contributions in *ZaöRV* 64 (2004), 255 et seq.

3 See R. Wolfrum, "Introduction of the Workshop", note 2, at 255; H. Neuhold, "Law and Force in International Relations – European and American Positions", note 2, 263, T. M. Franck, "The Power of Legitimacy and the Legitimacy of Power: International Law in an Age of Power Disequilibrium", *AJIL* 100 (2006), 88 at 90 et seq.; F. Fukuyama, *State Building: Governance and World Order in the Twenty-First Century*, 2004, at 142 et seq.

words to touch upon the question of legitimacy of international law in general. Actually this question has to be subdivided into two, namely whether it is appropriate at all to raise the question of legitimacy in international law and, if the answer is in the affirmative, what does legitimacy mean in the context of international law and where does it lead to.

In recent years the question of the legitimacy of international law has been discussed quite intensively.[4] The focus of the questions raised varies considerably. Only some of those questions will be mentioned here. Such questions are, for example, whether international law lacks legitimacy in general; whether international law or parts of it has yielded to the facts of power; whether adherence to international legal commitments should be subordinated to self-defined national interests; whether international law or particular rules of it, such as the prohibition of the use of armed force, have lost their power to induce compliance (compliance pull);[5] and what the relevance of non-enforcement or failure to obey is for the legitimacy of that particular international norm?

The fact that seemingly identical questions concerning the legitimacy of international law or parts of it are being raised sometimes camouflages the fact that their authors represent different approaches towards international law and thus pursue different objectives. Although this may be considered an over-simplification, four such schools of thought will be identified and addressed here.

One school of thought argues that international law lacks legitimacy – at least if compared with the legitimacy of national democratic governance – and therefore that less authoritative weight should be given to international law.[6] This school of thought, which actually may be per-

---

4 Amongst others, T. M. Franck, *The Power of Legitimacy among Nations*, 1990; M. Kumm, "The Legitimacy of International Law: A Constitutionalist Framework of Analysis", *EJIL* 15 (2004), 907; J. L. Goldsmith/E. A. Posner, *The Limits of International Law*, 2005; A. Buchanan, *Justice Legitimacy, and Self-Determination: Moral Foundations for International Law*, 2004; H. L. Hart, *The Concept of Law*, 1961; Franck, note 3, 88.

5 Franck, note 3, at 93.

6 E. A. Young, "The Trouble with Global Constitutionalism", *Texas International Law Journal* 38 (2003), 527 at 544; Goldsmith/Posner, note 4, at 13; M. J. Glennon, *Limits of Law, Prerogatives of Power: Interventionism after Kosovo*, 2001, at 84; J. Rabkin, *Law Without Nations? Why Constitutional Government Requires Sovereign States*, 2005, at 69-70, for whom the potential dan-

ceived as reviving ideas voiced by Carl Schmitt[7] and his school, seems to be driven by the consideration that international law is to be seen from the perspective of national law or national interests. The Carl Schmitt school's view of international relations is State-centred, international law being perceived as directly controlled by each individual State.[8]

Another school of thought seems to argue that, as a result of global developments, international institutions should be remodelled with a view to increasing or even establishing their legitimacy to meet the new global challenges by setting up organs which may exercise parliamen-

---

ger seems to lie in the authoritarian potential for people to begin to follow an international system that is not backed by a democratic constitutional structure.

[7] Nationalsozialismus und Völkerrecht [1934], in: Carl Schmitt, Frieden oder Pazifismus, Arbeiten zum Völkerrecht und zur internationalen Politik, edited by Günther Maschke, 2005, 391-421. He says: „Die innerstaatliche Ordnung ist Grundlage und Voraussetzung der zwischenstaatlichen Ordnung, jene strahlt in diese aus, und es gibt überhaupt keine zwischenstaatliche Ordnung ohne innerstaatliche Ordnung." (The internal normative order is the basis and the precondition of any normative order among States. The former influences the latter and an international normative order cannot exist without an internal one). This statement is introduced by the assertion that internal political changes in a State (the reference is to Germany and the German people) result in changes of the international legal community (*Völkerrechtsgemeinschaft*).

[8] For example, John H. Herz, "The National Socialist Doctrine of International Law and the Problems of International Organization", *Political Science Quarterly* 54 (1939), 536 at 539 summarizes the National Socialist doctrine as to reduce "international law to an ensemble of rules belonging exclusively to the German order of law. For Germany international law is only the law concerning its external relations which has been recognized by Germany and has been incorporated in its municipal law; its validity depends upon this incorporation and exists as long as this recognition lasts, for the competence of the national state cannot be limited by any norm binding its sovereign will" (references omitted). He emphasized that, in particular, Carl Schmitt argued strongly against the attempt to juridify international life and to over-emphasize law in international relations (at 548, referring to Nationalsozialismus und Völkerrecht, note 7, at 396). Certainly the philosophical starting point of Carl Schmitt and of modern critics of international law is a different one but the result is similar, namely that the relevance of international law to guide State conduct in international relations is given limited weight, if any weight at all, and that national interests, however formulated and motivated, should prevail.

tary and governmental functions[9] or by increasing the influence of NGOs.[10] This development is being seen as the institutional consequence of globalization. The objectives pursued by both schools of thought are diametrically opposed, since the former is concerned with the protection of the autonomy of democratically elected governments to act as required by State interests (at least as they perceive such interests), whereas the latter intends to replace or to supplement national governments by democratically legitimate world institutions. Nevertheless, they coincide at one point. Both have in common that they consider the legitimacy of international law from the point of view of the democratic legitimacy of national governance.[11] Whether or to what extent this starting point is appropriate for international law is open to challenge.

One may identify two further schools of thought. One raises the question of the legitimacy of international law with a view to enhancing the acceptability of the latter. This school is not concerned with the establishment of new international institutions but rather with adapting the traditional means of the development of norms and their content (determinacy, symbolic validation, coherence and adherence) to the needs of a globalized world.[12] The second school of thought in this context which, considering modern normative developments in international

---

[9] R. Falk/A. Strauss, "On The Creation Of A Global Peoples Assembly: Legitimacy And The Power Of Popular Sovereignty", *Stanford Journal of International Law* 36 (2000), 191; R. Falk/A. Strauss, "Towards Global Parliament", *Foreign Affairs,* Jan.-Feb. 2001; G. Teubner, "Globale Zivilverfassungen: Alternativen zu staatszentrierten Verfassungstheorien", *ZaöRV* 63 (2003), 1.

[10] P. Spiro, "Accounting for NGOs", *Chicago Journal of International Law* 3 (2002), 161; in detail S. Charnovitz, "Nongovernmental Organizations and International Law", *AJIL* 100 (2006), 348, who also discusses under which circumstances the input of NGOs may have a legitimizing effect (at 366 et seq.). See also R.O. Keohane/J.S. Nye Jr., "The Club Model of Multilateral Cooperation and Problems of Democratic Legitimacy", in: Robert B. Porter (ed.), *Efficiency, Equity, and Legitimacy: Multilateral Trading System at the Millennium*, 2001, 264 at 282.

[11] The term 'governance' as used in the context of this contribution means to embrace all forms of processes by which authority – not necessarily public authority – is being exercised; see World Bank, *Governance: The World Bank's Experience*, 1994, at XIV; different Christoph Möllers, "European Governance: Meaning and Value of a Concept", *Common Market Law Review* 43 (2006), 313 at 314 et seq.

[12] Franck, note 3, at 93 et seq.; references to Franck are frequent.

law as a form of international governance, advocates strengthening the national parliamentarian influence on the conduct of international relations which is traditionally thought to be the domain of governments. This approach is inspired by the consideration that international law has reached – at least in part – a different quality which may be referred to as international governance.[13] It perceives that governance, undertaken on whichever level, requires legitimacy.

The two latter approaches sketched out here start from the same point of view, namely that certain parts of international law may have a legitimacy deficit. They seek to cure this deficit at different levels, though. Whereas the first school of thought intends to improve the mechanisms of international law, the second attempts to strengthen the national legitimacy chain. The approaches advocated by these two schools of thought are not necessarily mutually exclusive; they assess and approach an identified problem from different sides and thus may complement each other.

The following contribution will deal with two issues, thus hoping to contribute to the current discussion. The contribution will briefly summarize the reasons why it is possible to speak of the development of international governance, and thus why the quest of legitimacy of international law has become an issue. This is done without questioning the relevance of international law as law. On this basis the contribution will discuss to what extent proceeding from a model of legitimacy as developed over the centuries for democratic national governance is adequate for international law.[14]

---

[13] Amongst others R. Wolfrum, "Kontrolle auswärtiger Gewalt", *VVDStRL* 56 (1997), 38, with further references.

[14] Critical in this respect J. H. H. Weiler, "The Geology of International Law – Governance, Democracy and Legitimacy", *ZaöRV* 64 (2004), 547 at 548, and M. Reisman, "The Democratization of Contemporary International Law-Making Processes and the Differentiation and Their Application", in: R. Wolfrum/V. Röben (eds.), note 1, 15.

II. Legitimacy and Public International Law Based on State Consent

1. On Legitimacy in General

The term legitimacy is being used differently, although it mostly means to refer to the justification of authority, this notion being understood as the equivalent of having the power to take binding decisions or to prescribe binding rules. Such decisions or rules may be general or specific in nature; this distinction may be of relevance for their legitimacy.

Different approaches to the elements which may induce legitimacy of a particular authority are discussed. Theoretically they may be source-, procedure- or result-oriented or a combination thereof.[15]

Authority can be legitimated by its source of origin. For public international law legitimacy rests – at least according to the traditional view – in the consent of the States concerned. According to this view international law is based upon the assumption that States have the ability to negotiate and to adhere to international agreements. By doing so they accept obligations *vis-à-vis* the other partners to that agreement or *vis-à-vis* a larger community. They also have the ability to commit themselves unilaterally.

Authority can also be legitimized if the decisions in question are taken in the course of procedures considered to be adequate or fair.[16] Rules concerning the composition or establishment of an institution and its rules concerning decision-making processes are to be seen from this point of view. Procedure, or rather adhering to a pre-agreed procedure, thus has a legitimising effect in international law as it has in national law.[17] In this respect we must mention that legitimacy may also depend on who participates in the decision-making process. For example, when professional judges consider expert opinions in their decision-making process this may increase the objective legitimacy of a judgment,

---

[15] For details see R.A. Posner, *The Problematics of Moral and Legal Theory*, 1999, 90 et seq.; on input and output legitimacy see F. Scharpf, *Regieren in Europa, Effektiv und demokratisch?*, 1999, 16-28.

[16] T. Franck, note 3, emphasizes the 'right process' (at 91); D. A. Wirth, "Reexamining Decision-Making Processes in International Environmental Law", *Iowa Law Review* 79 (1994), 769 at 798, points out that procedural integrity in itself is an important source of legitimacy for international law.

[17] N. Luhmann, *Legitimation durch Verfahren*, 2nd ed., 1989.

whereas opening up proceedings to allow interested third parties to participate by way of amicus curiae briefs may increase the subjective legitimacy of a decision.

Finally, it has been argued that authority can be legitimated or delegitimated by the outcome it produces. This is a crucial issue and one which deserves further consideration. If a particular body, such as the Security Council or an international court or tribunal, although established in accordance with the applicable rules and taking decisions according to the established procedure does not achieve results which the community as the addressee of such decisions considers to be adequate, this may, in the long run, lead to an erosion of its legitimacy. The fate of the UN Human Rights Commission is an example to this extent. Political dissatisfaction with the UN Human Rights Commission has led to the establishment of the Human Rights Council whose composition is different from that of the former Human Rights Commission. It is, in this context, of particular relevance that a member of the Human Rights Council may be expelled if it significantly and systematically violates internationally protected human rights. However, having said that, it cannot and does not mean that the legitimacy of an international body should be judged merely according to whether its decisions are considered to be satisfactory by a State, a group of States or a community to which they are addressed.

2. Legitimization through Consent by States

A discussion on legitimacy in international law should proceed from international treaties as the main source of international law. International treaty law is developed on a consensual basis. States representatives negotiate international rules which are subsequently adopted by the national institutions in a procedure designed by national law. Thus, it is for national law to ensure that there is a chain of legitimacy justifying the implementation of the ensuing international obligations through national institutions. As a matter of principle it is safe to say that – as far as consent-based international law is concerned – the legitimacy of the consequential implementation is to be established through nationally imposed mechanisms.

This raises a generic question, namely how such chain of legitimacy may be established where some of the participating States are not democratically structured. Does this mean that the international law in question lacks legitimacy for that reason and that one has to distinguish between international law as agreed among democratic States and other international law? This issue has been raised by some of those authors who question the legitimacy of international law and its legal relevance for the conduct of international relations.[18] From the point of view of international law several arguments may be advanced to challenge such an approach. Although one may identify an increasing tendency in international law to induce States to establish a democratic national structure by providing for democratic elections and to abide by the rule of law, international law does not provide automatic sanctions against States that are organized on a different basis. The more powerful argument against the view that international law lacks legitimacy if it results from an agreement with non-democratic States is that this would, as a result, jeopardize the possibility to influence such States through international law, for example, with a view to their adopting democratic governmental structures or adhering to international human rights standards. Finally, it must be pointed out that the lack of democratic legitimacy of one or more partners to an international agreement puts into question the implementation of such agreement in those countries, but not the substance of the international agreement as such.

The situation of customary international law is different depending upon what is considered the legitimizing source of customary international law. If customary international law is understood as a tacit agreement by the States concerned,[19] then its ultimate source is the consent of States. The situation is more complex if one considers the source of customary international law to be the fictitious consent of States.[20] It is, however, still possible under this approach to base customary international law upon voluntary acts of States which they undertake in the awareness of their implications for the possible development of customary international law.

---

[18] See the authors referred to in note 6 and also A. Buchanan/R.O. Keohane, The Legitimacy of Global Governance Institutions, in this volume, 25 at 38.

[19] G. Tunkin, *Theory of International Law*, 1974, at 123; see on this C. Tomuschat, "The Complementarity of International Treaty Law, Customary International Law, and Non-Contractual Lawmaking", in: R. Wolfrum/V. Röben (eds.), note 1, 401 at 405; according to Goldsmith/Posner, note 4, at 26, customary international law should be seen as behavioural regularities that emerge when States pursue their interests on the international stage.

[20] E. Suy, *Les actes juridiques unilatéraux en droit international public*, 1962, at 245 et seq.; B. Simma, *Das Reziprozitätselement in der Entstehung von Völkergewohnheitsrecht*, 1970, at 39 et seq.

When State consent is considered as legitimizing international legal commitments it is not always realised that such commitments may have differing meanings, which again influences the scope of consent. The consent of States can have specific and static meaning namely to refer to a particular clearly defined obligation and a more general or dynamic meaning referring to the establishment of a regime or a system of governance which – having been set up by consent – develops a legal life of its own, such as by formulating obligations.[21] The essential difference rests in the following: specific and static State obligations are honoured by one act or by preserving a particular situation; the obligation does not change over time. In contrast a general and dynamic commitment embraces a mandate for the established international body through which the substance and scope of the original obligation may be modified. These two options are not as clearly distinct as one may assume. They merge into one another at the edges. However, both options raise different questions concerning the legitimizing effect of State consent.

The consent of a State will undoubtedly be sufficient as a mechanism to invoke the legitimacy of the measure in question if the obligation is a specific and static one and can be implemented by an isolated act or omission. The same is true even if the obligation is of a continuing nature but the commitment does not change over time as far as its substance and scope is concerned. There is, de facto, the danger, though, that the legitimizing effect of the original consent may fade over time. This would be particularly true if, due to changing circumstances, the burden of implementing a given obligation increased significantly. Nevertheless, international law proceeds from the assumption that the establishment of continuous obligations is possible by a single original consent. The mechanism for re-establishing legitimacy if such obligation has changed over time and has thus become illegitimate is either through renunciation of or withdrawal from the obligation in question or having recourse to the *clausula rebus sic stantibus*. In particular the latter is intended, within some limits, to re-adjust continuing legal obligations to the equilibrium originally envisaged by the partners.[22] Another such mechanism is the review process provided for by an increasing number of international agreements.

---

[21] D. Bodansky, "The Legitimacy of International Governance", *AJIL* 93 (1999), 596 at 604.

[22] See G. Dahm/J. Delbrück/R. Wolfrum, *Völkerrecht*, Bd I/3, 2nd ed. 2002, at 743.

3. Consent, an Adequate Form of Legitimization of International Governance?

It is widely accepted that international law has changed in recent decades as far as its scope and its impact on national law, its addressees, the procedures through which international norms are being created and the value system upon which public international law is being based are concerned.[23]

Considering this factual situation it has been argued that – at least in some respects – international law has developed into some form of international governance which makes it necessary to reconsider its legitimacy.[24] If States have indeed agreed to establish regimes or systems of international governance endowed with quasi-legislative or adjudicative competences this constitutes a challenge to the legitimizing effects of the original consent through which the regime or system was set up.[25] The cases one may truly speak of international governance, to be compared with national governance, are rare.[26]

This neither abolishes the problem set out above nor ameliorates it, though. Apart from the few cases in which international institutions have been endowed with truly legislative functions, international law has developed subtle forms of establishing norms or influencing the national administrations efficiently, although perhaps not directly.[27] Finally, a growing number of international adjudicative bodies have recently been developed, the decisions of some of which directly affect individuals. For example, an adjudicative system has been developed under the world trade regime, whereas the WTO has neither legisla-

---

[23] See amongst others C. Tomuschat, "International Law: Ensuring the Survival of Mankind on the Eve of a New Century, General Course in Public International Law", *Recueil des Cours* 281 (1999), 10 at 63 et seq.; B. Fassbender, "Der Schutz der Menschenrechte als zentraler Inhalt des völkerrechtlichen Gemeinwohls", *Europäische Grundrechte-Zeitschrift* 30 (2003), 1 at 2 et seq.

[24] See for example V. V. Heiskanen, "Introduction", in: J.-M. Coicaud/V. Heiskanen (eds), *The Legitimacy of International Organizations*, 2001, 1 et seq.

[25] Weiler, note 14, at 557 et seq.

[26] A detailed analysis has recently been provided by J. Alvarez, *International Organizations as Law-Makers*, 2005, at 184 et seq.

[27] See, in particular, the examples provided by J. Alvarez, note 26, at 217 et seq.

tive[28] nor executive functions outside the realm of WTO. The legitimacy of the WTO has also been put into question.[29]

The reasons advanced are not necessarily identical; they may be rooted in a broad perception of the need for legitimacy or a broad understanding of what constitutes governance, or both.

But apart from these instances which exercise functions which at least in part resemble national governance, concerns about a legitimacy deficit have been raised with regard to international organizations in general because they affect the welfare of people in general and the chains of delegation between citizens and agents of global governance are too attenuated.[30]

The divergent views about legitimacy in international law or – more appropriately – about when and why the legitimacy of international law may be challenged make it necessary to deal in greater depth with the question of which forms of international governance require legitimization. Otherwise the danger exists that the notion of legitimacy will become a mechanism for denying the relevance of international law in all those cases where short-term national interests seem to recommend such an approach.

It is commonly acknowledged that international law increasingly supplements legal norms which used to have a national basis. However, this does not amount to governance in the sense used in respect of govern-

---

[28] Critical in this respect A. von Bogdandy, "Law and Politics in the WTO – Strategies to Cope with a Deficient Relationship", *Max Planck UNYB* 5 (2001), 609 at 618 with further references.

[29] R.O. Keohane/J.S. Nye, *The Club Model of Multilateral Cooperation and the WTO: Problems of Democratic Legitimacy*, Harvard University Center for Business and Government www.ksg.harvard.edu/cbg; A. von Bogdandy, "Verfassungsrechtliche Dimension der Welthandelsorganisation", *Kritische Justiz* 34 (2001), 247 at 267; id., "Legitimacy of International Economic Governance: Interpretative Approaches to WTO law and the Prospects of its Proceduralization", in: S. Giller (ed.), *International Economic Governance and Non-Economic Concerns: New Challenges for the International Legal Order, European Community Studies Association of Austria*, vol. 5 (2005), 103. At 106 it is stated: "From the static perspective, the drawback can be found in the fact that, although national (and consequently democratic) sovereignty is formally respected, the content of the rules is determined in intergovernmental negotiations. An open public discourse that can influence the rules, an essential element for democratic legitimacy according to most theories, is severely limited."

[30] Buchanan/Keohane, note 18, at 38 et seq.

ance exercised by States. Firstly international law has a sectoral approach compared to the general competences exercised by States.[31] Secondly international law supplements national law on the level of norm-setting, whereas the execution of such norms in general rests with States. Even the exercise of adjudicative functions on the international level is the exception. In spite of these differences the fact remains that States are increasingly bound by international norms. Hence referring to this as 'international governance' and requesting matching legitimization must mean seeking a legitimization which, in form and content, reflects the nature of international governance as well as interaction between State governments and the relevant international institutions.

In what follows some examples will be given to illustrate the increased scope of international law, modifications concerning addressees and in respect of the procedure for developing international norms. It is certainly a question whether and to what extent they meet the sustainability test concerning legitimacy by means of the original consent.

It is a fact that international law increasingly affects or even regulates areas which traditionally belonged to the realm of national law. This is particularly true for human rights issues, environmental law, economic law and even issues concerning national governance. The relevant international rules leave national governments only limited leeway as far as norm-setting is concerned. As an example one may refer to some more recent national constitutions which have even incorporated international human rights regimes in their totality.[32] Therefore one may say that the notion of 'domaine reservé' as referred to in Article 2, paragraph 7, UN Charter has lost, if not all, at least much of its traditional meaning.[33] There are very few legal issues left which may be considered

---

[31] J. Steffek, "Sources of Legitimacy Beyond the State: A View from International Relations", in: I-J. Sand/G. Teubner (eds.), *Transnational Governance and Constitutionalism*, 2004, 81 at 90.

[32] Interim National Constitution of the Republic of the Sudan, Republic of Sudan Gazette, Special Supplement no. 1722, 10 July 2005. This does not mean to say that the human rights situation in Sudan yet reflects international human rights standards. The incorporation of the international human rights instruments is rather to be seen as a reaction to the prevailing human rights situation.

[33] For a detailed analysis see G. Nolte, "Article 2 (7), MN 23 et seq.", in: B. Simma (ed.), *The Charter of the United Nations*, 2nd ed. 2002; somewhat less sceptical of the continuing meaning of Article 2(7) UN Charter G. Guillaume, "Commentaire, Article 2(7), para. 14 et seq.", in: J.-P. Cot/A. Pellet, *La Charte des Nations Unies*, 3ième édition, 2005.

to be absolutely immune to being influenced by international law. Although the international rules in question have to be implemented at national level, these rules are the outcome of an international process and reflect the will of an international body rather than that of a legislature representing the will of the people of a particular State.[34] This is not necessarily a consequence of globalization,[35] although this phenomenon has not only accelerated this process but also opened up additional areas for international regulation.[36] That international law increasingly limits the competences of States is particularly true for economic law, where international law increasingly prescribes to what extent national borders have to be permeable. The erosion of national competences as far as the protection of human rights is concerned; the protection of the environment or how to govern international commons has a somewhat different origin, although the underlying motive and the effects on national autonomy are structurally the same.

As already indicated international law increasingly addresses individuals directly or indirectly. The most recent example is Security Council Resolution S/RES/1672 (2006), 25 April 2006 in which sanctions were adopted and States were obliged to implement such sanctions. In this respect States are being transformed into enforcement agencies of the Security Council. It would not be fully correct to say that traditional international law addressed only States and had no impact on individuals, be it a positive or a negative one, except as a legal reflex. The *ius in bello* has always directly addressed individuals by either providing protection for certain groups (prisoners of war, wounded and shipwrecked, or civilians) or by limiting the means of waging war. The jurisprudence of the two international military tribunals after the Second World War reflects this, although the prosecution of war criminals dates back far further. This trend has been taken up again and strengthened by the es-

---

[34] D. Thürer, "Völkerrecht und Landesrecht – Thesen zu einer theoretischen Problemumschreibung", *Schweizerische Zeitschrift für Internationales und Europäisches Recht* 9 (1999), 217 et seq.; Buchanan/Keohane, note 18, at 33, take this as an argument for their assessment that democratic legitimization on the national level cannot balance the influence of the international bureaucracy.

[35] As to the notion of globalization and its effect on international law see, for example, A. von Bogdandy, "Globalization and Europe: How to Square Democracy, Globalization, and International Law", *EJIL* 15 (2004), 885 at 888 et seq.

[36] Kumm, note 4, at 913, seems to take a different position; Heiskanen, note 24, at 1, speaks of these issues being lumped together by the term globalization.

tablishment of the two ad hoc criminal courts and the establishment of mixed criminal courts and now the ICC. Another area in which international law addresses individuals is the regime concerning the protection of minorities. The protection of individuals which, to a certain extent, builds upon this has reached a further dimension after the Second World War; it has been broadened and institutionally consolidated. Reference is made in this respect to the universal and regional international human rights regimes, in particular the regional human rights courts. However, this development of international law into benefiting or obliging individuals has also affected economic law as evidenced by the jurisprudence of the various arbitral tribunals on investment disputes. International law also addresses corporations. This development is but a matter of consequence. Multinational corporations cross national borders and thus have to become addressees of international law or even partners to international organisations.[37]

As far as the procedure of norm-setting is concerned international law is now being progressively developed not only by international agreements but by other more flexible means.[38] In particular, international environmental law has made use of the mechanism that international treaties may be developed further by decisions of Meetings of States Parties. The international treaties in question mandate the Meeting of States Parties progressively to develop norms within their frameworks. The norms resulting therefrom are not merely of a technical nature but often constitute either additional obligations for States or even individuals or corporations or they accelerate the implementation of obligations already taken. For example, the Montreal Protocol on Substances that Deplete the Ozone Layer provides that controls on such substances may be tightened by a qualified majority vote.[39] The decision in question subjects the minority to the majority will since such adjustment measures are binding upon all parties to the Montreal Protocol. Certainly such norms have to be implemented in national law but the States have no discretion in that respect. Here again they act more like implementing agencies. Even Meetings of States Parties not endowed

---

[37] See A. Seibert-Fohr/R. Wolfrum, "Die einzelstaatliche Durchsetzung von Mindeststandards gegenüber transnationalen Unternehmen", *Archiv des Völkerrechts* 43 (2005), 153.

[38] Wolfrum/Röben, note 1.

[39] Article 2, para. 9; further examples are being provided for by G. Handl, "International "Lawmaking" by Conferences of the Parties and Other Politically Mandated Bodies", in: Wolfrum/Röben (eds.), note 1, 127.

with competences similar to that of the Montreal Protocol are beginning to develop policies for the progressive development of the treaty regime they are working under. For example, the Meeting of States Parties of the Convention on the Law of the Sea not only elects the judges to the International Tribunal for the Law of the Sea and decides on the budget of that Tribunal and the International Seabed Authority but also formulates policies in respect of marine law and policy. Certainly such policies can only be implemented through additional instruments the development of which depends upon the consent of States. Nevertheless such policy decisions of Meetings of States Parties result in a preformulation which may have a significant prejudicial effect on subsequent treaty law.

Further, international organisations have progressively developed their mandates by re-interpreting or adapting them to new situations; the new security strategy of NATO, for example, was the result of such development.[40] The legality of this strategy was, from the point of view of the prerogatives of the German Bundestag on accession to international treaties, challenged before the German Federal Constitutional Court.[41] The Court held that the original consent given by the German Bundestag also covered later tacit modifications. From the position advanced by Buchanan/Keohane,[42] namely that legitimacy must reflect the continuing consent of States in respect of the dynamic character of global institutions this decision is to be deplored.

The UN Security Council, referring to another example, not only interpreted its mandate broadly but also assumed new functions. Making use of its power under Chapter VII of the UN Charter, it has acted in at least two cases as an international legislator, against terrorism and against the proliferation of weapons of mass destruction, respectively.[43]

---

40 NATO Press Release NAC S(99)65, 24 April 2004.

41 Decisions of the German Federal Constitutional Court (BVerfG), vol. 104, 151.

42 Note 18 at 36.

43 S/RES 1373 (2001) 28 September 2001; S/Res. 1540 (2004), 28 April 2004, reaffirmed by S/RES 1673 (2006) 27 April 2006 in which States are reminded under Chapter VII UN Charter of their obligation to implement the obligations established by S/RES 1540; see in this respect the contribution of E. de Wet, "The Legitimacy of United Nations Security Council Decisions in the Fight against Terrorism and the Proliferation of Weapons of Mass Destruction: Some Critical Remarks", in this volume, p. 131 et seq.; G. Abi-Saab, "The Security Council as Legislator and as Executive in its Fight Against Terrorism and

The establishment of the two *ad hoc* criminal tribunals may also be qualified as acts of norm setting. Although law-making by the Security Council is undertaken in a process which is no different from that used in the process of taking Security Council decisions in general, and although the distinction between applying law and legislation is a gradual one,[44] it is evident that the decisions of the Security Council referred to have reached a different level. They are based on an interpretation of its mandate under Chapter VII of the UN Charter, which gives a broad meaning to the notion of 'threat to peace'. What transcends the traditional interpretation of Article 39 UN Charter are two things, namely that not only States but also groups of individuals may be considered a threat to international peace and that not only isolated incidents but also general situations may also qualify as such and trigger actions by the Security Council. Accordingly the decisions in question deal with a general situation and require States to take action not only to deal with a particular incident but to enact national legislation to face the general problem, namely terrorism and proliferation of weapons of mass destruction. This raises the question to be discussed in depth in the Seminar: whether the original consent of States expressed when ratifying the UN Charter constitutes an adequate mechanism to induce legitimacy. In dealing with this question one should consider whether States are reduced by such resolutions as S/RES 1673 to mere implementing agencies.

The examples given in respect of NATO and the Security Council are only indicative of a trend as far as the functioning of international organisations is concerned. This trend has resulted in strengthening the functions of international organisations as regards their member States. Certainly they remain derived institutions created by the will of national governments and acting under their control, and none of them has yet reached the independence of the European Union with an equally broad mandate. Such control of international organisations rests, though, with the national governments, whereas national democratic legitimacy is based upon, at least in principle, the people's consent. Even if the democratic character of many member States is taken into account as well as their democratic values, the connection between people and international organisations remains a mediated and remote one.

Against Proliferation of Weapons of Mass Destruction: The Question of Legitimacy", in this volume, p. 109 et seq.

[44] R. Higgins, *The Development of International Law through Political Organs of the United Nations*, 1963, at 5.

The broadening of the mandate of international organisations, combined with a more effective decision-making process and, in particular, the strengthening of their secretariats, results in an enhanced independence of such organisations, at the same time weakening the ability of governments to control them although their collective control is not put into question.[45] Even if one cannot speak of international governance in the strict meaning of the word, the legitimizing effect of the original State consent to the establishment of the international organizations in question and the involvement of State officials in the organs of those organizations may not be considered adequate to cover the new developments.

Examples of institutions which may assume greater responsibility somewhat detached from States are also treaty bodies, such as the Human Rights Committee established by the International Covenant on Civil and Political Rights. Their mandate is to monitor the implementation of an international agreement. Part of their mandate is also to provide for an interpretation of the provisions of the instrument whose implementation they monitor through General Comments or General Recommendations, respectively. Although it is a matter of discussion to what extent such interpretation is authentic and whether it may be considered as binding upon the parties to the relevant instrument it certainly carries considerable weight. The contribution of such General Comments or Recommendations should not be underestimated. For example, the US government criticized in harsh terms[46] the General Comment of the Human Rights Committee[47] on article 2, paragraph 1 of the International Covenant on Civil and Political Rights and the way in which the Group of Rapporteurs of the Commission on Human Rights had made use of it in its assessment of the prisoners at Guan-

---

[45] Weiler, note 14, at 550 refers to further examples. He states: "The regulatory regime is often associated with a bureaucratic apparatus, with international civil servants, and, critically, with mid-level State officials as interlocutors. Regulatory regimes have a far greater "direct" and "indirect" effect on individuals, markets and more directly if not always visible as human rights, come into conflict with national social values."

[46] Reply of the Government of the United States of America to the Report of the five UNCHR Special Rapporteurs on Detainees in Guantanamo. 10 March 2006 (available at http://www.asil.org/pdfs/ilib0603212.pdf).

[47] Human Rights Committee, General Comment No. 3 (2004), CCPR/C2/Rev.1/Add.13, para. 10.

tanamo Bay.[48] Leaving aside this criticism and concentrating on the generic problem it can hardly be denied that the influence of these bodies has increased. This raises the question whether the composition of such bodies, in particular the mode of election of their members, is adequate from the point of view of improving the legitimacy of their activities.

Further, it should be mentioned in this context that groups of experts or practitioners may contribute to the development of the body of international law. The *lex mercatoria* may serve as just one example.[49] An example from a different area of international law may further underline this point. The Commission on the Limits of the Continental Shelf – a body composed of experts – established pursuant to Annex II of the Convention on the Law of the Sea is mandated to assist coastal States in defining the limits of the outer continental shelf. The limits established in accordance with the recommendations of the Commission are final and binding.[50] This means norm-setting *erga omnes* in what may be qualified as a discourse between a State and an international group of experts. What should be mentioned in this context, too, is that only States Parties to the Convention on the Law of the Sea may benefit from this process. States which have refrained from joining the Convention have no means of claiming an outer limit to their continental shelf which will be recognized by the international community.

Finally, the establishment of new institutions on the settlement of international disputes, the revival of existing ones and the creation of new mechanisms for monitoring the implementation of international obligations is to be mentioned in this context. Such international courts, tribunals or compliance committees not only apply the relevant instrument *stricto sensu* but also add explicitly or implicitly to the understanding of the norm in question. Taking into consideration that international law, treaty law as well as customary international law, is by its very nature less concrete, the contribution of these institutions to the corpus of international law should not be underestimated. There is a trend for individuals to take an increasingly prominent role in international dispute settlement. This role was already well established in the context of investment disputes, but it is beginning to permeate the arrangements for international dispute settlement in international trade. The most noticeable contemporary step in providing direct access of

---

48 Situation of detainees at Guantanamo Bay E/CN.4/2006/120.

49 See F. Galgano, *Lex mercatoria*, 2001.

50 Article 76, paragraph 8, of the UN Convention on the Law of the Sea.

individuals to international dispute settlement procedures was provided for by the 1965 Convention on the Settlement of Investment Disputes between States and Nationals of Other States.[51] This international agreement makes arbitration and conciliation procedures available to foreign investors, and thus restrains them from having recourse to the traditional means of diplomatic protection.[52] This, in effect, minimizes state intervention in international disputes and underlines the individual's own responsibility in protecting its rights *vis-à-vis* other States. The system of settling disputes between individuals and States has been further developed under the regime of NAFTA and the EU.

The last three examples (treaty bodies, expert groups and international courts and tribunals) have one element in common. They are all composed of experts, the term being understood as 'a person of particular experience or knowledge' which has been recognized internationally. Is this factor, combined with the fact that they are elected for a limited period only by a clearly defined group of States, sufficient to induce the legitimacy of their impact on the formation of international law in general or in specific cases? If the answer is in the affirmative the use of experts could become an additional element inducing legitimacy.

4. Is there a Legitimacy Deficit for Some Areas of International Law and if so for What Reason?

Three trends may be identified in the actual development of international law: As far as the creation of norms is concerned a factual shift of competences from the national to an international level can be witnessed. It is perhaps imperative to acknowledge that such a 'shift of competences' is of a different nature compared to the shift of competences from the state to the federal level as provided by the constitution of a federal state. Nevertheless, such a shift is a reality as, for example, the WTO regime proves. According to that States may nationally introduce restrictions upon the freedom of trade in goods only if the conditions under article XX GATT are met. This shift may be characterized by the terms denationalization in favour of internationalization

[51] For the current status of ICSID Convention, Regulations and Rules see: http//www/worldbank.org/icsid/basicdoc.htm.

[52] F. Orrego Vicuña, *International Dispute Settlement in an Evolving Global Society: Constitutionalization, Accessibility, Privatization*, 2004, at 64 et seq.

and departiamentarisation in favour of strengthening the role of the executive. Another trend is that increasingly individuals, including corporations, have become addressees of international law. Finally, the role of the judicial settlement of legal disputes has been strengthened in this respect. What is common to all these new trends is that the direct influence of national governments, and even more so of the national legislature, on the shaping of international law in general or international law decisions has been reduced and the chain of legitimacy towards the people has been further weakened.

Do these changes in international law suggest that it is no longer sufficient to base it on the legitimacy of consensual obligations as was for long considered sufficient?[53] Is it now necessary for international law to meet the test of legitimacy modelled on democratic principles?[54]

It has to be accepted that in some areas international law has mutated into what may be qualified as international governance, to be compared with governance on the national level.[55] In respect of these areas – and only these areas – it is necessary to inquire into the legitimacy of the rules and decisions which result therefrom. Recourse to the legitimacy as provided for by the original consent of the States concerned does not seem to be sufficient for them. In all the cases referred to the original consent seems to be too attenuated to provide an unproblematic basis for legitimacy. There is one further problem to be taken into account. Negotiations undertaken to establish international institutions entrusted with or by their very nature capable of assuming governance functions on the international level, as well as the ensuing deliberations within these institutions, are undertaken by representatives of the executive. Therefore, transferring legislative competences to the international level by setting up such international institutions results not only in the denationalization of legal issues but equally in their deparliamentarization.[56] Looking more closely one has to acknowledge that the legitimacy deficit has different roots. Whereas in respect of international agreements which have received parliamentary approval but which are

---

[53] On this critical issue cf. Buchanan/Keohane, note 18, at 35 et seq.

[54] Critical in respect of the legitimizing impact of democratic procedure E. de Wet, note 43, 136.

[55] Weiler, note 14, at 550.

[56] It is particularly for this reason that F. Orrego Vicuña, "In Memory of Triepel and Anzilotti: The Use and Abuse of Non-Conventional Law-Making", in: Wolfrum/Röben (eds.), note 1, 497 at 506 warned of the possible misuse of the non-traditional forms of international law-making.

developed without such involvement of parliament the problems rests in the fact that the original parliamentary consent does not cover further developments, the situation in respect of international law originating from international organizations is different. Here one can hardly speak of parliaments having approved such norms.

The lack of legitimacy results from the fact that the original consent by States, including the involvement of the legislature, is conceived so as to endorse nationally concrete and static rather than general and dynamic commitments.

Although the national executive is meant to be in control of international organizations and other international bodies the influence of each single state executive is in fact limited. This is due to several factors: the growing influence of an international bureaucracy, the complexity of the subject-matter and the fact that the norm-creating process in such international organizations and bodies lacks transparency. The ensuing negative consequences for legitimacy in the original sense is intensified by the fact that the influence on the progressive development of the international norms in question is subtle and takes place in forms which do not make it necessary or even possible to involve the legislature.

This latter aspect is evident in particular when international organisations are broadening their functions through a wide interpretation of the original mandate.[57] Furthermore, there are few effective accountability mechanisms in place which could help strengthen legitimacy.

Finally, one has to accept that more international law directly addresses individuals – this includes cases where States have to implement the measures in question, are obliged to do so without having discretionary power in this respect and act like implementation agencies of the relevant international body.

III. Whether and How to Fill the Gaps in Legitimacy: Tentative Conclusions

It is necessary clearly to distinguish between situations where there is no gap in legitimacy concerning international law and where the issue of legitimacy of international law is invoked only as a Trojan horse to

---

57 See J.E. Alvarez, "Constitutional interpretation in international organizations", in: Coicaud/Heiskanen, note 18, at 104 et seq.

put the relevance of international law in question. This is the case, for example, in respect of all treaty-based international obligations where the ensuing obligation is a static one. The bulk of international treaty law would fall into this category, for example such classical international treaties as the Vienna Convention on the Law of Treaties, the Vienna Convention on Diplomatic Relations and even the Geneva Conventions for the Amelioration of the Condition of the Wounded and Sick in Armed Forces in the Field, for the Amelioration of the Condition of Wounded, Sick and Shipwrecked Members of Armed Forces at Sea, relative to the Treatment of Prisoners of War and relative to the Protection of Civilian Persons in Time of War, including the two Additional Protocols.

In comparison thereto a legitimacy gap may develop in respect of those instruments which are designed to be progressively developed, for example, through additional instruments which do not require parliamentary consent or more informally through meetings of States parties. International organizations may also fall into this category. However, whether or not a legitimacy deficit exists cannot be decided on an abstract basis, but only after a concrete assessment of each single case.

A legitimacy gap can be filled either on the international or on the national level or on both. There does not seem to be just one remedy.

It is doubtful whether it is necessary, possible or even advisable to attempt to invoke the democratization of international law in general.[58] First of all international governance has, hitherto, been an isolated phenomenon, although the trend is increasing. Apart from that it is incorrect to say that international law is lacking legitimacy in general. Improving the legitimacy of international governance should aim to find solutions within the existing matrix of international law; State consent and the national procedure establishing the legitimacy of international commitments reflect the fact that law is increasingly being developed and implemented on different levels. Implementation rests with the States as it rests with them to contribute the necessary legitimacy.

If there is agreement that the gap in the legitimacy chain can be identified to be at the link between the international and national levels it should be discussed which efforts are to be undertaken to reinforce this link or – in other words – to make this link commensurate with the governmental authority exercised on the international level. Such need arises in all cases where legislative measures or individual acts are taken

---

[58] Pointedly Weiler, note 14, at 552 and 560 et seq.

on the international level which replace otherwise possible equivalent legislative measures or decisions at national level. The consent, including the consequential approval of the competent national institutions as the major source of legitimacy, is to be construed in a way that covers the international commitment in its short as well as long term consequences.

There are multiple options which may be chosen to achieve that objective at national level. They cannot be identified and assessed in this contribution. They would all require the strengthening of the impact on and control of the legislature of the conduct of foreign relations. This could be undertaken in such a way as to cover international relations in general, thus reflecting the fact that the conduct of foreign relations – due to the changed circumstances – is the joint responsibility of the executive and the legislature.

Another option would be to provide for the legislature to have a qualified impact on the establishment of international organisations or fora likely to assume functions of international governance. In this context it is worth discussing, too, whether and to what extent non-governmental organizations may play a positive role in establishing legitimacy in respect of acts of international governance.

Additional approaches are to be sought on the international level. One central element is to strengthen the legal legitimacy of measures deriving from international governance, legal legitimacy being understood as the obligation to keep strictly within the frame of the original mandate. This refers to the option of inducing legitimacy through procedure. This would mean that as a matter of self-restraint the institution in question, be it the Security Council, an international organization or a Meeting of States Parties, does not attempt to broaden its mandate, and that it follows the procedures set out for decision-making. The logical consequence of enforcing legal legitimacy would be to strengthen the possibility of judicial review. This would be a matter of consequence considering the functions international governance is assuming. If international institutions are taking over governance tasks equivalent to those of national institutions and – one should add – to the detriment of the latter they should come under the same restrictions as national governance in States adhering to the principle of the rule of law. If, for example, the Security Council assumes legislative competences or even competences affecting the rights of individuals directly such increase in power calls for a counter-balance through judicial review on the international level.[59]

What is however important is to reconsider legitimacy in the context of international law. Is it really appropriate to copy from national constitutional law? International law has developed its own value system. It should be considered whether the new forms of international governance have their roots in the will of an international community united by such system[60] and gain their legitimacy by conforming to such values.

Finally it may be worth exploring whether the involvement of internationally recognized experts constitutes another additional mechanism of inducing legitimacy. This mechanism is the one followed by human rights treaty bodies and, more pointedly, by the Legal and Technical Commission of the International Seabed Authority. Although this Commission formally has merely consultative functions as far as the review of formal written plans is concerned, such recommendation may be overturned by the Council only by a qualified majority. When assessing international law in this respect one has to realize that recourse to expert opinions plays a significant role in international law. The composition of international courts or tribunals as well as the composition of the Appellate Body of the WTO may be seen from this perspective. Perhaps it is time to develop a systematic approach in this respect which, in particular, should also clarify how such experts are to be identified, the role of the national legislature and the correlation between expert advice and decisions to be taken on the national level.

---

[59] From this perspective the establishment of an international constitutional court as discussed by F. Orrego Vicuña, note 45, at 10 et seq. deserves further consideration.

[60] Critical Fukuyama, note 3, at 155 et seq.

The Legitimacy of Global Governance Institutions

*Allen Buchanan and Robert O. Keohane** **

'Legitimacy' has both a normative and a sociological meaning. To say that an institution is legitimate in the normative sense is to assert that it has *the right to rule* – where ruling is promulgating rules and attempting to secure compliance with them by attaching costs to noncompliance and/or benefits to compliance. Ruling in this broad sense does not require that the rules be backed by coercion, much less that the rule-maker claims a rightful monopoly on coercion within a jurisdiction, so it does not presuppose the state. Later we will see that the notion of the right to rule is subject to stronger and weaker interpretations, but for now it will suffice to say that an institution is legitimate in the sociological sense when it is widely *believed* to have the right to rule.[1] When

---

* This article originally appeared in Ethics & International Affairs 20, no. 4 (2006), pp. 405-437. It is reprinted here with the permission of the Carnegie Council for Ethics in International Affairs.

** Authors' note: The authors are grateful to Sahar Akhtar, Thomas Christiano, Michael Doyle, Nicole Hassoun, Nan Keohane, Avery Kolers, Joseph S. Nye, John Tasioulas and an anonymous referee for their helpful comments on earlier versions of this paper, and to William Alford, Ryan Goodman and Gerald L. Neuman for valuable criticisms and suggestions when such a version was presented at Harvard Law School, November 3, 2005. We are particularly grateful to comments by Charles Beitz and a number of other colleagues made at a workshop on the normative and empirical evaluation of global governance, Princeton University, February 17-18, 2006.

1 Fritz Scharpf points out that such a belief may be based on the processes used by the institution, which he denotes as "input legitimacy," or on the results achieved, "output legitimacy." See *Governing in Europe: Effective and*

people disagree over whether the WTO is legitimate, they are not disagreeing about whether they or others *believe* that institution has the right to rule; they are disagreeing about whether it *has* the right to rule.

For many students of international relations during the Cold War, imbued with the emphasis on interests of both realism and rationalism, legitimacy was not terribly important: foreign policy interests trumped such ideas.[2] Since the end of the Cold War, however, legitimacy has increasingly become a concern of students of world politics. Indeed, legitimacy has been the focus of both scholarly and policy debates, both on issues of military intervention[3] and on the *institutional legitimacy* of global governance institutions mandated to provide a measure of global governance. This paper is concerned with the normative dimensions of such institutional legitimacy: under what conditions should global governance institutions be considered legitimate?[4]

Democratic? Oxford: Oxford University Press, 1999. In our view, as will become clear below, both processes and outcomes are important.

2 The concept of legitimacy does not play a major role in leading Realist works on world politics during the Cold War. See Hans J. Morgenthau, *Politics Among Nations: The Struggle for Power and Peace,* fourth edition (New York: Alfred A. Knopf, 1967), Kenneth N. Waltz, *Theory of International Politics* (Reading, Massachusetts: Addison-Wesley, 1979), and Robert Gilpin, *War and Change in World Politics* (Cambridge: Cambridge University Press, 1981). A major exception to the generalization that issues of legitimacy were overlooked during the Cold War is Inis L. Claude, "Collective legitimation as a political function of the United Nations," *International Organization* 20:3 (1966), pp. 367-79. The English School of international relations theory, led by Martin Wight and Hedley Bull, constitutes another exception. For a contemporary English School analysis of legitimacy, see Ian Clark, *Legitimacy in International Society* (Oxford: Oxford University Press, 2005).

3 See the special issue of the *Review of International Studies,* volume 31, (December 2005), edited by David Armstrong and Theo Farrell, "Force and legitimacy in world politics," the discussion in Independent International Commission on Kosovo, *Kosovo Report* (Oxford: Oxford University Press, 2000), and especially *A More Secure World: Our Shared Responsibility,* Report of the High-Level Panel on Threats, Challenges and Change. United Nations General Assembly document A/59/565, 29 November 2004, paragraphs 204-209.

4 Ian Hurd has argued that legitimacy is an important means of social control, which introduces elements of authority into the "anarchy" of world politics. "Legitimacy and authority in international politics." *International Organization*, vol. 53, no. 2 (spring 1999), p. 399.

Concerns about the legitimacy of global governance institutions have deepened as their powers have grown. 'Global governance institutions' covers a diversity of multilateral entities, including the World Trade Organization (WTO), the International Monetary Fund (IMF), various environmental institutions such as the climate change regime built around the Kyoto Protocol, judges' and regulators' networks, the UN Security Council, and the new International Criminal Court (ICC).[5] These institutions are like governments in that they issue rules and publicly attach significant consequences to compliance or failure to comply with them – and claim the authority to do so. Nonetheless, they are not governments because they do not attempt to perform anything approaching a full range of governmental functions, they do not seek to monopolize the legitimate use of violence within a permanently specified territory, and their major actions require the consent of states.

The legitimacy of global governance institutions matters for several reasons.

First, although they do not control major means of coercion and only rarely attempt to exercise direct authority over individuals, it is difficult to consider them voluntary. For a society to be integrated effectively into the world economy, its government must belong to the WTO, which in turn requires accepting a large number of quite intrusive rules. Poor countries are likely to have great difficulty attracting foreign investment if they defy the IMF or the World Bank. Increasingly, the rules made by and through global governance institutions affect what were formerly regarded as domestic practices, and cannot easily be evaded. Second, some global governance institutions significantly constrain state sovereignty. During the 1990s the United Nations exercised

---

5 A large and growing literature exists on global governance. For a sampling of perspectives, see the following edited collections: Aseem Prakash and Jeffrey A. Hart, eds., *Globalization and Governance* (London: Routledge, 1999); Joseph S. Nye and John D. Donahue, eds., *Governance in a Globalizing World* (Washington: Brookings, 2000); Gary P. Sampson, eds., *The Role of the World Trade Organization in Global Governance* (Tokyo: United Nations University Press, 2001); David Held and Anthony McGrew, eds., *Governing Globalization* (London: Polity Press, 2002); Rorden Wilkinson, ed., *The Global Governance Reader* (London: Routledge, 2005), and David Levi-Faur and Jacint Jordana, eds., "The Rise of Regulatory Capitalism: the Global Diffusion of a New Order," *Annals* of the American Academy of Political and Social Science, volume 598 (March 2005). For a discussion of governmental networks, including judicial networks, see Anne-Marie Slaughter, *A New World Order* (Princeton: Princeton University Press, 2004).

effective rule in East Timor, Bosnia and Kosovo; and the Appellate Body of the World Trade Organization can make judgments binding on members in international law, without their consent. Hence the question arises as to whether such institutions are compatible with the right of self-determination, so far as this right is exercised through the powers of sovereignty. Third, these institutions affect the well-being and opportunities of tens of millions of people, most of whom are at best dimly aware of their existence and know little of their origins and functions. Loan decisions by the World Bank or decisions on resource allocation by the Global Fund to Fight AIDS, Tuberculosis, and Malaria are matters of life and death for people in Africa and Asia. WTO policies on agricultural subsidies and import duties can dramatically affect the welfare of farmers around the world.

In Section I we explain the valuable social function that legitimacy assessments can perform. We argue that legitimacy assessments are not reducible to claims about self-interest, show that justice and legitimacy ought to be kept distinct, and identify the conception of legitimacy that is central for global governance institutions. Finally, we distinguish between the *conception* of legitimacy suitable for global governance institutions and the *standards* such institutions must satisfy to be judged to be legitimate according to that conception. In Section II we consider three widely-discussed standards: state consent, the consent of democratic states, and global democracy. Section III identifies a set of desiderata that a standard for the legitimacy of global governance institutions ought to satisfy and then goes on to propose what we call the Complex Standard and to show how it satisfies the desiderata.

We aim to stake out a middle ground, between an increasingly discredited statist conception of legitimacy and the unrealistic view that legitimacy for these institutions requires the same democratic standards that are now applied to states. Our approach to the problem of legitimacy integrates conceptual analysis and moral reasoning with an appreciation of the fact that global governance institutions are novel, still evolving, and characterized by reasonable disagreement about what standards of justice they should meet. Because both standards and institutions are subject to change as a result of further reflection and action, we do not claim to *discover* the necessary and sufficient conditions for legitimacy through pure conceptual analysis and moral reasoning. Instead, we offer a principled *proposal* for how the legitimacy of these institutions ought to be assessed – for the time being.

I. Assessing Legitimacy

The social function of legitimacy assessments

Global governance institutions are valuable because they create norms and information that enable member states and other actors to coordinate their behavior in mutually beneficial ways. They can reduce transaction costs, create opportunities for states and other actors to demonstrate credibility, thereby overcoming commitment problems, and provide public goods, including rule-based, peaceful resolution of conflicts.[6] However, an institution's ability to perform these valuable functions may depend on whether those to whom it addresses its rules regard them as binding and if others within the institution's domain of operation support or at least do not interfere with its functioning. It is not enough that the relevant actors agree that *some* institution is needed; they must agree that *this* is the institution that is worthy of support. So, for institutions to perform their valuable coordinating functions a higher-order coordination problem must be solved.[7]

Once an institution is in place, on-going support for it and compliance with its rules is sometimes simply a matter of self-interest from the perspective of states, assuming that the institution actually achieves coordination or other benefits that all or at least the more powerful actors regard as valuable.[8] Similarly, once the rule of the road has been established and penalties are in place for violating it, most people will find compliance with it to be rational, from a purely self-interested point of view. In the latter case, no question of legitimacy arises, because the sole function of the institution is coordination and the choice of the particular coordination point raises no issues on which people are likely to disagree. However, although coordination is one of the most important benefits they confer, global governance institutions are not pure coordination devices in the way in which the rule of the road is. Even though all may agree that some institution or other is needed in a specific domain (e.g., the regulation of global trade) and all may agree that

---

6 Robert O. Keohane, *After Hegemony: Cooperation and Discord in the World Political Economy* (Princeton: Princeton University Press, 1984 [20th anniversary edition, 2005]).

7 James D. Fearon, "Bargaining, enforcement, and international cooperation," *International Organization* 52, no. 2 (spring 1998): 269-306.

8 This is a major theme of Russell Hardin, *Liberalism, Constitutionalism, and Democracy* (Oxford: Oxford University Press, 1999).

any particular institution is better than the noninstitutional alternative, different parties, depending upon their differing normative perspectives, will find some feasible institutions more attractive than others. In particular, there may be disagreements about what the distributive effects of a given institution are or ought to be. The fact that all acknowledge that it is in their interest to achieve coordinated support for some institution or other may not be sufficient to assure adequate support for one particular institution.

The concept of legitimacy allows various actors to coordinate their support for institutions by appealing to their common capacity to be moved by what might be called *normative reasons*, as distinct from purely strategic or exclusively self-interested reasons, under conditions in which there is serious and persisting normative disagreement. However, if the concept of legitimacy is to perform its coordinating function, actors must not insist that only institutions that are *optimal* from the standpoint of their own normative views are acceptable, since this would preclude coordinated support in the face of diverging normative views. Similarly, actors must not assume that an institution is worthy of support only if it is *perfectly just*, since this requirement would ensure that in our imperfect world, the needed support would never materialize. To attain the valuable benefits of institutions, therefore, we need a standard of legitimacy that is both accessible from a diversity of normative standpoints and less demanding than justice. The needed evaluative perspective must appeal to various actors' capacities to be moved by normative reasons, but without presupposing more normative agreement than exists.

Legitimacy and Self-Interest

It is one thing to say that an institution promotes one's interests and another to say that it is legitimate. As Andrew Hurrell points out, the rule-following that results from a sense of legitimacy is "distinguishable from purely self-interested or instrumental behaviour on the one hand, and from straightforward imposed or coercive rule on the other."[9] Sometimes self-interest may speak in favor of treating an institution's rules as binding; that is, it can be in one's interest to take the fact that an

[9] Andrew Hurrell, "Legitimacy and the use of force: can the circle be squared?" *Review of International Studies* 31 (special issue, December 2005), p. 16.

institution issues a rule as a weighty reason for complying with it, independently of a positive assessment of the content of particular rules. This would be the case if one is likely to do better, from the standpoint of one's own interest, by taking the rules as binding than one would by evaluating each particular rule as to how complying with it would affect one's interests. But if one's *only* reasons for taking the institution's rules as binding were those of self-interest, it would add nothing to say that the institution is legitimate. Yet clearly it makes sense to ask whether an institution that promotes one's interests is legitimate. So legitimacy, understood as the right to rule, is a normative notion, but not one that reduces to rational self-interest. To say that an institution is legitimate is to imply that it has the right to rule even if its ruling is not in accordance with the best interests of everyone who is subject to its rule.

It is important to achieve coordinated support for institutions on the basis of normative reasons, rather than on the basis of purely self-interested reasons. First, the appeal to normative reasons is instrumentally valuable in securing the benefits that only institutions can provide because, as a matter of psychological fact, normative reasons matter to us when we try to determine what our practical attitude toward particular institutional arrangements should be. For example, we care not only about whether an environmental regulation regime reduces air pollutants and thereby produces benefits for all, but also whether it fairly distributes the costs of the benefits it provides. Given that we disagree as to which institutional arrangement would be optimal, we need to find a shared evaluative perspective that makes it possible for us to achieve the coordinated support required for effective institutions without requiring us to disregard our most basic normative commitments. Second, and perhaps most important, if our support for an institution is based on reasons other than self-interest, it may be more stable, because what is in our self-interest may change as circumstances change. Normative commitments can preserve support in the face of shifting balances of power.

For legitimacy to be an issue in the first place there must be considerable normative disagreement; yet for agreement on legitimacy to occur there must be sufficient agreement on what sorts of considerations count as normative reasons for evaluating the institution in question. The domain of the concept of legitimacy, then, is the space between the thorough-going normative agreement that makes questions of legitimacy otiose and the thorough-going normative disagreement that precludes coordinated support for institutions on any basis other than that of a *modus vivendi*. The concept of legitimacy is grounded in a complex belief, namely, that while it is true that institutions ought to meet standards more demanding than mere mutual benefit (relative to the noninstitutional alternative), they can be worthy of our support even if they do not maximize our own interest and even if they do not measure up to our highest normative standards.[10]

Understanding the social function of legitimacy assessments helps us to identify which concept of legitimacy – which interpretation of the notion of the right to rule – is appropriate. Two alternatives are worth considering. According to the first, weak interpretation, an institution has the right to rule if and only if its agents are morally justified in carrying out their institutional roles. According to the second, stronger interpretation, two additional conditions must be satisfied: those to whom the institution addresses its rules must have content-independent reasons to comply with them, and those within the domain of the institution's operations must have content-independent reasons to support the institution or at least not to interfere with its functioning. Furthermore, in both cases the content-independent reason must be a normative reason: it cannot simply be that one will be subject to the use of force if one does not comply with or support compliance the institution's rules. In other words, the content-independent reasons must be grounded in features of the institution other than its ability to coerce; in that sense, the content-independent reasons must be normative, not coercive.

Our account of the social function of legitimacy assessments suggests that the second, stronger interpretation of the right to rule best captures what is usually at stake in real-world debates about the legitimacy of global governance institutions. When someone asserts or denies that a particular global governance institution is legitimate, part of what is at stake is whether those who occupy key roles in the institution are morally justified in performing the functions attached to those roles, including formulating rules and attempting to ensure that they are complied

---

[10] Legitimacy can also be seen as providing a "focal point" that helps strategic actors select one equilibrium solution among others. For the classic discussion of focal points, see Thomas C. Schelling, *The Strategy of Conflict* (Cambridge: Harvard University Press), chapter 3. For a critique of theories of cooperation on the basis of focal point theory, and an application to the European Union, see Geoffrey Garrett and Barry Weingast, "Ideas, interests and institutions: constructing the European Community's internal market," especially pp. 178-185, in Judith Goldstein and Robert O. Keohane, eds., *Ideas and Foreign Policy* (Ithaca: Cornell University Press, 1993).

with. But that is not all: there is the issue of whether states or other collective entities to which the institution addresses its rules ought to take those rules as binding, independently of a positive assessment of the content of each particular rule. Legitimacy disputes concern not merely what institutional agents are morally permitted to do but also whether those to whom the institution addresses its rules should regard it as authoritative.[11]

There is also the question of whether individuals ought to support their governments when the latter take the rules to be binding or whether individuals may rightly protest their states' compliance with the institution's rules or attempt to sabotage it. The debate about the legitimacy of global governance institutions, then, engages both the perspective of states and that of individuals. Yet, regardless of which perspective is at issue, the key point is that legitimacy assessments focus upon the proper practical attitude toward the institution as a source of rules rather than merely upon whether the institution's agents are morally justified in trying to rule. Legitimacy in the case of global governance institutions, then, is the right to rule, understood to mean both that institutional agents have the moral right to make rules and that people subject to those rules have normative, content-independent reasons to follow them.

We have stressed that agreement on standards for legitimacy can facilitate valuable coordination of support for global governance institutions. However, if it becomes widely understood that an institution does not measure up to the standards, then the result may be lack of coordination, at least until the institution changes to conform to the standards or a new institution that better conforms to them replaces it. Thus it would be misleading to say simply that the function of legitimacy judgments is to achieve coordinated support for institutions; rather, its function is to make possible coordinated support based on normative reasons, while at the same time supplying a critical, but realistic mini-

---

[11] Because there are stronger and weaker senses of 'the right to rule', legitimacy judgments can be ambiguous. In this paper we are concerned with the grounds for asserting that a global governance institution is legitimate, where this conveys more than that the institutional agents have the right to rule in the weak sense, that is, that their attempting to rule is not morally impermissible. An institution can fail to be legitimate (lack the right to rule in the stronger sense) and yet not be illegitimate (not lack the right to rule in the weaker sense, that is, not act impermissibly in attempting to rule). So, given this ambiguity of 'legitimacy', it is a mistake to infer from the statement that an institution is not legitimate that it is illegitimate.

mal normative standard by which to determine whether institutions are *worthy* of support.

Justice and legitimacy

The foregoing account of the social function of legitimacy assessments helps clarify the relationship between justice and legitimacy. Justice is an ideal standard, whereas legitimacy expresses a threshold value, in a non-ideal world, for the conditions under which an institution has the right to rule. Justice and legitimacy are therefore closely related; but collapsing legitimacy into justice confuses a non-ideal with an ideal standard and undermines the valuable social function of legitimacy assessments. There are two reasons not to insist that only just institutions have the right to rule. First, there is sufficient disagreement on what justice requires that such a standard for legitimacy would thwart the eminently reasonable goal of securing coordinated support for valuable institutions on the basis of normative reasons. Second, even if we all agreed on what justice requires, withholding support from institutions because they fail to meet the demands of justice would be self-defeating from the standpoint of justice itself, because progress toward justice requires effective institutions. To mistake legitimacy for justice is to make the best the enemy of the good. Yet if an institution is sufficiently unjust, there will not be sufficient normative reasons to support it, because whatever moral reasons there are for supporting it will be overwhelmed by its extreme injustice. And as we will see, to *remain* legitimate, a global governance institution must provide for continuing deliberation about what global justice requires and how the institution ought to contribute to it.

II. Competing Standards of Legitimacy

So far we have identified the proper conception of legitimacy for application to global governance institutions (the right to rule on the stronger interpretation), explained the circumstances of legitimacy and the social function of legitimacy assessments, argued that legitimacy is not reducible to being in accordance with self-interest or with the ability to coerce, and distinguished between legitimacy and justice. Having explicated our *conception* of legitimacy, we now explore *standards* of legitimacy: the conditions an institution must satisfy in order to have the right to rule. In this section we articulate three candidates for the appropriate standard of legitimacy: state consent, consent by democratic states, and global democracy.

State consent

The legitimacy of policies or laws is often thought to be a matter of pedigree, of whether they came to be through the right sort of process. Similarly, institutions are sometimes said to be legitimate if they were created by the right sort of process, and, more specifically, if they were created by legitimate institutions, the idea being that legitimacy can be transferred, as it were. In international legal scholarship it is often assumed that global governance institutions are legitimate if they are created through state consent. Call this the International Legal Pedigree View (the Pedigree View, for short). If this view were correct, the problem of assessing the legitimacy of these institutions would be easily solved: we would need only to determine whether they were created by states, in accordance with the international law of treaties. A more sophisticated version of the Pedigree View would require the periodic reaffirmation of state consent, on the grounds that states have a legitimate interest in determining whether these institutions are performing as they are supposed to.[12]

The Pedigree view, on both its variants, fails because it is hard to see how state consent could render global governance institutions legitimate, given that many states are nondemocratic and systematically violate the human rights of their citizens and for that reason are themselves illegitimate. State consent in these cases cannot transfer legitimacy for the simple reason that there is no legitimacy to transfer. To assert that state consent, regardless of the character of the state, is sufficient for the legitimacy of global governance institutions is to regress to a conception of international order that failed to impose even the most minimal normative requirements on states. Indeed, once we abandon that deeply defective conception of international order, it is hard to see why state consent is even a *necessary* condition for legitimacy.

---

[12] For a more detailed discussion, see Allen Buchanan, *Justice, Legitimacy and Self-Determination: Moral Foundations for International Law* (Oxford: Oxford University Press, 2003), especially chapter 5.

It might be argued, however, that even though the consent of illegitimate states cannot itself confer legitimacy, there is an important instrumental justification for making state consent a necessary condition for legitimacy: doing so provides a check on the tendency of stronger states to exploit weak ones. In other words, persisting in the fiction that all states – irrespective of whether they respect the basic rights of their own citizens – are moral agents worthy of respect serves an important value. However, this conception of the state, what Charles Beitz calls the Morality of States view, is not a fiction that those who take human rights seriously can consistently accept.

The proponent of state consent might reply as follows: "My proposal is not that we should return to the pernicious fiction of the Morality of States. Instead, it is that we should agree, for good cosmopolitan reasons, to regard a global governance institution as legitimate only if it enjoys the consent of all states." However, withholding legitimacy from global governance institutions, no matter how valuable they are, simply because not all states consent to them would purport to protect weaker states at the expense of giving a legitimacy-veto to tyrannies. The price is too high. Weak states are in a numerical majority in multilateral institutions. They are less threatened by the dominance of powerful states within the institutions than they are by the actions of such powerful states acting outside of institutional constraints.

The consent of democratic states

The idea that state consent confers legitimacy is much more plausible when restricted to democratic states. However, on reflection the mere fact of state consent, even when the state in question is democratic and satisfies whatever other conditions are appropriate for state legitimacy, is not sufficient for legitimacy in the case of global governance institutions.

From the standpoint of a particular weak democratic state, participation in global governance institutions such as the WTO is hardly voluntary, since the state would suffer serious costs by not participating. Yet "substantial" voluntariness is generally thought to be a necessary condition for consent to play a legitimating role.[13] Of course, there may be rea-

[13] For a perceptive discussion of how consent to new international trade rules in the Uruguay Round (1986-94) was merely nominal, since the alternatives for poor countries were so unattractive, see Richard H. Steinberg, "In the

sonable disagreements over what counts as substantial voluntariness, but the vulnerability of individual weak states is serious enough to undercut the view that the consent of democratic states is by itself sufficient for legitimacy.

There is another reason why the consent of democratic states is not sufficient for the legitimacy of global governance institutions: the problem of reconciling democratic values with unavoidable "bureaucratic discretion" that plagues democratic theory at the domestic level looms even larger in the global case. The problem is that for a modern state to function, much of what state agents do will not be subject to democratic decisions and saying that the public has consented in some highly general way to whatever it is that state agents do is clearly inadequate. The difficulty is not in identifying chains of delegation stretching from the individual citizen to state agents; instead, the problem is that at some point the impact of the popular will on how political power is used becomes so attenuated as to be merely nominal. Given how problematic democratic authorization is in the modern state and given that global governance institutions require lengthening the chain of delegation, the assertion that the consent of democratic states is sufficient for the legitimacy of the latter is unconvincing.

Yet even if the consent of democratic states is not sufficient for the legitimacy of global governance institutions, it may appear to be necessary. Indeed, it seems obvious that for such an institution to attempt to impose its rules on democratic states without their consent would violate the right of self-determination of the people of those states. However, matters are not so simple. A democratic people's right of self-determination is not absolute. If the majority persecutes a minority, the fact that it does so through democratic processes does not render the state in question immune to sanctions or even to intervention. One might accommodate this fact by stipulating that a necessary condition for the legitimacy of global governance institutions is that they enjoy the consent of states that are democratic *and* that do a credible job of respecting the rights of all their citizens.

This does not mean that *all* democratic states must consent. A few such states may willfully seek to isolate themselves from global governance (Switzerland only joined the UN in 2002). Furthermore, democratic states may engage in wars that are unnecessary and unjust, and resist

---

shadow of law or power? Consensus-based bargaining and outcomes in the GATT/WTO. *International Organization*, volume 56, no. 2 (spring 2002): 339-374.

pressures from international institutions to desist. It would hardly delegitimize a global governance institution established to constrain unjust warfare that it was opposed by a democratic state that was waging an unjust war For these reasons we cannot simply assume that the consent of all democratic states is an unexceptionable necessary condition for the legitimacy of all global governance institutions. A more reasonable position would be that there is a *presumption* that global governance institutions are illegitimate unless they enjoy the on-going consent of democratic states. The intuitive idea here is that the on-going consent of rights-respecting, democratic states helps to make global governance institutions accountable, by linking them, though indirectly, to publics who can hold their own states accountable. Let us say, then, that on-going consent by rights-respecting democratic states constitutes *the democratic channel* of accountability and that the well-functioning of this channel is generally necessary for legitimacy.[14]

However valuable the democratic channel of accountability is, it is not sufficient, for two reasons. First, not all the people who are affected by global governance institutions are citizens of democratic states, so even if the on-going consent of democratic states fosters accountability, it may not foster accountability to *them.* If – as is the case at present – democratic states tend to be richer and hence more powerful than non-democratic ones, then the requirement of on-going consent by democratic states may actually foster a type of accountability that is detrimental to the interests of the world's worst-off people. For this reason, and because of the problem of bureaucratic discretion, the idea that the legitimacy of global governance institutions requires democracy on a grander scale may seem plausible.

Global democracy

Because democracy is now widely thought to be the gold standard for legitimacy in the case of the state, it may seem obvious that global governance institutions are legitimate if and only if they are democratic. And since these institutions increasingly affect the welfare of people everywhere, surely this must mean that they ought to be democratic in

---

[14] How the requirement of on-going consent should be operationalized is a complex question we need not try to answer here; one possibility would be that the treaties creating the institution would have to be periodically reaffirmed.

the sense of giving everyone an equal say in how they operate. Call this the Global Democracy View.

The most obvious difficulty with this view is that the social and political conditions for democracy are not met at the global level and there is no reason to think that they will be in the foreseeable future. At present there is no global political structure that could provide the basis for democratic control over global governance institutions, even if one assumes that democracy requires little direct participation by individuals. Any attempt to create such a structure in the form of a global democratic federation that relies on existing states as federal units would lack legitimacy, and hence could not confer legitimacy on global governance institutions, because, as has already been noted, many states are themselves undemocratic or lack other qualities necessary for state legitimacy. Furthermore, there is at present no global public – no worldwide political community constituted by a broad consensus recognizing a common domain as the proper subject of global collective decision-making and habitually communicating with one another about public issues. Nor is there consensus on a normative framework within which to deliberate together about a global common interest. Indeed, there is not even a global consensus that some form of global government, much less a global democracy, is needed or appropriate. Finally, once it is understood that it is *liberal* democracy, democracy that protects individual and minority rights, that is desirable, the Global Democracy View seems even more unfeasible. Democracy worth aspiring to is more than elections; it includes a complex web of institutions, including a free press and media, an active civil society, and institutions to check abuses of power by administrative agencies and elected officials.

To be legitimate, global governance institutions must incorporate democratic principles, in particular, what we call broad accountability below; and generally they must have the consent of democratic states. Our theory is therefore emphatically democratic. Yet we do not require that global institutions be democratic on the domestic analogy. [15] More

---

[15] Critics from both Left and Right disagree. For an argument from the Left that multilateral institutions are not democratically legitimate, see Robert A. Dahl, "Can international organizations be democratic?" In Ian Shapiro and Hacker-Cordón, eds., *Democracy's Edges* (Cambridge: Cambridge University Press, 1999), pp. 19-36. For an argument from the Right that reaches a similar conclusion, see Jeremy A. Rabkin, *Law without Nations? Why Constitutional Government Requires the Sovereign State.* Princeton: Princeton University Press, 2005. In the workshop at Princeton in February 2006, John Ferejohn drew a distinction between "reason-based" legitimacy to legitimacy based on

specifically, they need not include global electoral processes in which all individuals participate. If global governance institutions must be authorized by a global democracy to be legitimate, then none are legitimate and none are likely to be legitimate for the foreseeable future. Yet global governance institutions provide benefits that cannot be provided by states and, as we have argued, securing those benefits may depend upon these institutions being regarded as legitimate. We therefore reject the assumption that to be legitimate these institutions must be authorized by a global democracy.

We are now in a position to identify at least one condition that a standard of legitimacy for global governance institutions should include: the on-going consent of democratic states. For reasons already indicated, however, such consent is not sufficient. Accordingly, our proposal for a standard of legitimacy must be more complex.

III. A Complex Standard of Legitimacy

Desiderata for a standard of legitimacy

Before further elaborating our proposal, it will be useful to identify the characteristics that a standard of legitimacy for these institutions should have. Our discussion of the practical function of legitimacy assessments and our critique of the three dominant views on the standard of legitimacy for these institutions (state consent, democratic state consent, and global democracy) suggest the following desiderata. (1) The standard must provide a reasonable basis for coordinated support for the institutions in question, on the basis of normative reasons that are widely accessible in spite of the persistence of significant normative disagreement: in particular, disagreement about the requirements of justice. (2) The standard must not confuse legitimacy with justice but nonetheless must be consistent with the intuition that extreme injustice is incompatible with legitimacy. (3) The standard must take the on-going consent of democratic states as a presumptive necessary condition, though not a sufficient condition, for legitimacy. (4) Although the standard should not make authorization by a global democracy a necessary condition of legitimacy, it should nonetheless be consonant with the key

---

popular will. In his phrase, in discussing global governance, we do not attempt to "go across the bridge" from reason-based to will-based legitimacy.

values that underlie the demand for democracy. (5) The standard must properly reflect the dynamic character of global governance institutions: the fact that not only the means they employ, but even their goals, may and ought to change over time. Finally, (6) the standard must address the problem we encountered earlier: the limitations of accountability through the on-going consent of democratic states, due to the attenuated chains of delegation between citizens and agents of global governance institutions. So the standard of legitimacy must incorporate some additional way of providing accountability.

Normative disagreement and uncertainty

The first item on the list of desiderata is complex and warrants further explication and emphasis. We have noted that a central feature of the circumstances of legitimacy is the persistence of normative disagreement about (i) what the proper goals of the institution are (given the limitations imposed by state sovereignty properly conceived); (ii) what global justice requires; and (iii) what role if any the institution should play in the pursuit of global justice. Normative disagreement is not unique to global governance institutions. At least under modern conditions, disagreements about what justice requires and the role of the state in the pursuit of justice occur within the state. For example, some citizens may think that the state should provide comprehensive health care for all, while others reject this or other welfare functions for the state, and this disagreement may be rooted in deeper disagreement about what justice requires.

However, there are two circumstances in the case of global governance institutions that exacerbate the problem of normative disagreement. First, in the case of the state, democratic processes provide a way of accommodating these disagreements, by providing a public process that assures every citizen that she is being treated as an equal, through the electoral process, while as we have seen democracy is unavailable at the global level. Second, although there is a widespread perception, at least among cosmopolitans broadly speaking, that there is serious global injustice and that the effective pursuit of global justice requires a significant role for global institutions, it is not possible at present to provide a principled specification of the division of institutional labor for pursuing global justice. In part the problem is that there is no unified system of global institutions within which a fair and effective allocation of institutional responsibilities for justice can be devised. How responsibilities for justice ought to be allocated among global institutions and between states and global institutions depends chiefly on the answers to two questions: what are the proper responsibilities of states in the pursuit of global justice, taking into account the scope of state sovereignty (because this will determine how extensive the role of global institutions should be); and second, what are the capabilities of various global institutions for contributing to the pursuit of global justice? But neither of these questions can be answered at present, in part because global governance institutions are so new, and in part because people have only recently begun to think seriously about achieving justice on a global scale. So the difficulty is not just that there is considerable normative disagreement about the proper goals of global governance institutions and about the role these institutions should play in the pursuit of global justice; there is also normative *uncertainty*.[16] Whatever the standard of legitimacy for global governance institutions is, it must some how accommodate *the facts of normative disagreement and uncertainty.*

The standard of legitimacy we propose is complex. To be legitimate, we argue, a global governance institution must have certain *attributes*, but also must stand in certain *relationships* to entities outside the institution. We have already noted one key relationship: the channel of accountability that the ongoing consent of democratic states makes possible. We argued that the democratic channel is presumptively necessary for legitimacy, but not sufficient. What more is needed? In our view, the democratic consent condition needs to be supplemented with substantive criteria that specify the attributes a global governance institution must have to be legitimate. We begin with a set of institutional attributes that have considerable intuitive appeal: minimal moral acceptability, comparative benefit, and institutional integrity.

Three substantive criteria

Minimal moral acceptability

Global governance institutions, like institutions generally, should not persist in committing serious injustices and if they do we should not

[16] For a valuable discussion that employs a different conception of normative uncertainty, see Monica Hlavac, "A Developmental Approach to the Legitimacy of Global Governance Institutions" (unpublished paper).

take their rules as binding or otherwise support them. We believe that the primary instance of a serious injustice is the violation of human rights. We also believe that the most plausible conception of human rights is what might be called the basic human interest conception. This conception, which we can only sketch in broad outlines here, builds on Joseph Raz's insight that rights generally are normative relations (in particular, duties and entitlements) which, if realized, provide important protections for interests.[17] Given this conception of what rights are, it is clear that to justify the claim that R is a right, one must identify an interest, support the claim that the interest is of sufficient moral importance to ground duties, explain why the duties are owed to the right-holders, and make the case that if the normative relations in question are satisfied, significant protection for the interest will be achieved. On this view, certain rights are properly called human rights because the duties they entail provide especially important protections for basic human interests, given the standard threats to those interests in our world.[18]

---

[17] See Raz, *The Morality of Freedom, cited above.*

[18] Drawing on John Tasioulas's illuminating application of the interest-based conception of rights to the case of *human* rights, we can outline the basic form that arguments for various human rights would take, according to the basic interest conception of human rights. (Tasioulas, "The Moral Reality of Human Rights,"unpublished article).

(1) All human beings are entitled to be treated in a manner that acknowledges their equal fundamental moral worth.(The Moral Equality Principle)

(2) Treating all human beings in a manner that acknowledges their equal fundamental moral worth requires a serious commitment on the part of all individuals, both in their conduct as individuals and through the operation of their institutions, to protecting the basic human interests of all human beings, that is, to ensuring the conditions for a decent or minimally good life for every human being (so far as this commitment is compatible with the facts of human psychology and with the fact that what we owe to others is limited by the permissibility of a degree of partiality toward ourselves and our personal attachments).

(3) X (e.g., physical security, access to materials needed for subsistence, not being tortured, etc.) is a basic human interest; that is, X is generally a condition for having a minimally good or decent human life.

(4) A serious commitment to the reasonable protection of every human being's interest in X requires the acknowledgement of duties and/or the imposition of duties (for example, through the operation of institutions) to ensure that every human being is provided with X.

What the standard threats are can change over time. For example, when human societies create legal systems and police and courts to enforce laws, they also create new possibilities for damaging basic human interests. For this reason, the content of particular human rights, and even which rights are included among the human rights, may also change, even though the basic interests that ground them do not. For example, all human beings, regardless of where they exist, have a basic interest in physical security, but in a society with a legal system backed by the coercive power of the state, adequate protection of the interest in physical security requires rights of due process and equal protection under the law.

Unsurprisingly, there is disagreement among basic interest theorists of human rights as to exactly what the list of human rights includes and how the content of particular rights is to be filled out. However, there is agreement that the list includes the rights to physical security, to liberty (understood as at least encompassing freedom from slavery, servitude, and forced occupations), and the right to subsistence. Assuming that this is so, we can at least say this much: global governance institutions, and institutions generally, are legitimate only if they do not persist in violations of the least controversial human rights. To require that global governance institutions not persist in the most basic human rights violations is certainly minimal as a requirement for legitimacy. Yet in view of the normative disagreement and uncertainty that characterize our attitudes toward these institutions, it might be hard at present to reach agreement on a more extensive set of rights that they are bound to respect. It would certainly be desirable to develop a more meaningful consensus on stronger human rights standards. What this suggests is that we should require global governance institutions to respect minimal human rights, but also to expect them to meet higher standards as we gain greater clarity about the scope of human rights.

---

(5) Because the duties in question are grounded in the fundamental equal moral worth of each human being, they are owed to the individual simply as a human being

(6) If duties to provide X to every human being are owed to every human being simply as a human being, then X is a human right.

(7) (Therefore) there is a human right to X.

The notion of a serious commitment employed in premise (2) relies on Amartya K. Sen, "Elements of a Theory of Human Rights," *Philosophy & Public Affairs*, Vol. 32 (Fall 2004), p. 322.

For many global governance institutions, given the sorts of functions they perform, the proper expectation is that they should respect human rights, not that they should play a major role in *promoting* human rights. Nonetheless, a theory of legitimacy cannot ignore the fact that in some cases the dispute over whether a global governance institution is legitimate is in large part a disagreement over whether it is worthy of support if it does not actively *promote* human rights. This certainly seems to be true of the heated controversy over the legitimacy of the WTO. While some critics contend that the WTO actually violates human rights (for example, the right to subsistence, through its policies on import duties and agricultural subsidies), others claim that even if it does not violate human rights, it ought to promote protection of them, for example, by requiring trade agreements to include universal labor standards for safety and health, and for limitations on child labor. A proposal for a standard of legitimacy for global governance institutions must take into account the fact that some of these institutions play a more direct and substantial role in securing human rights than others.

When we see the grievous injustices or our world and appreciate that ameliorating them requires institutional actions, we are quick to attribute obligations to institutions and then criticize them for failing to fulfill those obligations. However, it is one thing to say that it would be a good thing if a particular global governance institution took on certain functions that would promote human rights; it is quite another to say that it has a duty to do so *and* that this duty is of such importance that failure to discharge it makes the institution illegitimate. There are two mistakes to be avoided here. The first is "duty dumping," that is, arbitrarily assuming that some particular institution has a duty simply because it has the resources to fulfill it and no other actor is doing so.[19] Duty dumping not only makes unsupported attributions of institutional responsibility; it also distracts attention from the difficult task of determining what a fair distribution of the burdens – among individuals and institutions – for protecting the human rights in question would be. The second error derives from the first: if one uncritically assumes that the institution has a duty to provide X and also assumes that X is a central matter of justice (as is the case with human rights), then one may conclude that the institution's failure to provide X is such a serious injustice as to rob the institution of legitimacy. But the fact that an institution could provide X and the fact that X is a human right does not

---

[19] Allen Buchanan and Matthew DeCamp, "Responsibility for Global Health," *Transnational Medicine*, forthcoming.

imply that in refraining from providing X the institution commits a serious injustice. That conclusion would only follow if it were established that the institution has a duty of justice to provide X. Merely pointing out that the institution could provide X – or even showing that it is the only existing institution that can do so – is not sufficient to show that it has a duty of justice or any duty at all to provide X.

We seem to be in a quandary. Contemporary institutions have to operate in an environment of normative disagreement and uncertainty, which limits the demands we can reasonably place on them to respects or protect particular human rights. Furthermore, to be sufficiently general, an account of legitimacy must avoid moral requirements that only apply to some global governance institutions. These considerations suggest the appropriateness of something like the minimal moral acceptability requirement, understood as refraining from violations of the least controversial human rights. On the other hand, the standard of legitimacy should somehow reflect the fact that part of what is at issue in disputes over the legitimacy of some of these institutions is whether they should satisfy more robust demands of justice. In other words, the standard should acknowledge the fact that where the issue of legitimacy is most urgent, there is likely to be deep normative disagreement and uncertainty.

In our view, the way out of this impasse is to build the conditions needed for principled, informed deliberation about normative issues into the standard of legitimacy itself. The standard of legitimacy should require minimal moral acceptability, but should also accommodate and even encourage the possibility of *developing* more demanding requirements of justice for at least some of these institutions, as a principled basis for an institutional division of labor regarding justice emerges. Later in this section we explain how global governance institutions can be structured so as to facilitate principled, informed deliberation about whether the bar for minimal moral acceptability should be raised. For now we only want to stress that minimal moral acceptability, explicated in terms of the non-violation of human rights, is a plausible presumptive necessary condition for legitimacy for all global governance institutions.

Comparative benefit

This second substantive condition for legitimacy is relatively straightforward. The justification for having global governance institutions is primarily if not exclusively instrumental: we value them because of the benefits they bring, rather than regarding them as intrinsically valuable. The basic reason for states or other addresses of institutional rules to take them as binding and for individuals generally to support or at least not interfere with the operation of these institutions is that they provide benefits that cannot otherwise be obtained.

'Benefit' here is comparative. The legitimacy of an institution is called into question if there is an institutional alternative, providing greater benefits, that is feasible, accessible without excessive transition costs, and meets the minimal moral acceptability criterion. The most difficult issues, as discussed below, concern trade-offs between comparative benefit and our other criteria. Legitimacy is not to be confused with *optimal* efficacy and efficiency. The other values that we discuss are also important in their own right; and in any case, institutional stability is a virtue. Nevertheless, if an institution steadfastly remains instrumentally suboptimal when it could take steps to become significantly more efficient or effective, this could impugn its legitimacy in an indirect way: it would indicate that those in charge of the institution were either grossly incompetent or not seriously committed to providing the benefits that were invoked to justify the creation of the institution in the first place.[20] This suggests a third substantive presumptive condition for legitimacy: institutional integrity.

Institutional integrity

If an institution exhibits a pattern of egregious disparity between its actual performance, on the one hand, and its self-proclaimed procedures or major goals, on the other, its legitimacy is seriously called into ques-

20 For instance, as of the beginning of 2006 the United Nations faced the issue of reconstituting a Human Rights Commission that had been discredited by the membership of states that notoriously abuse human rights, and even by Libya serving as chair in 2003. In March 2005 Secretary-General Kofi Annan called for the replacement of the Commission on Human Rights (53 members elected from slates put forward by regional groups) with a smaller Human Rights Council elected by a two-thirds vote of members of the General Assembly (see his report, "In Larger Freedom," A/59/2005, paragraph 183). As of the beginning of January, no agreement had been reached on this proposal, but Secretary-General Annan's chief of staff, Mark Molloch Brown, was quoted as saying that "For the great global public, the performance or nonperformance of the Human Rights Commission has become the litmus test of U.N. renewal" – in other words, crucial to its sociological legitimacy. See *New York Times*, January 1, 2006, p. 1.

tion. The United Nations Oil-for-Food scandal is a case in point. The Oil-for-Food Program was devised to enable Iraqi oil to be sold, under strict controls, to pay for food imports under the UN-mandated sanctions of the 1990s. The purpose was both to prevent malnutrition in Iraq and to counter Iraqi propaganda holding the United Nations responsible for the deaths of hundreds of thousands of Iraqi children, without relieving the pressure on Saddam Hussein's regime to get rid of its supposed weapons of mass destruction. Yet it led to a great deal of corruption.[21] The most damning charge is that neither the Security Council oversight bodies nor the Office of the Secretary-General followed the UN's prescribed procedures for accountability. At least when viewed in the light of the historical record of other, perhaps less egregious failures of accountability in the use of resources on the part of the UN, these findings have raised questions about the legitimacy of the Security Council and the Secretariat.

It also appears that an institution is presumptively illegitimate if its practices or procedures predictably thwart the credible pursuit of the very goals in terms of which it justifies its existence. Thus, for example, if the fundamental character of the Security Council's decision-making process renders that institution incapable of successfully pursuing what it now acknowledges as one of its chief goals – stopping large-scale violations of basic human rights – this impugns its legitimacy. Randall Stone has shown that the IMF during the 1990s inconsistently applied its own standards with respect to its lending, systematically relaxing enforcement on countries that had rich and powerful patrons.[22] Similarly, if the WTO claims to provide the benefits of trade liberalization to *all* of its members, but consistently develops policies that exclude its weaker members from the benefits of liberalization, this undermines its

---

[21] Oil-for-Food became a huge program, permitting the Government of Iraq to sell $64.2 billion of oil to 248 companies, and enabling 3614 companies to sell $34.5 billion of humanitarian goods to Iraq. Yet more than half of the companies involved paid illegal surcharges or kick-backs to Saddam and his cronies, resulting in large profits for corporations and pecuniary benefits for some program administrators, including at least one high-level UN official. For the report of the Independent Inquiry Committee into the United Nations Oil-for-Food Program (the Volcker Committee), dated October 27, 2005, see http://www.iic-offp.org/story27oct05.htm, last accessed January 1, 2006.

[22] Randall W. Stone, "The political economy of IMF lending in Africa." *American Political Science Review*, volume 98, no. 4 (November 2004): 577-591. See also Stone, *Lending Credibility: The International Monetary Fund and the Post-Communist Transition.* Princeton: Princeton University Press, 2002.

claim to legitimacy. If an institution fails to satisfy the integrity criterion, we have reason to believe that key institutional agents are either untrustworthy or grossly incompetent, that the institution lacks correctives for these deficiencies, and that therefore the institution is unlikely to be effective in providing the goods that would make it rational for us to take its directives as binding.

Integrity and comparative benefit are related but distinct. If there are major discrepancies between an institution's behavior and its prescribed procedures and professed goals, then we can have little confidence that it will succeed in delivering the benefits it is supposed to provide. However, integrity is a more forward-looking, dynamic virtue than comparative benefit, which measures benefit solely in terms of the current situation. If an institution satisfies the criterion of integrity, there is reason to be confident that institutional actors will not only deliver the benefits that are now taken to constitute the proper goals institutional activity, but also that they will be able to maintain the institution's effectiveness if its goals change.

Epistemic Aspects of Legitimacy

Minimal moral acceptability, comparative benefit, and institutional integrity are plausible presumptive substantive requirements for the legitimacy of global governance institutions. It would be excessive to claim that they are necessary conditions *simpliciter*, because there might be extraordinary circumstances in which an institution would fail to satisfy one or two of them, yet still reasonably be regarded as legitimate. This might be the case if there were no feasible and accessible alternative institutional arrangement, if the noninstitutional alternative were sufficiently grim, and if there was reason to believe that the institution had the resources and the political will to correct the deficiency. How much we expect of an institution should depend, *inter alia*, upon how valuable the benefits it provides are and whether there are acceptable, feasible alternatives to it. For example, we might be warranted in regarding an institution as legitimate even though it lacked integrity, if it is nonetheless providing important protections for basic human rights and the alternatives to relying on it are grim. In contrast, the fact that an institution is effective in producing incremental trade liberalization, would not be sufficient to rebut the presumption that it is illegitimate because it abuses human rights.[23] Our three substantive conditions are best thought of as what Rawls calls "counting principles": the more of them an institution satisfies, and the higher the degree to which it satisfies them, the stronger its claim to legitimacy.[24] All three conditions are always relevant, but trade-offs between them must frequently be made. In determining such trade-offs, the relative weights of the three principles may vary, depending upon the context. Our complex standard, then, is a *general* standard, meant to be applied in a way that is sensitive to particular circumstances.

However, even if the three substantive conditions are generally necessary for the legitimacy of multilateral institutions, there are two epistemic reasons why they are not jointly sufficient. The first is *the problem of factual knowledge*: being able to make reasonable judgments about whether an institution satisfies any of the three substantive conditions requires considerable information about the workings of the institution and their effects in a number of domains. However, some institutions may not only fail to supply the needed information, they may, whether deliberately or otherwise, make such information either impossible for outsiders to obtain or obtainable only at prohibitive costs. Even if the institution does not try to limit access to the relevant information, it may not be accessible, in suitably integrated, understandable form.

The second difficulty with taking the three substantive conditions as jointly sufficient for legitimacy is *the problem of normative disagreement and uncertainty* noted earlier. Even if there is sufficient agreement on what counts as the violation of human rights, there are on-going disputes about whether at least some global governance institutions should meet higher normative standards than this minimal one. As emphasized earlier, there is not only disagreement but also uncertainty as to the role that some of these institutions should play in the pursuit of global justice, chiefly because we do not have a coherent idea of what the institutional division of labor for achieving global justice would look like. To expand on an earlier example: some argue that the WTO's goals should include not only "liberalizing trade" and making trade "fairer," but also more direct action to combat poverty and disease, for example, through policies that support universal labor standards or make life-saving medicines more affordable through modifications in

---

23 We are indebted to Andrew Hurrell for this example.

24 John Rawls, *A Theory of Justice* (Cambridge: Harvard University Press at the Belknap Press, 1971).

the intellectual property rights regime it has put into place. Yet whether the WTO should play these roles may depend upon what is assumed about the roles of other global institutions and of states, in the pursuit of global justice.

Furthermore, merely requiring that global governance institutions not violate human rights is unresponsive to the familiar complaint that they are unfairly dominated by rich countries and that even if they provide benefits to all, the richer members receive unjustifiably greater benefits. However, although all parties may agree that fairness matters, there are likely to be disagreements about what fairness would consist of, disputes about whether fairness would suffice or whether equality is required and about how equality is to be understood and even over what is to be made equal (welfare, opportunities, resources, etc.). So, quite apart from the issue of what positive role, if any, these institutions should play in the pursuit of global justice, there is disagreement about what standards of fairness they should meet internally.

We shall argue that the proper response to both the problem of factual knowledge and the problem of normative disagreement and uncertainty is to focus on what might be called the *epistemic-deliberative* quality of the institution, the extent to which the institution provides reliable information needed for grappling with normative disagreement and uncertainty concerning its proper functions. To lay the groundwork for that argument we begin by considering two items that are often assumed to be obvious requirements for the legitimacy of global governance institutions: accountability and transparency. We agree with conventional wisdom that accountability and transparency are crucial. But we also seek to demonstrate the limitations of these notions, as they are commonly understood. Doing so will pave the way for our account of epistemic-deliberative quality.

Accountability

Critics of global governance institutions often complain that they lack accountability. To understand the strengths and limitations of accountability as a gauge of legitimacy, we start with a skeletal but serviceable analysis of accountability. Accountability includes three elements: (1) standards that those who are held accountable are expected to meet; (2) information available to accountability-holders, who can then apply the standards in question to the performance of those who are held to account; and (3) the ability of these accountability-holders to impose sanctions: to attach costs to the failure to meet the standards. The need for information about whether the institution is meeting the standards accountability-holders apply means that a degree of transparency regarding the institution's operations is essential to any form of accountability.

It is misleading to say that global governance institutions are illegitimate because they lack accountability and to suggest that the key to making them legitimate is to make them accountable. Most global governance institutions, including those whose legitimacy is most strenuously denied, include mechanisms for accountability.[25] The problem is that existing patterns of accountability are inadequate from a normative standpoint. Consider, for example, the World Bank. This institution has traditionally exhibited a high degree of accountability, but it has been accountability to the biggest donor countries, and the Bank therefore has to act in conformity with their interests, at least insofar as they agree. This kind of accountability does not ensure meaningful participation by those affected by rules or due consideration of their legitimate interests. A high degree of accountability in this case may serve to perpetuate the defects of the institution.

So accountability *per se* is not sufficient; it must be the right sort of accountability. At the very least, this means that there must be effective provisions in the structure of the institution for holding institutional agents accountable for acting in ways that ensure satisfaction of the minimal moral acceptability and comparative benefit conditions. However, accountability understood is this narrow way is not sufficiently *dynamic* to serve as an assurance of the legitimacy of global governance institutions, given that in some cases there is serious disagreement about what the goals of the institution should be and, more specifically, about what role if any the institution should play in the pursuit of global justice. The point is that what the *terms of accountability* ought to be – what standards of accountability ought to be employed, who the accountability holders should be, and whose interests the accountability holders should represent – cannot be definitively ascertained without knowing what role, if any, the institution should play in the pursuit of global justice.

---

[25] Ruth W. Grant and Robert O. Keohane, "Accountability and abuses of power in world politics." *American Political Science Review,* vol. 99, no. 1 (February 2005): 29-44. See also Robert O. Keohane and Joseph S. Nye, Jr., "Redefining Accountability for Global Governance," in Miles Kahler and David A. Lake, eds., *Governance in a Global Economy: Political Authority in Transition* (Princeton: Princeton University Press, 2003): 386-411.

Therefore, what might be called narrow accountability – accountability without provision for contestation of the terms of accountability – is insufficient for legitimacy, given the fact of normative disagreement and uncertainty. Because what constitutes appropriate accountability is itself subject to reasonable dispute, the legitimacy of global governance institutions depends in part upon whether they operate in such a way as to facilitate principled, factually-informed deliberation about the terms of accountability. There must be provisions for revising existing standards of accountability and our conception of who the proper accountability holders are and whose interests they should represent.

Transparency

Achieving transparency is often touted as the proper response to worries about the legitimacy of global governance institutions.[26] However, to suggest that transparency ensures legitimacy is inadequate. First, if transparency means merely the *availability* of accurate information about how the institution works, it is insufficient even for narrow accountability, that is, for ensuring that the institution is accurately evaluated in accordance with the current terms of accountability. If information about how the institution operates is to serve the end of narrow accountability it must be (a) accessible *at reasonable cost*, (b) properly integrated and interpreted, and (c) directed to the accountability-holders. Furthermore (d) the accountability-holders must be adequately motivated to use it properly in evaluating the performance of the relevant institutional agents. Second, if, as we have suggested, the capacity for critically revising the terms of accountability is necessary for legitimacy, information about how the institution works must be available not only to those who are presently designated as accountability-holders, but also to those who may contest the terms of accountability.

Broad transparency is needed for critical revisability of the terms of accountability. Both institutional practices and the normative principles that shape the terms of accountability must be revisable in the light of critical reflection and discussion.[27] Under conditions of broad transpar-

---

26 Ann Florini, *The Coming Democracy* (Washington, DC: Island Press, 2003).

27 For a discussion of the role of critical revisability in practical reasoning, with parallels to theoretical reasoning, see Allen Buchanan, "Revisability and Rational Choice," *Canadian Journal of Philosophy*, vol. 5, no. 3, 1975, pp. 395-408.

ency, information produced initially to enable institutionally-designated accountability holders to assess officials' performance may be appropriated by agents external to the institution, such as NGOs and other actors in transnational civil society, and used to support more fundamental criticisms, not only of the institution's processes and structures, but even of its most fundamental goals and its role in the pursuit of global justice.

One especially important dimension of broad transparency is *responsibility for public justification*. Institutional actors must offer public justifications of at least the more controversial and consequential institutional policies and must facilitate timely critical responses to them. Potential critics must be in a position to determine whether the public justifications are cogent, whether they are consistent with the current terms of accountability, and whether, if taken seriously, these justifications call for revision of the current terms of responsibility. To help ensure this dimension of broad transparency, it may be worthwhile to draw on the notice and comment procedures of administrative law at the domestic level.[28]

Earlier we noted that although comparative benefit, minimal moral acceptability, and integrity are reasonable presumptive necessary conditions for legitimacy, it may be difficult for those outside the institution to determine whether they are satisfied. We now want to suggest that broad transparency can serve as a proxy for satisfaction of the minimal moral acceptability, comparative benefit, and integrity criteria. For example, it may be easier for outsiders to discover that an institution is not responding to demands for information relevant to determining whether it is violating its own prescribed procedures, than to determine

---

28 See Richard B. Stewart, "Administrative Law in the Twenty-First Century," *New York University Law Review* vol. 78, no. 2 (2003), pp. 437-60; Benedict Kingsbury, Nico Krisch, and Richard B. Stewart, "The Emergence of Global Administrative Law," *Law and Contemporary Problems* vol. 68 (2005), pp. 15-61. See also Daniel Esty, "Toward good global governance: the role of administrative law." Paper presented at a conference on global administrative law, New York University, April 21-23, 2005. See also John Wickham, "Toward a Green Multilateral Investment Framework: NAFTA and the Search for Models," *Georgetown International Environmental Law Review* vol. 12, no. 3 (2000), pp. 617-46; James Salzman, "Labor Rights, Globalization, and Institutions: The Role and Influence of the Organization for Economic Cooperation and Development," *Michigan Journal of International Law* vol. 21, no. 4 (2000), pp. 769-848; OECD, "Getting to Grips with Globalization: The OECD in a Changing World (Paris: OECD Publications, 2004).

whether in fact it is violating them. Similarly, it may be very difficult to determine whether an institution is comparatively effective in solving certain global problems, but much easier to tell whether it generates – or systematically restricts access to – information needed to try to determine whether it is. If an institution fails to cooperate in making available to outsiders the information that would be needed to determine whether the three presumptive necessary conditions are satisfied, that should count against its legitimacy.

Legitimate global governance institutions should possess three epistemic virtues. First, because their chief function is to achieve coordination, they must generate and properly direct reliable information about coordination points; otherwise they will not satisfy the condition of comparative benefit. Second, because accountability is required to determine whether they are in fact performing their current coordinating functions efficiently and effectively requires narrow transparency, they must at least be transparent in the narrow sense. They must also have effective provisions for integrating and interpreting the information current accountability-holders need and for directing it to them. Third, and most demanding, they must have the capacity for *revising the terms of accountability*, and this requires broad transparency: institutions must facilitate positive information externalities to permit inclusive, informed contestation of their current terms of accountability. There must be provision for on-going deliberation about what global justice requires and how the institution in question fits into a division of institutional responsibilities for achieving it.

Overcoming informational asymmetries

A fundamental problem of institutional accountability is that insiders generally have better information about the institution than outsiders. Outsiders can determine whether institutions enjoy the consent of states, and whether states are democratic; but it may be very difficult for them to reach well-informed conclusions about the minimal moral acceptability, comparative benefit, and integrity conditions. Our emphasis on epistemic issues is well-suited to illuminate these problems of asymmetrical information.

First, as we have already noted, in some cases information that is more accessible to outsiders can serve as a reliable proxy for less accessible information. For example, outsiders may observe that an institution is not meeting the requirements of broad transparency, even it they do not know what is transpiring within it. Broad transparency, as we observed earlier, requires provisions for making widely available, beyond the boundaries of the institution, information about what the current standards of accountability are, who the current accountability holders are, and whose interests they are serving. It also entails providing timely public justifications for the more controversial and significant policy decisions. Faced with similarly severe uncertainty about the quality of a car, the potential buyer of a used car facing a seller with more information can infer poor quality from the seller's unwillingness to let him have the car thoroughly checked out by a competent mechanic engaged by the buyer.[29] Likewise, outsiders to an institution are justified in imagining the worst if insiders refuse to provide crucial information about their deliberations in a timely fashion. Second, there may be an asymmetry of knowledge in the other direction as well, and this can have beneficial consequences for institutional accountability. Consider an issue area richly populated with independent nongovernmental organizations (NGOs) that seek to monitor and criticize national governments and global governance institutions and to suggest policy alternatives.[30] Suppose that in such a domain there is a division of labor among external epistemic actors. Some individuals and groups seek information about certain types of issues, while others focus on other aspects, each drawing on distinct but in some cases overlapping groups of experts. Still others specialize in integrating and interpreting information gathered by other external epistemic actors.

The fact that the information held by external epistemic actors is dispersed will make it difficult for institutional agents to know what is known about their behavior or to predict when potentially damaging information may be integrated and interpreted in ways that make it politically potent. The institutional agents' awareness of this asymmetry will provide incentives for avoiding behavior for which they may be

---

29 For the classic discussion of the problem of asymmetrical information and institutional responses to it, see George A. Akerlof, "The market for lemons: quality uncertainty and the market mechanism." *Quarterly Journal of Economics*, August 1970, 84 (3), pp. 488-500.

30 The issue area of the environment – with the World Wildlife Federation, Sierra Club, Greenpeace, Environmental Defense, and many more organizations active – is an example of a domain with many external epistemic actors. So is human rights – consider Amnesty International, Human Rights Watch, and organizations designed to oppose torture. Other areas, such as world poverty or development, or health, also are thickly populated with external epistemic actors.

criticized. A condition of *productive uncertainty* will exist: although institutional agents will know that external epistemic actors do not possess the full range of knowledge that they do, they will know that there are many individuals and organizations gathering information about the institution. Further, they will know that some of the information that external epistemic actors have access to can serve as a reliable proxy for information they cannot access. Finally, they will also know that potentially damaging information that is currently harmless because it is dispersed among many external epistemic agents may at any time be integrated and interpreted in such a way as to make it politically effective, but they will not be able to predict when this will occur. Under these conditions, institutional agents will have significant incentives to refrain from behavior that will attract damning criticism, despite the fundamental asymmetry of knowledge between insiders and outsiders.

This is not to say that the effects of transparency will always be benign. Indeed, under some circumstances transparency can have malign effects. As David Stasavage points out, "open-door bargaining ... encourages representatives to posture by adopting overly aggressive bargaining positions that increase the risks of breakdown in negotiations."[31] When issues combine highly charged symbolic elements with the need for incentives, conflicts between transparency and efficiency may be severe. Organizations may refrain from actions that might promote their goals, merely because they could not easily be justified to a public paying only limited and intermittent attention. For example, a number of environmental experts think that the best way to maintain healthy populations of elephants would be to cull the herds routinely and use the proceeds from selling ivory to hire game wardens and reward local populations for not destroying the animals or their habitats. However, any multilateral institution that was branded as "killing elephants" would face severe political difficulties. Similar issues have arisen with whaling. International agreements on whaling have progressively shifted from trying to promote sustainable use to banning whaling altogether, to the distress of Norwegians, Japanese and groups in other countries for

---

31 David Stasavage, "Open-door or closed door? Transparency in domestic and international bargaining." *International Organization,* volume 58, no. 4 (Fall 2004): 667-704. For a discussion of the impact of the transparency introduced into WTO proceedings by third-party involvement, see Marc Busch and Eric Reinhardt, "Three's a Crowd: Third Parties and WTO Dispute Settlement." Unpublished paper, September 2005.

which whaling has been a traditional occupation.[32] The moral and environmental issues are complex; but for our purposes, the point is that under conditions of broad transparency it would be very difficult, regardless of the merits of the question, for any international organization now to take a pro-whaling position.

Our claim is not that outcomes are necessarily better the more transparent institutions are. Rather, it is that the dispersal of information among a plurality of external epistemic actors provides some counterbalance to informational asymmetries favoring insiders. There should be a very strong but rebuttable presumption of transparency, because the ills of too much transparency can be corrected by deeper, more sophisticated public discussion, whereas there can be no democratic response to secret action by bureaucracies not accountable to the public. Broad transparency is conducive to the principled revisability of institutions, to their improvement through increasingly inclusive criticism and more deeply probing discussion over time.

Institutional agents generally have incentives to prevent outsiders from getting information that may eventually be interpreted and integrated in damaging ways and to deprive outsiders of information that can serve as a reliable proxy to assess institutional legitimacy. The very reasons that make the epistemic virtues valuable from the standpoint of assessing institutional legitimacy may therefore tempt institutional agents to ensure that their institutions do not exemplify these virtues. However, institutional agents are also aware that it is important for their institutions to be widely regarded as legitimate. Outsiders deprived of access to information are likely to react as does the prospective buyer of a used car who is prevented from taking it to an independent mechanic. That is, they will discount the claims of the insiders and may even refuse to agree to a bargain – that is, they may judge the institution to be illegitimate. So if there is a broad consensus among outsiders that institutions are not legitimate unless they exemplify the epistemic virtues, institutional agents will have a weighty reason to ensure that their institutions do so.

---

32 See Ronald B. Mitchell and Patricia M. Keilbach, "Situation Structure and Institutional Design: Reciprocity, Coercion and Exchange." *International Organization* volume 55, no 4 (Autumn 2001): 905-908, and references therein.

Contestation and revisability: links to external actors and institutions

We have argued that the legitimacy of global governance institutions depends upon whether there is ongoing, informed, principled contestation of their goals and terms of accountability. This process of contestation and revision depends upon activities of actors outside the institution. It is not enough for the institutions to make information available. Other agents, whose interests and commitments do not coincide too closely with those of the institution, must provide a check on the reliability of the information, integrate it, and make it available in understandable, usable form, to all who have a legitimate interest in the operations of the institution. Such activities may produce positive feedback, in which appeal to standards of legitimacy by the external epistemic actors not only increases compliance with existing standards but also leads to improvements in the quality of these standards themselves. For these reasons, in the absence of global democracy, and given the limitations of the democratic channel described earlier, legitimacy depends crucially upon the activities of *external epistemic actors* in what might be called the *transnational civil society channel of accountability*. The needed external epistemic actors, if they are effective, will themselves be institutionally organized.[33]

All three elements of our complex standard of legitimacy are now in place. First, global governance institutions should enjoy the on-going consent of democratic states. That is, the democratic accountability channel must function reasonably well. Second, these institutions should satisfy the substantive criteria of minimal moral acceptability, comparative benefit, and institutional integrity. Third, they should possess the epistemic virtues needed to achieve the on-going contestation and critical revision of their goals, their terms of accountability, and ultimately their role in a division of labor for the pursuit of global justice, through their interaction with effective external epistemic agents.

The complex standard views the legitimacy of global governance institutions as both dynamic and relational. Its emphasis on the conditions

33 We use the term "external epistemic actor" here broadly, to include individuals and groups outside the institution in question who gain knowledge about the institution, interpret and integrate such knowledge, and exchange it with others, in ways that are intended to influence institutional behavior, whether directly or indirectly (through the mediation of the activities of other individuals and groups).

for on-going contestation and critical revision of the most basic features of the institutions captures the exceptional normative disagreement and uncertainty that characterize the circumstances of legitimacy for this type of institution. While acknowledging this normative disagreement and uncertainty, the complex standard includes provisions for developing more robust normative requirements for institutions over time. The complex standard also makes it clear that whether the institution is legitimate does not depend solely upon its own characteristics, but also upon the epistemic-deliberative relationships between the institution and epistemic actors outside it.

A place for democratic values in the absence of global democracy

Earlier we argued that it is a mistake to hold global governance institutions to the standard of democratic legitimacy that is now widely applied to states. We now want to suggest that when the complex standard of legitimacy we propose is satisfied, important democratic values will be served. For purposes of the present discussion we will assume, rather than argue, that among the most important democratic values are the following: (1) equal regard for the fundamental interests of all persons, (2) decision-making about the public order through principled, collective deliberation, and (3) mutual respect for persons as beings who are guided by reasons.

If the complex standard of legitimacy we propose is satisfied, all three of these values will be served. To the extent that connections between the institutions and external epistemic actors provide access to information that is not restricted to certain groups but available globally, it becomes harder for the institution to continue to exclude consideration of the interests of certain groups, and we move closer toward the ideal of equal regard for the fundamental interests of all. Furthermore, by making information available globally, networks of external epistemic actors are in effect addressing all people as individuals for whom normative reasons, not just the threat of coercion, determine whether they regard an institution's rules as authoritative. Finally, if the complex standard of legitimacy is satisfied, every feature of the institution becomes a potential object of principled, principled, informed collective deliberation, and eligibility for participation in deliberation will not be restricted by institutional interests.

Having articulated the complex standard, and indicated how it reflects several key democratic values, we can now show, briefly, how it satisfies the desiderata for a standard of legitimacy we set out earlier. (1) The complex standard provides a reasonable basis for coordinated support of institutions that meet the standard, support based on normative reasons that are widely accessible in the circumstances under which legitimacy is an issue. To serve the social function of legitimacy assessments, the complex standard only requires a consensus on the importance of not violating the most widely recognized human rights, broad agreement that comparative benefit and integrity are also presumptive necessary conditions of legitimacy, and a commitment to inclusive, informed deliberation directed toward resolving or at least reducing the normative disagreement and uncertainty that characterize our practical attitudes toward these institutions. In other words, the complex standard steers a middle course between requiring more normative agreement than is available in the circumstances of legitimacy and abandoning the attempt to construct a more robust, shared normative perspective from which to evaluate global governance institutions. In particular, the complex standard acknowledges that the role that these institutions ought to play in a more just world order is both deeply contested and probably not knowable at present. (2) In requiring only minimal moral acceptability at present, the complex standard acknowledges that legitimacy does not require justice, but at the same time affirms the intuition that extreme injustice, understood as violation of the most widely recognized human rights, robs an institution of legitimacy. (3) The complex standard takes the on-going consent of democratic states to be a necessary, though not a sufficient condition for legitimacy. (4) The complex standard rejects the assumption that global governance institutions cannot be legitimate unless there is global democracy, but at the same time promotes some of the key democratic values, including informed, public deliberation conducted on the assumption that every individual has standing to participate and the requirement that key institutional policies must be publicly justified. (5) The complex standard reflects a proper appreciation of the dynamic, experimental character of global governance institutions and of the fact that not only the means they employ but even the goals they pursue may and probably should change over time. (6) The complex standard's requirement of a functioning transnational civil society channel of accountability – an array of overlapping networks of external epistemic actors – helps to compensate for the limitations of accountability through democratic state consent.

Conclusion

We characterize our view as a *proposal* for a standard of legitimacy for global governance institutions, not as a discovery, through pure normative-conceptual analysis, of the conditions of legitimacy. This characterization reflects our understanding of the social function of legitimacy assessments about global governance institutions. These institutions are quite new and still evolving. They exist in a world in which there is a relatively recent but growing commitment to global justice and an increasing capacity for beginning to achieve it, but also a great deal of disagreement about exactly global justice requires, as well as uncertainty about the appropriate allocation of institutional responsibilities for pursuing it. Few would deny that global governance institutions supply important benefits that neither states nor traditional treaty-based relationships among states can provide. Yet normative disagreement about them is so pronounced that there is a risk that they will not continue to enjoy the support needed for them to function effectively. Under these conditions a principled proposal for a standard of legitimacy could, if it garners sufficient support, serve as a focal point for provisional support while at the same time providing guidance for improvement and leverage for stimulating institutional change. Given the benefits and the imperfections of existing global governance institutions, there is an urgent need for a shared evaluative perspective that is sufficiently critical, yet not so demanding as to make coordinated, normatively-based support unlikely. Our hope is that the complex standard we propose is a first step toward meeting this need.

Legitimacy of Legislative and Executive Actions of International Institutions

Alain Pellet

I have been kindly asked by the organizers of this Symposium to deal with a vast, difficult and, possibly, impossible topic. This is why I will first explain why I will not deal with my assigned topic. Then I will try to deal with it. And finally, if time and your patience allow, I will try to draw some conclusions – here again wider than my assigned topic.

I. Some Introductory Points

Paradoxical as it may seem, I have had more difficulties in identifying the meaning of the word "actions" in my topic than that of the word "legitimacy". "Legitimacy" has for long not been a common word in the language of law in general, and certainly not of international law. It was of concern only for a very few international lawyers, of various "ideological" origins it is true to say, since, by way of example, Tom Frank[1] was neighbouring Myres McDougal,[2] which is clearly "counter

---

1 "Why a Quest for Legitimacy?", *UC Davis Law Review* 21 (1987), 535 or "Legitimacy in the International System", *AJIL* 82 (1988), 705-759; for a more recent presentation: "The Power of Legitimacy and the Legitimacy of Power: International Law in an Age of Power Disequilibrium", *AJIL* 100 (2006), 88-106.

2 See e.g.: Myres S. McDougal and Harold D. Lasswell, "The Identification and Appraisal of Diverse Systems of Public Order", *AJIL* 53 (1959), 1 et seq.; Harold D. Lasswell and Myres S. McDougal, *Jurisprudence for a Free Society,*

nature". However it seems now to be well established that legitimacy is part of the legal debate in the international sphere even though there are some uncertainties, to say the least, about the precise meaning of the word – which I interpret in less of an idealistic way than the previous speakers even if, like them, I accept that legitimacy is subject-oriented; but I will return to this in a few minutes.

Now, the word "actions" raises different issues and I have wondered what precise meaning the organizers of our seminar, whom I take this opportunity to thank heartily both for their initiative and for their invitation, had in mind when formulating the topic. "Actions" could be an equivalent for "measures" as referred to in Chapter VII of the UN Charter; but Chapter VII seems to differentiate between "measures" on the one hand – the word is used both in Article 40 ("Provisional Measures") and Article 41 ("Measures not involving the use of armed force") – and "actions", since Article 42 reserves the word "action" for military measures. For its part, Article 14 authorises the General Assembly of the United Nations to "recommend measures [not actions] for the peaceful adjustment of any situation".

A further difficulty is that I am supposed to speak not just of "executive actions" but of "legislative actions" as well. "Action" as used in Art. 42 of the Charter could be assimilated to "executive action", but surely not, at least from an orthodox and traditional point of view, to "legislative action". But, to tell the truth, I must admit that I see no real basis for the use of such terminology, which reflects, if I may say so with the utmost respect for the organizers of our seminar, an excessively state-oriented view of what international law is. As aptly explained by Weiler, "[a]nalogies to domestic law are impermissible, though most of us are habitual sinners in this respect"[3] – including the best among us; I am thinking in particular of Georges Abi-Saab's remarkable course at the Hague Academy, which rests on this, unfortunate for me, distinction between executive, legislative and judicial functions in international society.[4] I strongly suggest that there is no such thing in international society as the *séparation des pouvoirs*, the separation of powers. And this certainly has to do with our topic today.

1992; see also: Inis L. Claude, "Collective Legitimization as a Political Function of the United Nations", *International Organization* 20 (1966), 367-379.

[3] J.H.H. Weiler, "The Geology of International Law – Governance, Democracy and Legitimacy", *ZaöRV* 64 (2004), 550.

[4] "Cours général de droit international public", *Recueil des cours*, vol. 207 1987-VII, 11-463.

Within the State, the separation of powers is seen as one of the fundamental elements of democracy, as is very forcefully expressed in Article 16 of the French 1789 Declaration: "*Toute société dans laquelle la garantie des droits de l'homme n'est pas assurée ni la séparation des pouvoirs déterminés n'a pas de constitution,*"[5] which clearly meant, in the minds of the French revolutionaries, that such a society is not democratic. And democracy certainly has something in common with legitimacy, at least at the domestic level. But here again, I have strong doubts that it is so at the international level, and for two different reasons.

First, there is definitely no such thing as the separation of powers in the international sphere. It may be the case that some organs of some institutions have something which looks like executive or legislative functions. But these functions would hardly be separated from each other. Just take the Security Council of the United Nations. It has a "command power". But I would certainly hesitate to define the Council as an executive or legislative organ. It can decide – and even though it has for long hesitated to make decisions of a general and, in a way, abstract nature, it has now taken the plunge, at least in two particular matters: terrorism and the proliferation of weapons of mass destruction. This will be dealt with tomorrow morning by Georges Abi-Saab and Erika de Wet;[6] but even in these two fields, the resolutions adopted by the Counsel are certainly not a manifestation of a purely legislative power, in that it is turned into action. But nor can the Security Council be seen as a pure executive body since, on the one hand, it implements its own decision and, on the other hand, it is entirely dependent on "the forces of Members of the United Nations" to implement the actions it decides upon under Article 42, and it can only "call upon the Members of the United Nations to apply" the measures it decides under Article 41. I suggest that this is neither "executive" nor "legislative"; it is something which is very peculiar to the international sphere.

---

[5] "Any society in which no provision is made for guaranteeing rights or for the separation of powers, has no Constitution".

[6] See below in this book E. de Wet, "The Legitimacy of United Nations Security Council Decisions in the Fight against Terrorism and the Proliferation of Weapons of Mass Destruction: Some Critical Remarks", p. 131 et seq.; G. Abi-Saab, "The Security Council as Legislator and as Executive in its Fight Against Terrorism and Against Proliferation of Weapons of Mass Destruction: The Question of Legitimacy", p. 109 et seq.

The second reason I am definitely uncomfortable with my topic – and, on this, I certainly do not concur with Professor Keohane[7] – is that I think that the very notion of democracy is simply meaningless at the international level or, perhaps more accurately, that trying to transport democracy at the international level makes the very concept of democracy itself meaningless.

Even though this may seem very general and not purely focused on my topic, I wish to pause for a short while on this, especially because Professor Wolfrum clearly raised the question when he wrote in his introductory paper to this seminar: "Is it now necessary for international law to meet the test of legitimacy modelled on democratic principles."[8] But I think that he himself gives the right answer when he writes just two pages later: "It is doubtful whether it is necessary, possible or even advisable to attempt to invoke the democratisation of international law in general."[9] I entirely concur with this view and would probably go even further: democracy has little to do with international society; indeed, virtually nothing. And I feel that it is extremely confusing to speak of democracy or democratisation of international society as well as of the United Nations, which now give a quite reliable image of the international (restrictively defined as interstate) society.

Weiler, in his interesting article in the *Zeitschrift für ausländisches öffentliches Recht und Völkerrecht*, 2004, on international law governance, democracy and legitimacy goes as far as evoking "the tragedy of democracy in the international legal order."[10] This may be too dramatic an expression. But it is certainly true that international law is based on the sovereignty of the State and not on democracy.[11] And it is true, for

---

7 A. Buchanan and R.O. Keohane, "The Legitimacy of Global Governance Institutions", in this volume, at p. 36.

8 See above in this book p. 20.

9 See above in this book p. 22.

10 *Op. cit.*, note 3, at 561.

11 See *ibid.*, at 548. See also, for various views: Hans Kelsen, *Das Problem der Souveränität und die Theorie des Völkerrechts*, 2nd ed., 1928; "Sovereignty and International Law", *Georgetown Law Journal* 48 (1960), 627; Charles Chaumont, "Recherche sur le contenu irréductible du concept de souveraineté internationale de l'État", *Hommage d'une génération de juristes au Président Basdevant*, 1960, 114-151; P. Guggenheim, "La souveraineté dans l'histoire du droit des gens", *Mélanges offerts à H. Rolin. Problèmes de droit des gens*, 1964, 134-146; M. Virally, "Une pierre d'angle qui résiste au temps: avatars et pérennité de l'idée de souveraineté" in: I.U.H.E.I., *Les relations internationales dans*

example, that "one state, one vote" is entirely different from "one human being, one vote". If, as I strongly contend, democracy is the "government for the people by the people" it has indeed nothing in common with the sovereignty principle, at least as it stands in the international sphere.

If we were to transpose democracy at the international level this would mean that China would have to be allocated 1 billion and some hundred million votes. India more than 1 billion, and Nauru 8,000 votes. And even this would not be enough: China would itself have to become a truly democratic state; this may happen in a more or less remote future, but it is clearly not the case for the moment. Therefore, I would suggest that, subject to some qualifications to which I will come later,[12] we had better leave democracy aside at the global level for the time being.

With all this in mind, let me try to come closer to my topic by stating three general propositions:

- first, while legitimacy is not a common word in the language of law, it is not without relation to legality; I would suggest that this relationship goes both ways:
- on the one hand (and this is my second proposition), law being the result of a "successful political process"[13] which defines how policy goals are converted into binding standards, rules of law will only (or, at least, more easily) appear, and be seen, as lawful when they are legitimate; and
- third, on the other hand and reciprocally, legality is part of the legitimisation process in that, in the usual circumstances, behaviours which are in conformity with legal rules are seen as legitimate, while those which are unlawful will appear to be illegitimate; unless the law is widely seen as manifestly unjust, a behaviour's legality almost certainly guarantees its acceptance as legitimate.

This also shows – and this is why I do not entirely concur with the general approach of legitimacy which has been introduced by the two pre-

---

un monde en mutation, 1979, 179-195; J. Verhoeven, "L'État et l'ordre juridique international", *RGDIP* 82 (1978), 749-774; A. Truyol-Serra, "Souveraineté", *Archives de philosophie du droit* 35 (1990), 313-326; J. Combacau, "Pas une puissance, une liberté: la souveraineté internationale de l'État", *Pouvoirs* 67 (1993), n° 7, 47-58.

12 See below, p. 80 et seq.

13 "Une politique qui a réussi" (Émile Giraud, "Le droit positif – ses rapports avec la philosophie et la politique", *Méls. Basdevant*, note 11, 234).

vious speakers[14] – that legitimacy cannot be assimilated with fairness or with justice, as was very brilliantly shown by Thomas Frank in his Hague Academy Course in 1993.[15]

This approach can be illustrated by two different sets of examples regarding, first, the economic international institutions and, second, the use of force.[16]

II. International Economic Institutions

As regards economic institutions, whether the IMF, the World Bank or the WTO, we have probably very striking examples of the discrepancy between legitimacy in the strict sense on the one hand and fairness on the other hand.

All three institutions are vested by their respective Statutes with the power to take action in the bold sense I have accepted:

- the Bank lends money to Member States,
- the IMF can authorise its Members to purchase the currencies of other Members through the policies it defines,[17]
- while the WTO has very little decision-making power, it can nevertheless enforce its rules through the famous mechanism of the Dispute Settlement Body (DSB).

In all three cases, legal techniques (and indeed very different legal techniques) ensure the legitimacy of the decisions of those three international institutions.

The World Bank – that is the IBRD and its affiliate bodies, the IDA and the IFC – ensures the legitimacy of its actions by means of most classi-

---

[14] R. Wolfrum, "Legitimacy of International Law from a Legal Perspective: Some Introductory Considerations", 1 et seq.; A. Buchanan and R.O. Keohane, "The Legitimacy of Global Governance Institutions", at 25, both in this volume.

[15] "Fairness in the International Legal and Institutional System – General Course on Public International Law", *Recueil des cours*, vol. 240, 1993-III, 41-44.

[16] In both fields, I will deal only with the global level, leaving aside European law and its institutions.

[17] See Article IV, Section 3, of the IMF Articles of Agreement.

cal legal tools, i.e. loans agreements. These agreements are seen as legitimate for the very simple reason that the consent of the beneficiary of the loan is given in conformity with the traditional law of treaties which, at least in a volontarist approach, fully preserves the State's sovereignty and, in particular, permits the national Parliament to give formal approval if this is required by the national Constitution.

The IMF Agreement ensures the legitimacy of its "conditionality" – that is the special conditions it imposes on its Member States using its resources – in a more subtle way. It does so through quite peculiar legal instruments, the "stand-by arrangements" which, from my point of view, are not agreements, nor treaties, but unilateral decisions of the Organisation, which are compulsory for the Fund itself, but *not* for the beneficiary (the State which "buys" the currencies).[18] Legally speaking, the latter remains free to comply or not with the conditions – if not, it loses the ability to use the Fund's resources but it does not entail its international responsibility. Here again, the legitimacy of the Fund's action is ensured by its formal respect for the States' sovereignty.

Regarding the WTO, things are different again. As I have said, it is doubtful whether the organization can make decisions binding on its Members, but it can nevertheless take action in order to impose on its Member States the obligation to respect its Statute and the correlative agreements, including the 1947 and 1994 GATTs. But the WTO does so, not through executive or legislative actions, but through the quasi judicial – and more judicial than quasi … – action of the DSB, which, by the way, does confirm that, at the international level, there is no separation of power: in the case of the WTO, the judiciary is the means by which action is taken.

Here again, the legitimacy of such action is ensured by legal technicalities, which lie on State sovereignty, of which the organizations want to appear as the servants. First, the implementation mechanism is activated by the State or by an Economic Union, not by the organization itself; and, second, the DSB does not decide on the sanctions to be applied in case of non-compliance: it simply authorizes the State victim to take action – that is, in fact, to adopt counter measures in the most classical sense. And we are just referred back to one of the most classical features

---

[18] See Joseph Gold, *The Stand-by Arrangements of the IMF*, 1970 or Patrick Daillier et Alain Pellet, *Droit international public (Nguyen Quoc Dinh)*, 7th ed., 2002, at 1080. *Contra*: Dominique Carreau et Patrick Juillard, *Droit international économique*, 2nd ed., 2005, at 594.

of the most classical international law, the right of each state to take the law into its own hands.

Of course, there are differences; these measures are authorized and framed by the Organisation. However, I suggest that all three cases (World Bank, IMF and WTO) call for common conclusions: the acceptability of the actions taken by the three organisations is guaranteed through mechanisms which formally safeguard the sovereignty of the States, and which are then part of the legitimacy process. At least if we assimilate legitimacy with social acceptability,[19] there can be little doubt that those actions are seen as legitimate by the international actors concerned.

In all three cases, this result is, no doubt, reached. And, in all three cases, it can probably be accepted that the legitimacy of the process stems from a complex combination of factors:

- the initial consent given by the interested States when they became members of the organization,
- fear of the negative consequences of non-compliance,
- the need to obtain aid from the organizations and to be held to be full members of the "community", and
- the additional lip-service paid to State sovereignty by the organizations (at least in the case of the Bank and the Fund) or, in the case of the WTO, the contradictory judicial process which is also a powerful means of enhancing the legitimacy of the action taken.

Another conclusion can also be derived from these three examples. They confirm that legitimacy and fairness are two very different things, since also in all three cases, it is quite apparent that States are not exactly happy to comply with the institutions' demands. There is no need to elaborate: economic need and fear of retaliation are not precisely signs of wilful acceptance. States, whether the addressees of the Organisation's decisions or the beneficiaries of the action, consent; but will and

[19] As very aptly explained by professor Ian Hurd in an illuminating article, "legitimacy … refers to the normative belief by an actor that a rule of law or institution ought to be obeyed. It is a subjective quality, relational between actor and institution, and defined by the actor's *perception* of the institution" ("Legitimacy and Authority in International Politics", *International Organization* 53 (1999), at 381 – italics in the original text).

consent are quite different notions.[20] And, indeed, if underdeveloped countries are less vocal today in their criticisms of the international economic order that they used to be in the 1970s or the 1980s, they certainly cannot be described as willing partners. They accept actions by international economic institutions as a fact of life, not as an expression of fairness. However, I would think that they do not challenge the legitimacy of those decisions.

Nor do they question the procedures followed, unfair as they may appear in several respects. This is quite obvious in respect to the twin Washington Organisations where the decision making power lies in a handful of industrialized countries – the United States, the European Union and some others – as a consequence of the shares system, which results in an unequal distribution of the votes inside both the IMF and the World Bank, a system which is seen as unfair by the Third World. Unfair but legitimate since it is expressly provided for in the Statutes of both organisations and, more deeply, because it is an exact reflexion of the unequal distribution of power among States.

These conclusions *mutatis mutandis* also apply to the actions of international institutions in the field of the use of force (and by force I now mean only military force in international relations).

III. The Use of Force by International Institutions[21]

A preliminary remark can be made however: scholars may be puzzled by the lack of legitimacy of the UN system for peace; the States do not really share these concerns. It is striking that the 2000 Millennium Declaration[22] does not include the words "legitimacy" or "legitimate". This

---

20 See Alain Pellet, "The Normative Dilemma: Will and Consent in International Law-Making", *Australian Yearbook of International Law* 12 (1992), 22-53.

21 This second part of my presentation is directly inspired by a paper I prepared for the United Nations Foundation during the elaboration of the Report of the High-Level Panel on Threats, Challenges and Change, *A More Secure World: Our Shared Responsibility* (A/59/565, 2 December 2004): "Legitimacy, Legality and the Use of Force" (reproduced on the website of the United Nations and Global Security Initiative – http://www.un-globalsecurity.org/pdf/Pellet_legit_use_of_force.pdf).

22 A/RES/55/2 of 8 September 2000.

is in strong contrast with the Report adopted by the High-Level Panel of "Eminent Persons", *A More Secure World*, which uses the word a number of times (16 my computer told me ...) and devotes to the question a full sub-section suggesting five guidelines supposed to reinforce the legitimacy of the actions to be decided by the Council: seriousness of threat, proper purpose, last resort, proportional means and balance of consequences.[23] However, significantly, the record falls to two mentions in the Secretary-General's Report, *In Larger Freedom*[24] – and these mentions are not related to the actions of the Security Council; and to one in the 2005 World Summit Declaration which contents itself with supporting an "early reform of the Security Council – an essential element of our overall effort to reform the United Nations – in order to make it more broadly representative, efficient and transparent and thus to further enhance its effectiveness and the *legitimacy* and implementation of its decisions"[25]; in other words, only the composition of the Council seems to be a matter of concern in relation to legitimacy.

Although I certainly do not share this precise concern and maintain that the actual composition of the Council makes it a reasonably legitimate body, I agree that the UN system for the maintenance and re-establishment of peace does not raise real issues of legitimacy – again compared with fairness. But the request for more fairness is not strong enough to undermine its legitimacy whatever the "eminent persons" may believe. In any case, I think that experts cannot be the real judges of legitimacy and, in this respect, I am not sure I agree with either Rüdiger Wolfrum or Professor Keohane.[26]

There is but little doubt that an armed action in conformity with either an authorization or a measure taken by the Security Council under Article 42 of the Charter or within the framework of Article 51 will be seen as lawful and, consequently, legitimate, while an armed attack falling outside these two hypothesis will qualify, by nature, as both illegal and illegitimate aggression. The sharp contrast between the two Iraqi wars in 1990-1991 on the one hand and 2003 on the other hand is telling in this respect. And this certainly explains why the United States, even reluctantly, sought the Security Council's blessing before attacking Iraq

---

[23] A/59/565, note 21, para. 204-209.

[24] A/59/2005, para. 70 and 116.

[25] A/RES/60/1, para. 153.

[26] See above, Wolfrum, note 14, at p. 24 and Buchanan and Keohane, note 14, at p. 47 respectively.

in March 2003. Similarly, the high degree of probability that the Security Council would not have authorized the contemplated uses of force by the U.S. in this case, or by NATO in Kosovo, also explains why, eventually, a vote in this organ was not requested: the rejection of a resolution authorizing the use of force would have made its illegality too apparent and, by way of consequence, would have jeopardized its legitimacy (that is its acceptability as a lawful act) even more. Pointing to the same direction, it is striking to note that, in making its case for the Iraq war to international audiences, even the Bush administration tacitly accepted this framework, citing Security Council resolutions dating back a dozen years as legal justification for military action; only to domestic audiences did it offer a "preventive" rationale without reference to the Charter.

By contrast, Security Council Resolution 1368 (2001) has certainly enhanced the legitimacy of the U.S. response in Afghanistan to the "horrifying terrorist attacks" of September 11, by making it indisputable that the situation was one of self-defence even though an authorization by the Security Council is clearly not required for the use of military force in the event of an armed attack. In a way, it is exactly the opposite since Article 51 implies that the inherent right of individual self-defence (*légitime défense* in French) comes to an end when "the Security Council has taken measures necessary to maintain international peace and security" – an achievement which is not defined in the Charter and which, to my knowledge, has never been clearly presented as such in any formal resolution of the Council. I note in passing that, while Resolution 1368 is probably the most clearly identified example of a legally superfluous Security Council resolution enhancing the legitimacy of self-defence – that is the unilateral use of force by a State or a collection of States victim of an armed attack, this is clearly not an isolated example. Just think, for example, of the whole of the first Gulf war[27] when resolution 661 (1990) of the Security Council, which initiated the whole process affirmed "the inherent right of individual or collective self-defence, in response to the armed attack by Iraq against Kuwait, in accordance with Article 51 of the Charter".

These examples clearly show that a blessing by the international organ on the use of force by a State – or by States – reinforces the legitimacy of its or their unilateral use of force – this absent any action by the international institution itself.

---

27 Or second Gulf war if you include the Iran-Iraq war.

Now, when the Security Council decides to act or to authorize actions under Chapter VII of the Charter, there is no doubt, leaving aside legal quibbles made by scholars that States generally speaking clearly see such actions as legitimate. A striking example is the behaviour of the Milosević regime during the war in Bosnia-Herzegovina. As clearly appeared from the recent pleading in the *Genocide* case before the ICJ involving Bosnia and Herzegovina and the then Serbia and Montenegro, Yugoslavia was, at the time, conscious that it had to seem to comply with the Security Council's resolutions condemning its involvement in Bosnia and Herzegovina. And as Brdjanin, one of the leaders of the government of the Republica Srpska, the Bosnian Serb secessionist entity, put it: Belgrade wished "to appease the requests of the international community to cease all involvement in the country" while maintaining its hidden aid to the entity.[28]

So, even the Milosević regime saw the resolutions of the Security Council as both lawful and legitimate. This – and many other examples could be given – clearly shows that even the "wrongdoers" have no doubt that they must comply with the decisions of the Security Council. In this respect at least the legitimacy of its actions is not challenged. But it does not mean that, at the global level, Security Council action is seen as "fair" and, here again, we meet this opposition, or, at least, the absence of full coincidence, between legitimacy and fairness.

However, legitimacy through the rule of law may be jeopardized if the fairness of the legal process itself is put into question. In the present situation, this is probably the case as far as actions decided by the Security Council are concerned. I see two main reasons for this discrepancy (corresponding to the only two cases in which the use of military force is lawful in the current state of international law):

(1) the voting rules applicable within the Security Council are seen as unfair since they give a handful of permanent Members a power of veto, which, rightly or not, seems unfair to a great majority of States and

---

[28] See ICJ, CR 2006/10, 6 March 2006 (Condorelli), at 26, para. 34; see also, e.g.: CR 2006/2, 27 February 2006 (Van den Biesen), at 46-47, para. 62-64 or at 51, para. 75; CR 2006/8, 3 March 2006 (Van den Biesen), at 57, para. 72-73 or at 59-60, para. 82-83; CR 2006/34, 20 April 2006 (Van den Biesen), at 28, para. 1 and at 29-30, para. 6-7 and *ibid.*, (Ollivier), at 70, para. 20; see also the pleadings by Serbia and Montenegro trying to prove that assistance by the FRY to RS "was perfectly compatible with the (...) provisions of the United Nations Charter" (CR 2006/17, 13 March 2006 (Brownlie), p. 23, para. 222); see also CR 2006/16, 13 March 2006 (Brownlie), at 44-45, para. 129.

public opinions all over the world – which weakens the moral authority of the decisions of this organ, including those authorizing the use of force; and

(2) the conditions for the use of the "inherent right of individual or collective self-defence" under Article 51 of the Charter are uncertain and open to question, Resolution 3314 (XXIX) of the General Assembly (1974) defining aggression being both debatable and optional for the Security Council.

On the other hand, the legal conditions for the lawfulness of the use of force are seen in some limited but highly influential circles – mostly the Bush Administration and the US conservatives – as abusively (and therefore illegitimately) restrictive, mainly because they do not offer a proper legal framework for the defence and reinforcement of the State's interests and do not authorize (the United) States to use force in assuring their (its) national security interests. The U.S. and some others are therefore induced to define unilaterally both their own legitimate interests (usually presented under a veneer of "values") and the means by which they are most properly safeguarded – at the expense not only of the UN collective security system and commonly accepted international law, but also of legitimacy as perceived by the rest of the World.

An interesting phenomenon is however that the putting into question of the fairness of the system as such has not – or has not yet – from my point of view, jeopardized the legitimacy of the specific actions decided or implemented under such a system.

However, it clearly stems from what I have just said that the current established process for legitimization of the use of military force through the United Nations is under strong criticism from various circles and different parts of the World – even if for very different and sometimes quite opposite reasons. In the current political climate it would seem unrealistic and hopeless just to defend the system as it stands – although from my personal point of view it is highly defensible. On the other hand, it seems rather futile and useless to suggest changes in the law written into the Charter which would clearly be unacceptable for either, or both, of the two opposed "camps" – if only because any change which calls for a revision of the Charter implies a vote and ratification by a two-thirds majority "of the Members of the United Nations, including all the permanent members of the Security Council."[29]

---

[29] Articles 108 and 109.

At the "normative" level, two directions could be explored, relating respectively to each of the two conditions for the lawfulness of the use of force under positive international law. *First*, something could probably be done with respect to Article 2, paragraph 4, of the Charter combined with Chapter VII. *Second*, the conditions of use of the inherent right of individual or collective self defence could be more clearly defined.

It is commonplace to recall that Article 2, paragraph 4, is not satisfactorily drafted, and the "codification" by Resolution 2625 (XXV) (1970) of the principle it lays down improves its understanding in only a limited way and, in any case, does not seem to fit the current state of international relations. It would be advisable to adapt and clarify the scope of this principle in a formal and consensual Declaration on the Legitimate Use of Force in International Relations, the main aspects of which could be inserted into a newly drafted Article 2, paragraph 4. The main themes of such a Declaration could be summarized as follows:

(i) the use of force in international relations or its threat is forbidden under all circumstances except when the conditions set out in the UN Charter are fulfilled (the current drafting of Article 2.4 does not say this straightforwardly);

(ii) the prohibition of the use of force in international relations includes any acts of reprisal, military intervention, and the organization of or aid to civil wars in other states and any acts of terrorism (this is already included in Declaration 2625 (XXV), but could be made clearer and more categorical);

(iii) whether lawful or unlawful, any use of force in international relations does not exempt the Parties, including military forces under UN command, from fully respecting the laws of war, including those pertaining to military occupation of a foreign territory (this is made necessary by the uncertainties in severalsituations where the differentiation between *jus ad bellum* and *jus in bello* is not clearly perceived).

It cannot be seriously maintained, leaving aside Article 107 – which has clearly become obsolete – that there is any legal ground for the use of force in international relations other than (i) self-defence (or, at least, reaction to another use of force[30]) and (ii) measures taken by the Security Council pursuant to Article 42, and there is no need or any realistic possibility to change this state of the law: "legitimate self-defence" is and must remain the only exception to the prohibition of the use of force in international relations. However, given the uncertainties in the

---

30 See below, p. 79.

current drafting of the relevant provisions of the Charter, there is room for varied interpretation. I suggest in particular that:

(i) the French (and Spanish) text of Article 51 should be brought into line with the English text (*attaque armée* replacing *agression armée*) in order to avoid misunderstandings such as the ones which happened after September 11; more widely, the use of the word "aggression" (for which no generally accepted and "operational" definition has ever been found) should be deleted from Chapter VII of the Charter and replaced by the less sensitive expression "armed attack";

(ii) it could be accepted that measures that do not amount to an armed attack but do involve a use of force justify a proportional use of force by the victim or victims (the question was left open by the International Court of Justice in *Nicaragua*[31] – more recently, the Court seems to have accepted the lawfulness of such a further step[32] that I nevertheless hesitate to encourage);

(iii) it should be understood that any pre-emptive use of force is subordinated to a decision by the Security Council, but Article 42 should be redrafted so that (or formally interpreted in such a way that) the current practice (debatable from a strictly legal point of view) of authorizing the use of force by a State or a group of States be clearly lawful.

Whatever the clarifications and cautious widening of the cases in which the use of force is lawful, the main question remains: who may decide? The answer to be found in the Charter is unambiguous: failing an armed attack the decision-making power belongs to the Security Council alone,[33] and this is also true in case of an armed attack since, as I have already said,[34] pursuant to Article 51 the inherent right of self-defence ends when the Council "has taken the measures necessary to maintain international peace and security". There should be no question that a State, whichever it is, cannot be a judge in its own case (*nemo judex in re sua*); otherwise the very idea of a collective security would vanish. However, it must be recognized that in the present state of the law the monopolistic situation of the Security Council may give rise to an incapacity to act, claims for efficiency substituting the law in the quest for legitimacy.

---

31 Judgment of 27 June 1986, *ICJ Rep.* 1996, p. 110, para. 210.

32 See the Court's Judgment of 6 November 2003 in the *Oil Platforms* case, *ICJ Rep.* 2003, p 187, para. 51, or pp. 191-192, para. 64.

33 Article 39.

34 See above, p. 72 et seq.

Leaving aside the numerous and unconvincing attempts to modify the composition or voting rules in the Security Council, three tracks probably deserve to be explored.

First, one could think of an "organized self-restraint" in the use of the veto. By this I mean that the five permanent Members should agree that, when not directly concerned by a given threat to the peace, breach of the peace or armed attack, they would abstain from using their veto right. This should be done through a formal and duly publicized memorandum of understanding.

Second, the celebrated Resolution 377 (V), "Uniting for Peace", should be revived. In reality, it has never been repudiated and all categories of States have used it at one time or another, which confirms its legitimacy even if the debate on its legality is still open. But the "Dean Acheson Resolution" has fallen asleep since the end of the Cold War. It should be seen as a practical means to overcome the paralysis of the Security Council and a powerful tool for enhancing the legitimacy of the use of force in such a case: the General Assembly is seen by most States as more "democratic" than the Council (as debatable as the very idea of "international democracy" is[35]) and the end of the confrontation between blocs should lessen fears of "automatic majorities."[36]

Third, but probably not least, deep thought should be given to the possibility of using the regional arrangements provided for in Chapter VIII not only as a means to achieve peaceful settlement of local disputes or to enforce measures decided on by the Security Council, but also "upstream", as forces of proposals and as an aid to decision-making by the Council. At a time when the legitimacy of both the Security Council and the United Nations as a whole is put into question, such a shift towards regional organizations (when they exist – but this could be an incentive to create new ones, in particular in Asia) could be a way to safeguard a sense of collective security in relation to the UN but within less discredited institutions. Moreover, those arrangements, being more proximate to the (potential) enemies, could, at the same time, be more efficient and more easily accepted than the UN seen as a remote "World Government".

In this respect, one could contemplate encouraging (or directing?) those regional arrangements to act as "peace watchmen" and to bring to the

---

[35] See above, pp. 64-66.

[36] See Alain Pellet, "Inutile Assemblée générale?", *Pouvoirs* 109 (2003), 43-60, esp. at 52-53.

attention of the Security Council potential threats to peace in the region. It should also be accepted that, in a case of unlawful use of force against one or several Member States of those regional organizations, they could have the first word (subject to confirmation by the Security Council) in determining whether there is a case for the use of force in self-defence and proposing specific measures to the Council; they could even provisionally enforce them until the Security Council has taken the necessary measures already envisaged within the framework of the African Union.[37]

The suggestions made above are intentionally limited to fields that are not yet totally explored or are in the works (such as the reform of the composition of the Security Council). I am strongly in favour of revisiting some important proposals for the reform of the UN which are far from having been completely implemented so far, such as the *Agenda for Peace* of former Secretary General Boutros-Ghali of 1992[38] and 1995[39] or the Brahimi Report of 2000;[40] their implementation would improve the efficiency of the UN and enhance the legitimacy of its action. However, I am firmly convinced that the current crisis is much less the result of the weaknesses of the legal framework than of the lack of political will of the various actors – and I have less in mind that of the U.S. than that of its partners which do not, or dare not, properly use the irreplaceable tool of regulation of the use of force provided for by the UN Charter.

However, once again, these proposals may enhance the efficiency of the Charter *system* for the maintenance or re-establishment of international peace and security, or reinforce its legitimacy, or make it look fairer, they must not hide the fact that, in the present state of international law and relations, the *actions* of the Security Council under this disparaged system are not seen by their main addressees – the States – as being illegitimate. Nor is it the case for public opinions. I would suggest that, on the contrary, the idea is well anchored that *only* actions based on the

---

[37] See in particular the Protocol relating to the Establishment of the Peace and Security Council of the African Union, Durban, 9 July 2002.

[38] *An Agenda for Peace. Preventive Diplomacy, Peacemaking and Peace-Keeping*, UN Doc. A/47/277 and S/24111, 31 January 1992.

[39] *Supplement to an Agenda for Peace: Position Paper of the Secretary-General on the Occasion of the Fiftieth Anniversary of the United Nations*, UN Doc. A/50/60-S/1995/1, 3 January 1995.

[40] Report of the Panel on United Nations Peace Operations, UN Doc. A/55/305-S/2000/809, 21 August 2000.

Charter are seen as legitimate. In other words, we face the paradox of a system the fairness of which is put in doubt while the actions taken in conformity with it not only are seen as legitimate but, even more, have a legitimizing effect.

IV. Some Concluding Remarks

Globally – and this holds true both for the use of force and the economic global system, I would think that the challenge to the fairness of the system is not important enough to undermine its legitimacy. The addressees, the beneficiaries of the "actions" decided on or undertaken by international institutions, feel that the decisions made are legitimate. But this also calls for some more specific conclusions.

First, generally speaking the actions of international institutions at the global level at least are seen as being legitimate – and this, in itself, is very telling. It shows that at the end of the 20th and the beginning of the 21st centuries, multilateralism is not seen as incompatible with sovereignty and is certainly accepted as more legitimate than unilateralism. The balance between sovereignty (or, more precisely, the formal respect for State sovereignty) and multilateralism seems even to be the reason why the system itself is felt to be legitimate.

This is certainly true for the use of force – if only because self-defence is better accepted when backed by a resolution of the Security Council. But this is also true in the economic field.

No doubt, the IMF or the WTO is unpopular and the decision-making processes in both institutions as well as in the World Bank are criticized and, often, felt as being unfair and inequitable. Nevertheless, multilateral institutions are seen as more secure and reliable channels for international aid than purely bilateral relations, and the reinforcement of the rules of the game in the field of trade through the WTO since 1994 has been accepted by the States as progress. There are two main reasons for this: (i) all Member States participate in the discussions for the adoption of new rules or the reinforcement of existing principles and the generalized practice of consensus gives all groups of States – if not all individual States – a chance to object to the adoption of illegitimate rules, while (ii) the implementation mechanism based on contradictory proceedings is widely accepted as legitimate and decently efficient.

Second, this acceptance of the actions decided by international institutions does not mean that the global system from which these actions emanate is itself seen as being fair. Neither the quota system in the Bretton Woods Agencies nor the right of veto in the Security Council is accepted as such. It remains nevertheless that, globally, States do comply with the outcomes of those processes and that the claims based on the unfairness of the system, whether made from inside the system, at the interstate relations level or coming from outside the system, from the so-called civil society, the NGOs, are not strong enough to delegitimate lawful action taken by an institution of the system. No State or group of States has voluntarily decided to step out or to stay apart from the system, and the concessions made by States in order to join the WTO are most revealing of their global acceptance of the rules of the game – whatever their reasons.

Not only is the international global system seen as legitimate, but admission to the system itself clearly appears as part of the legitimization of the States themselves.

Third, claims of illegitimacy of both the system and the actions taken in accordance with its rules and principles do not usually come from inside; they come from outside: they emanate from "public opinion" (an undefined notion, but an indisputable reality), and in particular the NGOs, which style themselves as the guardians of international morality.

This self-defined function is not to be underestimated: it offers a constant incentive for reforms and improvements and their claims are, in the long term, echoed by the system as a whole and the particular institutions which compose it, which probably makes it more legitimate and, consequently, more acceptable and sustainable.

Now, I think that my conclusions would certainly be more popular if I were of the view that the system and the actions taken in accordance with the system are illegitimate. But this view is neither reasonable nor tenable.

Before ending this rather general paper on a vast and fascinating topic, I offer some even more general conclusions on the very nature of legitimacy:

(i) first, fairness and legitimacy are two different concepts; of course, they are connected to each other, in that fairness of the procedure or its outcomes – that is the rules to be followed by the actors and the actions of the actors themselves – is probably part of the legitimacy of such rules and actions; nevertheless,

(ii) it is both intellectually acceptable and observable in practice that claims for the unfairness of these systems and actions are not strong enough to undermine their legitimacy – even though, in the long term, they could have this result; and

(iii) legitimacy in the international legal sphere is no doubt a fashionable concept, but I wonder whether, after all, it is that new.

It reminds me of a most classical discussion, well known to all of us, on the two elements of custom, which is said, and rightly so, to be based on general practice accepted as law. And I suggest that, after all, the very idea of legitimacy of the rules of law is nothing more than the good old *opinio iuris* of the addressee that the rules which are addressed to it are acceptable and must be obeyed. And this joins my deeply rooted conviction: the very test of law in general and of international law in particular is not the will of the States, nor is it pure relations of power, it is a subtle alchemy of a great variety of elements which at the end of the day result in a generalized *opinio iuris*, which founds both the efficiency and the legitimacy of the rule of law. This *opinio iuris* also explains why, in spite of so many criticisms, the global system and its actions are seen as being legitimate.

Now, and to put it bluntly, with respect, I am not sure that I agree with Rüdiger Wolfrum[41] that there is a deficit of legitimacy at the global level. This does not, however, mean that the system is fair. It just shows that it is not unacceptably unfair, which, I think, is different. This may be the wrong kind of legitimacy, to paraphrase Professor Keohane;[42] it is nevertheless *a* kind of legitimacy.

---

41 See Wolfrum, note 14, at p. 19 et seq.

42 See Buchanan and Keohane, note 14, at p. 42 et seq.

On the Legitimacy of International Institutions

Anthony D'Amato

I. The Concept of Legitimacy

In the draft paper I prepared before coming to grand old Heidelberg to participate in this conference, I began by taking the position that the word "legitimate" was hopelessly ambiguous. It seemed to be trying to occupy a space between "lawful" and "unlawful", yet that space is hard to measure or even imagine. Of course the ambiguity can be removed by eliminating the space – by stipulating that "lawful" and "legitimate" are synonymous. Black's Law Dictionary tells us simply that "legitimate" is that which is "lawful, legal, recognized by law, or according to law." Simple, but not helpful.

However, in listening to the distinguished participants during the conference, I became persuaded that a space all its own might exist for "legitimacy" in international law. I'm not at all sure that such a space exists in domestic law. But international law has some features that distinguish it from domestic law. Accordingly, in revising this paper for publication, I take the opportunity to begin it a different way, and to present what I believe is an unambiguous example in international law of a real difference between lawful and legitimate.

Legitimacy can sometimes usefully describe a space between international law and international politics. I will use as an example the distinction in international law between de jure and de facto recognition of governments. Although I will only discuss one real case, the principles involved can readily be extended to almost all other cases of recognition of governments.

The case I want to discuss is the situation that arose in 1936 when Italy, seeking to assert on the world stage its new fascist personality, abruptly invaded and conquered the state of Ethiopia. Emperor Haile Selassie, who embodied the Ethiopian government, fled to Great Britain.

Italy set up a functioning government in Ethiopia. Now the beleaguered country had two competing governments: the effective puppet government in Addis Ababa, and the government in exile consisting solely of the person of Haile Selassie. Great Britain, not wishing to reward Italy for its aggression, maintained its existing de jure recognition of Haile Selassie as the government of Ethiopia. The British Foreign Office stated after the Italian conquest: "an Envoy Extraordinary and Minister Plenipotentiary from His Majesty the Emperor of Ethiopia" is accorded recognition at the Court of St. James.[1]

Receiving an ambassador from a foreign government is the bright-line test of de jure recognition. Haile Selassie remained the "lawful" – not necessarily the "legitimate" – government of Ethiopia up until November 30, 1938, when Great Britain dismissed Selassie's Envoy and instead recognized the King of Italy as the de jure government of Ethiopia. Thus for the period 1936-1938, the only lawful government of Ethiopia was Haile Selassie. When he brought suit in a British court for monies owed to Ethiopia by a British corporation, the court had no choice but to accept Selassie as the person entitled to the monies in view of the fact that he was the lawful government of Ethiopia.

The complicating factor was the status of the King of Italy in Ethiopia during the period 1936-1938. The British Foreign Office took the abnormal step of actually designating the King of Italy as the de facto government of Ethiopia. To be sure, verbal designations of this sort are hardly conclusive of the international legal question. (There is no formal bright-line test, such as the exchange of ambassadors.) However, customary international law does in fact recognize the status of a de facto government as in some instances distinct from a de jure government. The Ethiopian case from 1936 to 1938 was indeed one of those instances.

Here is where the concept of legitimacy can be useful. The King of Italy in 1936-1938 was the legitimate government – the de facto government – of Ethiopia. Legitimate does not mean lawful. In a British court where title to Ethiopian assets are at issue, it is the lawful government, not the

---

1 *Haile Selassie v. Cable & Wireless, Ltd.*, 1938 L.R. Ch. 545. The fascinating proceedings in the British courts, stretching out over four cases that reversed each other, can be found in Anthony D'Amato, *International Law Coursebook* 5-17 (1994), also available at http://anthonydamato.law.northwestern.edu/ILC-2001/INTLAW02-2001-edited.pdf.

legitimate government, as we have seen, that must prevail. But what, then, does the term "legitimate de facto government" mean under international customary law?

One thing it does not mean is what many scholars have asserted it to mean: that the de facto status of a government simply is a temporary designation for a government that is on its way to becoming the de facto government. This cannot be correct as the following thought experiment will show. Suppose at some point in the 1936-1938 period, say in 1937, a combination of French and Dutch forces managed to drive out the Italian government and retake Ethiopia for Emperor Haile Selassie. In that event, we could not say that the de facto government of the King of Italy was simply a temporary stage on the way to its acceptance de jure. Instead, we would say that Selassie "remains" the lawful government of Ethiopia, and all talk about de facto governments would be dropped. In light of this simple thought experiment, we need another explanation for the term "de facto."

Suppose there are some British citizens who are trying to exit from Ethiopia but are restrained by the government. They get word to the British Foreign Office that they need help in getting an exit visa. Whom should the Foreign Office contact? Certainly not Haile Selassie, who is powerless and sitting in a hotel room somewhere in London. Clearly the Foreign Office must petition the de facto government of Ethiopia, which is in this case the King of Italy. For it is obviously the de facto government that has the requisite power to release or to detain the British citizens.

There are many similar situations that can arise: a British company wants to enter into a contract to construct a bridge in Ethiopia and wants to know its rights if it enters into a contract with the King of Italy. Or suppose some Ethiopian citizens temporarily in Great Britain want to obtain visas to enter Ethiopia. If the King of Italy is the functioning government of Ethiopia, then he must be dealt with in order to allow daily interactions with the conquered territory of Ethiopia. Any conflicts with Ethiopia (which the King renamed Abyssinia) can only be resolved, as a practical matter, if the King of Italy is a party. The fact that the King of Italy is not the lawful government of Ethiopia does not disable it from being a responsible party to these routine situations that can come up from time to time. Accordingly, it makes pragmatic sense to call the King of Italy the legitimate government of Ethiopia even as we continue to designate Haile Selassie as its lawful government.

What this example shows is the existence of a definite space in international legal discourse for the term "legitimate' as distinct from the term "lawful." More importantly, it shows that what is legal in international law is sometimes very close to what is political.[2] This is perhaps best exemplified by the way customary law is formed. When a rule of customary law is in the process of being formed, there was no prior rule on the subject (by definition). There was only a political controversy, resolved in some political fashion. Its resolution, however, is then adopted by the international legal system and called a "precedent" (or a "custom") under customary international law. Thereafter in similar conflicts governing rule will be identical to the original rule that was arrived at empirically in the first political controversy. Hence customary law is constructed directly upon the political practices of states.

Once we see how endemic is the conception of legitimacy in international law, we can begin to use it cautiously in describing phenomena that interface the legal and the political. Prominent among these phenomena are international governance institutions.

II. International Governance Institutions

David Mitrany prophesied in 1943 that international organizations and institutions would gradually take over the functions of government, leaving to the states only local governmental matters such as public health and safety.[3] His goal was to eliminate political divisions that caused conflict by overlaying states "with a spreading web of international activities and agencies, in which and through which all nations would be gradually integrated."[4]

Mitrany acknowledged that there was "no prospect that under a democratic order we could induce the individual states to accept a perma-

---

[2] Students who first encounter international law in law school can object strenuously that the King of Italy should not be able to shoot and bomb his way into the position of a legitimate government of Ethiopia. And indeed today a country cannot obtain title to territory by conquest. But back in 1936-1938 the question still seemed to be open. This does not mean that the Ethiopian example won't happen again; it only means that it will happen in non-conquest situations, such as two equally well situated and competing military groups competing for governmental control of a country that is temporarily without a government.

[3] David Mitrany, *A Working Peace System*, 1943.

[4] Id. at 27.

nent limitation of their economic sovereignty by an international authority."[5] Yet certain governmental functions – which individual states might find onerous, routine or boring – could very well be entrusted to international institutions. We might say that Mitrany was hoping to usher in world federalism quietly through the back door.

Today, if we look at the growing power and reach of international institutions, it might appear that Mitrany's dream is being realized. Such institutions include the World Bank, the International Monetary Fund, the Multilateral Investment Guarantee Agency, the Inter-American Development Bank, the Council of Europe, the European Union itself, NATO, the OAU, the World Trade Organization, GATT, the Shanghai Cooperation Organization, the International Sea-Bed Authority, and so on, criss-crossing the globe with treaty-regimes.

These are all lawful international institutions.[6] The United Nations Charter itself encourages the formation of regional organizations and specialized intergovernmental agencies. One might want to go on and say that these agencies and institutions are all surely "legitimate." But the question would then be: legitimate compared to what? Unless the term "legitimate" occupies some space of its own, as we saw in Part I, it would simply reduce to the semantic equivalent of "lawful."

Let us consider comparing the legitimacy of international institutions with customary international law. There is no doubt that customary international law is legitimate. By comparison, are international institutions less legitimate? Can we go so far as to say that they are in a sense illegitimate?

Customary international law is the only law in the world which applies equally to every state, big or small. By contrast, the internal laws of international institutions apply only to their members. Suppose the Asian Development Bank has 43 member states in a world currently consisting of approximately 190 states. The Bank for International Settlements has 55 member states, and the Inter-American Development Bank 47 members, and so on. Now, following a suggestion once made by Oliver Lissitzyn, we draw a circle on a sheet of paper and label it ADB.[7] We draw another circle that is somewhat larger than the first because it has more member states, and call it BIS. A third circle, labeled IADB, is be-

---

5 Id. at 33.

6 There exist of course unlawful international organizations such as Al Quaeda and other terrorist groups.

7 Oliver Lissitzyn, *International Law Today and Tomorrow*, 1965.

tween the size of the first two. These circles are drawn so they overlap. If two circle-regimes each have the same six states among their membership, then the degree of overlap of the two states is proportional to their six common elements.[8]

Instead of overlapping the circles according to membership, the overlap can be made more functional by making the overlaps signify jurisdictional competences. For example, there is probably a considerable overlap between the jurisdiction of the Asian Development Bank and that of the Shanghai Cooperative Organization, or between GATT and the WTO. These overlaps would be difficult to ascertain, and yet even a rough approximation might prove useful for some purposes.

I have omitted the international institution called the United Nations. With a membership of nearly all the states in the world, it is larger than all the other circles and indeed includes those circles within its circumference. Yet we can be misled by looking at the United Nations as an inclusive organization. Its real power lies in the Security Council, and more so among the five permanent members within the Council. Although largely blocked by Cold-War vetoes from 1945 until 1990, the Council has emerged with a vengeance in the past decade and a half. Indeed, unless the International Court of Justice modifies or overrules its ill-advised preliminary decision in the Lockerbie case, the Security Council may have succeeded in arrogating to itself the power to modify the treaty arrangements and jurisdictional competences of all other international institutions.

III. World Government

We are a long way from David Mitrany's vision. He would have had no overlapping circles. Every institution would take up a specific governmental function such as banking, investment, mineral resources of the sea-bed, world trade, and copyright protection, and all states would be members of these institutions. It is certainly an impractical vision for today's world. Just to take one example, the World Bank is presently funded by loans made to it by the voluntary decisions of some of its members. If there were one World Bank, lending would cease because the rich nations would have to relinquish oversight of their loans to the

---

8 Lissitzyn himself, however, carried this idea too far. He said that international law was nothing but the overlapping circle-regimes.

majority of states. The loans would then seem too risky to make. Hence the World Bank would have to resort to taxation in order to raise money. But taxation would be a huge step toward centralized world government, and nations today are not willing to contemplate such a step.

Yet we may be proceeding toward world government anyway. The use by these international institutions of executive and legislative powers, even though only affecting their own members, inevitably spills over their jurisdictional competences to constrain the choices and the powers of other international institutions. As some of these institutions increase their power and others are reduced to shell organizations, we may see a slow-motion movement toward a world government to be eventually composed of a coalition of themselves. Yet a the world government that serves the interests of the most powerful interest groups will inevitably use its police power to suppress dissent, impose cultural uniformity and infiltrate the underclass anywhere in the world. This time around, as compared to Pax Romana 2000 years ago, the coalition government will have the brutal efficiency of advanced technological means of warfare, centralized communications and the unchallenged power to regulate currency and print more of it at the government's discretion. In terms of individual freedoms we may arrive at a situation like the claim of the President of the United States that he may use his executive power, in the name of national security, to listen in to private telephone conversations or open and read anyone's mail. A world government might be an unrestrained government. It could either claim "emergency" powers in a continuous emergency, or amend its own constitution.

The road to world government is a one-way street. Once that government arrives, there will be no counterforce in the world to take it down – no "humanitarian intervention" so to speak.

Compared to customary international law, I would argue that the law made by international institutions is illegitimate. It is a top-down law as compared with customary international law, which is bottom-up. We know how international institutions make law: they have a legislative branch and an executive branch. It is worth spending a moment to make some additional comments on how international law makes customary law.

IV. Formation of Customary International Law

In the beginning, before nation-states, international law existed only as a potential; it had no actual existence because it lacked substance. The substance would come from the new nation-states. But this presented an immediate problem: if what states did became what they should do, then everything states did would be lawful. Some kind of filter had to be imposed in order to distinguish some of the practices of states as law-creating from other practices that would either be irrelevant to law or counter to it. Yet this raises a second problem: before there are any rules of international law at all, how can we say some state practices could be counter to the law?

Since there are no pre-existing rules by definition, we must assume that of all the possible rules that could be incorporated into international law, only those rules will be incorporated that are compatible with the idea of law. Law is an invention designed to channel the behavior of persons toward peace and stability and away from anarchy.[9] Anarchy is the enemy of law. Thus the new international legal system will be attracted to state practices that imply rules that promote peace and stability.

Suppose a controversy breaks out between two states. If the controversy is later resolved short of war, then its resolution must be deemed "peaceful." The new international legal system will adopt the rule that governed the resolution of the dispute. The adopted rule becomes a rule of customary international law. Indeed, this outcome is exactly what the other states in the system want. They do not want any controversy to escalate into general conflagration; rather, they want it contained within the interaction of the two states. Thus the inferred operative rule governing that containment is a rule that all the other states will implicitly adopt as a rule of customary international law that will henceforth apply to all states. The "rule" that we infer to have been operative in producing the conflict-resolution thus automatically constitutes a rule of international customary law. As more controversies are settled short of war, the rules implicitly governing the resolution of those conflicts are added to the corpus of international customary law. The addition is

---

9 Based on my work-in-progress as well as on a paper delivered at a previous Max Planck Institute Conference. See Anthony D'Amato, "International Law as an Autopoietic System", in: Rüdiger Wolfrum & Volker Röben, *Developments of International Law in Treaty Making*, 2005, 335.

automatic; international customary law simply *constitutes* the rules that tame the forces of anarchy.

The process I have just described is not rule by the majority, nor rule by consent, nor rule by consensus, nor the rule of a representative democracy, nor any form of top-down governance. Rather, it is very much like the process of common-law formation in domestic law. Two individuals get into a dispute; the dispute is resolved by order of a court; and the court's judgment becomes a precedent for all other individuals had no part in the initial lawsuit but who just happen to find themselves within the ambit of that precedent. It is simply a matter of the common law "learning" to achieve peace by borrowing its norms from peaceful resolutions of conflicts. The only difference between this process of common-law formation and the formation of international customary law is that the latter (at least in the formative years) lacks an authoritative "court" to impose a settlement upon the parties. But this is not necessarily a shortcoming, for there are times when a judicially imposed "settlement" aggravates rather than settles a conflict. A conspicuous example is the Dred Scott decision of the United States Supreme Court in 1856, allowing the extension of slavery into the new territories of the United States.[10] The Court's unfortunate decision was a major factor leading to the outbreak, four years later, of the Civil War. The Dred Scott case has been thoroughly vitiated as a precedent. In brief, it is the fact of peaceful conflict-resolution, rather than the method by which it was achieved, that controls its adoption by the overarching legal system, whether it be the domestic legal system or the international legal system.

We find therefore that customary international law consists of norms or rules that earned their way into the corpus of customary law by proving their compatibility with other rules and the peaceful resolution of conflicts. Customary international law turns out to be an inductive process of retaining the results of the resolution of millions of international conflicts. These resolutions, these compromises, these results represent stable solutions to bilateral and multilateral conflicts, achieved usually through negotiation but sometimes simply by letting the problem die of its own weight as attention became focused elsewhere. When negotiation is involved, it will always help one side to show that the proposed rule to govern the controversy at hand is the one that is closest to other existing rules in the system. If a proposed rule is compatible with a half-dozen neighbor rules, then the system of rules is more likely to be co-

[10] 60 U.S. (19 How.) 393 (1857).

herent and hence preserved if the proposed rule is adopted. This would then be a very strong argument in the negotiation in favor of the proffered rule. In short, customary international law is doing its work even though the particular rule at issue is not (yet) listed in its set of rules.

V. Conclusion: Inclusivity v. Exclusivity

Rules and practices of international institutions may seem benign in their intended effects upon non-member states. Yet realism dictates that we should look beneath the surface of purported altruism. A regional bank, for example, may have investment policies in non-member countries that seem to further the latter's interests, and yet the real party in interest may be the bank itself. For example, building hydroelectric power stations in an underdeveloped country may appear to be in the latter's best interests, but we can be fairly confident that if it were not in the investment bank's financial interests the station would not be built at all.

International institutions are top-down, exclusive circle-regimes superimposed upon the globe. In this respect they do not have the equality and democratic bottom-up quality of customary international law. The more than international institutions prosper and grow, the closer we may be getting to a coalition of those institutions that proclaims itself the government of the world. In such a world, customary international law would disappear. As I suggested earlier, the problem with world government is that it is irreversible. If it turns out to stifle individual freedoms and abolish human rights, there will be no counterforce to overturn the government and reclaim those rights and freedoms. Hence I think we should reserve the term "legitimacy" to customary international law and keep a vigilant eye upon the practices of "lawful" international institutions.

Discussion Following Presentations by Rüdiger Wolfrum, Robert Keohane, Alain Pellet and Anthony D'Amato

R. Keohane: I found Professor Pellet's commentary very interesting, but since he had the benefit of my paper and Professor Wolfrum's and not vice-versa, I wanted to give three responses.

My first response is to the notion that "the very notion of democracy is meaningless at the international level". I noticed that he says notion of democracy. One needs to distinguish then between the principles of democracy and its actual practice in domestic politics. The funny thing about his discussion was that he criticized the observation that the notion of democracy is relevant and that his examples were China having 1,3 billion votes, which of course would be a matter of institutionalising the domestic analogy. But they're not the same thing. My position is that indeed democracy is highly relevant, not at all meaningless at the international level, but it's the principles of democracy which have to be adapted in a way that's different from the domestic analogy. The actual practices of domestic democracies are, if not irrelevant, at least not directly applicable. Unless we make a distinction between the principles of democracy and its institutionalisation domestically we can't make sense of the issue.

The second issue is that Professor Pellet said that "democracy has nothing to do with international society". But here we have to distinguish between a descriptive claim and a normative claim. He was making a descriptive argument, but it deviated substantially into a normative argument. Yes, indeed, international law is based on sovereignty, and indeed, sovereignty has nothing to do with democracy. It was invented by absolutist theories in an absolutist age. But neither of these statements has any normative force. They're simply descriptive statements. Descriptively, the problem with Professor Pellet's argument, for me is that it's static and backward looking. International governance is changing rapidly and sovereignty is in fact being undermined whether he likes it or not. And the responsibility to protect doctrine is the most recent one which was approved even though the word legitimacy wasn't used by the UN General Assembly last year. The last proposition I would take issue with is that legitimacy and fairness are identical. They are not identical because fairness is close to justice and, as I said, Legitimacy is a threshold concept, a non-ideal concept. But it seems to me that to carry out a coherent or complete descriptive analysis one would have to look at the political context, for example public opinion, which he did mention at the end of his talk. And in a democratic era, international law institutions will only thrive if they're defensible in the democracies as fair. So there is a very close connection between fairness and what Daniel Bodansky and also Buchanan and I refer to as sociological legitimacy, i.e. public beliefs in the legitimacy of institutions. So one needs to understand therefore sociological legitimacy, the beliefs that publics have got the rights of institutions to rule before one can understand whether institutions are indeed legitimate in a descriptive sense. Thanks for giving me a chance to make these responses.

H. Neuhold: While some of us question the difference between legality and legitimacy, I am one of those who believe in its relevance. However, I have to agree that a precise definition of the concept of legitimacy is not easy. I therefore have one or the other question to put to our speakers, in particular to Professor Rüdiger Wolfrum whose paper I find most useful. In light of his statements in this paper,[1] if one of the decisive criteria is the satisfactory outcome of the norm-creating process, what is the standard for determining the satisfactory or adequate character of the rule concerned, who decides, and how is satisfaction/dissatisfaction assessed and measured? Is this the same criterion as the notion of justice used by Professor Robert Keohane? I found Robert Keohane's distinction between justice as the ideal and legitimacy as the real world intriguing, but am afraid that it might add to the considerable confusion which already characterises the debate.

R. Howse: I have a couple of questions for Professor Keohane, both about his paper and a couple of things he said in the presentation that I couldn't actually find in the paper although I may not have read it carefully enough.

One of the things that he said in the presentation that puzzled me, and I wondered what it meant, was that one could have standards of human rights and democracy that were somehow delinked from a concept of

---

1 R. Wolfrum, "Legitimacy of International Law from a Legal Perspective: Some Introductory Considerations", in this volume, p. 6.

justice, that justice is an ideal concept and that rights and democracy are about some sort of minimum standard that is somehow not informed by an ideal concept of justice. And I didn't understand this move because it's hard to imagine ideas like rights and democracy having a normative force that doesn't depend upon an ideal conception of justice. Some ideal conception of justice. So I just didn't understand that. I guess that also I found in the paper as well that it was not clear what sort of work this minimum legitimacy is supposed to do. Is it supposed to allow the institutions to exist legitimately? Or is it supposed to somehow put the substantive decisions and outcomes of the institutions beyond open democratic contestation? And if it's the second, you know I would have very serious worries about buying into any kind of minimum standard of legitimacy. And if one just takes the standard, the human rights component of the standard, it seems in a way, the way it's articulated in the paper, close to trivial to say that international institutions should observe or not violate the most uncontroversial human rights. What would that mean – that international institutions shouldn't commit genocide or engage in torture? Now, there may be some instances where one could argue the UN should have state responsibility for certain things that peacekeepers have done, but apart from these very rare instances, it seems to me that this criterion can't do much legitimating work since the whole debate about legitimacy of international institutions is not really about the problem of their going around committing genocide or violating norms on torture or entirely uncontroversial kinds of human rights.

E. Riedel: First of all let me thank all the four presenters for their excellent exposés this afternoon and really highlighting one of the key issues of current international law and I dare say international relations. I really enjoyed the presentations. I will say right from the outset that I very much side with Rudiger Wolfrum's position for various reasons. But I did not see such great differences between his approach and that of Professor Keohane, and also to a certain extent what Anthony D'Amato said in the end. But I do see some differences as far as Alain Pellet's position were concerned and I suppose it was the intention to juxtapose them. But I do feel that the differences are not as great as they were made out to be for our purposes.

Just briefly, the question of legitimacy, the moment you take that word into your mouth, you are convinced that something other than "might is right" exists. Otherwise, you would not use the word legitimacy. So, some form of justification of authority having the power to take binding decisions, as Rüdiger Wolfrum said right at the beginning, is probably the starting point. But the five or six examples that he gave from various fields of international law probably require different answers. He said merely referring to constitutional law or European law is not enough when the question of legitimacy is raised, for instance in relation to international economic law, international environmental law and international human rights law or human rights law in general. When that does not work, then clearly the veil of sovereignty is pierced and some legitimacy issues are raised. But he then went on to discuss the role of the Security Council, particularly in its most recent form when the Security Council assumes quasi-legislative functions regarding individuals, and then actually as in the Afghanistan situation assuming legislative functions, which it had not done to such an extent before. Here, Rüdiger Wolfrum says at this stage it needs some underpinning, I would call it judicial or expert underpinning, and then I saw a couple of raised eyebrows as I looked round when the word "experts" came up. You think of bureaucrats, you think of technocrats, and as an alternative to democracy clearly that is not meant, and I would add a word of caution: the treaty bodies that were mentioned, in particular Art. 21 of the ICCPR in relation to Guantanamo Bay is perhaps a case in point. There is some sort of interpretative authority bordering on legislative function. I quoted it directly from the text. I have some misgivings about that. Is it really interpretative power or is this not more in the sense of – I am looking at Mr Habermas – is this not more discourse offerings to States that are engaging in the discourse to defend, to justify, to legitimise whatever they are doing? And from the point of view of those that conduct that discourse, is it not just an *invitatio ad offerendum* more than a quasi-legislative act? But apart from that, I fully agree with his notion.

Mr Keohane added when you deal with the word democracy, you have to look at questions of – and I only pick the last two of his five criteria – accountability and transparency. Now clearly, it is a very different cup of tea when you talk of it at the international level from when you talk about this at the domestic level. But the interesting developments that have been outlined by other people are that at the international level we are using the notions of democracy or democratisation in order to supplement and to give added legitimacy to the system. And are there self-steering mechanisms? And that is a question to all four panellists. Are there self-steering mechanisms of the system that do the trick so that individual unilateral actors find it more difficult to act? Is it something like – as political scientists call it – reflexive institutionalism? Or do we have to revert to other notions? The question of legitimacy always boils down to the fact that if you want to raise the question of democracy you have to use the domestic notions and transfer them by analogy to the international level. Thus you will be able to see how it is domestically applied, but without further parameters not how it is democratised at the international level. Thank you very much.

M. Herdegen: In the light of the four inspiring presentations which we have just heard, I am somewhat intrigued by the normative function of what we call legitimacy and its somewhat delicate relationship to legality under international law. We have been told quite often that certain actions such as NATO's humanitarian intervention in the Kosovo conflict are "illegal but legitimate". I have never found this analysis very helpful and tend to consider it even as irrelevant. But I am interested in the views of our speakers. If legitimacy as a factor generating a pull to compliance in normative terms is to be taken seriously as an objective basis for a value judgement, it can refer only to values that are inherent in the existing legal system. If that is true there is no space for legitimacy above or opposed to international law. The normative pull to compliance would flow from the pedigree of the concrete rights and obligations, from rules asserted as being in accordance with recognized rules of formation of international law. This perception seems to explain also why we are so very intrigued and concerned about issues of legitimacy: This concern is obviously linked with a crisis within our existing system of formation of new rules, a crisis of our regime of sources of international law. Nowadays, it is much easier in the international law discourse to advocate a destabilization of certain customary rules than 20 or 30 years ago. We seriously discuss or even assume the legality of humanitarian intervention although we know exactly that well over 130 states have expressed their opposition to this concept. Not only do we have a crisis in the formation, in the destabilization of customary law, we also have new dramatic developments in the formation of new treaty rules. With treaties now considered as "living instruments", we witness approaches to the interpretation of treaties that fall well away from the historic and actual will of many of the ratifying States. The question I should like to put to our speakers is whether, in the light of the recent dynamics in international law, the traditional regime for the formation of new rules still stands up to scrutiny. Should dynamic treaty interpretation, processes of deduction and extrapolation not only be based on a given methodology, but also be related to concurrent State practice and legal opinions prevalent in the community of

States? In this context, I tend to side with the analysis of Alain Pellet because I tend to think that the basic foundation of legitimacy in international law still is the consent of States. Of course, states have consented to human rights standards, to *ius cogens*, they have consented to sovereign equality, to territorial integrity. But this consent relates to values and principles on a fairly high level of abstraction. If we come to balance these principles in case of conflict, if we engage in processes of deduction and extrapolation, this consent may be evaporating. The crucial standard, I suggest, is a sound blend of actual or latent consent on one hand and a recognized methodology for evolutive interpretation, balancing and extrapolation. Thus, treaty interpretation, the more it moves away from the wording and the original intent, the more it should be based on actual consent, as reflected in State practice and the *opinio iuris* of at least significant sectors of the international community concerned.

W. Heintschel v. Heinegg: To the question of legitimacy: first of all, we often look at the Kosovo campaign when it comes to the relevance of legitimacy in international relations. Obviously states make use of that argument if they know that what they are doing is not necessarily in accordance with the existing law. On the other hand, there is the other scenario we have not talked too much about – apart maybe from Professor Keohane – where states make use of the legitimacy argument: it is not only that states do not wish to be held accountable. In general, states know exactly what the law is about, and they know that somebody would be entitled to tell them what they ought to do and what they should not do. But they do not like this – as all human beings do not like being told what they should or should not do. In order to escape the unpleasant situation of being accused of having breached the law, they refer to legitimacy simply because they are aware that they do not have a legal argument. This works both ways: for those who want to go beyond the existing law or for those who want to complain about the existing law. Legitimacy is a perfect public relations argument. But let us assume that it is more than a public relations argument. Indeed, what else is it then than just denoting a phase of the creation of international law. Like, for example, humanitarian intervention. Maybe today it is only legitimate and it may become legal in some distant future. We do not know that. But in any event, it would only denote a phase of the creation or formation of some norm of international law. Finally, being a simple positivist I do not believe in natural law approaches or some metaphysical approaches to international law. If we look at international law as it stands, I think there is a good point in saying that any international organization is legitimate for a simple fact: not just because states have agreed with the creation of that international organization. It is more than that, because states have also agreed about the purpose the international organization in question is to serve. As long as the means and measures taken by that international organization serve the purpose and as long as they are adequate and necessary for arriving at that purpose, who will then doubt not only the legality but also the legitimacy of the actions taken? Thank you very much.

C. Bradley: Thanks to the panellists for what I found to be very helpful introductory remarks to this topic. Since we are still in the early stages of the symposium, I thought I would ask if it's alright to put an introductory type of question, one that's been troubling me just as a preliminary matter. I have difficulty, and maybe there are different views about it among the panellists, about exactly which perspective we are starting from when we ask the question about what is legitimacy. Whose perspective are we using? I actually had the sense that sometimes we are talking about different possibilities, sometimes systemic points of view, and sometimes individual nation states' points of view. Maybe one could also talk about individual citizens' points of view, which may be different from their states' views, even in democracies. So here's my question to test this out, and I was surprised that the papers didn't have more about the question, given all the controversy that has surrounded it in the academic literature, which is the connection between legitimacy and the idea of state interest, individual state interests. There's been a lot of discussion in the academic literature about whether there's really any difference between international law and legitimacy and state interests. And I'd be interested in the panel's views about that. The old claim that used to be made about legitimacy was that it would enhance compliance, as mentioned already in the speakers' comments, and people meant by that compliance even when it's not otherwise in the states' interest to comply and they're not being forced to do it. That may be the panellists' points of view, but I have trouble with that proposition. I have difficulty understanding ultimately the claim, i.e. if it's really not in even the long-term interest of nation states to participate in the international criminal court or another international organization or to comply with international regimes in certain respects, I don't understand the argument that, well it's legitimate, so you should nevertheless go against your long-term interest as a state. On the other hand, I can understand the point that the legitimacy factors described by the panellists may enhance the argument for long-term self-interest, because they show that systemic values will be promoted and that the system will not be biased against the state. That's obviously a different way of thinking about this, and I'd be interested in the panellists' thoughts about that.

W. Benedek: I would like to congratulate the organizers for choosing such an interesting topic, which, I think, is very relevant for the evolution of the international legal system and which, additionally, forms a bridge between our discipline of international law and the discipline of political science. This is why the presence of Professor Keohane today is very valuable. I wish to ask the panellists about one aspect: what is the relevance of the constituency or the community of legitimacy we are talking about? Actually, nobody has really mentioned that. But I think that it makes a difference whether you are talking about a community of states or about all the world citizens in general or only about the stakeholders in a particular legal process. And I think that legitimacy also has to be related to that in some respect. The reason why we are talking more about legitimacy these days is the widening of the stakeholders. It is, further, the widening of the sources of international law. If you wish to see acceptance and compliance, this wider range of stakeholders – including international civil society – plays an important role. It needs to be acting in the same direction. Because, as we could see very well, particularly in the WTO process, international civil society has the power of delegitimization. They can also stop certain processes. And if you look at the WTO experience with essential medicines, you can see that NGOs together with states from the South have actually managed to change the rules. Or you can look at the field of services trade, where again NGOs were very relevant for getting the European Communities to remove public services from the international negotiations, at least on their side. Then you can see that this constituency, this part of international society is able to have a certain influence. And you can see that non-trade issues have increasingly been recognized at least by the secretariat of WTO. Director-General Pascal Lamy has recently given an important example, when he referred to "humanizing globalisation" and meant that the economic aspect has to be complemented with social, ecological and other considerations. He mentioned the Millennium Development Goals as well, although the WTO could argue that it is outside the United Nations and therefore not bound by them. This shows that the WTO cannot escape from these international obligations.

We might also have to distinguish different forms of legitimacy. Democratic legitimacy is something we should be particularly concerned about. It means the inclusion of all those who are affected by the decisions taken, although this is hardly to be found in reality. Also, legitimacy is not something which we can talk about in the absolute. I think it is the issue of getting a higher degree of legitimacy and not the issue of having it or not. In this context the issue of values plays a role as well. If legal regulations or if international institutions are in line with certain values (or at least do not contradict certain basic values) they will be considered more legitimate and will therefore enjoy a higher degree of acceptance and compliance. As mentioned by Professor Wolfrum in the end, there is a community of values which makes a difference, but it would be of substantial interest to me if we could delve a bit deeper into the relevance of this international community of values for the concept of legitimacy.

T. Eitel: I was rather wondering whether what so far I have been understanding by the word legitimacy is different from what seems to be the sense given here to this word by the panellists. Here legitimacy is used, it seems to me, as almost an equivalent of lawfulness, which in my understanding is more legality. To legitimacy we come when we are looking for justifications, for excuses even, regarding behaviour that is widely considered illegal. I have in my ear resounding statements that this or that is illegal, but it is legitimate. And I wonder whether that is *démodé* or whether that is something which is still actual. In that context, legitimacy is in a higher realm, in a more philosophical sense I think, in the realm of good and evil or something like that, dealing more with equity than with law. Then I have a difficulty with what I understood to be your opinion, Professor Keohane, as far as democracy is concerned. Also Professor Wolfrum referred to it. To me democracy is ... well, a very good system of running a state, of governance, but I was afraid that you were trying to do away with Art. 2 para. 1 of the UN Charter where it says that all states – and there is nothing said about democracy – are, in dealing with whatever they are dealing with, in sovereign equality. And I am opposed to a notion that already now democratic states are better than ... well, let's say monarchies or whatever, autocratic states. We may not like them that much, but if international law is to regulate international relations we must not bring into the system notions like differences of value of states that are either democratic or not democratic.

And, finally, only a footnote to what Professor Pellet said: In my understanding, the Security Council is not implementing its own decisions. They are either implemented by the Secretary-General or they are – look at sanctions – implemented by states, by member states. I don't think that the Security Council itself is implementing its decisions. Thank you.

A. Pellet: As for what you said, Professor Keohane, regarding democracy, I maintain that democracy brings us to human beings and that democracy is something too precious and too important to turn to fit any case. I think that transposing the word in the international society in fact undermines its content itself. We should avoid mixing everything with everything.

In this respect I'm very sensitive to what Professor Benedek said about "constituencies". I think that all depends on what kind of constituency you are speaking of. We must accept that when we speak of international institutions we are speaking of *interstate* institutions and, between States, sovereignty, not democracy, is relevant. I don't understand why you should introduce there the concepts of democracy, human beings, NGOs, etc. I'm afraid that this mania to mix all with everything is rather confusing.

I have a problem with the experts I must say. And in this respect I think that Eibe Riedel will not expect me to concur with him. Experts are very dangerous people. They have – or pretend to have – a self-proclaimed legitimacy. I'm afraid that this confiscation of legitimacy by experts is at least as dangerous as the trends they are supposed to neutralize. And for me the same holds true for the NGOs. What is their legitimacy? Again, it is first a self-proclaimed legitimacy. And I think that this question of the legitimacy of the actors is by itself a very wide and difficult question. And maybe it could be the subject of our next colloquium here...

Now, many of you have given me an occasion to try to clarify my ideas – for me as well as for the audience – on the relations between fairness, legitimacy and legality. And in this respect, I try also to answer Hanspeter Neuhold, Professor Herdegen and Professor Bradley. I would suggest that probably fairness is something which is subjective, it is the good and the bad or the good and the evil as perceived by a subject. It is prospective as well. Legitimacy is objective-subjective, in that it is a perception of a subject, but it is not a preference by the subject, precisely I think that the legitimacy rubs out the preference. You think it is legitimate, whether you like it or not. And this makes a great difference between legitimacy and fairness. And then you have legality, I think legality is objective-objective. If a norm fulfils the criteria for legality, you must comply. To summarize: fairness is prospective, legitimacy is descriptive and legality is perspective.

Just a word to answer to Professor Eitel and Professor Herdegen. I do not think that the distinction between what is legal and what is legitimate is *démodé* at all. You can indeed have illegal but legitimate actions, you can have legitimate and legal actions as well as illegal and illegitimate ones. Thus, the first Iraqi war in 1990 was both legal and legitimate, Kosovo was illegal and legitimate, and the US aggression in Iraq was illegal and illegitimate. I have no problem with that. The distinction is, without any doubt, absolutely meaningful.

One last word on a small point. I think Professor Heintschel von Heinegg said international organizations are legitimate or could be seen as legitimate by definition, since, after all, they are created to achieve the given purpose of their founders. Well, yes and no. International organizations are like all legal institutions and maybe like all human institutions; they can be legitimate, and they certainly are legitimate in their creators' eyes when they are established. But (i) this might not be the case in the perception of non-members (we come back to the fruitful idea of "constituencies"); and (ii) their purpose can become progressively illegitimate. It happens that I am the legal advisor of a very interesting organization, which is the World Tourism Organization. Tourism is seen as a legitimate activity. It could perfectly easily happen that one day or the other it would be seen as a terrible activity, which destroys human society etc. So I don't entirely agree that just because you create international organizations it will be legitimate forever. I think that it can become unlegitimate or illegitimate one day or the other.

R. Keohane: There were many questions directed at me. I'll try to be concise. I want to start with two general points. It's not surprising that since I am a political scientist my view seems to be different from that of many people in this audience, which is one reason why I wanted to come. There are two big points that I want to make before answering.

The two general points are that globalisation in my view is empowering, differentially empowering certain private actors, particularly corporations and financial groups. If international law or international governance stands still it won't be neutral, those groups will benefit.

And the results will be bad for democratic values based on equal human rights. So we shouldn't be under any illusion that the system is working just fine and we are in a static world. We are in a very dynamic changing world. And therefore we should question and criticize all appeals to tradition. And I've heard many of those today. We should be very suspicious of all appeals to tradition that claim that because international law has worked well for hundreds of years it will keep working well in a very different era.

The second premise of my thinking on this issue, which is different I think from that of many people in this room, is that in my view the basis of the right to rule lies squarely in democratic theory, not in the tradition of international law. The fact that something is inscribed in international law is to me neither here nor there with respect to whether it confers the right to rule. It only tells you that some set of actors in the past institutionalised the rule. That may or may not be a good reason to follow it. So in my view, international law is not inherently legitimate. (I know this may bring thunder and lightning down on me in this room or put me alone in one of those soccer stadiums which are so plentiful in Germany. I won't divulge my hotel address!) Democracies in my view should have superior status. They do, I think, have superior normative status. So here we simply disagree, Professor Eitel, on that issue. I do agree with Professor Pellet that the legality-legitimacy distinction is very important as it must be if you take this premise of mine.

So that in a sense those constitute my response to Professor D'Amato. It seems to me that his presentation is a combination of being unbelievably sanguine about the state of the world and the state of our current legal system. I don't think it's in good shape. And secondly, it seems to me, there is almost a paranoia about the danger of some oligarchic grouping of states running the world oppressively. But no such oligarchic rule has ever succeeded in world politics. The thieves always fall out with each other. You can count on that, that's one thing you don't have to worry about. There are a lot of worries in the world, but the worry that somehow the great powers would agree and impose rules on everybody else is not going to happen as long as world politics is as fragmented as it is and remains in political structure.

Now, in specific response to Professor Howse: you misunderstood my argument. My argument is that justice and legitimacy are different because legitimacy is a threshold value and justice is an ideal value. Justice of course is closely linked to rights and democracy. Democratic theory and theory of rights is the basis for justice as well as on a lower threshold the basis for legitimacy. Legitimacy is always provisional, so therefore institutions could always be illegitimate if they behaved badly. So all my conception does is give institutions that have so far passed the test some sort of provisional right to have their regulations respected unless there are good reasons not to.

Professor Bradley, it's a good question about interest. It won't surprise you that I squarely endorse the view that legitimacy is important because it can help institutionalise long-term interest. I don't see it as opposed to interests. As a political scientist, I think states act largely on their interests. This statement, however, begs the question as to what those interests are; how they conceptualise them.

To Professor Benedek, a very good question about the relationship ... what's the constituency? This really gets to the core of the issue between the sociological and the normative view of legitimacy. Normatively, I believe, since I'm a democrat, that it's individuals that really matter. That individuals' views matter. On the other hand, I also said that you can only design an institutional system in a way that's consistent with contemporary political reality, which means you have to take into account the beliefs of people and how those beliefs are weighted by power. So, descriptively, government views are weighted heavily and have to be taken into account. So you have to worry more about the views of the Chinese government than the views of Professor Keohane on issues of legitimacy. So, the trick is that non-ideal normative legitimacy needs to be consistent with sociological consideration. That was the point of talking about the revisability of standards. As the sociological situation changes, if a change is favourable one could in principle stiffen or tighten the criteria for legitimacy.

And, finally, I want to respond to Professor Habermas' very good question and point. I agree entirely that my discussion of accountability doesn't solve the problem. And the reason it doesn't solve the problem is that accountability is a power term and I can't solve the basic fact of world politics, which is that there are huge inequalities of power. And they're played out in the way the system operates and the way institutions operate. So, yes, it illuminates more than it solves. But I think there is a potential partial solution or a move toward a solution. So it seems to me that there are in the system now incremental moves through both interpretation and sanctions, naming and shaming is one of the sanctions. Toward bringing some accountability into the system, it's not very much but it's better than nothing. And specifying criteria for legitimacy seems to be a crucial aspect because you need standards of introducing some degree of accountability. Let me give you an example: the recent furore of a couple of years ago over the WTO and patent protection for drugs, when it became clear that the intellectual property standards of the WTO were preventing people in Africa who needed anti-viral treatment from receiving it because patent protection raised the price so much of those drugs. What ensued reflected a rough accountability system. There was a set of standards which were basically of minimal human rights. People have a right to life in a sense that if there are drugs available that could save their lives they should not be barred by poverty from having them. That standard was used to criticize the rules and the drug companies. And what happened was that under this criticism the WTO changed the rules and the drug companies backed down. I am not saying that these accountability mechanisms were always so successful, just that the episode illustrated the operation of a rough accountability mechanism, which remains imperfect because there are so many power inequalities. Thank you.

A. D'Amato: Professor Keohane is quite right that thieves can fall out with each other. World organizations and coalitions may be less permanent than they look. But then the question is, why accord them legitimacy? It seems to me that legitimacy has to be earned the hard way: by accepting human rights as a constraint upon the very institution that wants legitimacy. It's like saying that a good government is one that downsizes: in other words, the downsizing government is so good that we want less of it. My main fear about world government is that it could be irreversible except for the slim hope of thieves falling out with each other. Let me now address the topic of democracy. It strikes me as interesting, if not peculiar, that European scholars are much more inclined to import democracy into international law than are American scholars. This is despite the fact that the leader of this movement, Tom Franck, is an American. Well, maybe he's really a Canadian, and maybe Canadians are really Europeans. In any event, my disagreement with Tom is almost as wide as the Atlantic Ocean. His view of democracy is that it is a process, whereas I believe that what makes democracy work is human-rights limitations on that process. The process view of democracy is two wolves and a sheep voting on what to have for dinner. But if what really is important is human rights – the sovereignty of the individual – then perhaps the Franckian idea of democracy as primarily a process is a false signpost for the evolution of international law. Perhaps Professor Keohane would agree with my position; his use of the term "individualism" may be a surrogate for human rights. Thus, if it makes sense, as Professor Wolfrum advised in his opening remarks, to place at issue the legitimacy of international law itself, then I think we have to take the road labelled "human rights" and not the road called "democracy."

R. Wolfrum: I will try first of all to reiterate what I've said or what I meant to say about legitimacy. It has been qualified, I believe, by Alain as being subjective. No! It is not. The test of legitimacy is an objective term to the extent that it goes back to the source of the procedure. This I believe is objective. But it can have a subjective connotation, namely when it comes to the result. Let me say a word about that; this has been touched upon by Hanspeter Neuhold and Professor Habermas. Can we really argue that we don't like a result and for that reason something is illegitimate? This also touches upon the interest. I would say no. We have this double check – objective and subjective test. And if something comes from the right source, proper source or through the right procedure, even if one state doesn't appreciate the result, too bad. The long-term interest—and this is what Professor Bradley was hinting at—the long-term interest should induce the given state to comply with the respective measure, for the reason that in another issue the result may be in favour of that given state and others may dislike it. Therefore, it gives a certain safety net if one relies on that.

My second remark is addressed to Alain. You said there is no separation of power in international law. If you put it that way I do agree. I think you meant it differently. We have legislative, adjudicative and executive functions. Here we may disagree. And you can clearly make a distinction between the three as far as adjudicative functions is concerned. International treaties are for me a substitute for laws on the national level, and negotiating and adopting international treaties is one of the means of exercising prescriptive powers.

My next point deals with the question of values. Professor Benedek and others referred to that and I confess I was rather brief on this subject matter. May I elaborate on that issue somewhat. International law is based on a value system represented, in particular, by the human rights system and those regimes which are designed to protect the interests of the international community rather than reciprocal interests of the member states concerned. Measures taken by international organizations in whatever form, even not meeting the traditional sources, are legitimized as long as they keep within this value system. This I consider source-oriented legitimacy.

Finally, let me come to the experts and the legitimizing effect they may have. I expected objections to that aspect of my introduction. May I respond to Professor D'Amato that I didn't just speak of experts, but of experts who have been recognized as international experts in a given procedure. These are two elements: expertise plus the international recognition, mostly they're being elected. Professor Riedel is elected as far as I recall for four years and Professor Treves for nine as a judge. After nine years, there's a new decision. This election for a limited period is a source of legitimacy for the pronouncement either of judgments or statements and the impact the judgments and statements may have on the development of the international law. This election procedure is for me the mechanism which protects against what you were referring Professor D'Amato to as bureaucrats. The latter are not experts; I make a significant distinction between these two types of people.

The Security Council as Legislator and as Executive in its Fight Against Terrorism and Against Proliferation of Weapons of Mass Destruction: The Question of Legitimacy

Georges Abi-Saab

I. On the Meaning of "Legislative" and "Executive" Functions in International Law

The subject I was asked to address is the legitimacy of Security Council legislative and executive action against terrorism and the proliferation of weapons of mass destruction. The exact title on the programme uses the formula "the Security Council as legislator and executive…".

Yesterday, Alain Pellet, referring specifically to my *Cours général* of 1987 at the Hague Academy,[1] criticized the use of the tripartite division of legal functions into legislative, judicial and executive, because, he says, this division does not exist in international law, as there is no international legislature. On this point, that there is no international legislature, I totally agree with him. Indeed, the whole problem with international law, its congenital weakness, is that there is no power (or rather centralized power) to divide in the first place, not to speak of its devolution "from above" to specialized bodies (*corps constitués*), that would be the repositories of, and could be referred to, as the legislative, the judicial and the executive powers or merely as the legislature, the judiciary and the executive.

However, we must here distinguish between **powers** and **functions**. A legal system can only manifest itself and prove its existence by perform-

1 *Recueil des Cours*, vol. 207 (1987 VII), chap. VI-VII, pp. 127 ss.

ing certain types of activities or functions, however haphazardly it does it, namely the creation and modification of norms, the ascertainment of their application in specific situations and the enforcement, if need be, of such determinations and other executory or enforceable legal decisions.

Thus defined, these are "functions" in the sociological or phenomenological sense of the term; the definition being based on the mere observable description from the outside of the content and modalities of the legal activity. It is in this sense and not in that of the formal constitutional separation of powers that I use the term "legislative function".

These functions are exercised in societies where power is centralized – leaving aside the pure Hobbesian model where all powers are concentrated in the hands of one person or entity, the leviathan – through devolution "from above" to certain organs, according to a pre-established constitutional scheme, that at the same time operates the division of labour between them, in other words, the formal separation of powers.

Where power is not centralized, political scientists, borrowing from biologists, say "the function creates the organ". In international law, this can be effected "from below", by agreement of the subjects to create an organ (to perform the function in one instance, in a series of instances or in general). But sometimes, when no such agreement is sought or reached and no organ already exists, the function "squats" in whatever organ it can find. As in the Middle Ages, when certain persons were supposedly possessed by the spirits, international law "takes possession" of whatever organ or mechanism it can get into in order to exercise its vital functions and manifest its existence as a living legal order.

In such cases, international law operates like a climbing plant, latching on to any support it can find in its quest for light. It is a legal system in permanent search for structures or institutions to enable it to function as such; the same with its constant efforts to firm up the hold of its substantive rules on society, like an invertebrate species trying to develop a spine on its own; but without centralized power this is a very difficult ambition to realize. International law is still rather at the stage of soft shell or spine. But this is the whole idea of evolution, in nature as in law.

This brings me to our subject today. The phenomenon of legal functions "possessing" or "squatting in" organs which were not originally established for the performance of such functions raises severe problems of legality and legitimacy. For, regardless of the initial design behind the establishment of the organ, the legal activity that constitutes the exercise of the "new" (or "squatting") function, has to fall squarely within the jurisdictional bounds of the organ; which is a problem of legality. But even if it does, the propriety or appropriateness for the organ to exercise this function may still be questioned, if it goes against the legitimate expectations of the society or the community that established the organ to do something else; which is a question of legitimacy. And both questions entail a greater burden of legal justification.

II. On "International Governance Regimes"

Rather than treating the subject of "legitimacy in international law" in general, Professor Wolfrum in his introductory essay focuses on the question of the legitimacy of what he calls "international governance regimes". He thus provides us with a narrative or a theory which, I assume, we are supposed to verify in the context of the different subjects that we are asked to treat.

Briefly, as I understood it, Professor Wolfrum's narrative proceeds from the premise that the ultimate source of legitimacy in international law, and – I assume – the basis of obligation, is state consent (a premise that can be questioned, but not here). The obligations consented to are of two kinds. The first are specific and static, *i.e.* "punctual" obligations that are discharged at one point in time, and thus their content cannot change over time. The second are of a more general and dynamic nature, the contents of which are specified over time, as those involving the creation of or participation in international institutions, the activities of which may lead to substantial modifications in the scope and substance of the original obligations of member States.

It is in relation to the second type that the question of legitimacy arises; and it is precisely this type of obligation that underlies the "international governance regimes". These regimes, which have proliferated in recent decades, are endowed with quasi-legislative and judicial functions. They serve as conduits of contemporary trends of international law (in response to globalisation pressures), to extend its scope by increasingly regulating matters that were traditionally considered as falling within the domestic jurisdiction of States. In consequence, the ensuing regulations also increasingly address, more or less directly, individuals within those States, and affect their daily lives as well as their rights and obligations.

Thus, States sign law-making organic treaties establishing international governance regimes, which develop lives of their own and undertake proliferating legal activities that touch individuals within their boundaries. The more these activities develop, the more they distance themselves from the initial consent; hence the waning legitimizing effect of this consent. Professor Wolfrum sees another problem of legitimacy in this development, namely that the normative production of these regimes which replaces (at least to a degree) or is superimposed on national legislation takes place outside any democratic control or participation by the legislatures of member States. Hence the search for ways and means, first for reviving or enhancing initial consent in relation to the ongoing activities and their outcomes; and secondly for achieving a measure of democratic control over the legislative outcomes of international governance regimes. In both cases, the search aims at enhancing the legitimacy, and consequently the "compliance pull", of these regimes as regards member States as well as their citizens who are affected by the outcomes of these regimes.

This is one way of representing the recent evolution of international law that gave rise to "international governance regimes" and the problems of legitimacy they entail. But it is not the only possible narrative. An alternative one (that sheds more light on the subject I have to treat) explains the same phenomena by the marked post-war move, in international legal regulation, from an "international law of co-existence" to an "international law of co-operation" approach, to use Wolfgang Friedmann's famous distinction.[2]

The "international law of coexistence" is the "epitome" of the so-called "westphalian model", the classical international law ensuing from the Peace of Westphalia. It is a legal structure that came about in order to manage the disintegration of a community, which was called by Vinogradoff "the world state of medieval Christendom."[3] This world State, with its underlying double allegiance, may have been a myth. Still, it represented an ideological or value-based community; a community that was formally shattered, first by the Reformation, then by the Wars of Religion. When neither of the two camps managed to prevail and impose its "truth" upon the other, they sought a way out of these long drawn-out wars, through a legal structure, in the manner of an armistice

2 For further elaboration, see *ibid.* Chap. IX, p. 319; G. Abi-Saab, "Wither the International Community ?", *EJIL*, vol. 9 (1998), p. 248.

3 P. Vinogradoff, "Historical Types of International Law", *Bibliotheca Visseriana*, vol. 1 (1923), p. 53.

agreement, that would allow the coexistence of potentially antagonistic units. In other words, those of David Mitrany, the task of this legal system was to keep its subjects "peacefully apart", rather than to bring them "actively together."[4] The way of achieving this result, skirting round their differences, was through the new twin parameters of allocation of power: the principles of sovereignty and equality.

According to the first, each prince has the last word or is the last instance within his territorial and functional domains; and does not depend on any higher authority. But for the system to be sustainable in the presence of a plurality of princes, they have to recognize the same attributes to each other, regardless of their differences of size, power, wealth, ideology or religion. Thus emerges, to suit the system's needs, the model of the hermetic states, Arnold Wolfers's "billiard ball" States, equal and opaque, that one cannot see or pretend not to see inside, and which can only touch from the outside.

There is no community or common interest among the subjects of this system, except in minimum rules of the game that permit each to play against the others in order to gain at their expense. And the obligations it imposes are mainly passive ones that can be summarized in one mega injunction not to trespass on the territorial or functional ambits of other sovereigns.

The "international law of cooperation" approach, in its premises and logic, is the exact reverse of that of the "law of coexistence". It is premised on the assumption that there are certain common needs (values or interests) that cannot be satisfied, or adequately satisfied, except by a common endeavour. It consequently aims at "bringing the subjects actively together", imposing on them positive obligations to do (rather than abstain from doing) and to do together. But if the abstentions of the mouse and the elephant have the same nature and effect, their actions are hugely different, and tasks must be allocated and obligations adapted to abilities and needs; hence the necessity of institutions to manage the common endeavour, taking charge of the division of labour (and deserts) as well as of the follow-up of implementation. This is why the law of cooperation is closely associated with the emergence and growth of international organizations.

Small islands of the law of cooperation started modestly to appear within an ocean of the law of coexistence in the wake of the industrial revolution, during the latter part of the 19th century, particularly in the

---

4 D. Mitrany, *A Workable Peace System*, 1943.

field of international communications (river commissions, administrative unions). Great efforts were subsequently made to extend this approach to the central problems of international law, those of war and peace, particularly via the League of Nations; unfortunately without much success.

The Charter of the UN, coming at the end of the Second World War, carried with it a new vision, that of the victors of the Second World War, or their blueprint, for the post-war international society. Legally speaking, it is true that the Charter is based on the parameters of the law of coexistence, its first principle being "sovereign equality" (art. 2, para. 1). But in its "Purposes", it goes a long way towards the law of cooperation, in two ways. For a start, the first purpose of the Charter (art. 1, para. 1) is "the maintenance of international peace and security". To that end, the Charter undertakes to establish what Karl Deutsch calls a "security community"[5] on the global level, by providing a detailed legal regime of peaceful settlement of disputes and collective security designed according to the law of cooperation approach, which was normal for an organization born out of war. In addition, the third purpose of the UN is promoting international cooperation in the economic, social and cultural fields, as well as that of human rights, obviously through the establishment of international cooperative regimes. But here, in contrast with the maintenance of international peace and security, the Charter itself merely earmarks the fields of cooperation, leaving the establishment of the regimes to the subsequent activities of the organization.

Such regimes were indeed established and developed, sometimes beyond what could have been initially envisaged, as in the case of human rights. But in other fields, particularly the economic one, their development has been patchy. This is because, once established, these regimes pick up speed and develop an inner dynamic of their own, depending on the driving force of their participants (inner push) and the perceived needs and responses of their environment (outer pull), in the process producing the changes in international law that Professor Wolfrum describes in his introductory Report.

Both these narratives, Professor Wolfrum's and mine, describe the evolution of international cooperative governance regimes from the outside, but do not tell us much about the enabling and restraining role of

---

[5] K. Deutsch et al., *Political Community and the North Atlantic Area: International Organization in the Light of Historical Experience*, Princeton U.P. 1957.

law in this dynamic movement. This calls for an analysis from another perspective (from the inside, that of their constitutive instruments) and using a different set of tools, those of the jurist; which raises the question of legality. However, it has to be done without losing sight of the environment and how it perceives and receives this evolution; which is a question of legitimacy. However, these two questions are not totally separate. Indeed, one can hardly see, if at all, how "legitimacy" can be discussed without reference to "legality".

III. On "Legitimacy" and "Legality"

What is the relationship between "legitimacy" and "legality"? Are they identical, as strict positivists would tell us? And, if not, are they mutually supportive or antinomical?

Going through the torrential stream of recent writings on legitimacy, mainly from the US, leaves one with the impression that much of it is consciously or unconsciously seeking an escape route from "legality". In other words, most of those writers consider that addressing the legitimacy of an act or a situation (or a process, rule or organization), and proposing criteria for that purpose (which differ from author to author, but strangely look very much like counter-factual legal models), absolve them from examining its legalities.

This is in total contrast with the concept and role of legitimacy that emerges from Professor Wolfrum's initial Report, when he raises the question of the widening gap between international governance regimes and initial consent to them, and where legitimacy intervenes to reinforce the waning legality ensuing from increasingly remote consent. A concept that tallies with the seminal work of Professor Tom Franck on the subject which goes back to 1990, where he defines legitimacy as those "factors that affect our willingness to comply voluntarily with commands."[6] In other words, it is the response to the question: what are the factors that lead people to consider law as law and that it should be complied with, apart from coercion, or beyond the Austinian definition of law as "a command backed by threats"? Factors that, according to Franck, generate a "pull toward compliance" (or "compliance pull").

In the same vein, Professor Frowein considers that "legitimacy ... refers not to the lawfulness in the strict sense, but to a higher justification of

---

6 T. Franck, *The Power of Legitimacy among Nations*, 1990, p. 150.

what is being done by lawful means"[7]. Thus, legitimacy lies at one remove, upstream, from legality, and explains its anchorage or rooting in society. It is not an alternative that can replace legality.

This is why I would discard from the discourse of legitimacy any attempt to use it as a means to dodge or get round the law; as a *passe-droit*, a licence trumping legality or a "justification" of its violation (*cause d'exonération*, "circumstance excluding wrongfulness").

Of course, law can and has to change in response to social needs and demands, which determine, at least to a degree, the social perception of its legitimacy. But such change cannot be effected through Michael Reisman's "media-made law", gushing out of opinion polls and op-eds in the press.[8] It has to go through the proper, objectively recognizable and commonly perceived channels of law creation and change.[9]

IV. On the Legality of the "Executive" and "Legislative" Action of the Security Council against Terrorism

With this understanding of the concept of legitimacy, it becomes necessary, before applying it to the executive and legislative action of the Security Council against terrorism, to examine the legality of this action according to the Charter.[10]

I shall concentrate on legislative action. Executive action is more straightforward. Moreover, the executive action relevant to our subject is that taken in application of the "legislative" prescriptions or action of the Council. Thus, its legality and legitimacy hinge, at least in large part, on the legality and legitimacy of the latter.

---

[7] J. Frowein, "Issues of Legitimacy around the United Nations Security Council", in: Frowein et al. (ed), *Liber Amicorum Tono Eitel*, p. 122.

[8] W.M. Reisman, "The Democratization of Contemporary Law-Making Processes and the Differentiation of their Application", in: R. Wolfrum/V. Röben (eds.), *Developments of International Law in Treaty Making*, 2005, p. 15.

[9] *Cf.* G. Abi-Saab, "Comment", *ibid.* p. 31.

[10] The literature on the subject abounds. Two recent books deserve particular attention: Catherine Denis, *Le pouvoir normatif du Conseil de Sécurité des Nations Unies: portée et limites*, 2004; Erika de Wet, *The Chapter VII Powers of the United Nations Security Council*, 2004.

1) What do we mean by "legislation" or "legislative action" in this context? Obviously, it is not merely the taking of mandatory decisions, binding on the subjects to whom they are addressed. Nor is it the mere enactment of norms, if we go by Kelsen's understanding of "norm" (an understanding I do not share) as covering any normative prescription mandating or permitting a certain conduct, whether it is limited to one specific instance, like a court judgement, or is meant to set a general standard of behaviour.

To me, and in general, legislation *stricto sensu* signifies the enactment of prospective, general and abstract rules of conduct that bind all the subjects in the unlimited future, whenever the contingencies they provide for obtain; *i.e.* enacting rules of general international law. Can the Security Council "legislate" in this sense? In order to answer this question we have to review, however briefly, the spectrum of "powers granted to the Security Council" (the language of art. 24/2) by the Charter of the United Nations, and see whether they can be interpreted as accommodating, explicitly or implicitly, such a power to legislate.

2) As mentioned earlier, the Charter provides a detailed legal regime for the "maintenance of international peace and security" (the first "purpose" and function of the UN), with both normative and institutional components; entrusting the Security Council with the "primary responsibility" (again, the language of article 24) for its implementation; a regime that lays down the legal parameters and bounds of Security Council action in this field, encompassing its action against terrorism.

The Charter confers on the Security Council extensive powers in discharging this responsibility. They are not limited to the "soft power" of recommendation and diplomatic action (of intercession), under Chapter VI on the "pacific settlement of disputes", covering the "preventive" side of the function. For once we move to the "remedial" side by way of the collective security system of Chapter VII, the powers change radically. Indeed, according to article 39, in the event of a "threat to the peace, a breach of the peace or an act of aggression", and on the Council's own "determination" of the existence of such a situation, it transforms itself into an "international executive" endowed with the "hard power" of taking mandatory decisions (binding on Member States, but also non-Member States, and even non-State entities) and the application of coercive measures whether forcible or not (those of arts. 41 and 42).

3) In the exercise of this very large spectrum of powers, the Security Council enjoys a very wide freedom of decision and action. But, to quote the Appeals Chamber of the ICTY in the *Tadic* case, "This does

not mean that its powers are unlimited". I cannot resist here reciting in full the reasoning of the Appeals Chamber that underlies this statement:

> "The Security Council is an organ of an international organization, established by a treaty which serves as a constitutional framework for that organization. The Security Council is thus subjected to certain constitutional limitations, however broad its powers under the constitution may be. Those powers cannot, in any case, go beyond the limits of the jurisdiction of the Organization at large, not to mention other specific limitations or those which may derive from the internal division of power within the Organization. In any case, neither the text nor the spirit of the Charter conceives of the Security Concil as *legibus solutus* (unbound by law).
>
> In particular, Article 24, after declaring, in paragraph 1, that the Members of the United Nations 'confer on the Security Council primary responsibility for the maintenance of international peace and security', imposes on it, in paragraph 3, the obligation to report annually (or more frequently) to the General Assembly, and provides, more importantly, in paragraph 2, that:
>
> 'In discharging these duties the Security Council shall act in accordance with the Purposes and Principles of the United Nations. The specific powers granted to the Security Council for the discharge of these duties are laid down in Chapters VI, VII, VIII, and XII.' (Id, Art. 24(2)).
>
> The Charter thus speaks the language of specific powers, not of absolute fiat."[11]

4) Turning back to legislation (and whether it fits within the large spectrum of powers "granted to the Security Council" by the Charter, and proceeding by successive approximation, it is necessary to deal first with certain activities of the Security Council which may appear like legislation, in the sense that they involve laying down general normative prescriptions, but are distinguishable from legislation *stricto sensu* as defined above.

The Council can (in fact it has to) regulate its own conduct, by adopting its Rules of Procedure, (Art. 30), although it is still working, more than 60 years after the establishment of the UN, under "provisional rules", because of the initial stalemate over the problem of the "double veto".

---

[11] *ICTY*, IT-94-AR72 (Appeals Chamber, Interlocutory Judgement on Jurisdiction of 2 October 1995), para. 28.

This regulatory power is part of the internal governance of the Organization (what is called in French *le droit interne des organisations internationales*) supposedly with no significant legal effect on the substantive rights and obligations of Member States. But how far can this "regulatory power" go? You may remember that in the wake of the first Gulf War and the euphoria of what George Bush Senior called "the first war for international law", a first Security Council Summit Meeting was convened on 31 January 1992. At the end of this meeting, John Major (for the UK) read a Presidential Statement entitled "The Responsibility of the Security Council in the Maintenance of International Peace and Security"; declaring that the Council would henceforth adopt an extensive interpretation of "threats to peace" to cover what he called "systemic threats", such as environmental upheavals or massive flows of refugees.

Can the Council thus create *per se* categories of "threats to peace", and proceed, as it did, to discuss at length what it would do or what should be done, in such contingencies; a pattern it also follows in treating what it calls "thematic items", like "child soldiers"?

This tendency was heavily criticized as "over-reaching" or trespassing into "legislation"; criticism that may be partly true. But it is less worrisome, in my submission, than the extremely lax (not to say erratic) manner in which the Security Council uses the concept of "threats to peace", however subjective and political it may be.[12] It suffices to recall here the *Lockerbie* incident, where suddenly, 8 years after the fact, the Council found that it constituted a "threat to peace", on the eve of a decision by the ICJ in the matter, and with the clear intent of preempting a certain judicial course of action, which it did.

That the Council declares beforehand what types of contingencies it will consider as "threats to peace" and how it purports to handle them, pertains in a general way to legislation. But it is legislating for itself. It binds or limits, rather than extends, its own discretion, increasing the foreseeability of its future action while reducing to the same extent the risk of capriciousness and abuse of power. On condition, of course, that the Council sticks to its own directives and applies them in a consistent

12 Cf. *Tadic, ibid.* Para. 29: "While the 'act of aggression' is more amenable to a legal determination, the 'threat to peace' is more of a political concept. But the determination that there exists such a threat is not a totally unfettered discretion, as it has to remain, at the very least, within the limits of the Purposes and Principles of the Charter".

manner. For one of the main criticisms of the Council is its selectivity and inconsistent treatment of like situations.

In any case the resolutions and Presidential declarations carrying these general directives are not formally binding on the membership (nor beyond) and thus lack an essential element of legislation.

5) With the adoption of Res. 1373 of 28 September 2001, barely two weeks after the September 11 attacks, in the words of Paul Szasz, "The Security Council starts legislating;"[13] or so it seemed to many commentators.

Indeed, the format of the resolution lends credence to such a conclusion. For while it was called for by the September 11 events, its language is general (not limited in time or to a particular situation) and without any express reference to those events. It is also mandatory; addressed to all States ("All States shall…"); directing them to take certain measures at the national law level against terrorism and to report to the monitoring subsidiary organ it established, the Counter-Terrorism Committee (CTC).

It is noteworthy that the provisions dealing with financing terrorism are taken from the International Convention for the Suppression of the Financing of Terrorism. In other words, the resolution, by its own fiat, purports to impose on all States conventional obligations they may not have subscribed to.

A similar pattern was later followed in Res. 1540 of 2004, on the prevention of the spread of weapons of mass destruction to non-State entities.

Is this legislation in the above-mentioned sense of the term? Can the Security Council legally legislate? If not, what is the legal status of these two resolutions? And what can be done to buttress their status whether in terms of legality or of legitimacy?

6) If we go by the Charter, the answer to the question "Can the Security Council legally legislate?" is, in my submission, definitely in the negative, as neither the text nor the context of the Charter allows for such a possibility.

Article 24 which "confers" on the Security Council the "primary responsibility for the maintenance of international peace and security", after providing in its paragraph 2 that "[i]n discharging those duties shall act in accordance with the Purposes and Principles of the UN",

---

13 *AJIL* 96 (2002), p. 901.

adds significantly: "*The specific powers* granted to the Security Council for the discharge of these duties, are laid down in Chapters VI, VII, VIII and XII" (emphasis added).

As these are "specific powers", *i.e.* specifically "granted", they have to be expressly provided for. Nowhere in the Charter, and more particularly in Chapter VII – which is the only one directly relevant to our subject and which confers on the Council the exceptional powers of taking mandatory decisions and coercive measures – is it expressly stated or suggested that the Council can use these powers other than to handle a specific crisis or situation, e.g. to enact general and abstract prospective rules in detachment from a discrete set of circumstances limited in time or space.

Nor does such a legislative power fit into the general context or economy of the Charter and the place of Chapter VII in it.

Chapter VII provides for the UN response to exceptional circumstances or events threatening the international public order; similar to "public emergencies" on the national level which, once proclaimed, usually confer exorbitant powers on the Executive, to face up to these emergencies. But because of their exceptional nature, these powers are usually carefully circumscribed and limited to the treatment of the emergency at hand that justified the proclamation of the state of emergency.

The same is true of the activation of Chapter VII, which is triggered by the Council's own determination of "the existence of any threat to the peace, breach of the peace or act of aggression". The use of the indefinite pronoun "any" (the French version uses the indefinite article "*une* menace ..."), makes it abundantly clear that what is envisaged is a particular or specific situation falling, in the Council's judgement, within one of the three categories referred to in article 39.

What does this triggering of Chapter VII specifically entail? Article 39 is very precise as to the exceptional powers that the Security Council can exercise as a result of this determination:

> "The Security Council *shall* determine ... and *shall* make recommendations, or *decide what measures shall be taken in accordance with Articles 41 and 42*, to maintain or restore international peace and security."[14]

---

[14] Emphasis added. The use of the mandatory *shall* indicates that the Charter envisages the implementation of Chapter VII as a "function" in the public law sense of the term of conferring jurisdiction and powers on an organ, not as

In other words, once the determination is made, the Council *has* to act in response ("and shall..."), either by continuing to exercise its normal powers under Chapter VI by making non-binding "recommendations", or – and here lies the extension of powers operated by Chapter VII – by taking "decisions". But this is not an unlimited extension, a blank cheque. It is expressly circumscribed by the same provision that authorizes it, by limiting its ambit *ratione materiae* to the application of the coercive measures provided for in articles 41 and 42.

Can these measures be construed to include "legislation"? Obviously legislative action does not fit into article 42, which provides for measures of a military nature, involving the use of armed force.[15]

The same is true of the measures of article 41 not involving the use of armed force. It is true that the list provided by this article is illustrative and not exhaustive, and that these measures are defined negatively by what they are not ("not involving the use of armed force"). But it is also clear from the language of the article, the examples it provides and its general context that the measures envisaged are concrete preventive or enforcement measures, the object of which is "to maintain or restore international peace and security" in the particular crisis or situation which called, in the judgement of the Security Council, for their adoption. A profile poles apart from the incomparably all-embracing scope of prospective, general and abstract legislation.

---

a right or faculty to be exercised or not exercised at its discretion, but as a charge or duty to be discharged *every time* the circumstances provided for obtain (the use of the indefinite pronoun *any* before "threat to the peace, breach of the peace or act of aggression" makes this abundantly clear); with a view to achieving the object and purpose of the function (*i.e.* "to maintain or restore international peace and security", art. 39) in that particular instance. As is well known, one of the major criticisms addressed to the Security Council is its extreme selectivity (or double standards) in handling like situations. See *supra* I.

[15] Nor *a fortiori* can legislation be considered as one of the "provisional measures" of article 40 which by their very nature and as the name indicates are "provisional" *i.e.* of a temporary character (contrary to legislation), and which are intended to serve as a *stand-still* or a *holding operation*, by the Council "before making the recommendations or deciding upon the measures provided for in Article 39". Moreover, these provisional measures are "without prejudice to the rights, claims or position of the Parties concerned" (again contrary to the very essence and effect of legislation) and their mandatory character is subject to controversy.

This textual interpretation is comforted by the general context of Chapter VII and the role it assigns to the Security Council within the general economy and architecture of the Charter.

Article 24 which confers on the Security Council the primary responsibility for the maintenance of international peace and security opens with the phrase "In order to ensure prompt and effective action by the United Nations". Indeed, the Security Council appears to have been intentionally conceived as an organ with a limited but high powered membership, capable of handling specific crises and conflict situations efficiently and expeditiously. But precisely because of these characteristics, which make up its virtues in carrying out this responsibility, it is totally ill-suited to the task of articulating general and prospective norms for the international community; a task that requires lengthy reflection and preparation and the widest possible participation and adherence; and which was not entrusted to the Council anyway, but to the General Assembly, for these very same reasons (albeit in the much diluted form of "encouraging the progressive development of international law and its codification" of article 13).

7) All the same, several lines of argument were put forward to justify the Security Council's legislative action; some on legal grounds, others on purely practical and pragmatic ones.

a) The first legal argument used is that of *implied powers*. But "implied powers" is not a mere slogan; it is a technical legal concept drawn from constitutional law that has its own conditions and parameters. Implied power is an ancillary power that proves necessary for the exercise of the expressly granted powers, like the incidental (or inherent) jurisdiction of tribunals that enables them to exercise their principal jurisdiction. It is a power subordinate to (or *infra*) the express power and of a much narrower scope (merely providing a missing screw or cog, necessary for the exercise of the express power). It is not, and cannot be, a *meta* power that transcends and subsumes the express power, as legislation would be in relation to the specific measures provided for in articles 41 and 42 of the Charter.

A parallel and related argument is to say that legislative action of the Council does not have to be based on a specific article, but on the *general powers of the Council under Chapter VII*; an argument that finds some support in the fact that the Council now rarely cites a specific article when it invokes Chapter VII. However, if the Security Council sometimes does not expressly specify the Charter article on which its decisions under Chapter VII are based, this does not mean that such a basis does not exist or is not needed.

Postulating "general powers" goes against article 24/2 which speaks of "the *specific powers* granted to the Security Council", and of the role of Chapter VII in the Charter as a grant of "exceptional" or "exorbitant" emergency powers, that have to be treated as such.

The Appeals Chamber of the ICTY addressed this issue in its *Tadic* decision of 1995 in the following terms:

> "A question arises in this respect as to whether the choice of the Security Council is limited to the measures provided for in Articles 41 and 42 of the Charter (as the language of Article 39 suggests), or whether it has even larger discretion in the form of general powers to maintain and restore international peace and security under Chapter VII at large. ... The language of Article 39 is quite clear as to the channelling of the very broad and exceptional powers of the Security Council under Chapter VII through Articles 41 and 42. These two articles leave to the Security Council such a wide choice as not to warrant searching, on functional or other grounds, for even wider and more general powers than those already expressly provided for in the Charter."[16]

b) Another line of legal justification is based on *subsequent practice* and *acquiescence.* It is argued that the Security Council has established its legislative power by taking legislative action, and that States have acquiesced in it by complying, particularly by reporting, as required, to the CTC (Counter-Terrorism Committee).

Here again, and assuming that what the Council did was legislative action (an assumption that can be questioned, a matter to which I shall return later on), we have to distinguish between "action" and "practice". The fact that the Council has acted does not guarantee that its action is lawful or that this action will necessarily constitute legally significant "practice" that contributes to the evolution of the law. What makes the difference is the legal perception and reception of that action by others, *i.e.* the international community, which gives it precedential legitimacy as a new rendering of the law or proscribes it as a violation of that law. The more so if we are speaking not of practice in general but of "subsequent practice" as a principle of interpretation of treaties. In this case, the new reading of the treaty has to be revealed through the subsequent practice of the whole of the conventional community.

The new reading or interpretation of the Charter we are speaking of here is one that would allow the Security Council to legislate in general,

---

16 *Supra* note 11, para. 31.

not merely to take energetic action bordering on legislation in one particular case. Can we say, on the basis of the two above-mentioned resolutions, that the subsequent practice of the membership of the UN reveals such a common understanding or reading of the Charter? And can such subsequent practice be assumed simply from the so-called "acquiescence" of States by their submitting reports to the CTC or cooperating with it?

We have to keep in mind the very exceptional circumstances in which resolution 1373 was adopted: the generalised traumatism caused by the 11 September events, and the widespread feeling of imminent threat, aptly described by Michael Reisman as "the shared perception of a common danger, not simply to individual States, but to a system of world public order."[17] Indeed the real threat of transnational or globalised terrorism became tragically palpable and apparent, the same as the need for a global response at a corresponding level. All States felt threatened, including the "usual suspects" in the eyes of the West, the Arab and Moslem countries that have been the victims of some of the worst terrorist attacks and whose rulers stand on the front line of potential terrorist targets.

Resolution 1373 purported to provide the awaited global response. It is not astonishing in these circumstances, whether it qualifies as legislation or not (a question to which I shall return later), that governments in general or as a class who called for such a response would by and large implement it and report to or collaborate with the CTC.

They did so (though protesting here and there about some of its aspects) not because they recognized or acquiesced in the exercise by the Security Council of a general legislative power of which this case is but a particular instance; nor even necessarily because of its formal mandatory character under Chapter VII; but mainly because they found that it corresponded to their felt needs or interests; in other words, they were willing to cooperate because they accepted it; an acceptance that is limited to the specific contents of this particular resolution.

The limited precedential significance of Resolution 1373 as to the possession by the Security Council of a general power to legislate is corroborated by the circumstances surrounding the adoption of the second resolution 1540 of 2004 on the spread to non-State actors of weapons of mass destruction; a resolution of a much narrower scope, dealing basi-

---

[17] W.M. Reisman, "In Defense of World Public Order", *AJIL* 95 (2001) p. 834.

cally with the traffic destined to non-State actors. Here, there is no directly felt personal threat, creating a sense of "holy alliance" among governing elites all over the world. Strong voices were raised – those of India, Pakistan, and several other members of the Non-Aligned Movement – not particularly against the concrete measures taken, but to dissipate any larger implication that the Council can legislate.

c) The pragmatic or practical arguments justifying the exercise of legislative power by the Council are mainly two, the first of which is that the Security Council is a *political organ* that cannot be expected to act like a Tribunal or be shackled in the discharge of its extremely important functions and in the exercise of its wide discretion by legal niceties and technicalities.

The answer to this simplistic argument was given by the ICJ as early as in 1948, in the following terms:

> "The political character of an organ does not release it from the observance of the treaty provisions established by the Charter when they constitute limitations on its powers or criteria for its judgement."[18]

Almost 50 years later, the Appeals Chamber of the ICTY applied the same reasoning to the Security Council in the 1995 *Tadic* decision that I quoted earlier.[19]

d) More serious is the second practical or pragmatic argument, which is that in any case there is no way – no judicial, procedural or institutional means – to review or control the legality of decisions of the Security Council, which thus remains the sole judge of its own action.

This is true, but not completely true. It is true that there is no preestablished mechanism of control of legality of Security Council decisions. But the absence of such mechanism does not make action in violation of the Charter legal. Constitutional law is not justiciable in many jurisdictions. This does not mean that the constitution can be ignored.

As far as the Security Council is concerned, and apart from the internal restraining effect of its voting system, certain possibilities do exist of controlling the legality of its decisions and actions from the outside. In the first place, the General Assembly can challenge the Council's actions through censure, question their legality through a request for an

---

18 ICJ, A.O. on *Admission to Membership of UN*, 1948, p. 64.

19 *Supra*, note 11 and accompanying text.

advisory opinion addressed to the ICJ or curtail them through its control of the UN budget.

Secondly, the issue may be raised before an international tribunal as an incidental question in a case before it. The *Lockerbie* case provided such an opportunity, but the ICJ shied away from it. However, the Appeals Chamber of the ICTY did not baulk in the *Tadic* case from passing on the legality of Security Council action, although it is itself a creation of the Council.

Thirdly, challenge can be made in regional fora, such as the OAU or the Organisation of Islamic Conference, which both found that sanctions against Libya were *ultra vires* and recommended to their members not to comply with them. The same is true of the European Parliament which is currently examining aspects of blacklisting by the CTC.

Fourthly, the issue can also be raised before national tribunals or in national parliaments, considering that Security Council action was *ultra vires* or contrary to *jus cogens* and should not be heeded. For, in the final analysis, ultimate accountability lies in the respect accorded to the Council's decision: if the Council stretches or abuses its powers beyond credibility, Member States – who, in Article 24/1, "confer[red] on the Security Council primary responsibility for the maintenance of international peace and security, and agree[d] that in carrying out its duties under this responsibility the Security Council acts on their behalf" – retain the residual power to revoke this mandate and simply ignore the *ultra vires* decisions of the Council by not complying with them.

V. On the Status of Security Council Resolutions 1373 and 1540: How to Enhance Legitimacy

In the absence of legislative power, what is the status of Resolution 1373 (and later on Resolution 1540)?

My answer, written in the wake of the September 11 events, is the following:

> "Security Council resolution 1373 of 28 September 2001 comes nearest to a declaration of an 'international state of emergency' to face up to these events, establishing a temporary regime under Chapter VII to take measures against terrorism in this particular emergency …

> We should recall, however, that the crisis situation opened by the 9/11 events was characterized by the Security Council as constituting a 'threat to international peace and security' not merely because of the combined attacks against the US, but even more so because of the high degree of efficiency and capacity for harm of transnational terrorism that was revealed by these attacks and the acute threat it has become to world public order at large. The measures taken by the Security Council are intended to respond as well to these larger aspects of the crisis, with a view to containing and eventually eliminating this generalized looming threat; which probably explains the general language of the resolution."[20]

In other words, I consider that these resolutions are specifically addressed to the crisis that broke out with September 11, rather than being general legislation; a particular crisis, in spite of its global scope, which is still with us. And if we pursue the analogy with an internal declaration of a state of emergency where the Executive is usually given exceptional powers such as to rule by decree, we note that these powers are limited in time, beyond which limit they have to be submitted to parliament for ratification, or lapse. Here we have no parliament, though the General Assembly comes somewhat close to one. But the Charter did not cast it in that role. Still, beyond the specific crisis or situation, the prescriptions of the Security Council cannot hang in the air. They would lapse or would have to be transformed into norms of general international law. But such transformation cannot be brought about by the Council's enactment or fiat alone (this would bring us back, full circle, to legislation). It has to come "from below", through the "cumulative process" of international law.

Thus, the way to enhance or gain legitimacy for Security Council legislative action is not by seeking to obtain acquiescence or recognition of the Council's power to legislate (from above), but by working on the output or product of this activity, the resolution, on a case by case basis, and by ensuring that it meets the conditions that maximize the chances of its normative content being transformed, through the "cumulative process" of international law, into norms of general international law.

I have long been studying the process of transformation of General Assembly resolutions into law, and "normative resolutions" into general international law; and identified three indices that reveal and gauge the

---

[20] G. Abi-Saab, "The Proper Role of International Law in Combating Terrorism", *Chinese Journal of International Law* 1 (2002), p. 305 at p. 310.

degree of such transformation.[21] They can usefully be applied to the resolutions of the Security Council as well.

These three indices are

i – the degree of consensus obtaining in the body politic over the content of the normative statement; consensus taken here not in its procedural but its substantive sense of conviction or acceptance;

ii – the degree of specificity of the normative statement that makes it readily applicable as law; and

iii – the existence and effectiveness of a follow-up or monitoring mechanism generating continuous pressure for compliance.

If we apply these three indices for example to Resolution 1373, we find that if at first blush it seems to score highly; a closer look, however, reveals a more mitigated result.

i – As to the specificity of the normative statement that makes it readily applicable, in spite of the peremptory language requiring concrete action by States, the content of this action and its implementation depend completely on what the States would, or are willing to, do at the level of municipal law.

ii – As concerns the follow-up mechanism, which is an essential part of all governance regimes, given the total dependence for implementation on state action at the municipal law level, the CTC could not function as a coercive mechanism vis-à-vis States (though it did so as regards individuals and private entities, through blacklisting, which affects States by ricochet). Thus, in a revealing statement of 4 October 2002, Sir Jeremy Greenstock, the first Chairman of the CTC, "emphasized that the CTC is designed not to single out and judge individual States but rather to work cooperatively with States to help them meet their obligations under Resolution 1373."[22]

---

[21] G. Abi-Saab, in: *Les résolutions dans la formation du droit international du développement, Geneva*, IUHEI, 1971, pp. 9-10; "The Legal Formulation of a Right to Development", in: *The Right to Development on the international Level* (Colloquium of the Hague Academy of International Law), The Hague, Sijthoff, 1979, pp. 159-161; "Progressive Development of Principles and Norms of International Law Relating to the New International Economic Order : Analytical Study" (Annex to the Report of the Secretary General to the General Assembly) UN Doc.A/39/504/Add.1 (1984), par. 21-27; "Cours général", *supra* note 1, pp. 154-183.

[22] Report of the SG A/60/825/27 April 2006, Uniting against Terrorism: Recommendations for a Global Counter-Terrorism Strategy, para. 82.

iii – As to the degree of substantive or political consensus, because of the generalized feeling of the threat of terrorism and the holy alliance among ruling elites against it, this particular resolution mustered a reasonable amount of it, though not by any means general consensus. In particular, the blacklisting practices of its creature, the CTC, elicited much criticism and resistance.

In general, however, and by way of conclusion, when it comes to the transformation of Security Council resolutions into general international law, it is this criterion of consensus that is the hardest to satisfy. This is because the Council itself is suffering from an acute loss of legitimacy as a result of its increasingly non-representative character of the membership of the Organization as a whole. And it is precisely the consensus of this membership of the Organization as a whole that is needed to transform an edict of the Council into a norm of general international law.

The Legitimacy of United Nations Security Council Decisions in the Fight against Terrorism and the Proliferation of Weapons of Mass Destruction: Some Critical Remarks

Erika de Wet[*]

1. Introduction

In November 2003, during the conference on *Development of International Law in Treaty Making*, the current author concluded that Security Council practice in the post Cold War era has swayed between complete inaction and overreaction.[1] This extreme situation is a reflection of the reality that decision-making within the Security Council in the post Cold War era is driven by the (short term) political interests of the only remaining super-power and its closest allies – interests which are frequently being pursued at the expense of the international community as a whole and at the expense of international law.[2] Moreover, it is unrealistic to believe that this situation will change in the near future.

---

[*] B. Iur.; LL.B.; LL.D. (University of the Free State, South Africa); LL.M. (Harvard); Habil. (Zurich); Professor of International Constitutional Law, University of Amsterdam, The Netherlands; Extraordinary Professor, North-West University (Potchefstroom Campus), South Africa. The contribution also forms part of a so-called VICI project of the Netherlands Organisation for Scientific Research (NWO), titled The emerging international constitutional order: the implications of hierarchy in international law for the coherence and legitimacy of international decision-making.

[1] Erika de Wet, "The Security Council as a Law Maker: The Adoption of (Quasi)-Judicial Decisions", in: Rüdiger Wolfrum & Volker Röben (eds), *Developments of International Law in Treaty Making*, 2005, 225.

[2] Ibid.

For the time being, the international community remains confronted with a Security Council that will only engage in law-making activity if and to the extent that it serves the interests of a few powerful states and, where necessary, at the expense of the very norms on which the United Nations is based. The choice is thus likely to remain between total inaction and overreaction. It is difficult to know which one would be most detrimental to long term peace and security and the legitimacy of the Charter system.[3]

This conclusion expresses a concern about the increasing sense of a "right to rule" on the part of powerful states who seem to assume that power equals legitimacy, or rather that "might is right". It also reveals the growing discomfort of those directly affected by the decisions of the ruling class, but who remain without any (effective) mechanism to influence the decision-making process, or the impact of the decisions on their functioning. Stated differently, there is a growing sense that the decisions of the Security Council increasingly lack legitimacy, which can be defined as the extent to which the decision in question is accepted as being representative of the opinion of those being affected by it.[4] In relation to decisions of the Security Council, this would include other Member States of the United Nations and, increasingly, private individuals and other private entities.

Legitimacy is to be distinguished from legality, which implies that Security Council decisions have to be taken in accordance with the law of the Charter of the United Nations (the Charter). The following passages will exclusively focus on the legitimacy of certain Security Council decisions that have been adopted in the fight against terrorism and the proliferation of weapons of mass destruction. The discussion will reveal that legality does not necessarily imply legitimacy. Even if one were to accept that (most of) the decisions discussed below were

---

[3] Ibid.

[4] Eric Stein, "International Integration and Democracy: No Love at First Sight", *American Journal of International Law* 95 (2001), 491. See also Nico Krisch, "More Equal than the Rest? Hierarchy, Equality and US Predominance in International Law", in: Michael Byers & Georg Nolte (eds), *United States Hegemony and the Foundations of International Law*, 2002, 152. See also Mattias Kumm, "The Legitimacy of International Law: A Constitutionalist Framework Analysis", *European Journal of International Law* 15 (2004), 915.

adopted in accordance with the law of the Charter, their legitimacy remains questionable.[5]

The subsequent analysis will commence with a closer scrutiny of the concept of legitimacy. Thereafter it will apply the benchmarks identified to certain Security Council sanctions regimes pertaining to international terrorism and weapons of mass destruction, all of which were adopted under Chapter VII of the Charter. The first of these regimes include the Iraqi sanction regime that was imposed after Iraq's invasion of Kuwait on 6 August 1990 and lasted until 22 May 2003. As is well known, Resolution 661 of 6 August 1990 commenced the most comprehensive sanctions regime in the history of the United Nations. It resulted in the suspension of Iraq's customary trade and financial relations, including restrictions on the sale of Iraqi oil and the freezing of the country's assets.[6] In addition, it instituted an arms embargo, and provisions requiring verification that Iraq destroyed or disposed of its chemical and biological weapons of mass destruction.[7] This embargo was finally terminated by the Security Council in Resolution 1483 of 22 May 2003.

The second sanctions regime to be evaluated in terms of its legitimacy concerns the so-called *Al-Qaeda* sanctions regime, resulting from Resolution 1267 of 15 October 1999 and subsequent resolutions.[8] In accor-

---

[5] For an extensive discussion of the legality of decisions of the Security Council, see Erika de Wet, "The Chapter VII Powers of the United Nations Security Council" (2004). For a more general discussion on the legitimacy of Security Council decisions, see Steven Wheatley, "The Security Council, Democratic Legitimacy and Regime Change in Iraq", *European Journal of International Law* 17 (2006), 531-551; Jane Boulden, "Double Standards, Distance and Disengagement: Collective Legitimization in the Post-Cold War Security Council", *Security Dialogue* 37 (2006), 409-424.

[6] SC Res 661 of 6 August 1990, para 20.

[7] Andrew K. Fishman, "Between Iraq and a Hard Place: The Use of Economic Sanctions and Threat to International Peace and Security", *Emory International Law Review* 13 (1999), 702 at 713. See also SC Res 687 of 3 April 1991, paras 7 - 10, which included a more detailed listing of proscribed items including conventional arms, weapons of mass destruction, ballistic missiles and services related to technical support and training. See also Report of the International Committee of the Red Cross, *Iraq: A Decade of Sanctions,* 1999, 2-3, at www.icrc.org.

[8] See SC Res 1333 of 19 December 2000; SC Res of 15 January 2002; SC Res 1390 of 16 January 2002; SC Res 1452 of 20 December 2002; SC Res 1455

dance with this sanctions regime, member States are obliged to freeze the assets of *Usama bin Ladin*, individuals and undertakings associated with the *Al-Qaeda* movement. These resolutions further authorized the relevant sanctions committee (hereinafter referred to as the *Al-Qaeda* Sanctions Committee) to maintain an updated list, based on information received from member states and regional organizations, of the individuals and undertakings designated as being 'associated' with *Usama bin Ladin* and the *Al-Qaeda* organization.[9]

Finally, the contribution will focus on the legitimacy of the two "legislative" regimes adopted up to date.[10] The first of these, Resolution 1373 of 28 September 2001, determined any act of international terrorism to be a threat to international peace and security and dictated that all States should act to prevent and suppress the financing of terrorist acts. In addition, it obliged them to refrain from providing safe havens to terrorists and to cooperate in the prosecution of perpetrators of international terrorism.[11] The second legislative regime refers to the one adopted under Resolution 1540 of 28 April 2004 that obliged Member States to take a range of steps aimed at preventing the proliferation of nuclear, chemical and biological weapons, as well as their delivery systems and related materials, including by non-state actors.[12]

---

of 17 January 2003; SC Res 1456 of 20 January 2003; SC Res 1526 of 30 January 2004; SC Res 1617 of 29 July 2005; SC Res 1699 of 8 August 2006.

9 SC Res 1333 of 19 December 2000, para 8(c) and SC Res 1390 of 16 January 2002, para 5(a).

10 The reference to "legislative regimes" relates to their general and abstract nature. Instead of responding to a specific incident of terrorism or proliferation of weapons of mass destruction, they respond to the general threat implied by these situations by creating legal obligations for States in the area of international law. See Axel Marschik, "Legislative Powers of the Security Council", in: Ronald St. John MacDonald & Douglas Johnston (eds), *Towards World Constitutionalism*, 2005, 474.

11 Matthew Happold, "Security Council Resolution 1373 and the Constitution of the United Nations", in: Paul Eden & Therese O'Donnell (eds), *September 11, 2001. A Turning Point in International and Domestic Law?*, 2005, 618.

12 Gabriel H Oosthuizen & Elizabeth Wilmshurst, "Terrorism and Weapons of Mass Destruction: United Nations Security Council Resolution 1540", Chatham House BP 04/01, September 2004, 2, available at http://www.riia.org/.

2. Conceptualizing Legitimacy

In the current context, legitimacy should be understood as the extent to which the decision of (an organ of) an international organization such as the Security Council is accepted as being representative of the opinion of those affected by it. For many authors such representativeness can be achieved by procedural means. It is closely connected to the process by means of which the decision in question came into being and, in particular, the democratic quality of that process.[13]

Many critics regard decisions of international institutions such as the United Nations as representing an illegitimate, super-imposed normative system that takes place beyond any form of democratic control or accountability.[14] They see international organizations as being governed by an elite group of national officials in coalition with international secretariats whose staff at times act independently of the member states of the international organization.[15] In addition, they regard the proliferation of non-governmental organizations (NGOs) that interact with powerful international organizations as self-elected elite advocates of special causes, unrepresentative of the general public and engaged in an unholy alliance with international bureaucrats and sympathetic states, forming a romance of questionable legitimacy.[16] The impact of this illegitimacy becomes even more palpable when the law of the international organizations is enforced directly in the domestic legal order without the national parliament's imprimatur – especially where a member state is outvoted in the international organization that produced the directly applicable decision.[17]

---

13 Stein, note 4, 491. Krisch, note 4, 152. Kumm, note 4, 915.

14 Stein, note 4, 491; Jed Rubenfeld, "The Two World Orders", *Wilson Quarterly* 27 (2003), 28; see also Rüdiger Wolfrum, "Legitimacy of International Law from a Legal Perspective: Some Introductory Considerations", p. 1 et seq.; Allen Buchanan & Robert O. Keohane, "The Legitimacy of Global Governance Institutions", p. 25 et seq., both in this volume.

15 Stein, note 4, 491.

16 *Ibid.* For a sceptical approach to multi-lateralism, see in particular Kenneth Anderson, "The Ottowa Convention Banning Landmines, the Role of International Non-governmental Organizations and the Idea of International Civil Society", *European Journal of International Law* 11 (2000), 91-120; see also B.S. Chimni, "International Institutions Today: An Imperial Global State in the Making", *European Journal of International Law* 15 (2004), 19 et seq.

17 Stein, note 4, 491.

The author submits that one can criticize these arguments for their mythologizing of national democratic governance as a model for international governance.[18] They seem to assume that there is one national model of democratic governance that can set threshold conditions for the legitimacy of international governance. In doing so, these arguments overlook the fact that there is no single actualized form of liberal democracy which could easily be identified as the ideal model of governance. In addition, they overlook the fact that democracy does not necessarily equate with legitimacy.[19]

First, whilst there may be agreement that liberal democracy implies periodic multi-party elections,[20] it remains difficult to distill a common essence of what this implies in concrete terms. Democracy can mean many different things, including popular democracy, representative democracy, or pluralist democracy, to name but a few.[21] Second, even to

---

18 José Alvarez, "Multilateralism and Its Discontents", *European Journal of International Law* 11 (2000), 410; Philip Allott, "The Emerging International Aristocracy" *New York University Journal of International Law and Politics* 35 (2003), 309; See generally Miguel P. Maduro, "Europe and the Constitution: What if this is as Good as it Gets?", in: Joseph H.H. Weiler & Marlene Wind (eds), *European Constitutionalism beyond the State*, 2000, 83 et seq.; Joseph H. H. Weiler, "Does Europe need a Constitution? Reflections on Demos, Telos and the German Maastricht Decision", *European Law Journal* 1 (1995), 219 et seq.; Yves Mény, "The People, the Elites and the Populist Challenge", *European University Institute Jean Monnet Chair Paper RSC 98/47*; ibid., "De la démocratie en Europe", *Journal of Common Market Studies* 41 (2003), 1 et seq.; Deirdre Curtin, "Civil Society and the European Union: Opening Spaces for Deliberative Democracy", in: *Collected Courses of the Academy of European Law*, 1999, 185 et seq.; Armin von Bogdandy, "Globalization and Europe: How to Square Democracy, Globalization and International Law", *European Journal of International Law* 15 (2005), 885 et seq.; Carlos Closa, "Constitution and Democracy in the Treaty Establishing a Constitution for Europe", *European Public Law* 11 (2005), 145 et seq.

19 Allott, note 18, 309. See also Armin von Bogdandy, "Demokratie, Globalisierung, Zukunft des Völkerrechts – eine Bestandsaufnahme", *Zeitschrift für ausländisches öffentliches Recht und Völkerrecht* 63 (2003), 858-59.

20 Christian Pippan, "Book Review", *European Journal of International Law* 15 (2004), 212.

21 Daniel Bodansky, "The Legitimacy of International Governance: A Coming Challenge for International Environmental Law?", *American Journal of International Law* 93 (1999), 599; Allott, note 118, 319-20; Stein, note 4, 492. See also Juliane Kokott, "Souveräne Gleichheit und Demokratie im Völkerrecht", *Zeitschrift für ausländisches öffentliches Recht und Völkerrecht* 64 (2004), 528.

the extent that such a common essence can be distilled on the national level, it has not yet been convincingly explained why the concept of democracy would in and of itself be determinative for the legitimacy of any form of governance. Even in well established democracies the legitimacy of the decision-making process has been undermined by the fact that national democracies tend to exclude many who are affected by their policies, simply because they are not part of the *demos* as understood in a particular ethno-cultural sense. However, it is questionable whether such ethno-cultural definitions of *demos* are compatible with the founding principles of constitutional democracies which aim at the full representation and participation of all affected by the decision-making process.[22] It thus becomes questionable whether the substance of the national democratic legislative decision-making process would necessarily reflect the actual wishes of the majority of those affected by it.[23]

Furthermore, even in instances where groups are officially represented in the governmental decision-making process, the legitimacy of the process suffers from the lack of the *de facto* access of many of these groups to the public debate leading up to the governmental decision-making process; as well as the lack of transparency of the decision-making process itself; and the (perceived) lack of independence and expertise of the decision-makers in question.[24] One should therefore take care not to assume that the overcoming of the democracy-deficit of the international decision-making process would necessarily result in the overcoming of its legitimacy-deficit.[25] For the acquisition of legitimacy is not merely a matter of expanding the scope of the polity, but also concerns the quality of representation and participation.[26]

At this point it is also necessary to remember that the structural differences between the composition of the international community (the global *demos* or international polity)[27] and national communities make

---

22 Maduro, note 18, 83.

23 Alvarez, note 18, 411.

24 Alvarez, note 18, 410-11; see also Bodansky, note 21, 617 et seq.

25 See also Maduro, note 18, 85.

26 Maduro, note 18, 85.

27 But see Bodansky, note 21, 600 who denies the existence of a global 'demos'. Cf. Thomas Cottier & Maya Hertig, "The Prospects of 21st Century Constitutionalism", *Max Planck Yearbook of United Nations Law* 7 (2003), 287 et seq.

it questionable whether democracy could ever have the same meaning internationally as it does domestically.[28] Consequently, those who regard the national democratic model as an essential pre-requisite for legitimate decision-making would be reluctant to accept that the international legitimacy deficit could ever be overcome. However, if one accepts that democracy does not necessarily result in legitimate decision-making either, it becomes plausible to ask whether the international legitimacy deficit can be overcome through measures other than democratic decision-making.[29]

Viewed in this light, it is inappropriate to dismiss out of hand the possibility of legitimate decision-making by international organizations or their organs. Instead, one should acknowledge that the legitimacy deficit is a continuing challenge intrinsic to any political decision-making process, regardless of whether it is of a domestic or international nature.[30] Addressing it necessitates, as a first step, more transparency of the decision-making process, as well as accountability towards those affected by the outcome of the decisions.[31] A core element of accountability would arguably be the contestability of the decision in question, in both political and legal terms.[32]

In addition, international organizations should encourage broader participation during the decision-making process. This would, for example, include (informal) sessions with those member States who do not form part of the decision-making organ, but who are nonetheless bound and affected by its decisions. It could also include sessions with NGOs acting on behalf of groups affected by Security Council decisions.[33] Whilst it may be wrong to equate those NGOs already present in the (interna-

---

[28] Bodansky, note 21, 613. He *inter alia* questions whether the principle of sovereign equality of states could serve as a justification for the translation of the concept of 'one person one vote' into 'one state one vote', as it would grant disproportionate influence to small states representing only a fraction of the world's population.

[29] Cottier & Hertig, note 27, 309-10; see also Bodansky, note 21, 617 et seq.

[30] Alvarez note 18, 411.

[31] See Kumm, note 4, 926.

[32] See also the contribution of Allen Buchanan & Robert O. Keohane, "The Legitimacy of Global Governance Institutions", in this volume, p. 25 at 51 et seq.

[33] Therese O'Donnell, "Iraqi Sanctions, Human Rights and the United Nations Security Council", in: Paul Eden & Therese O'Donnell (eds), *September 11, 2001. A Turning Point in International and Domestic Law*, 2005, 723.

tional) political arena with all of civil society affected by the decisions of an organ such as the Security Council, they do constitute a part of civil society that deserves to be heard.[34].

Finally, it is worth considering whether efficiency could be regarded as a legitimating factor. It is arguable that the efficiency of a Security Council decision, to be understood as achieving the result intended by it within a reasonable period of time, could in and of itself compensate for the fact that the decision-making process was deficient in terms of contestability, transparency and participation.

3. Implications for Security Council Decisions Pertaining to Terrorism and Weapons of Mass Destruction

When applying the criteria of contestability, transparency, participation and efficiency to the decisions of the Security Council, the matter is complicated by the fact that these criteria have to be applied to both the Security Council itself and its sanctions committees. For each respective sanctions regime the Security Council also creates a sanctions committee for the purpose of monitoring its implementation.[35] The following passages will analyse the legitimacy of the relevant Security Council decisions pertaining to international terrorism and weapons of mass destruction, as well as those of the relevant Sanctions Committee.

---

[34] James Hathaway, "America, Defender of Democratic Legitimacy?", *European Journal of International Law* 11 (2000), 124-125. Instead of criticizing vocal NGOs for making use of the collective exercise of free speech for mobilizing decision makers within post-national constitutional regimes, one should concentrate on expanding the accessibility of this form of public participation to as many non-state actors as possible.

[35] SC Res 661 of 6 August 1990, para 6, provided for a Sanctions Committee which had to oversee the implementation of the sanctions. These Sanctions Committees (which proliferated after 1990), are set up as subsidiary organs of the Security Council under Article 29 of the Charter and replicate Security Council membership. See Margaret Doxey, *United Nations Sanctions: Current Policy Issues*, 1999, 41; Tono Eitel, "The United Nations Security Council and its Future Contribution in the Field of International Law", *Max Planck Yearbook of United Nations Law* 4 (2000), 67; Dorothee Starck, *Die Rechtmässigkeit von UNO-Wirtschaftssanktionen in Anbetracht ihrer Auswirkungen auf die Zivilbevölkerung*, 2000, 86 et seq.

3.1. The (Lack of) Contestability

The contestability of Security Council decisions by Member States is significantly reduced by the fact that, as a general rule, only the Security Council itself (as opposed to the individual Member States) can terminate decisions taken under Chapter VII of the Charter.[36] In addition, when adopting them, the Security Council is not obliged to determine when and how the sanctions will end.

The principle that Member States do not have the power to terminate binding enforcement measures imposed under Chapter VII of the Charter follows from the principle of the 'parallelism of competence', which is a general principle of administrative law. It determines that when a constitutive instrument invests a certain decision-making competence in a given organ, without expressly stipulating how such a decision may be revoked, the power of revocation lies with the same organ.[37] If one applied this principle to the Charter, it would mean that only the Security Council could terminate enforcement measures under Chapter VII, since the Charter does not provide any other procedure for doing so.[38] Furthermore, if Member States had a general right to determine for themselves whether the aim of the enforcement measures had been achieved, they would most likely come to very different conclusions depending on their geo-political interests. This would lead to major legal uncertainty that would undermine the effective functioning of the United Nations collective security system.[39]

---

[36] For exceptions to this rule, see extensively De Wet, note 5, 382 et seq.

[37] See Eric Suy, "Some Legal Questions Concerning the Security Council", in: Ingo von Münch (ed), *Festschrift für Hans-Jürgen Schlochauer zum 75. Geburtstag*, 1981, 684. See also David D Caron, "The Legitimacy of the Collective Authority of the Security Council", *American Journal of American Law* 87 (1993), 578; Brigitte Reschke, "Der aktuelle Fall: Die Aufhebung der Sanktionen gegen Haiti", *Humanitäres Völkerrecht* 3 (1994), 136.

[38] See Reschke, note 37, at 136.

[39] This reasoning was also reflected by the reaction of the General Assembly and the Security Council to the United States unilateral termination of the mandatory sanctions against Southern Rhodesia on 12 December 1979 (S/13688 (1979). The General Assembly responded by adopting GA Res 192 of 18 December 1979, which affirmed that it was within the exclusive authority of the Security Council to revoke mandatory sanctions imposed by that organ and that a unilateral termination of sanctions violated states' obligation under article 25 of the Charter. The Security Council, for its part, still considered it necessary

Second, the law of the Charter does not oblige the Security Council to determine when and how the sanctions will end when adopting them, and in practice they are often adopted without a particular time limit attached to them.[40] This means that a separate Security Council decision is needed to terminate the economic sanctions that will also have to be taken in under Chapter VII. This follows from the principle of the parallelism of forms, which is well established in the Charter system.[41] This is problematic to the extent that a Chapter VII resolution can only be adopted if there is consensus amongst the five permanent members to this effect. As a result, the termination of the embargo can be blocked by the 'reverse veto' of a permanent member.

The practical reality therefore is that, once adopted, an open-ended Security Council decision remains incontestable, as long as it has the support of one permanent member. This was clearly illustrated by the maintenance of the comprehensive, open-ended sanctions regime against Iraq between the first and second Gulf Wars, despite the criticism of a growing number of states in light of its harsh consequences for the civilian population.[42] Even though the exercise of the reverse veto by permanent members was not in and of itself illegal, it is doubtful whether the sanctions regime was still representative of the membership of the United Nations by the turn of the century.

The lack of contestability also arises within the sanctions committees where the veto power is effectively extended to each Member, since these committees function by means of consensus.[43] The impact of this

---

to terminate the sanctions in SC Res 460 of 21 December 1979 See also Reschke, note 37, at 136-37; Suy, note 37, 685-86.

[40] See Reschke, note 37, at 136.

[41] This principle, which normally supplements the rule of the 'parallelism of competencies', determines that the same type of act by the same organ is required to revoke the decision that had been taken. The Security Council has since 1990 consistently terminated its enforcement measures by means of Chapter VII resolutions. In fact, SC Res 460 of 21 December 1979, which terminated the sanctions against Southern Rhodesia, constituted the only instance in which the terminating resolution was not explicitly adopted under Chapter VII of the Charter.

[42] See De Wet, note 5, 227 et seq. and sources quoted there.

[43] Michael P. Scharf & Joshua L. Dorosin, "Interpreting UN Sanctions: The Rulings and Role of the Yugoslavia Sanctions Committee", *Brooklyn Journal of International Law* 19 (1993), 774; see also Lutz Oette, "Die Entwicklung des

lack of contestability is aggravated by the fact that the decisions of the sanctions committees tend to move beyond the boundaries of the inter-state paradigm for which the Security Council and its sub organs were intended, as they increasingly affect the basic human rights of individuals. This already became apparent from the sanctions regime in place against Iraq, where the sanctions committee created under Resolution 660 (1990) was also responsible for authorizing humanitarian exceptions to the embargo. By granting humanitarian exceptions, the sanctions committee attempted to mitigate the impact of the sanctions on the socio-economic rights of the Iraqi civilian population, including their right to food and healthcare.[44]

However, due to the veto power of each member a large number of requests for exemption were prevented or placed on hold,[45] with serious implications for the implementation of the humanitarian programme.[46] By the turn of the century it was obvious that the humanitarian exemption policy of the Iraq sanctions committee was succeeding in sufficiently safeguarding neither the right to life of Iraqi infants, nor the right to health of the civilian population in general. Even so, none of the affected individuals or their representatives could directly contest any of the sanctions committee's decisions pertaining to the humanitarian programme, as the sanctions committee's inter-state character did not facilitate such a possibility.

The lack of contestability is even more acute in relation to decisions of the *Al-Qaeda* sanctions committee, which directly targets individuals

---

Oil for Food-Programs und die gegenwärtige humanitäre Lage in Irak", *Zeitschrift für ausländisches öffentliches Recht und Völkerrecht* 59 (1999), 842.

44 This was already authorized in SC Res 666 of 13 September 1990, para 1. See extensively De Wet, note 5, 232 et seq.

45 The Secretary-General *inter alia* suggested that for items placed on hold, the Sanctions Committee should provide written and explicit explanations within 48 hours. This would enable the applicants to provide any additional information required by the Sanctions Committee. See S/1999/4, para 122.

46 S/1999/986, para 101; S/2001/1089, paras 6 and 127; see Human Rights Watch, Letter to the United Nations Security Council, 4 January 2000, paras 7 and 23, available at www.hrw.org/; Human Rights Watch, Explanatory Memorandum Regarding the Comprehensive Embargo on Iraq. Humanitarian Circumstances in Iraq (2000), para 20, available at www.hrw.org/; S/1999/4, para 127. Cf Oette, note 43, 853-54; Gian Luca Burci, "Interpreting the Humanitarian Exceptions through the Sanctions Committees", in: Vera Gowlland-Debbas (ed), *United Nations Sanctions and International Law*, 2001, 150.

and other private entities suspected of involvement with the *Al-Qaeda* network. Despite the fact that such targeting has the effect of a criminal charge and severely limits the right of the individuals to enjoy their property, they cannot directly contest their blacklisting before the sanctions committee (or any other forum).[47] According to the Guidelines of the Sanctions Committee for the Conduct of its Work (hereinafter the Guidelines),[48] affected individuals or undertakings can submit requests for de-listing to the sanctions committee only via their respective States of residence or citizenship[49] or the so-called Focal Point in the secretariat of the United Nations.[50] These requests are subsequently reviewed by the *Al Qaeda* sanctions committee itself.[51]. Since the sanctions committee reaches decisions by consensus,[52] it means that removal from the list can be prevented by the objection of one single member. In addition, the blacklisting is of an open-ended (indefinite) nature, as there is no sunset clause attached to the blacklisting procedure.[53] The net effect is that the affected individuals can remain on the sanctions list for an indefinite period of time, without having had the opportunity to challenge their listing.

As far as the legislative regimes provided for by Resolution 1373 (2001) and 1540 (2004) are concerned, the issue of contestability may be less

---

47 For the legal implications of such targeting see De Wet, note 5, 352 et seq.; see also extensively Bardo Fassbender, *Targeted Sanctions and Due Process* (United Nations Office of Legal Affairs, New York, 2006),. 4 et seq., available at http://www.un.org/law/counsel/Fassbender_study.pdf.

48 Latest version adopted on 12 February 2007, available at www.un.org. Hereinafter referred to as Guidelines.

49 Guidelines, note 48, para 8(e).

50 Guidelines, note 48, para 8(d).

51 *Ibid*, at para 3(b). The Focal Point was created in SC Res 1730 of 19 December 2006, para 1 ff. The Focal Point does not engage in any substantive review of the request but merely serves as an administrative unit that passes on de-listing requests to the Sanctions Committee.

52 *Ibid*, at para 4(e).

53 SC Res 1333 of 19 December 2001, paras 23 and 24, initially imposed these measures for 12 months. However, thereafter SC Res 1390 of 16 January 2002, at para 3, extended these measures for an indefinite period of time. The indefinite character of these sanctions was overlooked in the decision of *Ahmed Ali Yusuf & Al Barakaat International Foundation v Council of the European Union & Commission of the European Communities*, 21 September 2005, paras 299 ff; T-306/01 available at http://eur-lex.europa.eu/.

problematic than it appears at first sight. On the one hand, they impose an open-ended regime on member States, as they were also adopted without any time limit attached.[54] The problem of contestability of the (termination) of the relevant regime therefore remains present at the level of the Security Council. On the other hand, closer scrutiny reveals that both regimes leave states a significant discretion with regard to their implementation. In this context it is of particular interest that Resolution 1373 (2001) does not attempt to define terrorism, but allows each jurisdiction the discretion to determine its own definition. It further calls on states to implement the regime provided for by it in accordance with international human rights obligations.[55] As a result, States are in a position to provide some form of domestic contestability by implementing the measures with the involvement of their parliaments and by safeguarding fair trial procedures where individual rights are affected by the implementing measures.[56]

Second, the committees created under these regimes have thus far refrained from moving beyond the inter-state paradigm, i.e. from adopting measures against individuals or other private entities. Moreover, although it has "named and shamed" 85 countries that were lagging behind in reporting by October 2003,[57] the CTC has predominantly functioned as technical assistance bodies that rely heavily on the voluntary cooperation of states, as will be enlarged upon in section 2.2. The same applies to the Non-Proliferation Committee. In essence therefore, one

---

[54] See Marschik, note 10, 474.

[55] See e.g. SC Res 1456 20 January 2003; SC Res 1535 of 26 March 2004. The CTC was, unfortunately, very reluctant to appoint a human rights expert that could assist it in monitoring member States' compliance with international human rights norms when adopting counter-terrorism measures. Although such an expert was eventually appointed in 2005, his exact mandate remains unclear. See Alexander Marschik, "The Security Council's Role: Problems and Prospects in the Fight against Terrorism", in: Guiseppe Nesi (ed), *International Cooperation in Counter-Terrorism*, 2006, 72. See Eric Rosand, "Security Council Resolution 1373, the Counter-Terrorism Committee and the Fight against Terrorism", *American Journal of International Law* 97 (2003), 340.

[56] However, some authors argue that exactly because of this discretion, SC Res 1373 (2001) can easily be misused to target individuals or minority groups for political reasons. Marschik (in Nesi), note 55, 72-73.

[57] S/2003/1056, 03-59396 (E) 031103; Eric Donnelly, "Raising Global Counter-Terrorism Capacity: The Work of the Security Council's Counter-Terrorism Committee", in: Paul Eden & Therese O'Donnell (eds), *September 11, 2001. A Turning Point in International and Domestic Law*, 2005, 777.

could argue that the discretion left to states in implementing the regimes provided for under Resolution 1373 (2001) and Resolution 1540 (2004), combined with the predominantly voluntary nature of the monitoring bodies set up by these resolutions, have reduced the impact of their lack of contestability at the level of the Security Council itself.

3.2. (The Lack of) Transparency and Participation

From the perspective of the legitimacy of Security Council decision-making, a different point of concern relates to the (lack of) transparency and participation in the decision-making process. Although transparency and participation are two separate concepts, they often go hand in hand and can, in the present context, be considered as two sides of the same coin.

It is well-known that the work of the Security Council is clouded in secrecy. Security Council debates and decisions are very often a mere formality, since they confirm what has already been decided in secret consultations, for which no records are available.[58] Although the debates of the public and private meetings provided for in Rule 48 of the Provisional Rules of Procedure of the Security Council[59] are documented, the discussions during the many informal meetings remain unrecorded.[60] The net result is that the Security Council meets in public only to adopt resolutions already agreed upon in informal meetings, without giving any insight into the motives underpinning its decisions.[61] Such secrecy also implies a reluctance to include non-members

---

[58] Bernhard Graefrath, "Die Vereinten Nationen im Übergang – Die Gratwanderung des Sicherheitsrates zwischen Rechtsanwendung und Rechtsanmassung", in: Klaus Hüfner (ed), *Die Reform der Vereinten Nationen*, 1994, 44. See also Bardo Fassbender, "Uncertain Steps into a Post Cold War World: The Role and Functioning of the UN Security Council after a Decade of Measures against Iraq", *European Journal of International Law* 13 (2002), 389.

[59] S/96/Rev.7 (1983), at www.uno.org.

[60] Eitel, note 35, 59; see also Frederic L Kirgis, "The Security Council's First Fifty Years", *American Journal of International Law* 89 (1995), 518.

[61] For example, there were various reports of the United States promising rewards and threatening punishment so as to influence the vote on SC Res 678 of 29 November 1990, authorizing the use of force against Iraq. There were also alleged promises of or demands for financial help to/ by Colombia, Ivory Coast, Ethiopia and Zaire; an agreement with the Soviet Union not to include

of the Security Council (let alone NGOs!) in the decision-making process.

This secrecy and exclusivity also extend to the work of the sanctions committees, notably those created to monitor the sanctions regime against Iraq and *Al Qaeda*. In addition to functioning by consensus, both committees meet/met behind closed doors and are/were under no obligation to give reasons for their decisions.[62] In the case of Iraq the sanctions committee systematically refrained from explaining why it refused to implement all the proposals of the Secretary-General and other United Nations missions to Iraq concerning expansion of the humanitarian programme.[63] The justification given for this refusal was that a veil of confidentiality was necessary to protect the members of the Security Council from undue political pressure. If it were lifted, the argument goes; the members responsible for negative decisions regarding humanitarian exemptions could be subjected to unjust or excessive political pressure from affected countries, businesses or persons.[64]

Even though there is merit in this argument, the case of Iraq illustrated that the harm resulting from such confidentiality can outweigh the advantages. In the light of the severe consequences that the sanction regime has had for the right to life and the right to health within Iraq, the lack of transparency contributed to the delegitimation of the sanctions regime as a whole.[65] Similar criticism pertains to the functioning of the *Al Qaeda* sanctions committee. Given the direct impact of its blacklisting for inter alia the right to property and the right to a fair trial of the individuals concerned, improved consultation with the relevant states,

---

Estonia, Latvia, and Lithuania in the November 1990 Paris summit conference; and an agreement with China to lift trade sanctions in place since the Tiannamen Square incident and to support a World Bank loan of USD 114.3. Also, as result of Yemen's negative vote, the United States allegedly cut its substantial annual aid to that state. See Caron, note 37, 563-64; also see Eitel, note 35, 230, at 59; Graefrath, note 55, at 44; Kirgis, note 60, 518.

[62] See, for example, the Guidelines, note 48, para 3(b).

[63] See De Wet, note 5, 226 et seq. and sources quoted there.

[64] Hans-Peter Kaul, "Sanktionsausschüsse des Sicherheitsrates: Ein Einblick in Arbeitsweise und Verfahren", *Vereinte Nationen* 44 (1996), 98.

[65] Fishman, note 7, 689.

as well as transparency in relation to the listing and de-listing procedures would be essential for acquiring any degree of legitimacy.[66]

The lack of transparency and inclusiveness in the working methods of the Security Council was also very prominent during the adoption of Resolution 1373 (2001). This resolution was adopted within just over 48 hours after the United States began consultation with the other four permanent members on 26 September 2001. The draft resolution, which was circulated informally amongst Security Council members the next day, was adopted in a formal public meeting lasting only five minutes on 28 September 2001.[67] During this meeting no member of the Security Council spoke on the draft resolution or explained its vote, neither was any non-member consulted or present at the meeting.[68] This working method was subsequently criticized by non-members, who called for a more transparent and interactive approach from the Security Council.[69]

However, despite this criticism, all states seemed to have acquiesced in the regime provided for by Resolution 1373 (2001), as all Member States submitted a first report on steps taken for its implementation by May 2003.[70] The willingness of states to give effect to the regime set out in Resolution 1373 (2001) is most likely the result of the lack of any definition of international terrorism in the resolution itself.[71] In addition, the Sanctions Committee created by this regime (the so-called Counter Terrorism Committee/ CTC) has consistently taken a cooperative approach, assisting member States to identify their particular needs and matching these needs with expert advisers.[72] In essence there-

---

66 S/2006/154, par. 13; see also http://www.un.org/News/Press/docs/2006/sc8730.doc.htm.

67 Stefan Talmon, "The Security Council as World Legislature", *American Journal of International Law* 99 (2005), 187.

68 Marschik, note 10, 485.

69 Talmon, note 67, 187; see also Costa Rica in A/56/PV.25 (2001), 3. See also the Philippines S/PV/4950 (2001), 2, who stated that those who are bound should be heard.

70 Marschik, note 10, 474, 480; Donnelly, note 57, 765.

71 Rosand, note 55, 339.

72 Rosand, note 55, 335. The expertise of the advisers assisting the CTC includes legislative drafting; customs law and practice; police and law enforcement and illegal arms trafficking. While the CTC self does not provide assistance, it has set up an easily accessible electronic database to help states looking for information, experts and model legislation. See Oosthuizen & Wilmshurst, note 12, 7.

fore, the work of the CTC resembles more that of a technical assistance body than a sanctions committee in the traditional sense.

As far as the adoption of Resolution 1540 (2004) is concerned, it may seem that the Security Council has followed a more inclusive and transparent procedure. On 22 April 2004 it facilitated an open meeting where Security Council members and more than 30 non-members from different regions commented on the draft resolution.[73] However, the extent of participation facilitated by this meeting remains debatable, as only a few nominal changes were subsequently made to the draft before its adoption on 28 April.[74] The decisive negotiations seemed to have occurred behind closed doors and essentially amongst the permanent membership.[75] Even so, the resolution was adopted unanimously and most States seem to have acquiesced in its adoption through submitting reports to the Non-Proliferation Committee.[76]

The initial two year mandate of the sanctions committee (the Non-Proliferation Committee) established by Resolution 1540 (2004), has since been extended to 2008.[77] As in the case of the CTC, the Non-Proliferation Committee combines the monitoring of state reporting on the implementation of Resolution 1540 (2004) with cooperation in the form of outreach, dialogue and the provision of technical expertise.[78]

On the whole, one may be tempted to conclude that the cooperative working methods of the CTC and Non-Proliferation Committee may compensate, to some extent, for the legitimacy deficit incurred through their manner of adoption. However, this may be too optimistic a conclusion. The reality is that the wider membership of the United Nations

---

[73] The non-members included Ireland (speaking on behalf of the EU), Malaysia (speaking on behalf of the large Non-aligned Movement grouping), South Korea, Japan, Argentina, Nigeria, South Africa, Jordan, Israel and India. Oosthuizen & Wilmshurst, p. 9.

[74] Oosthuizen & Wilmshurst, note 12, 3; Marschik, note 10, 485.

[75] Oosthuizen & Wilmshurst, note 12, 9.

[76] Of the non-members of the Security Council, India was the most outspoken critic. It reacted formally to the adoption of the resolution by expressing its concern at the legislative role of the Security Council. See S/2004/239 of 28 April 2004. Pakistan, as a Security Council Member at the time of adoption, also warned that an unrepresentative body such as the Security Council cannot legislate for the world. See S/PV.4956, at 3; Marschik, note 19, 479 – 480.

[77] SC Res 1673 of 27 April 2006, at para 4.

[78] Oosthuizen & Wilmshurst, note 12, 6.

feels that the Security Council controls the organization's work pertaining to counter-terrorism and the proliferation of weapons of mass destruction too tightly, while the large majority of States are excluded from participation.[79]

3.3. (Lack of) Efficiency

When considering the legitimacy of Security Council decisions and those of its sanctions committees, one also has to consider the efficiency of the measures in question. If the relevant measure had the intended effect within a reasonable time, this might compensate to some extent for shortcomings pertaining to transparency, participation and contestability. On the other hand, inefficiency could serve to delegitmate measures – including those that live up to the requirements of contestability, transparency and participation.

At the time of writing, the efficiency of all four sanctions regimes discussed above remains questionable. It is common knowledge that the sanctions regime against Iraq, which was in place for more than a decade, did not succeed in effecting the disarmament of *Saddam Hussein's* regime without inflicting undue hardship on the civilian population.[80] By the turn of the century (i.e. after nine years of sanctions) it was clear that the Iraqi government had succeeded in using the civilian population as a shield to deflect the impact of the sanctions away from it in order to ensure its own survival.[81]

Similarly, it remains to be seen whether the blacklisting procedure of the *Al Qaeda* Committee has significantly reduced the flow of funds to terrorist networks.[82] National authorities have encountered difficulties

---

[79] Marschik (in Nesi), note 55, 80.

[80] Human Rights Watch, Explanatory Memorandum, note 46, para 24; Cf. Starck, note 35, 361-62. Eitel, note 35, 66; Fassbender, note 58, 295.

[81] See O'Donnell, note 33, 705; John Mueller & Karl Mueller, "Sanctions of Mass Destruction", *Foreign Affairs* 52 (1999).

[82] By 2006 about USD 200 million in assets of persons and entities with ties to terrorist networks including *Al Qaeda* had been frozen. However, it remains difficult to determine how much of this can be attributed to the Security Council requirements to freeze assets. See Eric Rosand, "The UN Security Council's Counter-Terrorism Efforts", in: Roy S. Lee (ed), *Swords into Plowshares: Building Peace through the United Nations*, 2006, 79-80.

in enforcing embargoes against individuals and other entities, for reasons ranging from the lack of political will to the complexity of the Guidelines, lack of resources, technical capacity and coordination difficulties at the national level.[83] The inflexibility of the sanctions regime further prevents quick adaptation to new developments, such as the change in *Al Qaeda's* financing methods to circumvent the original controls. Moreover, international cooperation has been inadequate, because States are hesitant to share confidential information on individual terrorists in a United Nations sanctions committee.[84]

As for the CTC and Non-Proliferation Committee, one should be careful not to equate the submission of reports with effective compliance, as reporting in itself is no guarantee that states are also complying with the substantive obligations contained in Resolution 1373 (2001) and 1240 (2004).[85] Moreover, closer scrutiny reveals that with the passage of time a certain compliance fatigue has set in. Initially, all states responded to the deadline for first reports to the CTC. Most states also responded to a call for a second round of reports, in which they had to respond to questions of the CTC pertaining to the first reports.[86] However, by June 2004, 71 States had not met the deadline set by the CTC for further reporting.[87] In addition, there are huge discrepancies in both the length and quality of the reporting.[88] Similar problems plague the Non-Proliferation Committee, to which 129 States had submitted a first national report by May 2006, whereas 62 still had to do so. In response to examination of their first national reports, 83 States had provided additional information.[89] By this time many States had raised the issue of "reporting fatigue" and openly questioned the utility of the reporting process.[90]

It is also doubtful whether the CTC has the capacity to supervise effectively the implementation of Resolution 1373 (2001), despite its "revi-

---

83 Marschik, note 10, 472.

84 Marschik, note 10, 472; Happold, note 11, 684.

85 Talmon, note 67, 191.

86 Rosand, note 55, 397.

87 Talmon, note 67,191.

88 Donnelly, note 57, 766.

89 http://www.un.org/News/Press/docs/2006/sc8730.doc.htm

90 http://www.un.org/News/Press/docs/2006/sc8730.doc.htm. The point had also been made that the extensive reporting requests took away essential resources that could otherwise have been spent on implementation.

talization" by Resolution 1535 (2004). This resolution complemented the 15 CTC members representing the Security Council member States (the Plenary) with a Bureau composed of a Chairperson and Vice-Chairpersons and a Counter-Terrorism Executive Directorate (CTED). Within the CTED a group of 20 technical experts is charged with assessing the progress made by States in implementing the substantive obligations arising from Resolution 1373 (2001).[91] However, it is highly doubtful whether a mere 20 individuals with limited financial resources and a mandate (initially) limited to 2007 can effectively monitor the adoption and implementation by 192 member States of highly complex legislation and other measures, ranging from criminal and financial legislation to border and export controls.[92]

These challenges may also provide some explanation for why the CTC is, five years into its mandate, still very much concerned with the first of the three stages of its work, namely reviewing whether States have adequate legislation in place.[93] As similar challenges face the Non-Proliferation Committee, both these committees are heavily reliant on the voluntary cooperation of States in order for them to succeed in their goals. Neither do they possess the capacity to rebuke those States which do not cooperate.[94]

This fact touches on an anomaly represented by the regimes of the CTC and the Non-Proliferation Committee, namely the use of Chapter VII decisions in a context in which enforcement of the relevant resolutions against recalcitrant states would be almost impossible to achieve. Adopting binding measures in a situation in which it is obvious that the relevant monitoring committees are not in a position to enforce effectively any of the substantive obligations envisaged by the measures in question, constitutes a contradiction in terms. It does not enhance the (perception of the) efficiency of the measures concerned and could eventually undermine the authority of the Security Council as a whole.

Finally, it is worth noting that the lack of efficiency of sanctions committees is further aggravated by their proliferation in numbers combined with the lack of continuity in their composition. They are all es-

---

[91] See also Donnelly, note 57, 761.

[92] Rosand, note 55, 335; Donnelly, note 57, 777.

[93] Talmon, note 67, 191. The second and third stages concern the institution of effective executive machinery for implementing the legislation; and the examination of the efficacy of the legislation.

[94] See also Talmon, note 67, 187.

tablished on an *ad hoc* basis and draw their representatives from the permanent missions in New York that are subjected to constant personnel change. In addition, five new permanent members take their seats on the Security Council every year.[95] This lack of continuity frustrates attempts to develop coherent monitoring policies within and amongst the different committees and ultimately also the efficient enforcement of their respective mandates. These deficits plague not only the "classic" sanctions committees such as the Iraq and *Al Qaeda* Committees, but also the more technical assistance oriented committees such as the CTC and the Non-Proliferation Committee. [96]

4. Conclusion

The above analysis reveals that the variety of measures taken by the Security Council during the last 15 years in order to combat terrorism and weapons of mass destruction have been haunted by legitimacy deficits of various degrees. Deficits pertaining to contestability, transparency and participation, as well as efficiency have tainted Security Council resolutions themselves, as well as the work of monitoring committees established by these resolutions. These challenges seem to be particularly acute in instances where the Security Council decision or that of one of its monitoring committees moves beyond the inter-state paradigm and directly affects individual human rights. In addition, there is the risk that some of the monitoring committees remain paper tigers with overly ambitious mandates the effective enforcement of which is severely limited by the structural limitations inherent in their composition and working methods.

Since no formal reform of the Charter system itself can be expected in the near future, it would be up to the Security Council itself to restructure – within the constraints of the current Charter system – its working methods and those of the respective monitoring bodies in a manner that takes heed of the legitimacy deficits illuminated above. Unfortunately, however, the Security Council has thus far been reluctant to take

---

[95] Doxey, note 35, 41. See also Eitel, note 35, 68. Cf Mariano J. Aznar-Gómez, "A Decade of Human Rights Protection by the UN Security Council: a Sketch of Deregulation?", *European Journal of International Law* 13 (2002), 229.

[96] Rosand (in Lee), note 82, 81.

over (in any consistent or comprehensive fashion) recommendations which have repeatedly been made in this regard since the end of the Cold War.

For example, the problems pertaining to the lack of contestability of Security Council decisions could be reduced if the Security Council subjected its sanctions regimes to time limits (sunset clauses). Since the Security Council will then need an additional Chapter VII decision to extend the sanctions regime – as opposed to terminating it – there is less chance that a sanctions regime that violates basic human rights would be perpetuated.[97] Although the Security Council has occasionally shown itself willing to attach sunset clauses to sanctions regimes, it has not followed this policy in a consistent manner.[98] The foregoing analysis reflects that in particular in relation to measures pertaining to international terrorism and weapons of mass destruction, it has resorted to open-ended (and therefore effectively incontestable) sanctions regimes.

Ironically, this problem has to some extent been aggravated by targeted sanctions which were intended to tailor sanctions in such a manner that they affected only those responsible for the threat to international peace and security, as opposed to innocent civilians.[99] However, as the black-

[97] Eitel, note 35, 66; See also Lutz Oette, "A Decade of Sanctions against Iraq: Never Again! The End of Unlimited Sanctions in the Recent Practice of the UN Security Council", *European Journal of International Law* 13 (2002), 97. At 101-02 he noted that some countries fear that time limits would undermine the effectiveness of the sanctions. According to this argument, the limitation of the duration of the sanctions might encourage the target to endure the short-term damage and attempt to prevent the renewal of sanctions at the end of the period, without having complied with the demands of the Security Council. (For arguments to this effect, see the statements of the United States and the Netherlands in S/PV.4168 5 ff (2002)). However, in the absence of time limits, members of the Security Council may not be willing to vote for the initial imposition of sanctions at all. In addition, the inclusion of a time limit does not in itself create a presumption against the renewal of sanctions.

[98] Some early examples include the ban on the import of rough diamonds from Sierra Leone which was limited to 18 months (SC Res 1306 of 5 July 2000, para 6); and the ban on rough diamonds from Liberia that was subject to a limitation of 12 months (SC Res 1342 of 7 March 2001, paras 6 and 10). The Security Council also initially limited the arms embargo against Eritrea and Ethiopia to 12 months (SC Res 1298 of 17 May 2000, paras 6 en 16), as well as that against the Taliban (SC Res 1333 of 19 December 2000, paras 23 and 24); and in the case of Liberia to 14 months (SC Res 1343 of 7 March 2001, para 9).

[99] An example of tailored measures *inter alia* is those against UNITA in the 1990s. These included an arms embargo and a ban on oil sales against UNITA

listing of the *Al Qaeda* Committee has illustrated, such tailoring opens up new challenges in relation to the balancing of international peace and security with human rights protection, including the contestability of such sanctions by those directly affected by means of a fair trial.[100]

A different, but closely related issue concerns the call for replacing the current sanctions monitoring system by a single, permanent and better resourced body that is responsible for planning and monitoring sanctions.[101] This monitoring system should review the human rights implications of economic embargoes on a regular basis, with particular emphasis on its impact on vulnerable groups. In addition, it should introduce some form of transparency into the sanctions monitoring system by, for example, providing detailed reports to the Secretary-General and the General Assembly.[102] From this perspective, the more open and cooperative working methods of the CTC and Non-Proliferation Committee are to be welcomed.

Finally, it is worth keeping in mind that there are no instant solutions to international terrorism and the proliferation of weapons of mass destruction. If nothing else, the doubtful efficiency of the measures discussed above illustrates that the Security Council may not be the best instrument for addressing these challenges. Instead, more traditional methods such as treaty-making and negotiating within the General Assembly, as well as addressing the root causes of international terrorism, may prove to be more successful in the long run.

(SC Res 864 of 15 September 1993, para 19); the restriction on traveling of UNITA's senior members, the banning of UNITA flights and the insuring and servicing of UNITA aircraft (SC Res 1127 of 28 August 1997, para 4); the freezing of UNITA funds within other countries (SC Res 1173 of 12 June 1998, para 11); and the banning of the import of diamonds and the provision of mining services to areas which are not under the control of the Angolan government (SC Res 1173 of 12 June 1998, para 12).

[100] See Fassbender, note 47, 28 et seq.

[101] Doxey, note 35, 40.

[102] In this context one should mention that since 1999 the Security Council's report to the General Assembly has included a report on the work of each Sanctions Committee. The Security Council suggested these reports as a method for making the work of the Sanctions Committees more transparent in S/1995/234, para 1. In S/1996/54, para 1, the Security Council also encouraged the Chairperson of each Sanctions Committee to give an oral briefing to interested member states after each meeting. Gasser, above note 24, at 903; Doxey, note 35, at 45.

Discussion Following Presentations by Georges Abi-Saab and Erika de Wet

W. Heintschel v. Heinegg: I disagree with both speakers. Professor Abi-Saab, you have not elaborated on the fact that, in accordance with Art. 39 of the Charter, the Security Council has to deal with any threat to the peace, and I emphasize "any". Moreover it is necessary to distinguish between duties and powers. First, there is the duty to deal with any threat to the peace, and then come the powers which the Security Council may exercise.

In view of that I cannot but feel pity for the Security Council. Of course, there were two events, Korea, which was an accident rather, and the second was Rhodesia in the 1960s where the Security Council for the first time made use of its powers under Chapter VII by imposing an oil embargo upon Southern Rhodesia and entitling the UK to enforce it. Nobody really took any notice of that. Then, it took until 1990/91 before the Security Council seemed to make use of its powers under Chapter VII, and suddenly there was this euphoria – as you rightly mentioned, Professor Abi-Saab. However, this euphoria then very quickly changed into disappointment. Especially for those who had expected something different to emerge from that initial, or rather second, use of Chapter VII powers. The disappointment was very quickly accompanied by legitimacy. Legitimacy was the argument against what the Security Council did. I am astonished about why we are so impatient. What the Security Council has achieved during the last 15 years is very impressive. What the Security Council has done, it has done with the consent, or at least with the acquiescence, of states. Since you are mentioning Resolution 1540, well, there were some states grumbling a little bit, like India. But there were no official protests, there was no official statement by those countries that doubted the legality of 1540. Thank you very much.

A. Zimmermann: I will try to be brief. I have four remarks and/or questions.

The first relates to what Georges Abi-Saab said on subsequent practice. I was not quite sure whether you referred to subsequent practice of the

Security Council as such or rather to subsequent practice of States, members of the Security Council. If you did refer to the practice of the Security Council as such, you did by the same token at least implicitly refer to the advisory opinion of the International Court of Justice in 'Certain Expenses'. According to the Court, it is for each organ first *prima facie* to determine its own competencies. Yet, I myself would perceive this practice rather as one of those States represented in the Security Council plus as the practice of the other general membership of the organization following up on those resolutions.

Now, if we have a look at Security Council resolution 1540, basically all member States have reported to the Council. Indeed even those States reported which beforehand had uttered concerns about the aforementioned resolution. Could one not at the very least consider this as subsequent legitimacy being granted by those States saying: "Well, we might not particularly like it, but we take it for granted that the Security Council can do that..." and that therefore – to speak in the words of Alain Pellet – it is at least not completely intolerable.

The second point relates to what Erika de Wet said. Provided I understood her correctly, we should make a distinction between the Security Council acting and the Sanctions Committee acting. Now, if we look at recent practice, we realize that the Security Council itself may have blacklisted certain specific persons. It does it directly. I therefore do not particularly see that distinction that Erika de Wet might have tried to draw.

My third remark relates to Security Council resolution 1540. And I think we have to take into consideration that Chapter VII does not operate in a legal vacuum. *First*, we have to take it for granted that the Charter of the United Nations generally and its Chapter VII more specifically take the list of sources of international law as an axiomatic starting point, and in particular that there are treaties to be concluded by States. I believe the main problem with Security Council resolution 1540 lies in the fact that it was trying to impose treaty obligations upon member States of the United Nations via Chapter VII, and I think this is simply not possible.

And last but not least, you referred to the participation by the general membership in the drafting, or post-drafting or pre-drafting of Security Council resolution 1540. You argued that any such participation did not make any difference. You argued that they could have said what they did say, but that it did not make any difference. Yet, if we take another example, if we take Security Council resolutions 1422 and 1487, concerning deferrals under Article 16 of the Statute of the International

Criminal Court. There was really a vast list of critiques by the general membership concerning Security Council resolutions 1422 and later 1487. And I think it's not without reason that Security Council resolution 1487 was not prolonged and I think it was not only due to Abu Ghraib and the incidents that took place in Abu Ghraib, but also to the general feeling within the membership of the United Nations that Security Council resolutions 1422 and 1487 were simply not legitimate. Thank you very much.

W. Benedek: I think it's quite interesting that we are discussing the legitimacy of decisions of the Security Council, because one would maybe imagine that this is really a question more of legality than of legitimacy. What is the "value added" of talking about legitimacy? First, it tells us that even a body like the Security Council is not outside such considerations. Referring to three criteria Professor Wolfrum mentioned yesterday, there seems to be a problem of inclusivity in relation to the question of the source. From the perspective of the question of procedure, we have the problem that basic criteria of fair trial and due process are not taken into consideration. Erika de Wet also showed us, as far as the outcome is concerned, a lack of effectiveness, and therefore another criterion of legitimacy has not been met. This means that we can actually criticize the decisions of the Security Council under such criteria, and it makes sense to do so. Certainly, what I missed a bit was an elaboration of the question to what extent this can be excused by an emergency situation, i.e. necessity. This is also recognized in the Articles on State Responsibility as one of the circumstances precluding wrongfulness.

I was a bit surprised that we did not hear anything about the issue of the inclusivity of the Security Council itself in view of the fact that Germany and some other states wanted to make it more inclusive. Maybe this would also be a good idea. Thus, I believe that the legitimacy of the Security Council itself should be discussed. To what extent is it representative of the world of today? In relation to this question we can see that the developments are moving in different directions. There is the G8, which has just met in St. Petersburg. The G8 would be a very good case to be discussed for its legitimacy as this is a self-appointed group, which legitimizes itself mainly by its power or outcomes. On the other hand, it would be interesting to look at the legitimacy of the General Assembly, which is an assembly of states. Some of you might know that there are efforts at the moment to create a United Nations parliamentary assembly in order to establish a body with more democratic legitimacy. This is something which even the European Parliament has supported. So I think there are some other wider issues of legitimacy of these bodies which would also be worth discussing.

R. Keohane: I wanted to focus on Professor de Wet's very interesting paper – to compliment her first on it and then ask her a question.

First the compliment. It seems to me that you've shown the value of the concept of legitimacy beyond the notion of legality as well as the value in a practical way of having criteria for assessing it. You have three, Buchanan and I have five, but they come down to very much the same thing. And so we've seen an illustration of the value of not simply analysing an issue: is it legal or does it have state consent? But are the procedures in your terms inclusive and transparent and is there the ability for compensation and accountability in our terms? I think that's a valuable example of why this conference is worthwhile and why it's worthwhile not to stop with legality or not to stop with the pedigree view of legitimacy that is simply a matter of state consent.

My question for you is really focused on the issue of what Buchanan and I call "comparative benefit". If the arrangements for the Sanctions Committee on the Security Council are not legitimate, and they are problematic as you say on each of your criteria, would any other arrangements – the General Assembly and national parliaments sounds very weak to me, sounds like it might not meet the comparative benefit criteria at all, you might not have any regime at all in effect. Is there a design for a superior system that you have in mind to replace the Security Council based Sanctions Committee? Thank you.

J.A. Frowein: I think the discussion hitherto has already shown how tricky and difficult, and of course to a certain extent dangerous, the juxtaposition or the putting against each other of the two notions of legitimacy and legality really is. And German constitutional history can of course show these dangers very well. I'm not going to go into that. Nevertheless, with Professor de Wet and Professor Keohane I am of the opinion that the question must be put, in particular where you have a legally valid mandate given to a non-inclusive body. And that is of course the Security Council. In that respect the example given by Professor Zimmermann just a moment ago concerning the ICC resolutions is a very good example for a development where, although there were doubts concerning legality, and I think very well founded doubts, nevertheless states have then by unanimity accepted in two resolutions the system. But then the legitimacy was found to be lacking to such an extent that even the US did not any longer press it to the very end. That is a good example where the pull-off legitimacy finally came to the right result.

I would like to add one question concerning the listing procedure, which was mentioned by Professor de Wet. The listing procedure is an example of a completely illegitimate use by the Security Council of its powers. One can again have great doubts concerning the lawfulness in some respects, but in particular concerning the fact that it needed more than two years to come up with a delisting procedure of any importance and the complete misunderstanding prevailing apparently in the Security Council as to the need for judicial review and judicial protection. In that respect the Court of First Instance also failed, as Professor de Wet said. I wonder to what extent the question of legitimacy must not be put exactly at the corner of the adoption or finding faults in municipal law or in regional law. At this corner or at this really crucial point, the issue of legitimacy must be put again. Thank you.

Y. Dinstein: I am not going to address the central issue of legitimacy because I shall do that later in the day and I do not want to speak twice on the same subject. Let me just mention, *à propos*, that no one has yet managed in actuality to have delegitimized any Chapter VII resolution adopted by the Security Council. This is a matter of record. And I will put it to you that the chances of such delegitimization ever happening successfully in the years ahead are very slim.

What I mainly want to address now is an issue raised by Professor Abi-Saab. He gave us a very good presentation, but regrettably I do not agree with his conclusions. So far, the Security Council has adopted not two but four Chapter VII resolutions amounting to legislation. The two earlier resolutions were adopted in 1993 and 1994 as regards the establishment of the two International Criminal Tribunals on the former Yugoslavia and Rwanda respectively. At the time, a number of scholars blew the whistle and wrote with outrage about the Security Council arrogating to itself powers that are not explicitly granted to it pursuant to the UN Charter (a name that comes immediately to mind is that of Professor Arangio-Ruiz from Italy). However, Georges, on that occasion you were on the other side. As a judge at the ICTY, you were not impressed by the argument at all. Currently, you are emphasizing the difference between the mere setting-up of an *ad hoc* tribunal in a specific context and the creation of what you call "general prospective obligations of States", *i.e.*, new law – as was clearly done in Resolutions 1373 of 2001 and 1540 of 2004. For my part, I believe that it would be disingenuous to pretend that the Statutes of the ICTY and the ICTR carry no consequences for countries other than the former Yugoslavia and Rwanda. Surely, the entire international community is affected by the specific language employed in the definitions of punishable crimes in those Statutes, as well as by the application of those definitions in the judgments of the tribunals established by the Security Council. By now, the question whether the Security Council has the power to legislate appears to me to have been overtaken by events. The Security Council exercises that power as a matter of course under Chapter VII. This is an illustration of "subsequent practice" of the Security Council which reshapes our understanding of its overall powers in accordance with the UN Charter (just as "subsequent practice" of the Council has recast the meaning of the phrase "concurring votes of the permanent members" in Article 27 of the Charter, in connection with the veto power).

No doubt, Resolution 1373 goes further than the resolutions of 1993/1994, and as soon as it was adopted it was hailed as a revolutionary step. Of the vast literature covering this crucial theme, allow me to refer you to a single important article written by the former President of the International Court of Justice, Judge Guillaume, published in the International and Comparative Law Quarterly. Guillaume states categorically that, by adopting Resolution 1373, the Security Council has assumed the role of a true international legislator. I should add, perhaps, that the Security Council is not free to enact new international law in every field and in every context: its powers are linked to Chapter VII, namely, to the maintenance or restoration of international peace and security.

Resolution 1373 deals with the specific topic of the financing of terrorism. What the Security Council essentially did was to take the main provisions of the 1999 International Convention for the Suppression of the Financing of Terrorism – which, in 2001, had very few contracting parties – incorporate them within the resolution and turn them into generally binding law. The interesting question is: what has happened as a result of Resolution 1373? The answer is twofold. First, most States have in the meantime become contracting parties to the 1999 Convention because it no longer matters whether they are in or out of the treaty net; in any event, they are all bound now by the same text through Resolution 1373. Secondly, all UN Member States were required by Resolution 1373 to submit reports to the Counter-Terrorism Committee, and – as we heard from Erika – all of them did that at least once: even Syria and Iran have sent in their reports. To my mind, this indicates that all Member States acquiesce in the exercise of the legislative power by the Security Council.

As for actual implementation, I disagree with Erika. In my opinion, implementation of Resolution 1373 through the CTC has been exceedingly successful, thanks to the centrality of the United States in the global banking system. Every bank in the world needs to do business with the United States, and recently some banks have agreed to pay tens of millions of dollars in penalties for having been caught through CTC work in handling (perhaps inadvertently) accounts traced back to terrorist organizations. No doubt, like everything in life, the functioning of the CTC could be further perfected. The CTC itself says so in its reports. But what has already been accomplished since Resolution 1373 is unprecedented. Resolution 1540 is obviously more recent, and more complex, so the jury is still out about its success. But, all in all, the legislative "subsequent practice" of the Security Council that started in 1993 is now too well-entrenched to be delegitimized.

M. Hartwig: I think the question of legitimacy is closely linked on the one hand to the question of authorization to act and on the other hand to the question of the qualification of the acting organ to comply with its tasks. Sometimes you may have doubts whether the Security Council is always qualified in the right way, especially in the fight against terrorism. Of course, we may be happy that it found a very swift answer, on 12 September 2001, in the fight against terrorism. But on the other hand, we can say: perhaps it was too swift, a day after the attacks in a very emotional environment, to take such far-reaching decisions, which to a certain degree reinterpreted existing international law and, to say the least, perhaps in a way not fully in line with the findings of the ICJ in the Nicaragua case. The Resolution of September 12, 2001 was even topped in 2004 by Resolution 1530 of March 11, 2004, when the attacks in Madrid took place. The very day the Security Council decided to put the blame on the Basque liberation movement, ETA. Unfortunately, it turned out to be wrong. In the end, we have the feeling that the Security Council was not focused on its main task, i.e. the maintenance of the peace of the world or in the world, but was participating in the electoral campaign in Spain.

The decisions concerning the blacklisting of terrorists were not always very happy. According to the first targeted sanctions resolutions against terrorists, the assets of these persons were frozen and the states were forbidden to pay any financial aid to persons who were on the lists. But what did it mean? The established regime would have entailed the consequence that the alleged terrorists had to starve to death. Therefore, no state was strictly applying these resolutions. There was the very famous decision of the European Court of First Instance of May 2002, in which it rejected the request for an interim award of the Swedish citizen, saying that there was no need for such an interim award because Sweden was paying social aid to this person. Would it mean that the violation of the Resolution was a justification for defending it? The UN Security Council changed the situation by adopting the resolution 1452 of December 2002 which provided for procedures to allow payments to persons on the list in need of financial support to make a living. This approach of trial and error is not adding to the foundation of the legitimacy of the UN Security Council Resolutions.

Another problem of legitimacy is whether the decisions of the Security Council are justified only by the respect for the procedure in the sense that, once the Council is acting within its competences it is right; the king can do no wrong. Perhaps there must be some material criteria which have to be applied in order to control even the Security Council. They are already mentioned in a decision of the European Court of First Instance of September 25, 2005. The court held that the resolutions must be in line with the *ius cogens*. Unfortunately, and this is quite telling, the content of *ius cogens* by now is very limited. Perhaps international lawyers shy away from giving such type of legitimacy to international law. As a result individuals have great difficulty in defending their rights against infringements by Security Council Resolutions. Thank you very much.

K. Doehring: In my view, Abi-Saab excellently demonstrated that the notion of legitimacy is unnecessary and useless in international law. The legitimacy of international law is recognition. And recognition of norms and of acts of international organizations forms part of legality. To look for legitimacy might result in destruction of legality. I wouldn't go as far as an American colleague, who told me that when students were asking whether a hard case shouldn't be solved by relying on the principle of justice, he replied: if you are looking for justice you should attend a course of divinity. So, nevertheless, I fear that the invocation of legitimacy would destroy legality. Of course, and I also said this some years ago, the Security Council may act *ultra vires*. That is possible. And then the acts are unlawful. But if we come to the conclusion that the Security Council acts *ultra vires*, then we are again in the area of questions of legality and not of legitimacy. And so, I think, we should be modest and say: legitimacy in international law, that's recognition;

yesterday Mr. Herdegen already invoked the question of consent in international law. And Abi-Saab, I think, did the same. Thank you.

S. Oeter: I could start by voicing disagreement with the previous speaker, Professor Doehring. I would not say that legitimacy is a completely unnecessary category, although I must admit that to a certain degree I agree with Professor Doehring that it is a very problematic enterprise to speak about legitimacy as if it were a purely legal category. I think yesterday it became quite obvious that we as lawyers have difficulties in leading a structured and meaningful discourse on legitimacy. And this is not a value judgement on the speakers yesterday, who I think did very well in discussing the topic. But behind the issue lies a structural problem: in essence, legitimacy is a category of political theory and of social science, and not a legal category. And in that sense, I found it fortunate that Professor Keohane was built into the panel and reminded us that beyond legal discourse there is a very elaborate debate on these categories.

Nevertheless, we tended to discuss legitimacy as a legal category and I would not say that this is completely wrong. Legitimacy may be in certain contexts a legal issue, a category of legal relevance. And I think the discussion today reminded us of one of these situations. Another one is the change of customary law when we are at a point when a lot of states are challenging a traditional rule and say: We don't share the traditional *opinio iuris*, we think the old rule is illegitimate, we need a new rule. There should be (or there is) an *opinio necessitatis* on a new rule. In such a situation we have a kind of legal relevance of legitimacy discourses. And the same is true in the example which was given to us this morning – the situation when an organ is overstepping its original mandate and we have, let us say, legal decisions, legal operations which are in a way illegal, beyond its original mandate. In subsequent practice the question arises. Do we nevertheless (as states) accept this kind of decision, this kind of activity, and are we willing to make it legal again by subsequent practice? We are again in a kind of legitimacy discourse of legal relevance. But I think we should be aware that these are limited discourses on legitimacy. This should not be misunderstood as saying that it doesn't make sense to lead a more general discourse on legitimacy. But this, I would say, is a matter of discourse that is clearly beyond pure legal discourses. And we should be aware, as lawyers, that this is a completely different kind of discourse. I think Erika reminded us in one context where we should lead that kind of meta-discourse in a much more structured and elaborate way, where legitimacy plays an enormous role – although we have difficulties in phrasing it adequately. And that's the link between international law and the operation of rules on the ground; in other words: the implementation of international law in the national legal systems. I think the general experience of international lawyers working on that topic of implementation is that in general this implementation only works if there is a general perception of legitimacy concerning the relevant international rules. Otherwise, we all too easily end up in a kind of symbolic game which doesn't really make a difference in the ground operation of law. But, and this is my last word on that, I think we have difficulty in phrasing that concern adequately in legal terms, because (without putting into doubt traditional doctrines on the role of international law in the national legal orders) we tend – to a certain degree with intent – to invisibilize that kind of legitimacy problem.

T. Eitel: Only a brief factual remark prompted by what was said by Matthias Hartwig, which I found a very interesting point. But the facts are, if I'm not mistaken, as follows: if money is frozen during the implementation of a Security Council resolution by national banks, the money, of course, is not transferred to the Security Council. It remains under national control and often states take money from these frozen accounts to serve their own interests. The case Matthias Hartwig was referring to finds an easy explanation as follows: the state by means of social security systems helps people from the sanctioned countries who get into need. And then the state takes money from the frozen account to keep itself out of trouble. And that is, in my understanding, the way these things are being dealt with. Thank you.

E. de Wet: In my response I will briefly address the most pressing questions addressed to me. First, it is necessary to distinguish between legality and legitimacy. On the one hand, it is very difficult to prove the illegality of a Security Council decision, especially if one keeps in mind that a strong presumption of legality is attached to those decisions. Therefore, if member States do not object to the illegality of a Security Council decision immediately, persistently and clearly, it would be difficult afterwards to claim that they did not acquiesce in the decision in question (which may have effectively expanded the power of the Security Council under the circumstances).

However, the fact that a sanctions regime is legal does not necessarily make it legitimate. In relation to the question raised by Professor

Zimmermann, I would respond that it is not of decisive importance whether the Security Council itself or its Sanctions Committee identifies the persons or entities on the sanctions list. The decisive factor is that the targeted sanctions in question represent a chain of decisions which usually begins on the level of the Security Council itself and then is continued within the Sanctions Committees. One should therefore focus not only on the legitimacy of the decisions taken by the Security Council itself, but also on those of its Sanctions Committees which are very powerful sub organs.

It may indeed also be the case that the Security Council members on occasion engage in in-depth consultations with other States when drafting binding resolutions. However, such consultation still seems to remain the exception to the rule and consultations with other States often do not amount to more than a *pro forma* meeting.

Concerning the points raised by Professor Keohane, I should stress that I am in favour of a strong Security Council. My criticism should therefore not be interpreted as suggesting that one should do away with the Security Council. It is exactly because it is the only existing international organ with binding powers in the area of peace and security that the need for the legitimacy of its actions is crucial. Stated differently, it is crucial that the Security Council itself adjusts its working methods and those of its Sanctions Committees by introducing elements of contestability, transparency and inclusivity during the processes of decision-making.

The current *modus operandi* of the Security Council reflects a serious lack of legitimacy. This, in turn, is bound to affect the efficacy of the Security Council in the long run, as the majority of members may not be inclined to continue implementing the decisions of an institution which they increasingly regard as illegitimate. Unfortunately, however, some permanent Members remain more concerned with the pursuing of short-term interests, at the expense of the legitimacy of the United Nations system as a whole.

Secondly, one has to accept that the Security Council cannot solve all pressing problems facing the international community. It is questionable whether it is the most suitable institution for dealing with questions pertaining to international terrorism and weapons of mass destruction, to which there are no instant solutions. The Security Council is not an international government and does not have the capacity to deal with these challenges in an enduring fashion. One should therefore accept its limitations and that many of these challenges require long-term solutions which ultimately have to be resolved through political negotiation in the General Assembly.

Finally, in response to Professor Dinstein, it is plausible to argue that the efficacy of the CTC could serve to redeem some of the procedural deficits by means of which this body came into being. However, one may question whether the results he referred to are truly due to the work of the CTC. Instead, many of the results may rather be due to the unilateral pressure of the United States government – pressure which would have existed regardless of the existence of the CTC or the legislative regime designed by Resolution 1373 (2001).

G. Abi-Saab: I shall try to combine my answers to the different questions and comments. First, on legality and legitimacy, I agree with much of what has been said, notably by Professor Frowein when he said that the question of legitimacy arises in particular for the Security Council because of its composition. It is not a representative organ, but a limited one. To me – I have said that at the outset – legality is the first rung or layer of legitimacy. If there is a strong controversy over legality, legitimacy is *a fortiori* and automatically impaired. But legitimacy goes beyond that. So, even when actions are taken within the clear bounds of formal legality, for example within the formal limits and respecting the formal conditions of the exercise of its jurisdiction by an organ, we may still have a problem of legitimacy. If in addition there is a controversy on whether these acts are legal or not, then we have a very severe crisis of legitimacy.

That is my first answer. And that also answers to some extent what Yoram has said. He said nobody has ever managed to delegitimise – I think what he meant was successfully to challenge the legality rather than the legitimacy of – a decision of the Security Council. This may be true, but such a challenge is not impossible. It can come up in the General Assembly, or as an incidental question before an international tribunal, as in the *Tadic* case at the ICTY in 1995. It can be raised before national tribunals or in national parliaments, considering that the Security Council action was *ultra vires* or contrary to *jus cogens* and should not be heeded. This is not impossible. The fact that we don't have a constitutional procedure of challenge or judicial review does not make all decisions of the Security Council automatically legal. Constitutional law in many countries is not justiciable. This does not make any violation of the constitution legal.

Secondly, I would contest Yoram's statement that the creation of the two *ad hoc* International Criminal Tribunals involved legislation. In a way, you know my arguments, they are clearly laid down in the *Tadic* judgement of 1995. Yoram says that the legislative element is in the definition of the crimes in the Statutes. But look at the Report of the Secretary-General and at the Statute. The Report of the Secretary-General is very clear. It says explicitly that it defines the crimes according to existing customary international law. So, it was a kind of codification; it may be good or bad codification, but it is not *de novo* legislation. The Tribunals themselves made a big effort whenever there was haziness to emphasize that they were applying pre-existing law, because of the principle of legality.

It is not the same with the ICC, where articles 8 to 10 were so much elaborated and played with that it was felt necessary to subject them, on an Egyptian proposal, to the rider of article 10 which provides that they are without prejudice to general international law. It is exactly the reverse situation from that of the *ad hoc* tribunals, where both the report of the Secretary-General and the jurisprudence insisted on their consistency with general international law.

Professor von Heinegg started by saying that article 39 speaks of any threat. I agree with that; this is why I ended by saying that there was in fact a kind of international public emergency brought about by the rise of global terrorism, and that it was a good thing that the Council reacted to it. Here also comes the element of necessity that Professor Benedek mentioned, which may explain certain excesses. Internally, in a public emergency, the Executive may get exceptional powers, for example the power to rule by decree. But ruling by decree is only for a limited time, beyond which the decrees have to be ratified by parliament or lapse. Here we don't have a parliament. It has to be replaced by the general acceptance of the product – the norms; acceptance by the generality of the Member States, which is another way of saying by the international community.

The example given by Yoram about the financing of terrorism is very good. What the Council did, taking up the repressive articles of the Convention and forgetting the ones protective of human rights, was an aberration. But it was somehow rebalanced by the increasing ratifications of the Convention by States. If the Council's action leads to increasing participation in conventions, that is all well and good. If not, I would still say that these rules would not stand in the air by the mere fiat of the Security Council. They have to be translated into general international law, not by way of the Council *pronunciamento* alone, but by general adherence to them.

This brings me to the question of subsequent practice raised by Professor Zimmermann. I agree with him that significant subsequent practice is necessarily the subsequent practice of all the membership of the UN. Subsequent practice of the Council as such, particularly when it comes to the interpretation and application of general norms, those of the Charter or general international law, cannot be attributed to the membership at large. Thus, if the Council acts in a certain way, for example interpreting abstention as an affirmative vote, i.e. interpreting article 27 of the Charter, it is necessary to establish that the membership as a whole, and not just that of the Council, has adhered to this interpretation in order for it to be considered as significant subsequent practice for the interpretation of the Charter.

In conclusion, I would like to come back to Professor von Heinegg, who started by saying that the record of the Council has been very impressive and that States have acquiesced in, and not protested against, it exceeding its powers and undertaking all sorts of activities during the last fifteen years. I would simply say that if we are speaking here about legitimacy as defined by Professors Franck and Frowein, going beyond legality to the factors that beget compliance outside coercion, then I think the Council would come out at best with a mitigated record, with as many errors as positive achievements.

This is why, Yoram, regardless of the existence or absence of institutional means of challenge, the epistemic community of international lawyers has vigilantly to exercise its critical function as the dispassionate monitor of legality and legitimacy in the international community.

Aspects of Legitimacy of Decisions of International Courts and Tribunals

Tullio Treves

Introduction: Legality and Legitimacy
Objective and subjective legitimacy

In considering the use of force outside the parameters of the U.N. Charter, the expression "illegal, but legitimate" has been used, in particular in the Goldstone report.[1] In that context, legitimacy as opposed to legality is used to indicate a judgement based on values different from those of conformity with the law. These values include moral principles such as the safeguarding of human life and dignity. "Legitimate" indicates a perception of acceptability in light of these values.

There are also other ways of looking at legitimacy. It seems particularly interesting to consider the notion put forward by Thomas M. Franck. He proposes that legitimacy be verified in light of correspondence with certain "indicators". These indicators, as put forward by Franck, are not directly of a moral nature. They belong to legal discourse, although lack of correspondence with them does not have as a consequence that legality in a specific case is put into question. Franck's indicators are: determinacy, symbolic validation, coherence and adherence.[2]

---

[1] Independent International Commission on Kosovo, The Kosovo Report: Conflict, International Response, Lessons Learned, 2000, at 164.

[2] T. Franck, *Fairness in International Law and Institutions*, 1995, at 30-46. In the following, I will refer to this book. Franck has, however, addressed legitimacy in a number of other works, especially *The Power of Legitimacy among Nations*, 1990; and, most recently, "The Power of Legitimacy and the Legitimacy of Power: International Law in the Age of Power Disequilibrium", *AJIL* 100 (2006), 88-106.

A judgement of legitimacy, especially if used according to the "Goldstone" meaning, when coupled with a judgement of illegality, expresses a criticism of the law, or a claim to change the law, or a claim to some form of justification. While "legality", i.e. conformity to the law, is a fundamental parameter of legitimacy both in the "Goldstone" and the "Franck" sense, a judgement of "legitimacy" or "illegitimacy" may also be used in addition to a judgement of "legality" (legal and legitimate, legal but illegitimate). In this case, when the requirements of legitimacy (used either way) are satisfied, something is added to "legality"; when they are not satisfied ("illegitimacy") something is subtracted from it; this "something" being a perception of acceptability.

In determining whether the requirements set out in the "indicators" of legitimacy proposed by Tom Franck are satisfied, different persons may of course reach different conclusions. This determination can nevertheless be considered an "objective" one as it is based on judgements that can be made on the basis of legal technique[3]. Even though the acceptance of these indicators as relevant may be seen to be based on a value judgement, in determining their applicability to a specific case no such judgement is necessary.

When used in the "Goldstone" sense, the judgement of "legitimate" or "illegitimate" is directly based on value judgements. In this sense, it can always be considered subjective. It seems, however, preferable to use this adjective only when the judgement is based on values held important by one State or by a group of States, and to indicate as "objective" such judgement when based on values broadly or generally shared. In most cases the values invoked to claim legitimacy or illegitimacy within the Goldstone meaning are broadly accepted, while what is not always broadly accepted is the judgement that these values must, in the specific case, prevail over other values not less broadly accepted. The borderline between subjective and objective judgement of legitimacy is thus not entirely clear, as subjective legitimacy is more often than not a claim that certain generally shared values should prevail over others in a specific case.

---

3 P.-M. Dupuy, "L'unité de l'ordre juridique international, Cours général de droit international public", *Recueil des cours*, vol. 297, 2002, 9 at 405, ftn. 813 observes that Franck's notion of legitimacy is closer to the notion of legality as traditionally understood in European political and legal philosophy than to the notion of legitimacy upheld by that philosophy.

I. Legitimacy of judicial decisions the legality of which is not questioned

When discussing legitimacy as regards judicial decisions, it seems particularly interesting to deal with the legitimacy of decisions the legality of which is not questioned. While not ruling out that there may be decisions the legality of which is questioned or questionable and the legitimacy of which may be discussed for that reason, the focus of the brief remarks that follow will be on factors that can add to or subtract from the legitimacy of a decision validly adopted.

In assessing the legitimacy of international judicial decisions, it may be interesting to consider a series of questions. The reader will recognize that these questions, although grouped in six clusters, follow the classification of legitimacy theories in three groups, as clearly put forward, for example, by Daniel Bodansky:[4] source-based theories (the first two clusters), process-based theories (the third and fourth clusters), and outcome-based theories (the fifth and sixth clusters).

The first cluster concerns the way the judicial body is established. The following questions may be considered:

- is a judicial body more legitimate when it is treaty-based, or when it is based on a Chapter VII resolution of the Security Council?
- is a judicial body that considers State-to-State disputes less legitimate if it has been established without the participation of some of the States which may become parties to cases before it (or the State that necessarily will be such a party)?

The second cluster has to do with the members of the judicial body. The following questions may be of interest:

- is a judicial body more legitimate when its members are elected or when they are designated?
- does the legal expertise of the members or the right political mix in the composition of the judicial body contribute more to the body's legitimacy?
- how important are the guarantees of impartiality and independence of the judicial body's members, and the record of their implementation, for the legitimacy of the decisions?

---

4 See D. Bodansky, in this volume, p. 309 at 310 et seq.

- how relevant is the quality of the previous judgements for the legitimacy of a specific decision?

The third cluster concerns the basis of jurisdiction. In particular, the following questions seem of interest:

- is a decision taken by a judicial body on the basis of a special agreement on jurisdiction more legitimate than one in which jurisdiction is based on a rule providing for compulsory jurisdiction or on the ICJ's optional clause?
- is a decision taken on the merits after a divisive battle has been fought on preliminary questions less legitimate than a decision taken when no such battle has been fought or when the preliminary questions have been solved by a broad majority of the judicial body?

The fourth cluster includes questions having to do with how judgements are reached. Among those to be considered are the following:

- are judgements made in proceedings in which one party has not appeared less legitimate than those in which all parties participate?
- are judgements made in proceedings in which there is a lack of balance in the means (human and material) at the disposal of the defence of the parties less legitimate than those where such balance exists?

The fifth cluster concerns the characteristics of the decision. Relevant questions seem to be the following:

- is the legitimacy of the decision influenced by the fact that it has been taken by an unanimous vote, or by a majority, or with the casting vote of the president?
- is the legitimacy of the decisions influenced by the presence of numerous declarations, separate or dissenting opinions?
- is the legitimacy of the decision influenced by lack of clarity of the operative part and/or of the reasons?
- is the legitimacy of a decision influenced by the fact that certain questions raised in the pleadings are not addressed or are addressed very shortly?
- is the legitimacy of a decision influenced by the fact that it addresses questions that have not been discussed, or which are irrelevant for the decision as it has been taken?
- is the legitimacy of the decision influenced by its consistency with previous judgements of the deciding body?

- is the legitimacy of the decision influenced by its taking into account of the existence, jurisdiction and jurisprudence of other international judicial bodies?

The sixth and last cluster has to do with the effects of the decision. The following question seems relevant:

- does the legitimacy of a decision have an influence on its implementation?

To address all these questions (and others that could be raised) in some detail would require extensive research and much more space than is available for the present paper. Raising these questions must be seen as an exploration of the territory to be covered in future studies. To draw a sketch of the possible answers would not be an impossible task, but the results might be misleading as based more on impressions than on fully fledged research. It seems preferable to consider two separate, specific, areas in the discussion of which the treatment of a few of the questions set out above may emerge.

I will try, first, to put international judicial decisions to the test of Thomas Franck's indicators of legitimacy. I will later focus on some examples of practices aimed at "legitimizing" or "de-legitimizing" international decisions within the Goldstone meaning of legitimacy.

II. Franck's tests of legitimacy and international judicial decisions

The decisions of judges are included, according to Franck, within the scope of the four indicators of legitimacy mentioned above, as these indicators concern "the legitimacy of primary rules, the ordinary rules, whether made by legislatures, bureaucrats, *judges* or plebiscites."[5] This notwithstanding, decisions of judges are not examined closely in Franck's analysis of the four indicators. This makes it particularly interesting to try this examination. What follows is an attempt to develop ideas taking Franck's indicators as a point of departure. Of course, I do not claim that these developments are entirely consistent with Tom Franck's thought or that he would agree with them.

Determinacy is the first of the four indicators. It consists in "the ability of a text to convey a clear message ... Rules which have a readily acces-

---

[5] Franck, *Fairness*, note 2, at 26.

sible meaning and say what they expect of those who are addressed are more likely to have a real impact on conduct."[6] Decisions of international courts and tribunals may fail this test if their operative part is unclear, avoids answering the questions addressed to the adjudicating body or if the reasons given are difficult to understand or may be subject to different interpretations. One can also wonder whether different reasons given for a certain position adopted, indicating that some apply only where other reasons are rejected, is consistent with this test.

The well known para. 2E of the operative part of the ICJ's advisory opinion of 8 July 1999 on the *legality of the threat or use of nuclear weapons* (adopted by seven votes to seven, with the casting vote of the President)[7] may be an example. In answering the rather clear question "is the threat or use of nuclear weapons in any circumstance permitted under international law?", the Court, in the key para. just indicated, states that: "the threat or use of nuclear weapons would generally be contrary to the rules of international law applicable in armed conflict, and in particular the principles and rules of humanitarian law". It adds that: "... the Court cannot conclude definitively whether the threat or use of nuclear weapons would be lawful or unlawful in an extreme circumstance of self-defense, in which the very survival of a State will be at stake". Even taking into account the difficulty of the question and its political impact, and the fact that the decision is an advisory opinion and not a judgement, it seems evident that the phrase "would generally be contrary" and the assertion that the Court "cannot conclude definitively" do not convey a clear meaning. The dissent of Judge Rosalyn Higgins argues exactly this point: "The findings in a judicial *dispositif* should be clear. I believe that para. 2E is unclear in its meaning". Such lack of clarity, in Judge Higgins' view, brings the Court to a *non liquet.* Judge Higgins also deplores the fact that the Court does not "show the steps by which it reaches its conclusions."[8] This view is shared in the declaration of one of the judges in the majority, Judge Ferrari Bravo, who states that the reasoning of the Court "is often difficult to read, tortuous and ultimately rather inadequate."[9]

---

6 Franck, *Fairness*, note 2, at 30-31.

7 ICJ Reports 1996, 226. Adoption with the casting vote of the President may by itself raise questions of legitimacy, as mentioned in the previous paragraph.

8 ICJ Reports 1996, 583, para.s 7 and 9 at p. 584.

9 ICJ Reports 1996, 282, at p. 283.

It may be argued that such lack of clarity takes something away from the Advisory Opinion's legitimacy. It could well be, however, that the other options open to the Court would have taken away something more. These options were, in particular, using its discretion in refusing to comply with the request of the General Assembly, and giving a clear, yes or no, answer to the question including the possible nuances that the expression "in any circumstance" contained in it could have permitted.

The second indicator of legitimacy proposed by Franck, *symbolic validation,* seems an inherent characteristic of international judicial decisions. The formality of the proceedings and of the reading of the judgement, the detailed character of the reasoning, the connections with the United Nations that exist in many international courts and tribunals, all signal that an international judgement, to use Tom Franck's words, "is a significant part of the overall system of social order."[10] From this viewpoint, it is unlikely that indications of illegitimacy can be found in the judgement of an international court or tribunal.

Coherence, the third indicator of legitimacy mentioned by Franck, if applied to international judicial decisions, would seem to require that decisions are in some measure predictable in light of previous decisions because like cases are treated alike and because "when distinctions are made, they must themselves be explicable by reference to generally applied concepts of differentiation."[11] Decisions taken – as happens quite often – on the narrowest possible ground, preferring what Georges Abi-Saab calls "solutions transactionnelles" to solutions based on principle,[12] may be expedient and politically acceptable, and so ultimately fair and legitimate, as Franck seems to imply.[13] They may nevertheless also be seen as subtracting something from the "legitimacy" of the decision as they avoid an assessment in light of the "coherence" indicator. The remark by Abi-Saab that this kind of decision may imply "une diminution significative du rôle de la Cour comme la plus haute instance judiciaire dans l'ordre juridique international,"[14] or that of Pierre-Marie Dupuy that it may jeopardize the Court's "rôle naturel de

---

[10] Franck, *Fairness*, note 2, at 34.

[11] Franck, *Fairness*, note 2, at 39.

[12] G. Abi-Saab, "Cours général de droit international public", *Recueil des Cours* 207 (1987-VII), 9, at 271.

[13] Franck, *Fairness*, note 2, at 331.

[14] Abi-Saab, note 12, at 272.

garant de l'unité d'interprétation du droit international,"[15] seem to point in the same direction.

In light of the multiplication of international courts and tribunals, and of the consequent multiplication of international decisions in which international legal rules are ascertained and interpreted, a further aspect of "coherence" as an indicator of legitimacy may be envisaged. An attitude of different courts and tribunals based on knowledge of each other's decisions, mutual respect, avoidance of unnecessary conflicts seems to contribute to the "coherence" of judicial decisions and thus to their legitimacy. Recourse by courts involved in cases in which other courts are or may also be involved to notions such as "comity" and "judicial economy" may be useful.[16] So may be the development of trans-judiciary general procedural principles or customary rules.[17]

A similar aspect of "coherence" may be envisaged in considering the relationship between the jurisdiction of the international judicial body that has adopted or may adopt a decision, and especially of the International Court of Justice, with the competence of an organ of the United Nations, such as the General Assembly and the Security Council. Concerns of legitimacy are probably to be seen in the attitude of the ICJ in the *Lockerbie* cases.[18] In recalling the *Lockerbie* provisional measures orders, in general terms Franck addresses this question, stating that: "the ICJ must give due weight to decisions of another organ interpret-

---

15 P.-M. Dupuy, note 3, at 476.

16 T. Treves, "Judicial Lawmaking in an Era of "Proliferation" of International Courts and Tribunals: Development or Fragmentation of International law?", in: R. Wolfrum/V. Röben (eds), *Developments of International Law in Treaty Making*, 2005, 587-620; id., "Le Tribunal international du droit de la mer dans la pléiade des juridictions internationales", in: O. Delas, R. Côté, F. Crépeau & P. Leuprecht (eds.), *Les juridictions internationales: complémentarité ou concurrence?*, 2005, 9-39.

17 See the stimulating essay by R. Kolb, "General Principles of Procedural Law", in: A. Zimmermann, Ch. Tomuschat & K. Oellers-Frahm (eds.), *The Statute of the International Court of Justice, A Commentary*, 2006, 793-835.

18 Case concerning questions of interpretation and application of the 1971 Montreal Convention arising from the aerial incident at Lockerbie, Libya v. United Kingdom, Libya v. United States, provisional measures, Orders of 14 April 1992; ICJ Reports 1992, 114 and Judgements on preliminary objections of 27 February 1998, ICJ Reports 1998, 9. (see in particular the dissent by Judge Jennings, p. 99, espe. p. 108).

ing its Charter-based jurisdiction."[19] A concern for legitimacy (and not only for avoidance of conflict) may also be seen in the provision of article 298, para 1 *c*, of the United Nations Convention on the Law of the Sea which permits a State party, by a declaration, to exclude from compulsory jurisdiction provided for disputes concerning the interpretation or application of the Convention, "disputes in respect of which the Security Council of the United Nations is exercising the functions assigned to it by the Charter of the United Nations...".

Adherence, the fourth indicator of legitimacy proposed by Franck, is based on the fact that rules "are demonstrably supported by the procedural and institutional framework within which the community organizes itself."[20] It would seem that this indicator of legitimacy is the closest to a test of legality. As regards decisions of international courts and tribunals, it would seem to include the fact that the court and tribunal has been established in application of legal rules and that it is competent according to the applicable rules. Concerns whether a court or tribunal was established in correct application of the existing rules, such as those discussed in the *Tadic* case by the International Tribunal for crimes committed in former Yugoslavia,[21] may certainly be considered, as they were in the *Tadic* case, from the point of view of legality. They may, however, also be seen as raising a question of legitimacy, which is an aspect of the question that can be envisaged in more general terms, regarding the use, and sometimes alleged abuse, of "legislative powers" by the Security Council.

III. Legitimacy of judicial decisions in light of their consistency with moral or political values

Coming now to legitimacy in the "Goldstone" sense, there can be many occasions on which a judicial decision may be argued to be "illegitimate" because it collides with values of a moral nature. Situations in which the jurisdiction of the judge, and consequently the scope of the judgement, can encompass only a limited part of a broad conflict may

---

19 Franck, note 2, at 331.

20 Franck, note 2, at 41.

21 Appellate Chamber, Decision on the Defence motion for interlocutory appeal on Jurisdiction, the Prosecutor v. D. Tadic, 2 October 1995, 35 *ILM* 32 (1996).

bring courts and tribunals to issue a judgement that some may see as illegitimate because it fails to address aspects of the conflict they consider essential in light of moral or political values. These values may often be incorporated in rules the application of which is beyond the limits of the jurisdiction of the court or tribunal. In these cases the concern for "legitimacy" as conformity with moral or political values collides with what we can call "the legitimacy of legality". In other words: the claim that the judicial decision should address certain issues and values even when they are beyond the limits of the court's jurisdiction, or are unnecessary to solve the dispute, collides with the argument that a value, the moral or political weight of which is considered essential, is that courts and tribunals do not, in their decisions, go beyond what has been brought before them according to the applicable rules.

In recent cases the ICJ has made statements in the situations just described linking the matter submitted to it to rules incorporating values it considers essential even when it decided that it lacked jurisdiction (or *prima facie* jurisdiction in provisional measures proceedings) or when the statements were of no legal relevance for the decision taken in the case.

In another study, I have labelled this kind of statement "political *obiter dicta.*"[22] In the context of the present paper, such statements can be called "legitimizing statements" as they can be seen as tools used by the Court to strengthen the legitimacy of the judgements or orders in which they are contained. A judgement or order that decides a case which emerges from a broad conflict that jeopardizes essential values such as those connected with loss of human life, genocide, use of force, on the basis of rather technical legal arguments such as those concerning lack of jurisdiction, may be more acceptable to the losing party and to public opinion if it contains statements – however unnecessary – that reaffirm these values. The same need of broad acceptability may well be an essential component of the decision-making process of the Court, as it may be easier for certain judges to concur with a decision taken on a basis not involving the application of rules incorporating moral values deemed essential if some mention of such rules is set out in the decision. It would seem that these judges, and also the losing State and public

---

[22] The Political Use of Unilateral Applications and Provisional Measures Proceedings, in: *Verhandeln fuer den Frieden, Negotiating for Peace, Liber Amicorum Tono Eitel*, Frowein, Schariot, Winkelmann & Wolfrum, eds., 2003, 463-481.

opinion are, through these statements, encouraged to see the decision as more legitimate.

The inclusion of "legitimizing statements" in recent decisions of the ICJ has to be seen in contrast with separate or dissenting opinions arguing in favour of the "legitimacy of legality", arguing, in other words, that these statements – independently of their legality, which in some cases is seen as doubtful – are unnecessary to support the decision and, especially, inopportune from the point of view of the proper exercise of the judicial function. These separate and dissenting opinions see the "legitimizing statements" included in the decisions with the purpose of connecting them with important legal and moral principles, as delegitimizing elements that subtract from the overall acceptability of judicial decisions. The subjective character of the idea of legitimacy of judicial decisions emerges clearly in this opposition of views, not because the values invoked are not broadly shared, but because of the difference as to which one should prevail.

Two examples from recent cases considered by the ICJ seem to illustrate the points just made. They are the 2002 Order in the *Armed Activities* (Congo v. Rwanda)[23] case and the 2003 judgement in the *Oil platforms* case (Iran v. United States).[24]

In the Congo v. Rwanda order the Court refused the requested provisional measures, stating that it did not have *prima facie* jurisdiction (lack of jurisdiction was later confirmed in the 2006 judgement on jurisdiction and admissibility[25]). Notwithstanding the fact that the *dispositif* stated lack of *prima facie* jurisdiction, the Court emphasized that parties "must act in conformity with their obligations pursuant to the United Nations Charter and other rules of international law"[26] and stressed "the necessity for the parties to these proceedings to use their influence to prevent the repeated grave violations of human rights and international humanitarian law."[27] In support of this approach Judge Koroma, in his declaration, indicated that "the Court, in accordance with its *obiter dicta* in the cited para.s, nevertheless discharged its re-

---

23 Order of 10 July 2002, 41 *ILM* 1175 (2002).

24 Judgement of 6 November 2003, Iran v. United States, 42 *ILM* 1334 (2003).

25 Case concerning armed activities on the territory of the Congo (new application 2002), judgement of 3 February 2006, 45 *ILM* 562 (2006).

26 Para. 56.

27 Para. 93. See also para.s 54 and 55.

sponsibilities in maintaining international peace and security" and stated that: "The position taken by the Court can only be viewed as constructive ... It is a judicial position and it is in the interest of all concerned to hearken to the call of the Court."[28]

The opposite view emerges in Judge Buergenthal's declaration.[29] Leaving aside his argument that these statements were inappropriate "as a matter of law,"[30] for our present purposes it is interesting to note that he placed himself on the terrain of legitimacy in considering them something detracting from the authority of the Court or inappropriate. He states that these statements "... despite their admittedly "feel-good" qualities, have no *legitimate* place in this Order."[31] In connection with the statement concerning the Court's responsibilities in the maintenance of peace and security, Judge Buergenthal states: "Of course, how could it be otherwise? Is it an *apologia* for the Court's lack of jurisdiction to do what it would like to do in this case? If so, I wonder whether it is appropriate."[32] He also stated: "Whether intended or not, the Court's pronouncements ... might be deemed to lend credence to the factual allegations submitted by the Party seeking the provisional measures. In the future they might also encourage States to file provisional measures requests, knowing that, despite the fact that they would be unable to sustain the burden of demonstrating the requisite prima facie jurisdiction, they would obtain from the Court some pronouncements that could be interpreted as supporting their claim against the other party."[33] These passages, among others, seem to be based on the "legitimacy of legality" rather than the legitimacy of the criticized statements of the Court.

In the judgement on jurisdiction and admissibility handed down in 2006 in the same case, the Court echoed the "legitimacy statements" made in the 2002 order. It stated, in particular: "Whether or not States have accepted the jurisdiction of the Court, they are required to fulfil their obligations under the United Nations Charter and the other rules of international law, including humanitarian and human rights law, and

---

28 41 *ILM* 1197 (2002) para. 16.

29 41 *ILM* 1199 (2002).

30 Para. 10.

31 Para. 4 (emphasis added).

32 Para. 6.

33 Para. 9.

they remain responsible for acts attributable to them which are contrary to international law.[34]

In the 2003 *Oil platforms* judgement the Court, in the first para. of the *dispositif*, found that

> "The actions of the United States of America against Iranian oil platforms on 19 October and 18 April 1988 cannot be justified as measures necessary to protect the essential security interests of the United States of America under Article XX, para. 1(*d*), of the 1955 Treaty of Amity, Economic Relations and Consular Rights between the United States of America and Iran, as interpreted in the light of international law on the use of force;"

The para. continues, finding further that:

> "the Court cannot however uphold the submission of the Islamic Republic of Iran that these actions constitute a breach of the obligations of the United States of America under Article X, para. 1, of that Treaty, regarding freedom of commerce between the territories of the parties, and that, accordingly, the claim of the Islamic Republic of Iran for reparation also cannot be upheld".

This rather peculiar *dispositif* reflects the reasoning of the Court. The submission by Iran was that the United States had violated its obligations under article X, para. 1, of the 1955 treaty, protecting freedom of commerce between the parties. The United States stated that it had not breached its obligations under article X, para. 1, while accepting that article XX, not precluding "measures necessary to fulfil obligations for the maintenance or restoration of international peace and security", could be considered as a defence, in case the Court had found otherwise. The United States did not insist on which article should be considered first. The Court chose to start from article XX, in light, *inter alia*, of the fact that "the original dispute between the parties related to the legality of the actions of the United States, in the light of international law on the use of force."[35] By a complex reasoning, in which it resorted to rules on the use of force through interpretation of the 1955 Treaty provisions in light of "any relevant rules of international law applicable in the relations between the parties" under article 31, para. 3c of the Vienna Convention on the law of treaties, the Court went on to examine the action by the United States (the bombing of Iranian oil platforms), concluding that it did not meet the requirements of self-defence

---

[34] Judgement of 3 February 2006 quoted above, para. 127.

[35] Para. 37.

and that consequently it could not be justified under the rules of international law on the use of force. Going on to examine such action from the viewpoint of a violation of obligations under article X, para. 1, the Court found that there was no such violation.

As mentioned, both findings are set out in the same point of the *dispositif* so that the fourteen judges voting in favour could not vote on the two findings individually. This may be seen as indirect evidence that a compromise was struck within the Court so that a broad majority could be mustered to reject the Iranian claim provided that, somehow, the judgement stated that the United States had not complied with the international law rules on the use of force.

From the declarations and separate opinions of most of the fourteen judges of the majority it emerges, however, that there was an important divergence as regards the path followed by the Court in giving legal form to the above indicated compromise. This divergence concerns legality as, in particular, some judges argue that the judgement violated the *non ultra petita* rule because the final submissions did not mention article XX. From the point of view that interests us in the present paper, however, the divergence concerns the policy followed in the judgement and shows in very clear terms different views of what enhances the legitimacy of a judgement and what detracts from such legitimacy.

Judge Simma, in his separate opinion, states:

> "I consider it of the utmost importance, and a matter of principle, for the Court to pronounce itself on questions of the threat or use of force in international relations whenever it is given the opportunity to do so."[36]

This statement seems to indicate that, whatever the constraints depending on the scope of the jurisdiction of the Court in the specific case, it is a policy requirement that matters as important as those concerning the use of force are addressed if connected with the dispute between the parties, even though not with the dispute as encompassed in the Court's jurisdiction. It would seem that, according to this view, the examination of questions relating to use of force enhances the legitimacy of the judgement.

The views expressed by judges Higgins, Kooijmans, Buergenthal and Owada in their separate opinions stress a totally different policy and notion of legitimacy. Their basic point, in legal terms, is that, as the Court found that there had been no violation of the invoked substan-

---

36 42 *ILM* 1429 (2003), para. 5.

tive article X of the 1955 Treaty, there was no need to examine the possible defence based on article XX and, in connection with it, on the rules on the use of force. The unnecessary consideration of this defence brought the Court to violate the *non ultra petita* principle. The legal discussion is, for our purposes, less interesting than the remarks on policy made by these judges, remarks from which an idea of legitimacy different from that of the judgement and of Judge Simma (again the "legitimacy of legality") emerges.

Judge Higgins states:

> "It cannot ... be "desirable" or indeed appropriate to deal with a claim that the Court itself has categorized as a claim relating to freedom of commerce and navigation by making the centre of its analysis the international law on the use of force. And conversely, if the use of force on armed attack and self-defence is to be judicially examined, is the appropriate way to do so through the eye of the needle that is the freedom of commerce clause of a 1955 FCN Treaty? The answer must be in the negative."[37]

Judge Kooijmans, among other arguments, holds, in his separate opinion, that:

> "... the inevitable effect of the prominent place given to Article XX, para. 1(d), and its interpretation in the light of general international law, combined with the first part of para. 1 of the *dispositif*, is that the Judgement reads more like a judgement on the legality of the use of force than as one on the violation *vel non* of a commercial treaty. One can only wonder what the effect will be on States which are parties to comparable treaties with a compromissory clause."[38]

Judge Buergenthal, in order to reach the conclusion that the Court violated the *non ultra petita* rule, states:

> "... the Court proceeds to convert a provision of the Treaty – Article XX, para. 1*(d)* – which was clearly relevant only as a defence had there been a violation of Article X, para. 1, into an opportunity to use Article XX, para. 1*(d)*, in order to render a decision on the international law on the use of force and thus to find the actions of the United States in breach of that law ... In my view, the Court's pronouncement on the issue not raised in the submissions of the Parties

---

[37] 42 *ILM* 1379 (2003), para. 26.

[38] 42 *ILM* 1391 (2003), para. 35.

> is not a statement entitled to treated as an authoritative statement of the law applicable to the actions of the United States."[39]

Judge Owada states:

> "The general problem of self-defence under international law is an extremely complex and even controversial subject both in terms of theory and practice. It is my considered view that while it is of the utmost importance for the Court to pronounce its authoritative position on this general problem in a proper context, it should do so in a context where it should be possible for the Court to deal with the problem squarely in a full-fledged manner, with all its ramifications both in terms of the law and the facts involved. Such is not the case with the present situation ..."[40]

The jurisprudence of the International Tribunal for the Law of the Sea gives another example of "legitimizing statements" and of the opposing position based on the "legitimacy of legality". This emerges from judgements in various cases based on the special procedure for the prompt release of vessels and crews set out in article 292 of the UN Law of the Sea Convention. In these cases, prompt release was sought for fishing vessels caught in the French and Australian exclusive economic zones of the southern Ocean while fishing in situations in which there were strong indications of "illegal, unreported and unregulated fishing."[41]

Professor Crawford, counsel for Australia in the *Volga* case, argued that: "*the Tribunal should at all times seek to act in aid of regional fisheries arrangements* which are the only way, now and in the long term, of preserving the world's fish stocks. ... .[42]" Similar requests were made in other cases.

---

[39] 42 *ILM* 1404 (2003), para. 9.

[40] 42 *ILM* 1417 (2003), para.s 38-39.

[41] On these cases, T. Treves, "'Straddling and Highly Migratory Flags' before the International Tribunal for the Law of the Sea", in: S. Charnovitz, D. P. Steger & P. Van der Bossche (eds.), *Law in the Service of Human Dignity, Essays in Honor of Florentino Feliciano*, 2005, 323-335, espe. 325-331.

[42] Emphasis added. Statement by Professor Crawford on behalf of Australia, The *Volga* Case, Russian Federation v. Australia, (Judgement of 23 December 2002, ITLOS Reports 2002, p. 10) Oral Proceedings, ITLO Seychelles v. France, judgement of 18 December 2000, ITLOS Reports 2000, 86.S/PV 02/ 02 12, at 21 (Dec. 12, 2002), http://ITLOS.org/cgi-bin/cases/case_detail.pl?id=11&lang=en.

The Tribunal was not insensitive to these appeals. Its response was, nevertheless, rather restrained. In the first two cases it resisted the temptation to make a "legitimizing statement" in consonance with these appeals. In the *Camouco* judgement the point was mentioned only in dissenting opinions.[43] In the *Monte Confurco* judgement the Tribunal summarized the arguments concerning the "general context of unlawful fishing in the region" and stated: "the Tribunal takes note of this argument."[44] In the judgement on the third case, the *Volga* case, the Tribunal again took note of this argument. It added, however, the following statement, which can be seen as a "legitimizing" one: "The Tribunal understands the international concerns about illegal, unregulated and unreported fishing and appreciates the objectives behind the measures taken by States, including the States Parties to CCAMLR, to deal with the problem."[45] The Tribunal thought it necessary, however, to state explicitly the reasons for the "legitimacy of legality" which, in its view, precluded going beyond such "taking note," "understanding," and "appreciating," even when challenged not to become "an unwitting accomplice to criminal activity."[46] It stated: "The Tribunal must, however, emphasize that, in the present proceedings, it is called upon to assess whether the bond set by the Respondent is reasonable in terms of article 292 of the Convention. The purpose of the procedure provided for in article 292 of the Convention is to secure the prompt release of the vessel and crew upon the posting of a reasonable bond, pending the completion of the judicial procedure before the courts of the detaining State."[47] In a fourth judgement, in the *Juno Trader* case, the Tribunal reverted to taking note of the concerns relating to "illegal, unreported and unregulated fishing."[48] This was probably in light of the fact that the indications of such fishing in the specific case were weaker than in the

---

43 Panama v. France, judgement of 7 February 200, ITLOS Reports 2000, 10, Anderson, J. & Wolfrum, J., dissenting at p. 50, 66.

44 Seychelles v. France, judgement of 18 December 2000, ITLOS Reports 2000, 86. at para. 79. Judge Anderson in his dissenting opinion states that: "This "factual background" is relevant in balancing the respective interests of France and the applicant".

45 The *Volga* Case, note 34 , at para 68.

46 Crawford, pleading for Australia. The *Volga* case, note 34, at 18.

47 The *Volga* case, note 34, at para 69.

48 Saint Vincent and the Grenadines v. Guinea-Bissau, Judgement of 18 December 2004, ITLOS Reports 2004, 4 at para. 87.

previous cases and that the fishing State had agreed in general terms with the concerns expressed on the subject by the detaining State.

Conclusion: legitimacy of judgements and judicial policy

The discussion of legitimacy of decisions of international courts and tribunals, at least as far as it could be conducted in the two sections above, seems to be about judicial policy and the perception of the implementation of such policy in public opinion in general and in the special public opinion of international courts and tribunals that is constituted by States.

Admittedly, "judicial policy" is a rather elusive term, difficult to define, notwithstanding the pioneering attempt made by Pierre-Marie Dupuy in an article published in 1995.[49] In light of Dupuy's contribution and of my own reflections, I think it correct to use this expression while having regard to the broad objectives to be pursued by an international court or tribunal in exercising its function. In particular, judicial policy has to do with the way in which the exercise of the judicial function should balance the function of settling disputes with that of stating, clarifying and developing international law. The latter aspect includes the discussion whether moral or political values and rules incorporating or supporting them should be mentioned and upheld even when this is not necessary for the decision on the dispute. In the case of the International Court of Justice, the latter discussion is intertwined with that concerning the responsibilities of the Court, as the "principal judicial organ of the United Nations", in the maintenance of international peace and security. While the positions in these discussions can be seen as different views on the legitimacy of judicial decisions, the result of the discussion is, or should be, the judicial policy of the court or tribunal.

There is, of course, a difference between, on one side, the values that make a decision legitimate in the view of one judge and the judicial policy a single judge would like to pursue, and, on the other, the notion of legitimacy and the judicial policy emerging from the decisions of a court or tribunal. A single judge can have clear ideas on the values he wishes to support and on the ways of furthering such values in judicial

[49] P.-M. Dupuy, "The Judicial Policy of the International Court of Justice", in: F. Salerno (ed.), *Il ruolo del giudice internazionale nell'evoluzione del diritto internazionale e comunitario*, 1995, 61-82.

policy. He may, for example, consider that the legitimacy of judgements is enhanced if all opportunities for stating lofty principles and invoking rules incorporating them are seized. He also may, for example, consider that the development of the notion of *jus cogens* and of its implications serves the same purpose. Another judge may be convinced that the most important component of the legitimacy of a judgement is that the judgement remains strictly within the limits of the jurisdiction conferred by the parties on the court or tribunal, and that the preferable judicial policy should be that of solving disputes without making pronouncements that are not strictly necessary for that purpose. Very seldom, however, will an idea of legitimacy and a consequent judicial policy emerge clearly in the result of the collective and collegial work of a court or tribunal. The differences between the cases examined, the differences in the composition of the court or tribunal through the years, the impact of the personality of different Presidents, and especially the compromises needed to reach decisions are all factors that tend to make the collective idea of legitimacy and the content of a judicial policy less evident.

It would seem, nevertheless, that one broadly held idea of legitimacy and the consequent judicial policy exists. It consists in the search for the broadest possible majority. The *Oil platforms* case considered above is a clear example. This policy has also, to a certain extent, been codified in the Resolution on the internal judicial practice adopted by the International Tribunal for the Law of the Sea. Under article 7, para. 2, of this resolution: "The Drafting Committee should prepare a draft judgement which not only states the opinion of the majority as it appears then to *exist but which may also attract wider support within the Tribuna*l."[50]

In light of this judicial policy, and of the idea of legitimacy it presupposes, the "legitimizing statements" considered above can be seen as compensation for substantive compromise results that appear unsatisfactory from the point of view of the values that have been sacrificed in order to reach a majority. As seen in the examples given above, these statements may be incorporated in the text of the judgement and form part of the compromise reached, or be expressed in declarations and in separate or dissenting opinions. Such opinions may tend, in some cases, to strengthen the "legitimizing statements" set out in the judgement and a reading of the decision reached somehow qualified by these statements: so, for example, judge Koroma's declaration in the *armed activi-*

---

[50] Emphasis added. The resolution, adopted on 31 October 1997, can be read in ITLOS, Basic Texts/Textes de base (2005), 2005, 71.

ties order of 2002, quoted above, or the separate opinion, also quoted above, of judge Simma in the *Oil platforms* judgement of 2003. In other cases, as in the declaration of Judge Buergenthal in the *Armed activities* order, and the separate opinions of the same judge and of judges Higgins, Kooijmans and Owada in the *Oil platforms* judgement, they may pursue the objective of offsetting the "legitimizing statements" set out in the judgement by exposing their irrelevance to the solution of the dispute and by opposing them with other criteria of legitimacy, so as to strengthen a reading of the decision which is unencumbered by complementary statements.

Aspects of Legitimacy of Decisions of International Courts and Tribunals: Comments

Rein Müllerson

Professor Tullio Treves[1] in his excellent paper speaks of two different approaches to the issue of legitimacy. As we have heard in presentations of various speakers at this symposium and as we will see further in my comments, there are even more quite legitimate ways of approaching legitimacy.

Tullio Treves distinguishes what may be called the Independent International Commission on Kosovo type of legitimacy (Goldstone legitimacy) "illegal, but legitimate", where legality and legitimacy are seen as different, non-overlapping concepts, and Thomas Franck's definition of legitimacy by means of four indicators: determinacy, symbolic validation, coherence and adherence. Since Professor Treves has clearly explained the meaning of these indicators, there is no need to dwell upon them in my intervention.

It has to be emphasized, however, that Franck's indicators apply, and in principle are applicable, only to legal norms or decisions, such as judgements of international courts and tribunals or arbitration awards. He defines legitimacy as "a property of a rule or rule-making institution which itself exerts a pull towards compliance on those addressed normatively".[2] Depending on the strength of these indicators (or properties), norms, judgements or awards may have stronger or weaker compliance pull. At the same time, the Goldstone approach to the issue of legitimacy is not applicable to legal norms and decisions based on them.

---

1 T. Treves, "Aspects of Legitimacy of Decisions of International Courts and Tribunals", in this volume, p. 169 et seq.

2 T. Franck, *The Power of Legitimacy among Nations*, 1990, p. 16.

Norms of international law, by definition, cannot be "illegal, but legitimate", though they may well be lawful, i.e. adopted in accordance with proper procedures and substantively not breaching any imperative norms of international law, but nevertheless lack legitimacy. Similarly, it is difficult to imagine that judgements or decisions of international judicial bodies are illegal, though they too may be seen by many as illegitimate. The Judgement of the ICJ in the South-West Africa Cases (Second Phase) of 18 July 1966 may serve as one such example. By 7 votes to 7, with the casting vote of the President, on the issue of the continuing existence of the mandate for South-West Africa and the duties and performance of South Africa as Mandatory the Court decided that Ethiopia and Liberia "could not be considered to have established any legal right or interest in the subject matter of their claims and accordingly decided to reject them". Such a perfectly lawful decision was seen by many as lacking any legitimacy. It was also a blow for the legitimacy of the institution, i.e. the ICJ, that had passed such a decision.

Let us imagine that in the winter of 2003 the Security Council had passed a resolution authorizing the use of all necessary means to enforce all previous Security Council resolutions on Iraq. Such a resolution would have made the war in Iraq perfectly legal from the point of view of even the most critically minded legal experts. Would it make it legitimate in the eyes of those who protest against the war in London, Berlin or Paris? Would such legality have meant anything to the Arab in the street? If anything, it would probably only have undermined the legitimacy of the United Nations even more.

Hence, decisions of international courts, tribunals and other institutions can be lawful while lacking legitimacy. On the other hand, when we speak of the behaviour or conduct of states or international institutions, we may arguably use the phrase "illegal, but legitimate".

What is legitimacy? Let me add my voice to the clarification or further obfuscation of this question. Legitimacy is a property or characteristic of something, which quite obviously has something to do with law, with international law in our case. That legitimacy is closely linked to law can be seen from the origins of the term, though, as we see further, the genetic link is not the only one between these notions. In Latin and in Roman law, *legitimus* meant "lawful, in accordance with law".

Ian Clark defines legitimacy as "political space marked out by the boundaries of legality, morality, and constitutionality".[3] Such an ap-

---

[3] I. Clark, *Legitimacy in International Society*, 2005, p. 20.

proach is preferable, first, because it does not balance law with legitimacy; secondly, such an approach can be used notwithstanding whether we speak of legitimacy of legal norms and decisions based on law or conduct of states or international institutions.

Legitimacy is a wider concept than the concept of lawfulness because it includes legality, i.e. lawfulness of norms, institutions, situations (orders) or behaviour of various actors. Lawfulness is one, in 'normal' cases the most important, element or aspect, of legitimacy. However, legitimacy is more than simply lawfulness. It also includes morality or a sense of fairness or justice. Although ideally these properties have to coincide, if not completely, then at least quite substantially, in practice they may clash, and in such a case we may indeed be able to say that something is illegal but legitimate or, vice versa, legal but illegitimate. However, such things should not be said lightly, at least by responsible agents. In that respect it is important to note that though the Independent Commission on Kosovo concluded that the NATO Operation Allied Force was "illegal, but legitimate", no NATO Government called the Operation illegal. As Nick Wheeler observes, 'At no point during the Security Council Debates in March 1999 did NATO Governments try to advance the argument that the bombing of the FRY was illegal but morally justified'.[4] Not only were moral arguments used to justify the use of force against the FRY but legal arguments based, for example, on the "creative" interpretation of Security Council resolutions, customary law right of humanitarian intervention or the combination of both were resorted to. For example, the UK Ambassador to the UN, Sir Jeremy Greenstock, not going into the details, nevertheless stated in the Security Council that the military intervention was "lawful on the basis of overwhelming humanitarian necessity".[5] A legal expert may distil from such a statement either a reference to a state of necessity or the right to use force for humanitarian purposes (humanitarian intervention), but it is clear that the British Government did not consider that it, or NATO for that matter, was acting illegally. British Foreign Secretary, Robin Cook, appearing before the House of Commons Foreign Affairs Committee in April 1999 was pressed by Diane Abbot MP on the legal grounds for NATO's action in Kosovo. He replied: '[t]he

---

[4] N. Wheeler, "Reflections on the Legality and Legitimacy of NATO's Intervention in Kosovo", in: Booth (ed.), *The Kosovo Tragedy: The Human Rights Dimension*, 2001, p. 154.

[5] T. Franck, *Recourse to Force: State Action against Threats and Armed Attacks*, 2002, p. 167.

legal basis for our action is that the international community [sic] states do have the right to use force in the case of overwhelming humanitarian necessity'.[6]

On the other hand, those governments (e.g., China and Russia) which considered the NATO operation illegitimate also considered it illegal, i.e. in the assessment of Operation Allied Force it was not so much a clash between these two concepts or properties (legality and legitimacy), as between differing perceptions of what was legal and what was illegal, what was legitimate and what was illegitimate. Moreover, even perceptions of most experts as to the legality of the Operation more or less coincided with their assessment of its legitimacy. As we will discuss further, it seems that one's assessment of the legality of certain acts is coloured by one's vision of its legitimacy and both governments and experts usually try to avoid such an intellectual or moral bifurcation. Therefore, clearly illegal acts cannot usually be seen as legitimate. Or, to put it another way, a strong sense of the legitimacy of certain behaviour leads one to mental gymnastics to justify such behaviour also in legal terms, and there is nothing hypocritical here; such a tendency to avoid clashes between various perspectives (positive, on the one hand, and negative, on the other) of one's assessment of the same situation or act is also too human.

As well as legality and morality Ian Clark includes in the concept of legitimacy what he calls constitutionality, "as a norm based on the political constraints that are voluntarily entered into within international society, and that have a basis recognizably different from legal and moral prescriptions, however much the political play may be rhetorically coloured by legal or moral language".[7] For a lawyer, at least, the term constitutionality is too closely related to the notion of legality (rather, as the highest form of legality), to use in this sense and context. However, it seems clear that there should be something else besides legality and morality in the property that exerts compliance pull in international relations. What may this be?

Henry Kissinger, writing about post-Napoleonic arrangements in Europe, opined in 1977 that legitimate is "an order whose structure is

---

[6] N. J. Wheeler, "Unilateral Humanitarian Intervention and International Law", Paper presented to the British International Studies Association Annual Conference held at the University of Bradford, 18-20 December 2000.

[7] I. Clark, note 3, p. 209.

accepted by major powers" as legitimate.[8] He did not talk here about legal, or not just about legal arrangements, though it is interesting to note that these arrangements were based on the very concept of legitimacy both of domestic regimes of participating states and their relations with each other. As Ian Clark correctly observes, the Vienna legitimacy had 'both an inward looking and an outward-facing aspect. Inwardly, legitimacy can be translated as a set of principles about the proper composition and constitution of individual states, so as to befit them for membership of international society. Outwardly, it manifests itself as a set of principles about the proper conduct of relations between states, in order to sustain a working international society'.[9] In that respect we may speak of consensus among major powers on certain rules of the game expressed in notions such as balance of power, spheres of interest or influence, various regimes that may be based both on legal and non-legal norms (e.g., OSCE arrangements). Today such consensus may be expressed, for example, by the G-8 plus China and India. Of course, today, in order to see whether something is legitimate, it is necessary to go beyond consensus accepted by only major powers. One has also to take account of consensus based on the commonality of cultural and value systems. However, in today's world, using Michael Waltzer's words, such consensus may be even thinner than the one between the governments of the G-8 plus China and India.

There are other significant differences between the legitimacy of the Vienna Congress at the beginning of the nineteenth century and legitimacy in today's international society, and they affect, first of all, the possibility of the exercise of hegemonic power either by a single state or even by a group of great powers. Contemporary international society has some particular characteristics, absent in previous international societies, which affect the exercise of hegemonic power, define its legitimacy and, notably, increase the need for such legitimacy. Today's world, where the United States may want to exercise hegemonic power, has at least two important features that differentiate it from all previous international systems and affect the exercise of any hegemonic authority. First, for the first time it is the whole world which, notwithstanding even its division into zones of peace and zones of turmoil or pre-modern, modern and post-modern states and international systems, forms a single international society. Previous international societies (whether the Ancient Greek city states, the Roman or Genghis Khan's

---

8 H. Kissinger, *A World Restored*, 1977, p. 145.

9 I. Clark, note 3, p. 90.

Empires or the European Westphalian system) were all territorially limited international societies. Even the Cold War international society, though encompassing practically the whole world, consisted of two competing sub-systems in which the authority of the respective hegemons was exercised over substantial, but nevertheless limited, parts of the system. The very hostility between opposing blocks served also as a factor helping to legitimize the hegemonic power of the block leaders.

The dual-divided hegemony (earlier there were also dual-joint hegemonies) during the Cold War could be exercised not only because the United States of America and the Soviet Union were militarily the two most powerful states, but also because the two clashing ideologies – the free-market and liberal-democratic ideology versus the communist ideology – served as factors legitimizing the hegemonic authority of the United States and the Soviet Union respectively. The communist ideology started to unravel even at the time when the Soviet Union was still militarily strong. The collapse of this legitimating factor spelt the end of any hope of transforming the empire: its ideological basis had collapsed.

To exercise hegemony in today's global international society one obviously needs more power, both economic and military, than would have been necessary in any previous limited international society, since today it would be necessary to carry the hegemonic burden on a global scale. As we see now, Washington notwithstanding its economic clout and military superiority has considerable difficulties in many regions of the world.

By the same token, it is more difficult for such a hegemon to have its power considered legitimate, if not by all states, peoples and their leaders (an impossible task), then at least by a sufficient majority of the world's states. Additionally, factors that would legitimize hegemony in today's world are different from those that would have legitimized it in previous international systems. In most ancient and not so ancient international societies, which were closer to the hegemonic end of the spectrum between hegemony and anarchy, one of the legitimizing factors was the hegemon's ability to guarantee at least relative order and security. For example, it has been noted that the security of trade routes and food supply, protection against barbarian raiders, provision of public goods (such as roads, promotion of *lingua franca*, standards for weights and measures) contributed to the emergence of empires.[10] The

---

[10] See B. Buzan/R. Little, *International Systems in World History,* 2000, at 177; see also A. Watson, *The Evolution of International Society,* 1992, at 37.

Great Silk Road in Central Asia indeed flourished under the Empire of Genghis Khan and his successors and became a route on which robbers, competing with various warlords, exercised control when Central Asia became divided into the small khanates of Khiva, Bukhara and Khokand. Although the Mongol Empire was indeed the biggest empire of its time even it was far from extending its sway over the whole Eurasian continent.

Religion, which has also been an important legitimizing factor in some empires (e.g., the Ottoman Empire), cannot be a legitimizing factor in a global international society of today. On the contrary, if used recklessly, religion divides rather than unites, or rather unites us against them, be they the blind forces of nature, as in pre-historic times, or other nations and religions, especially since the times when monotheistic religions started to prevail.

American, or generally the Western ideology of free-market liberal-democracy, the defence of which had legitimized the US hegemony over the First World and much of the Third World during the Cold War, has indeed been triumphant. However, this ideology is no longer sufficient for the legitimization of American, or even generally Western, hegemony all over the world. The reason for this is not just that in some societies there is significant resistance to the ideas of democracy, liberalism and human rights. American neoconservative author Andrew Sullivan, in a self-critical article[11] writing about what had gone wrong in Iraq, observes that 'the final error was not taking culture seriously enough. There is a large discrepancy between neoconservatism's skepticism of government's ability to change culture at home and its naivety when it comes to complex, tribal, sectarian cultures abroad'. It is indeed so.

Moreover, there is also a serious clash between unipolar power (even if exercised by the US together with some or even all of its NATO allies) and anarchophilia[12] – anarchophilia being the deeply entrenched belief that independent statehood is something intrinsically good while any degree of dependency and any form of inequality between states is even less unacceptable than, for example, inequality between individuals.

---

11 A. Sullivan, "What I Got Wrong About the War. As conservatives pour their regrets, I have a few of my own to confess", *Time*, 13 March, 2006, at 60.

12 Barry Buzan and Richard Little have defined 'anarchophilia', as 'the disposition to assume that the structure of the international system has always been anarchic, that it is natural, and (more selectively) that it is a desirable thing'; Buzan/Little, *International Systems*, note 10, at 440.

This means that people will often put up with dictators who speak the same language, worship the same god and are of the same genetic descent rather than welcome foreign liberators. It is not just that there is some truth in the saying that nations deserve their rulers but that outside liberation, if it is not from a alien occupation, is also a kind of humiliation for any proud nation.

Anarchophilia is based on the ideas of independence and the sovereign equality of states, which, in its origin, is not unrelated to the idea of freedom and equality between human beings. The emergence of the concept of equality between men (initially, of course, not amongst all men but only amongst some of them) was a powerful idea that almost inevitably, though slowly and gradually, led to the idea of equality between all men, then between men and women, and later between persons belonging to different racial or religious groups, and finally also between states. While the principle of sovereign equality of states reflects the division of humankind into different groups, the principle of respect for human rights and the very idea that there are at least some basic universal human rights reflect the unity of humankind.

The one-state-one-vote UN system, with its principles of sovereign equality of states and non-interference in their internal affairs, which is sometimes called a system based on liberal values and ideas, is only superficially similar to the one-person-one-vote liberal-democratic systems. Such 'liberal' international system that equally values and protects all the states notwithstanding their domestic characteristics, may indeed be necessary for a kind of order in international affairs, but at the end of the day such system also favours the perpetuation of undemocratic and illiberal domestic societies.[13] Democracy in interstate relations, if such a concept has any meaning there at all, is certainly a different kind of animal. That is why Allen Buchanan and Robert Keohane in their very interesting paper writing about the democratic legitimacy of global governance institutions do not use the term democracy to mean an interstate democracy, which indeed would be a contradiction in terms. They write: "The intuitive idea here is that the on-going consent of rights-respecting, democratic states helps to make global governance institutions accountable, by linking them, though indirectly, to publics

[13] There is no space in this book to do justice to the complicated issue of comparison of liberalism in domestic societies and in international society. Therefore, I refer to my *Ordering Anarchy: International Law in International Society*, 2000, at 60-63, where I analyse views of Martti Koskenniemi, Fernando Teson and John Rawls.

who can hold their own states accountable. Let us say, then, that ongoing consent by rights-respecting democratic states constitutes the democratic channel of accountability and that the well-functioning of this channel is generally necessary for legitimacy".[14]

However, notwithstanding differences in value between liberties of individuals and the independence of states, one would make a serious mistake if one were to neglect the influence of anarchophilia, i.e. the desire for independent statehood. In many regions of the world, the consolidation of independent statehood, for all kinds of reasons, both right and wrong, is a priority that prevails over other tasks such as the introduction and enlargement of individual liberties or even economic reforms. The anarchic Westphalian international society has difficulty drawing to a close even in Europe, where it emerged and developed. In many other parts of the world nationalism is on the rise, religious intolerance divides people even within states, and the idea of a universal empire is even more utopian than the idea that states, notwithstanding their differences in size, wealth and political systems, are (or at least should be) equal and independent in our interdependent, unequal and violent world.

This means that even benign hegemony will be met with resistance – while any hegemony, if not facing some opposition, has a tendency to become less and less benign; hegemony corrupts and absolute hegemony, almost by definition, corrupts absolutely. The American hegemony will be met with resistance not only by those who may lose out as a result of its utilization (the likes of Saddam Hussein or even the Saudi Royal family may stand to lose should Washington follow through its promise to promote freedom of religion and conscience, and defend it from encroachment by repressive governments[15]); the American hegemony will be resisted also by those who may well benefit from it. This is not only because in the past Washington has often abused its power; it is also because of the deeply entrenched ideas of equality and liberalism that have, rightly or wrongly (more often wrongly), been extended to relations between states – that is, because of our anarchophilia. As Barry Buzan and Richard Little write, "the strict territoriality and fierce commitment to sovereignty of the *modern* state strongly underpins anarchy, as does the doctrine of nationalism as the centrepiece

[14] A. Buchanan, R. Keohane, "The Legitimacy of Global Governance Institutions", in this volume, p. 38. Their article originally appeared in Ethics & International Affairs 20, no. 4 (2006), pp. 405-437.

[15] The National Security Strategy of the United States of America, at 4.

of political legitimacy. This is in sharp contrast to the unit effects in the ancient and classical world, where empire carried substantial legitimacy, and bandwagoning in pursuit of peace and order was as common as balancing to preserve independence.[16] In short, though the hegemonic power of even Alexander the Great, Genghis Khan or the Roman Empire had to be supported by hegemonic legitimacy, the nature of that legitimacy was rather different from, and in a way even less significant than, legitimacy, which would be needed for the support of hegemony in today's world. The emergence of the twin brothers of democracy and nationalism that are in a strange love-hate relationship,[17] as well as the extrapolation of liberal ideology to inter-state (inter-group) relations where it is welcomed by illiberal dictators, has made it impossible for anyone to exercise hegemony without the support of legitimizing factors that favour anarchy over hegemony. Today, hegemonic legitimacy has to take account not only of the idea of individual rights and liberties, but also of the idea of equality between states and respect for their independence. Therefore, for a balance to be struck, hegemony should enhance individual liberty without unnecessarily curbing the independence and formal equality of states.

Turning now to issues of the legitimacy of decisions of international courts and tribunals, it is obvious that these bodies, if they are not deciding on the basis of *ex aequo et bono*, cannot put aside law and decide on the basis of their understanding of legitimacy. However, this does not mean that legitimacy does not play any role in decisions of international judicial bodies.

Professor Franck did not just write about legitimacy but he also distinguished between what he called "idiot" and "sophisticated" norms of international law.[18] Most of the norms applied, for example, by the ICJ belong to the category of "sophisticated" norms, and in the interpretation of such norms the sense of legitimacy may play a significant role.

---

16 Buzan/Little, *International Systems*, note 10, at 333.

17 Writing about state-building in Western Europe, Adam Watson observes that 'the self-assertion of the middle class in Europe took two forms: the demand for participation in government, and nationalism' and that 'three related trends, towards nationalism, democracy and popular interest in external affairs, exercised an increasing influence on the European states system. ... The ideas of nationalism and democracy were related'; Watson, *The Evolution*, note 10, at 291. However, today nationalism is more often a limitation on democracy than its *conditio sine qua non*.

18 T. Franck, *The Power of Legitimacy Among Nations*, 1990.

Those judges and arbitrators in particular who prefer contextual analysis and interpretation of norms of international law may indeed try to see to it that decisions made by international judicial bodies are not only lawful, i.e. in accordance with international law, but also legitimate, i.e. that they are seen as just and fair. If there is more than one way to interpret and apply a legal norm in specific cases, judges or arbitrators may be consciously or even subconsciously guided by their understanding of legitimacy. As we mentioned above, one's sense of legitimacy colours how one understands law. Although law is, in a way, a more objective category than morality, sense of fairness or political expediency, it is not of course absolutely objective since there is simply no such thing as absolute objectivity. At best, law is an intersubjective category, and in this property of law lies its objectivity. Therefore, one's perception of what is lawful is inevitably coloured by one's sense of legitimacy.

In such situations legitimacy may contribute to the process of change of norms of international law. The moral and political vision of a judge or arbitrator inevitably colours his or her interpretation of law, and in such cases the concept of legitimacy is a channel through which contextual factors enter not only the process of decision making but also the process of legal change. This comment applies, of course, not just to decisions of international courts and tribunals. Governments in their international activities are much more than judges guided not only by legal norms but also by a sense of fairness and justice, and even more by political factors. Even if some NATO government officials may indeed have considered the bombarding of the FRY over Kosovo as not completely lawful but legitimate because of their sense of justice and also their understanding of political realities, such strong sense of legitimacy colours their *opinio juris* as to the use of force for humanitarian purposes. This is how customary international law changes.

Finally, there is an issue of what Tullio Treves calls "political obiter dicta" or "legitimating statements", in cases where a court or tribunal addresses certain issues and values even when they are beyond the limits of the court's jurisdiction.[19] The two differing approaches to the issue were most clearly expressed by Judges Bruno Simma and Rosalyn Higgins in their respective separate opinions in the Oil Platforms Case.[20] Judge Simma believes it to be "of the utmost importance, and a

19 Treves, note 1, p. 178-188.

20 ICJ, Case Concerning Oil Platforms (Islamic Republic of Iran v. United States of America), 6 November 2003.

matter of principle, for the Court to pronounce itself on questions of the threat or use of force in international relations whenever it is given the opportunity to do so'.[21] Judge Higgins, on the contrary, questions such an approach: '... if the use of force or armed attack and self-defence is to be judicially examined, is the appropriate way to do so through the eye of the needle that is the freedom of commerce clause of a 1955 FCN Treaty? The answer must be in the negative'.[22] Although it may be frustrating for international law students and even for their teachers that they do not find in ICJ judgements answers to the most burning legal questions since usually the Court has indeed refrained from discussing points of law in the abstract, i.e. if they have not been necessary to resolving the issues before the Court. I believe it has to remain so. The gist of the arguments of those who favour such broad 'legitimizing' statements is clearly expressed by Tullio Treves: "A judgement or order that decides a case which emerges from a broad conflict that jeopardizes essential values such as those connected with loss of human life, genocide, use of force, on the basis of rather technical legal arguments such as those concerning lack of jurisdiction, may be more acceptable to the losing party and to public opinion if it contains statements – however unnecessary – that reaffirm these values".[23] That may indeed be some consolation for a losing party and even some sectors of public opinion may appreciate it, but I very much doubt whether it increases the role of the ICJ, or any other international judicial organ for that matter, as the principal judicial organ of the United Nations. It often seems to be the case that the less one says, the more weight is given to one's words and *vice versa,* and even important truths may be lost if uttered by garrulous people. Had Alan Greenspan used every opportunity to make statements concerning interest rates or the state of the US economy, the world markets would not have reacted to every word he said. On a more serious note, taking into account the jurisdictional limits of international courts and tribunals based on state consent, it may be damaging for the legitimacy of their decisions if they were to make statements unnecessary for deciding concrete cases before such judicial bodies. It would be especially damaging for the judicial authority (and this is the most important aspect of their authority) of international courts and tribunals if they were to opine on issues of use

---

21 Paragraph 5 of Judge Simma's Separate Opinion.

22 Paragraph 26 of Judge Higgins' Separate Opinion.

23 Treves, note 1, p. 178.

of force or massive human rights violations using, for example, jurisdiction based on commercial treaties.

This does not mean that the Court should base its decisions on narrow technical grounds. Whenever broad general principles of international law are applicable in concrete cases, the courts and tribunals obviously interpret and apply them. Moreover, it is not inappropriate for them, and depending on circumstances it may be even necessary, to discuss contextual moral norms and political, strategic or economic realities.

Discussion Following Presentations by Tullio Treves and Rein Müllerson

J. Brunnée: I first of all wanted to thank both speakers for drawing our attention to the links between legality and legitimacy. It struck me throughout the discussions yesterday and also today that many speakers and commentators intervening from the floor seem to consider legitimacy to be an external lens that is to be applied to law and, as we heard today, an unnecessary or perhaps even an improper lens because it involves a political assessment rather than a legal one. So, again, I am grateful to you for trying to tease out some of the links between law and legitimacy. And my question is: as lawyers, are we not ceding important terrain much too easily by treating legitimacy simply as a political question? While some legitimacy questions may well be political, is it not the case that there is also a distinctly *legal* legitimacy? An internal lens, so to speak. And if that is so, then, as lawyers, we should be particularly well placed to participate in that discussion. When I say legal legitimacy, what I am referring to are factors such as the ones that have already been mentioned. They might include the idea of a right process for the adoption of legal norms or for legal decision-making. And they would also include criteria such as those that Professor Treves laid out in drawing on Tom Franck's influential work – coherence, determinacy, symbolic validation, and so forth. More generally speaking, you might refer to ideas such as norms requiring reasonable things, that they are not contradictory with one another, that like things are being treated alike, that rules are not retroactive, that they are transparent. These are all features that are largely procedural, rather than substantive or "political". And they describe the sorts of things that, I think, as lawyers we're familiar with and would be quite comfortable in associating with good law. Put slightly differently, these are the kinds of features that make law legitimate and, therefore, persuasive. That was also one of the themes that came out of the discussions yesterday about what it is that enables law to command particular respect. I would add, perhaps in distinction to the comments by the panellists, that in this sense legality and legitimacy are not necessarily the same thing. It is quite conceivable that there are formally valid rules that do not meet the legal legitimacy criteria that I have just described. And still, to repeat, when I stress the importance of these features, I am not talking about a substantive or political notion of legitimacy. I am not asking: was intervening in Kosovo the right thing to do or not? What I am referring to is a distinctively *legal* form of legitimacy, and I would be interested in comments on that proposition.

M. Benzing: I have a question concerning what Professor Treves has called "legitimizing statements" in the judgment on the indication of provisional measures in the *Armed Activities on the Territory of the Congo (Congo v. Rwanda) Case* and the judgment of the ICJ in the *Oil Platforms Case*. In *Congo v. Rwanda*, the Court reminded the parties of their obligations under international law, in particular their duty to prevent grave human rights violations notwithstanding the lack of jurisdiction. In the *Oil Platforms Case*, the Court reversed the order of examining the claim so as to be able to refer to the law of self-defence.

I wonder whether these judicial statements are not only legitimate or legitimizing but also legal in a strict sense. By this I mean that they may not be *ultra vires* but justified by the impact of *ius cogens* norms or, more generally, norms incorporating community interests on procedural and jurisdictional questions. The subject-matter of the *Armed Activities in the Congo Case* concerned massive violations of human rights and in the *Oil Platforms Case* infringements of the prohibition on the use of force, i.e. arguably *ius cogens* norms incorporating community interests. Admittedly, the ICJ said in *Congo v. Rwanda* that even where *ius cogens* norms are at issue, both states still need to consent to the exercise of jurisdiction by the Court. But I wonder whether, once jurisdiction is given and established in accordance with the principle of consent, *ius cogens* norms may extend or modify this jurisdiction. If so, one could argue that those "legitimizing" statements are legal even though, in making them, the Court went beyond the strict scope of consensual jurisdiction. Thank you very much.

H. Neuhold: I very much like the checklist presented by Professor Tullio Treves. An additional question I would like to raise concerns the relevance of these variables (as social scientists would call them) to the decision to violate a rule of international law. Professor Rein Müllerson rightly states that governments rarely, if ever, admit to a breach of their legal obligations, but in the internal debate the argument that the envisaged course of action is contrary to international law may be made, in particular by the legal advisor and his/her staff. My remarks also apply to the cases where judgments of the International Court of Justice are ignored.

Rein Müllerson should also be thanked for drawing our attention to the transformation of legal norms. If there is a mounting discrepancy between what is lawful and what is regarded as legitimate, pressure to change the law and bring it into line with legitimacy is likely to increase. A paradox which has always puzzled me can also be observed in domestic law despite its allegedly superior effectiveness compared with international law. If a norm is violated consistently and on a large scale because it is widely perceived as illegitimate, this rejection sets the stage for legal change, and yesterday's illegal act becomes today's legal behaviour. Examples coming to mind include abortion and, more recently, euthanasia in our domestic societies and legal orders.

Finally, let me suggest that the criteria listed by Tullio Treves also have an impact on compliance with "soft law". Just think of the impact of the determinacy of a UN General Assembly resolution and the majority by which it was adopted or the visibility and prestige of the organisation producing "soft law".

So there is an obvious need for further research and discussion in several directions.

A. Pellet: Several remarks, but short and in telegraphic style.

First, as regards the 1996 Advisory Opinion, it's clear that it is unclear, or that the message is unclear. But it is an advisory opinion. And I think that what would not have been acceptable in a judgement is much more acceptable in such an opinion. Even judges may not know, and there is no scandal in that.

Just another word on the relations between legitimacy and legality. In *Tadić*, the claim of illegality was clearly a challenge to the legitimacy of the Tribunal. In the first instance, there was an abrupt affirmation of the legality of the Tribunal based on purely legal reasoning. Interestingly, the Appeals Chamber clearly reinforced the legitimacy of the Tribunal by using much more sophisticated legal reasoning.

Thirdly, the *Oil Platforms* case. The question is not whether the ICJ must be seen as an academic forum. This is not the issue – and, in any case, the answer must clearly be in the negative. It is certainly true that the Judgment in that case was an obvious effort to find a majority – the last two Presidents (I don't speak of Dame Rosalyn Higgins yet), Judges Guillaume and Shi, were very anxious to find a wide majority. But the reasoning of the Court in *Oil Platforms* was also a means to enhance the legitimacy of the Judgment. And, as I was counsel for Iran in that case, I can tell you that the Judgment was extremely well received by the "losing" Party. Maybe it was not so for the US – but at least the US was the winning Party… As a matter of judicial policy things have probably been more subtle than could be thought at first sight.

Fourthly, personal opinions – I must say that I tend to share the usual view of Latin lawyers and certainly of French lawyers that the multiplication of personal opinions probably undermines, not the legal value, but the legitimacy of judgements.

More generally, Rein Müllerson wondered what the role of judges is in the process of evolution and change in international law. I am convinced that they have an extremely important responsibility in this process, especially since, at the international level, there is no legislator. International Judges, and especially the ICJ, can choose to encourage changes, as was done for example by the ICJ in 1951 in the *Reservations* Advisory Opinion. On the contrary, they can choose to put a brake on the trends for change or stop them. It was the case for the awful *Yerodia* Judgment, where the ICJ, without any need to do so, took the responsibility to stop a necessary and useful trend in the field of officials' immunities.

Last general remark: if I come back to my threefold distinction of yesterday, I think that the judgements by international tribunals are decisive in respect to legality; what they decide is legal, full stop. Secondly, usually their decision will be seen as legitimate; but here, there is room for plus or minus. Usually judgements will enhance the legitimacy of the rules on which they are based, but this will depend on the motivation, on the majority etc. And, lastly, they are neutral as far as fairness is concerned. If and when they apply unjust legal rules, both rules and the solution will remain just that: unfair, unjust; but they will nevertheless be legal. Just to give an example and to go back to the unfortunate World Court's Judgment in *Yerodia*, clearly what the Court decided was legal; I still maintain that it was unjust and unfair. There could be hundreds of judgements of this kind. I would nevertheless maintain my view that it was unfair.

R. Howse: This has been a very interesting session, and I merely wanted to brainstorm and push a view of the issues a bit further, and particularly based upon my own personal preoccupation, which is with the jurisprudence of the World Trade Organization. If indeed it's the case that democracy is important to legitimating international institutions, one question would be: is there a place for the application of the values of democracy in adjudication by international tribunals? And to give a concrete example from the context of the WTO, in one of its earlier rulings, the Appellate Body of the WTO was examining the relevance of the precautionary principle to a notorious case that involved a European ban on food injected with synthetic beef hormones. And the Appellate Body correctly said that the precautionary principle, whatever its status in international law, couldn't trump explicit treaty norms, but they also went on to say that it could be relevant to interpretation. And they made a statement about their openness to a precautionary principle in interpretation where they were dealing with the actions of, quote unquote, "responsible representative governments". In other words, the suggestions seemed to be that one might have a greater margin of appreciation for governmental activity that's under scrutiny by an international tribunal and perhaps a different standard of review if the government in question is acting as a representative government in response to the democratic well than otherwise might be the case. And I thought that would be an interesting example to sort of try and apply some of the ideas that, for example, Professor Keohane has been flagging to the activity, the judicial activity in and around international institutions.

The second point perhaps is just a kind of paradox. That in some sense this whole debate about whether you want to decide cases very narrowly without reference to broader principles, reference to them, I think, you know, shows a kind of dilemma within the notion of legitimacy. There's one concept of legitimacy of a judicial decision that might be that it's not a question or questionable, and so the tribunal succeeds if it can decide on such a narrow technical ground that the decision doesn't provoke public controversy. On the other hand, one might say that actually that is not an appropriate conception of legitimacy – that actually decisions may be more legitimate even if they become more contestable if they're more explicit about the underlying values at stake and the underlying normative concerns the tribunal has to wrestle with in the interpretive exercise. And again, it comes back to whether one believes public contestability is an important dimension of judicial legitimacy. And there I sense differences between what we'd call the Anglo-American tradition where people are very comfortable and it's a very normal thing to bring into public discussion and into the public space debates about judicial decisions in terms of political values and other traditions, where that seems to be almost like questioning the key prerequisites of disinterestedness and impartiality in judicial decision-making. So again, brainstorming rather than very precise questions or comments.

G. Ulfstein: I want to draw a link between what was said in the previous panel and this panel. Georges Abi-Saab of the previous panel referred to the law of coexistence and the law of cooperation. He said that certain issues are mostly relevant at international level, such as the use of force, and thus belongs to the law of coexistence. One may of course discuss legitimacy and also democratic control concerning such cases. But I think that questions about legitimacy and democratic control are more pertinent in the law of cooperation, when it comes to cases that traditionally or primarily belong to the domestic level. One example is human rights, where one can discuss the proper relationship between national courts and international courts and between the national legislator and the international legislator. Does the European Court of Human Rights interfere too much in details of national traditions, and to what extent does it apply too much of a dynamic approach in treaty interpretation? This is very relevant for the relationship between the domestic and the international levels. Therefore it is also a question about legitimacy and democratic control, about the proper procedures and also the outcomes. So I think that in discussing legitimacy in international law one should make a distinction between different subject areas, where a relevant distinction could be between the law of coexistence and the law of cooperation. Thank you.

M. Bothe: I would like to congratulate the organizers for having this subject included in the themes of the colloquium. This is not a matter of course. Isn't the judicial activity the one which by definition is concerned with legality only? But why are there obvious concerns about legitimacy, even in respect of this activity? The clue to the answer to that question lies in the practical impact of law and of legal institutions. Related to that question is the concept of the role of judges. You can say that lawyers should only argue about what the law is. Anything beyond this is not a lawyer's concern. But there is no denying the fact that the practical impact of the law and of a pronouncement of the law also matters – and this is a question of legitimacy. I think there are two ways of looking at judgments, and this has already been said earlier in the discussion. There are two kinds of standards for evaluating the impact of a judgment. The first kind of standard is the *lex artis*, the professional rules on how you write a judgment. The strict technical rules are: you write down only what is relevant for finding your result. If you do more you exceed the professional rules. Something like an *obiter dictum* is a bit strange in this context. Nevertheless, *obiter dicta* are common practice among courts. With good reasons, because there are other standards, i.e. standards of legitimacy which determine the impact court judgments may have on the social fabric. This is due to the fact that higher courts have constituencies which go well beyond the parties to a particular case.

This problem is related to the second question: is it the only function of a judge to decide a concrete case? Or is it the function of the judges of high courts, at least to a certain extent, to give guidance for future cases? This question is relevant not just for international courts. We have the same problem at the national level as well. Robert Howse has already alluded to that. We have famous cases of the German Constitutional Court where this role of giving guidance was seen as an essential point by the court. As far as international law is concerned, the judgment to be quoted in this respect is the one on the treaty between the Federal Republic and the German Democratic Republic on the basis of their relations. In the field of constitution law, the practice of judgments providing guidance started with a judgment on the legal regime of the audio-visual media and continued with the abortion and party finance cases. In the first case, the audio-visual media, there was a minister of justice saying that the court had in a shocking way departed from the path of the law. That was an argument about legitimacy, not about legality.

As for the International Court of Justice, I think Alain Pellet is right that you have to make a distinction between advisory opinions and contentious cases. In the case of advisory opinions it is clear that the court addresses the constituency of the United Nations. This is the very function of advisory opinions, a function of clarification of the law, but in a specific political context. The court has not forgotten this context, and should not forget this context. This accounts for some of the criticism voiced against certain advisory opinions, the Court being seen as too "politicized".

A short remark only on the oil platforms case, where I am in the same position as Alain Pellet because we were in the same team. The essential point is the legitimacy of this judgment. On the technical level, I agree with everything which Judge Treves said on that matter. But what would have been the result for the broader constituency of the court, for the international community at large, had the Court just said, 'Oh, we are sorry, for a narrow technical question concerning the application of the friendship and commerce clause of the treaty, the claim is unfounded', and had left out all debate about the legality of the use of force, which was at stake in the case?

Only two sentences on the question of Kosovo and Iraq. It is of course true that it is not possible to find any government member or official who said it was unlawful but legitimate. But you find many government members *not* having said that it was lawful, but having said only that it was legitimate. This includes The German Foreign Minister before the General Assembly of the United Nations. And I might reverse that: I interpret the position of the German government in relation to Iraq as saying that it was lawful but not legitimate. I don't ask for any comment from the Foreign Office on this proposition. Thank you.

G. Abi-Saab: Michael Bothe has said much of what I wanted to say. I would just add two small remarks. The first is about the attitude of the judge to changing law. We have that interesting *Icelandic Fisheries* case where, during the Conference on the Law of the Sea, the ICJ was faced with a claim for a fifty mile exclusive fishing zone. In these circumstances, the Court could not really have jumped the gun. It said in substance, "The matter is under consideration; change is probably under way. In the meantime, as a Court, I cannot anticipate the exact shape of things to come. So, I have to stick to existing law". Perhaps when things are in flux, but not subject to ongoing real negotiations, the Court may consider that it has more leeway. Alain gave the example of the *Reservations* advisory opinion. But there is also the famous *Nottebohm* case, where the Court came up with a novel solution that was not put to it by either party, and which was a little bit contrived.

This brings me to my second remark, which is on the question of judicial policy that Tullio formulated in terms of legitimacy. I had the fortune or the misfortune to squat in several fora as judge, judge ad-hoc, arbitrator, etc. As an international judge it is very interesting that whenever you move into a new or a different court, you know there is something in common with those you are familiar with; still, you feel you are moving into a different house. What is common – the fact that it is a house – is the concept of judicial function. What is different – location, orientation, layout, furniture, *courants d'air* – is judicial policy.

The difference in judicial policies is the result *inter alia* of the different constituencies that Michael mentioned. But it is also a function of how the tribunal perceives itself, its role and its place in the legal system. At the International Court, the *Platform* case, mentioned by Tullio, is a very good example. There the Court examined at length the issue of the use of force, though, according to the logic of its own reasoning, it had no need to do so, and finally decided the case on other grounds. Another example is the *East Timor* case in which Alain appeared, where the Court, before saying it had no jurisdiction, acknowledged the right of self-determination of the East Timorese people.

These examples bring out the fact that the Court is keenly aware of, and sensitive to, the very strict limits of its jurisdiction, ultimately based on consent; which is a question of legality. But when it comes to the question of legitimacy, i.e. propriety and judicial policy, it can allow itself some leeway, *un peu de jeu*. In both these cases, the Court had to act within the bounds of its jurisdiction and applicable law. But it felt compelled to say something about the wider and more fundamental legal issue underlying the case, such as the use of force and the limits of self-defence or the right to self-determination, being the principal judicial organ of the UN, and in fact of the international legal system. Hence what Tullio said about the legitimizing statements or *political dicta.* I think the Court could not have escaped saying something without destroying its image and even its self-image as guardian of the international legal system.

Now, there is a different type of courts, those which are part of institutionalized special regimes, for example the WTO Appellate Body – though I can't speak much about it – where you feel you are on a short leash, with special treaty law to apply and political organs and member States following closely how you interpret and apply it. At the same time, once you create an organ and you call it a tribunal, it has to act as a tribunal with some independence, in fact as much independence as is necessary for the exercise of the judicial function. Those opposing considerations make it much more difficult for the tribunal to venture beyond the specific questions which are put to it, and may lead to a judicial policy of strict constructionism, of interpretation which is rather literal. But even with strict constructionism, a tribunal cannot help sometimes turning to the general principles of law and international law as a matter of necessity and not just of policy.

On the other hand, at the ICTY, which was mentioned earlier, the judicial policy that emerged, at least at the creation, was that if you want to make the tribunal not only acceptable to its creator, the Security Council, but also legitimate in the eyes of the wider public, you have to insist for example that you are applying general international law on international crimes, and not just what was dictated to you by the Security Council in the Statute (and thus upholding the principle of legality and non-retroactivity).

All these factors play a role in the formulation of the judicial policy of a forum. But when there is a strong limit to jurisdiction, you cannot really play with it. Otherwise, the Court loses on both legality and legitimacy.

C. Bradley: Well, particularly in light of the last sets of questions, I thought I would emphasize a somewhat contrary view, and maybe a little bit contrary to Treves' presentation, although I think picking up on what Professor Müllerson was saying at the very end of his remarks. It occurs to me, and this is partly based on experience with domestic courts, that when courts are particularly weak and they lack significant enforcement machinery, and (contrary to the last remarks) when they are not embedded in a broader regime, there is a fairly strong connection in my view between a court like that and judicial restraint as a way of promoting and building legitimacy. And I haven't heard as much as I would have expected about restraint. Particularly, I would think of the ICJ as the paradigmatic example of a weak judicial institution. It has no independent enforcement machinery, it's not (unlike the WTO) built in a regime that otherwise induces parties to join and stay within the regime. Nevertheless, its record has not been one of restraint, at least in recent years. The result is a generally low level of legitimacy. And, contrary to Professor Pellet's views, I think the efforts to go beyond its mandate with advisory statements and opinions have only caused the ICJ more difficulties. So I think of examples ... maybe starting with the Nicaragua case, which I know is quite controversial. In that case, there were technical jurisdictional difficulties that were overlooked to some extent, and the unfortunate result was that one of the leading original proponents of the ICJ's compulsory jurisdiction pulled out permanently. More recently ... nobody mentioned the Israeli barrier decision. Maybe you would say well, that's advisory, but it was clearly a contentious case. It was a dispute between the Palestinians and the Israelis over security policy and was decided without one party's consent and in a form unlikely to produce compliance. As for the Oil Platforms decision – I understand how the Iranians might have appreciated some dictum that was helpful to them. But it was obviously quite gratuitous from the standpoint of judicial restraint, since one would not expect that a decision that was decided one way under a bilateral treaty could then be a vehicle for a broad essay about the proper uses of force. And when I think about Professor Keohane's and Tom Frank's legitimacy factors, such as avoiding the appearance of partiality, carefully connecting back to state consent, and making sure that you actually can obtain enforcement, all of them seem to be contradicted by the practice of the ICJ. And it doesn't have other machinery available to help it in that regard. So, what is the result empirically? Only one veto member in the Security Council is now a part of the compulsory jurisdiction of the ICJ. The Security Council I think has never enforced an ICJ decision. The docket of the ICJ has never been substantial. It went up for a brief period of time I think it's back down again. And states like the U.S. are no longer willing to consent to ICJ clauses in treaties, in large part because of concerns about bias. So as a method of promoting long-term respect for a weak institution, the ICJ's approach seems directly contrary to what one would suggest to a court in terms of wise strategy.

A. Zimmermann: I will only be making three relatively brief remarks. *First*, I was somewhat puzzled by the fact that issues of composition were being touched upon only briefly, if ever, by Tullio Treves, even more so since the very set-up of ITLOS and the composition of the bench of ITLOS itself can be perceived as an attempt to counter a perceived imbalance in the composition of the ICJ. In particular, if we take into account the fact that ever since 1946 the five permanent members of the Security Council have been represented on the bench of the ICJ despite the fact that there is no veto with regard to the election of the members of the bench and therefore no special role for the permanent members of the Security Council anyway.

On the other hand, what one should take into account is the role of judges *ad hoc* in increasing the legitimacy of international decisions. And finally, my last remark in that regard: there are almost no women or, if at all, only a very few women on the bench of international tribunals. And I think one can seriously question the legitimacy of those decisions if really this group of people is not represented as such, the International Criminal Court being one notable exception.

My second remark relates to what Matthias Herdegen said yesterday on the legitimacy of treaty development by international courts. I think what he missed was the principle of *compétence de la compétence*. If treaty parties set up a court, they by the same token also grant the court the power to also decide how far its competence reaches, including the possibility to perceive a given treaty as a living instrument. And more specifically with regard to the European Court of Human Rights and the European Convention on Human Rights, I think we have to take into account the very fact that the contracting parties in 1998 adopted the 11th Additional Protocol and soon the 14th Additional Protocol may enter into force. By doing so the contracting parties have ratified or reconfirmed the living-instrument approach the court has chosen ever since it was created.

My last remark concerns issues of coherence. Obviously, everybody agrees that courts should be consistent or coherent with their own previous decisions or with decisions of other international organs such as the Security Council or the General Assembly. But I think these are relatively easy issues. The most crucial issues come up when there is a discrepancy, a contradiction, between on the one hand an own decision on certain issues and a subsequent decision by the Security Council and the General Assembly making a different determination, for example on the issue of membership of the United Nations. What should then prevail? The previous decision by the very same court or the later determinations made by the other main organs of the organization on membership issues? Or what if the court made a certain determination on membership issues and later, in parallel cases, makes a different decision? What should then prevail? How should we decide the conflict which Alain Pellet at one point referred to as vertical versus horizontal consistency, the ongoing ICJ case between Bosnia and Herzegovina and Serbia and Montenegro being an example at hand? Is it really that the formal rule of *res judicata*, if it ever applies to issues of jurisdiction, should be sufficient to grant a court legitimacy in setting aside decisions it itself delivered almost ten years later, as compared to its own jurisdictional decision made in this very same case ten years earlier? Thank you very much.

R. Müllerson: I will be short because I think more questions were addressed to Tullio than to me. But the first question, by Professor Brunnée, was whether legitimacy is more a legal or a political concept? I believe that during this conference we have spoken more or less about two approaches to legitimacy. It would be correct to say that Tom Frank's approach is more within the legal framework. Tom writes about a legal concept of legitimacy. Though of course it necessarily has political implications, too. Tom writes about the legitimacy of international law, of norms of international law or decisions of international judicial bodies. Therefore, his discourse is more or less wholly within a legal frame because it is all about legitimacy of law. The other approach is a wider one because within it one can also talk about, say, legitimacy of political decisions made either by individual states or by the Security Council when it is using its wide discretionary powers. When in my presentation I spoke about the concept of legitimacy that included issues of legality, morality, fairness, justice and correspondence to existing political realities, I concentrated more on a political than legal concept of legitimacy because international law acts in the political environment and it has to take into account these political realities, too. Therefore, I believe legitimacy is both a political and a legal concept.

Now, the second question is about legitimating statements. I may have been slightly misunderstood because in my presentation I was very short on this issue. I don't think that international courts when they decide issues, whatever they may be, have to base themselves on so-called narrow legal grounds without applying or taking account of broad principles of international law (of course, if these principles are relevant for a concrete case). But let us take, for the sake of illustration, this symposium. It is devoted to issues of legitimacy, and let's assume that I am a specialist on global warming or that I have a keen interest in this issue. Therefore, instead of talking about legitimacy because, though this is an important issue, it is not as important as global warming, I would concentrate only on global warming. I don't think that this is a proper approach. Therefore, if the issue over which, say, the ICJ has jurisdiction is about the trade between two countries, not about the use of force, then issues concerning use of force are irrelevant for that case and should not be discussed on the merits. Even if this issue is a very important one, even if it is the most important issue in the world. If everybody speaks now about terrorism, this doesn't mean that we have to talk about it here, too. Or, rather, we may talk about it if it directly illustrates problems of legitimacy, but we should not be talking here about terrorism because it is probably the most important issue in today's world. What I wanted to say is the following: if some very important issues are not directly relevant for judicial decision-making, it would be better for the legitimacy of these tribunals and their decisions not to discuss these issues. They may be dealt with in separate opinions of some judges, but not in decisions of these courts or tribunals. Thank you.

T. Treves: I will try to go through the questions and I beg to be excused if I miss some or if I have misunderstood some.

As regards Jutta Brunnée's points, I agree that there's a legal legitimacy and that the test of legality is the first step for any analysis of legitimacy. But there are also criteria that go beyond pure legality.

As far as Professor Benzing is concerned, if I understood him correctly, he considers that perhaps the presence of ius cogens permits us to broaden the scope of the jurisdiction of a court. I would dissent from that, I don't think any question of substantive law permits one to change the legal basis of the jurisdiction of a court. The ICJ has stated this in its judgement of 3 February 2006 on the *armed activities in the territory of the Congo (new application 2002)*, at paragraph 125.

Coming to Professor Neuhold, I'm grateful for his invitation to me to work on my checklist. I hope I will be able to do so. Indeed, the elements which I hinted at, in drawing the checklist, as possible criteria for the legitimacy of judgements of international courts and tribunals might be among those that, in the innards of government, are weighted when the delicate decision to violate the law or not to comply with a judgement is taken, as it sometimes happens.

I come now to the important points raised by Alain Pellet. I agree with him and with Professor Bothe that the criteria to discuss and determine legitimacy may be different for an advisory opinion and for a judgement. But still, for instance, the element of determinacy is relevant also in an advisory opinion. May I also say that this holds true also as regards the concept of the constituency, which is very important in our discussion. The "constituency" of an advisory opinion is the General Assembly that requested it, while, in the case of a judgement, it is the parties that have brought the case to the Court. In advisory proceedings there is no real dispute in the traditional sense. Still, are we sure that even in an advisory opinion the only constituency is the requesting body? Probably not. In the *Wall* case for instance, as remarked on by Mr. Bradley, there were parties that were closer to the matter than the General Assembly. So it is a question of nuances and degrees. We can draw a line between contentious judgements and advisory opinions, but this line is bound to be a little bit blurred in many cases. I agree with the remarks of Alain Pellet about the *Oil Platforms* judgment. They coincide more or less with what I said. The developments concerning the use of force were made to bolster the legitimacy of the judgement, and I understand very well that Iran, although the loser of the case, was happy in reading it. Of course, what bolsters legitimacy for one side diminishes it for the other side. From the point of view of the court or tribunal, the problem is one of judicial policy, while from our point of view as scholars, or as independent observers, it is one concerning our assessment of the judicial policy.

I can now move to the points raised by Professor Howse. I agree that it is very important to consider the question of the constituency when we have the policy alternative between just settling the dispute and settling the dispute and deciding on the development of international law at the same time. Also here, we have to find a balance. A court that speaks only to the broad community and doesn't care about the two states that are litigating before it will most likely erode its legitimacy at least from the point of view of one of the two litigating states, perhaps from that of both, and in the long run might risk not being seen as a place where you would like to settle your disputes. Arbitration could be seen as a preferable course if a court acts too much as a political organ in its judgements.

All the remarks of Georges Abi-Saab are really illuminating, as they draw from the absolutely unique experience of his having been a member of many judicial bodies. We should all take note that every house has its different "perfume". All judges are judges, all perform the judicial function, but they orient their collective policy in different ways. It's very clear that the policies, including the approach and style, of the International Tribunal for the Former Yugoslavia, of the ICJ and of the WTO Appellate Body are very different. And I think Georges Abi-Saab's remark that specialized or regime tribunals, tribunals different from the ICJ, have less leeway in going for what I call legitimizing statements may be very correct. An empirical verification, especially in as far as the criminal tribunals are concerned, would be very interesting. In the narrow experience of the Law of the Sea Tribunal I think this view is confirmed. The approach of the Tribunal is perhaps more constructionist than that of the ICJ.

As far as the remarks by Curtis Bradley are concerned, I agree that judicial restraint is a factor relevant to promote legitimacy. Abstaining from "legitimizing statements" can be seen as a manifestation of this kind of restraint, even though, as I tried to show in my paper, others can see lack of restraint leading to an abundance of such statements as means supporting the legitimacy of a decision and of the court adopting it.

Lastly, I agree with Professor Zimmermann that the composition of the adjudicating body is an interesting element. I agree, in particular, that judges ad hoc may add to the legitimacy of judgments. In the experience of the Law of the Sea Tribunal, judges ad hoc have been extremely useful. The clearest example is that of the provisional measures adopted in the *Land Reclamation* case. They were supported by an unprecedented joint declaration of the two judges ad hoc. This made particularly strong and, I would say, legitimate, the rather bold prescriptions of the provisional measures order, which were oriented towards the management of the dispute with a view to helping the parties settle it. Such strength and legitimacy were confirmed by the successful settlement of the dispute on the basis of the process starting with the provisional measures order of the Tribunal.

The further point raised by Professor Zimmermann concerns the problem of coherence or non-coherence with decisions of non-judicial bodies such as, in particular, the Security Council. It is admittedly a difficult problem. After the controversial order on provisional measures, this problem has been somehow avoided by the ICJ in the *Lockerbie* case by postponing the real decision ... until the case was deleted from the list. There has been an attempt at preventing it in the Law of the Sea Convention. According to article 298, paragraph 1 (c), States may exclude from compulsory jurisdiction of the competent courts and tribunals cases that are under consideration by the Security Council. This provision does not solve the problem as a whole, as the exception to compulsory jurisdiction it introduces is merely optional, as it requires a specific declaration. This declaration has been used by, I would say, a dozen states or a little more. The provision indicates nonetheless that there is some awareness of this question. Thank you very much.

Codes of Conduct and their Implementation: the Question of Legitimacy

Helen Keller

A. Introduction

The process of globalisation has come with fundamental challenges for the effective and legitimate governance of transboundary affairs. On the one hand, the transnational nature of many contemporary policy issues exceeds the regulatory capacities of territorially defined national regulation; on the other, the traditional mode of ordering global affairs through classic international 'hard law' faces the inherent limitations of achieving the necessary political consensus. On the national level, economic developments in the 1980s seemingly have diminished the role of the state as the guardian of the public commons. It is against this background that, in the context of global capitalism, the issue of the regulation of transnational corporations (TNCs) in advancing corporate responsibility must be seen.

Bridled capitalism necessarily calls for the establishment of certain 'rules of the game'. Following only partially successful attempts in the 1970s to regulate corporate activity through *intergovernmental* codes, the 1990s saw a remarkable increase of interest in regulating corporate performance. In response to mounting pressures for increased corporate accountability (from consumer groups and other NGOs, and from potential public regulation, litigation or prosecution), voluntary private self-regulation was seen as a possible new way of filling the regulatory void opened up by globalisation. Indeed, the 1990s saw a proliferation of corporate codes of conduct and an increased emphasis on corporate responsibility. Recent developments in promoting corporate accountability involve new types of regulatory institutions – so-called multi-stakeholder initiatives (MSIs) – that attempt to address some of the limitations of corporate self-regulation. The proliferation of voluntary codes has led to a bewildering plurality of often competing standards, resulting in a regulatory system that is fundamentally *fragmentary* in character.

In the 1980s, Maitland stressed the "lasting appeal" of the "idea that we would be better off if we could rely on the promptings of a corporate 'conscience' to regulate corporate behaviour instead of the heavy hand of government regulation."[1] This paper sets out to explore the question whether voluntary codes indeed serve as effective and legitimate tools for promoting corporate accountability. Owing to the very diversity of the subject matter, assessments are inevitably ambivalent. The paper does not seek to provide a new study next to the prolific writings related to codes of conduct of other authors; rather it should be seen as an analysis and compilation of findings in light of the more specific topic of 'legitimacy'.

B. Concept of Codes of Conduct

Codes of conduct do not have any authorized definition. At a very basic level, they all aim to define standards and principles that ought to guide the behaviour of the addressee in a particular way. As such, they are *regulatory* instruments. They are not of recent vintage, yet it was not until the second half of the twentieth century, i.e. in the context of globalisation[2], that they rose to prominence as regulatory responses to the challenges posed by the globalisation of the world economy.[3]

---

1 Ian Maitland, "The Limits of Business Self-Regulation", *California Management Review* 27 (1985), 132.

2 Broadly speaking, globalisation may be defined as the shrinkage of distance on a world scale through the emergence and thickening of networks of interconnections – cutting across the political, cultural, social and economic fields; narrowly defined in an *economic* sense, we may refer by it to the globalisation of markets and the worldwide economic integration, (see, e.g., David Held/Anthony McGrew/David Goldblatt/Jonathan Perraton, *Global Transformations: Politics, Economics and Culture*, 1999; Robert Keohane/Joseph Nye, *Power and Interdependence*, 3rd ed., 2001.

3 Historically, codes of conduct "have been formulated with a view to guiding the behaviour of individuals, groups, organizations, governments, societies, and, most, recently, corporations." (Wesley Cragg, "Multinational Corporation,

They may respond to a broad range of regulatory concerns and be established at the initiative of governments, international organizations, individuals, and private organizations (NGOs, business entities). A distinguishing feature of codes of conduct is that they are voluntary in nature[4] rather than legally binding, and thus not legally enforceable. To the extent that they are issued by states, international organizations, non-governmental organizations (NGOs) and the International Chamber of Commerce, codes of conduct fall into the broad normative realm of *soft law*.[5]

While codes may be directed at states, a salient feature is their aim to regulate the *transnational* activities of *non-state actors*.[6] Indeed, the modern issue of codes of conduct is the question of how to effectively enhance the accountability of transnational corporations (TNCs[7]) in the international marketplace.

Globalisation, and the Challenge of Self-Regulation", in: John Kirton/Michael Trebilcock (eds.), *Hard Choices, Soft Law*, 2004, 213).

4 However, some trade and industry organizations make adoption of a code a precondition for company membership.

5 For a detailed and extensive discussion on the phenomenon of soft law, see Dinah Shelton (ed.), *Commitment and Compliance – The Role of Non-Binding Norms in the International Legal System*, 2000; Daniel Thürer, "Soft Law", in: Rudolf Bernhardt (ed.), *Encylopedia of Public International Law*, vol. IV (2000), 452-460.

6 Peter Willets, "Transnational Actors and International Organizations in Global Politics", in: John Baylis/Steve Smith (eds.), *The Globalisation of World Politics. An Introduction to International Relations*, 2nd ed., 2001, 357-383; Jan Aart Scholte, "Global Civil Society", in: Ngaire Woods (ed.), *The Political Economy of Globalisation*, 2000, 173-201; Thomas Risse, "Transnational Actors and World Politics", in: Walter Carlsnaes/Thomas Risse/Beth Simmons (eds.), *Handbook of International Relations*, 2002, 255-274.

7 There are variants to this term, such as multinational corporation (MNC) or multinational enterprise (MNE); a MNE has been characterized as "any corporation which owns (in whole or in part), controls and manages income generating assets outside its home country. [...] Thus, the MNE is a firm that engages in direct investment outside its home country." (Peter Muchlinski, *Multinational Enterprises and the Law*, 1995, at 12) or as an enterprise that is directed from its country of origin (or home country) and engages in economically significant activities within other states, known as host countries. What distinguishes it from other business enterprises is its "ability to exercise market power and influence in host countries by what may be termed remote control." (Hans Baade, "The Legal Effects of Codes of Conduct for Multinational Enter-

Codes of (corporate) conduct can be broadly defined as "commitments voluntarily made by companies, associations or other entities, which put forth standards and principles for the conduct of business activities in the marketplace."[8] They purport to shape corporate conduct in a certain way – through a catalogue of principles that define a set of relationships between the company and its stakeholders on a range of topics.

The introduction of private voluntary codes of (corporate) conduct can be seen as corporate and civil society attempts to fill some of the international regulatory voids that opened up in the wake of neoliberalism.[9] Voluntary codes have the advantage of transcending territorial confines, extending the application of prescriptive standards of socially accountable TNC behaviour overseas, to the operations of suppliers, subcontractors and other business partners where standards may be non-existent, incomplete, unenforced or ignored. In this sense, codes of conduct form part of an emerging *transnational normative regime.* Since private codes of corporate conduct are developed not by the national legislative in its formal position as lawmaker but by private, non-state actors, they constitute *informal* instruments, which, nevertheless, perform a *public* function, i.e. the protection and enhancement of social and ecological values. In this sense, they are *hybrid* norms.

---

prises", in: Norbert Horn (ed.), *Legal Problems of Codes of Conduct for Multinational Enterprises*, 1980, 3, 4). UN parlance, however, distinguishes between *multinational* and *trans-national*, the former term referring to enterprises owned and controlled by entities or persons from one country but operating across national borders, the latter to those owned and controlled by entities or persons from more than one country.

8 OECD, Codes of Corporate Conduct: An Inventory, Working Party on the Trade Committee, TD/TC/WP(98)74/Final, Paris, 1999, available at http://appli1.oecd.org/olis/1998doc.nsf/LinkTo/td-tc-wp(98)74-final, last visited 22 September 2006.

9 See Ans Kolk/Rob van Tulder, "Setting New Global Rules? TNCs and Codes of Conduct", in: *Transnational Corporations* 14 (2005), 2.

C. The Evolution of Codes of Conduct

I. The Rise of Codes of Conduct on the International Scene

1. Historical Outline

The early history of codes of conduct may be traced back to the nascent field of international humanitarian law. A pioneering role in issuing (self-regulatory) codes for business conduct was undertaken by the International Chamber of Commerce (ICC) with its *Code of Standards of Advertising Practice* (1931), which was accompanied by a number of other marketing-related codes.[10]

It is not until the 1970s, however, amid a climate of adversarial relations between TNCs and national governments, particularly those of developing countries, that codes of conduct gained major attention as regulatory responses to the negative impact of the increasing power and influence of TNCs. After the initial, post-World War II period in which many developing countries welcomed foreign direct investment (FDI), attitudes changed in the late 1960s as developing countries became increasingly critical of TNCs for their failure to operate in harmony with local economic, social and political objectives. Specifically, developing states perceived the growth of corporate power and influence as a threat to their sovereignty, which relates to the political climate of that time, i.e. the Third World demands for a New Economic International Order seeking to change the international economic system, seen to disfavour the fledgling, post-colonial states striving for political and economic independence. The ITTC scandal[11] in Chile was a defining incident in focusing international attention on the activities of TNCs in developing countries, giving rise to concerted calls for TNC regulation, which eventually led to the birth of the United Nations Centre on Transnational Corporations (1977) and its work on a comprehensive UN Draft

---

[10] Among the other ICC codes figure: the International Code of Sales Promotion (1987), the International Code of Environmental Advertising (1991), the International Code on Sponsorship (1992), the International Code of Marketing and Social Research Practice (1995), the International Code of Advertising Practice (1997), the International Code of Practice on Direct Marketing (1998), the Guidelines on Marketing and Advertising on the Internet (1998), and the International Code of Direct Selling (1999).

[11] *Infra* note 26.

Code of Conduct for TNCs.[12] While, owing to differences of interest between developed and developing countries, the drafting process eventually had to be discontinued in the early 1990s, other attempts at regulating TNCs that sought to establish more specific voluntary standards of socially responsible conduct for TNCs met with more success.

In 1976, the OECD issued the Guidelines for Multinational Enterprises[13] (MNCs) as part of a broader Declaration on International Investment and Multinational Enterprises; the ILO Tripartite Declaration on MNCs[14] was adopted the next year, establishing voluntary guidelines covering employment, training, working conditions and industrial relations. As international instruments of corporate social responsibility, they have been of limited effect; yet, they stand at the centre of the universe of corporate responsibility codes, at once establishing a comprehensive framework of aspirational standards of good corporate practice that serve as benchmarks, and laying the groundwork for future efforts. The 1970s saw not only the emergence of *intergovernmental* corporate regulation, but also the birth of the modern idea of *private self-regulation*, which is typically retraced to the 'Sullivan Principles'[15] (1977), a privately initiated set of standards designed to guide companies operating in South Africa with a view to employing business leverage to effectively change apartheid practices.

In the following years, further public initiatives emerged from within the UN family, such as the so-called *Set of Multilaterally Agreed Equitable Principles and Rules for the Control of Restrictive Business Prac-*

---

[12] At the national level, some 22 developing countries passed legislation controlling TNC activities in the late 1960s and 1970s, see Bob Hepple, "A Race to the Top? International Investment Guidelines and Corporate Codes of Conduct", *Comparative Labour Law and Policy Journal* 20 (1999), 347-363. For a survey of codes of conduct on the international level, *see* Thomas Reynolds, "Clouds of Codes: The New International Economic Order Through Codes of Conduct: A Survey", *Law Library Journal* 75 (1982), 315–354.

[13] *Infra* note 41. The OECD Guidelines cover the range of MNE activities, dealing general policies, information disclosure, competition, financing, taxation, employment and industrial relations, the environment, and science and technology. Mark Baker, "Tightening the Toothless Vise: Codes of Conduct and the American Multinational Enterprise, *Wisconsin International Law Journal* 20 (2001), 89-141.

[14] *Infra* note 37.

[15] *Infra* note 19.

tices, adopted by the UN general assembly in 1980.[16] Efforts were also made under the auspices of the United Nations Conference on Trade and Development (UNCTAD) to elaborate an *International Code of Conduct on Transfer of Technology*.[17] While adoption of the latter never came about, a more successful example is the WHO/UNICEF International Code of Marketing of Breast-milk Substitutes, which the World Health Assembly adopted in 1981.[18]

Apart from these initiatives, general interest in codes of conduct began to wither away in the 1980s, which coincided with the shift in governmental attitudes toward TNCs in the context of the neo-liberal doctrine of non-intervention, increased liberalisation and *deregulation* of business. In keeping with the "free market" philosophy, corporate self-regulation, i.e. the notion that the onus for regulating TNCs should rest with the companies themselves, gained momentum, and a plethora of company-written codes of conduct emerged in the 1990s.

---

16 G.A. Res. 35/63, U.N. GAOR Supp. (No. 48) at 123, U.N. Doc. A/35/48 (1980), *reprinted in* 19 I.L.M. 813 (1980), available at http://r0.unctad.org/en/subsites/cpolicy/docs/CPSet/cpset.htm. One of the objectives of this code is the creation, encouragement and protection of competition. Compliance by member countries, however, is voluntary; *see* Joel Davidow, "The Implementation of International Antitrust Principles", in: Rubin Seymour/Gary Hufbauer (eds.), *Emerging Standards of International Trade and Investment*, 1983, 119; Joel Davidow/Lisa Chiles, "The United States and the Issue of the Binding or Voluntary Nature of International Codes of Conduct Regarding Restrictive Business Practices", *AJIL* 72 (1978), 247-271.

17 On the issue of technology transfer *see* Andrés Guadamuz, "The Future of Technology Transfer in the Global Village", *Journal of World Intellectual Property* 3 (2000), 589-602.

18 *See* Kathryn Sikkink, "Codes of Conduct for Transnational Companies: The Case of WHO/UNICEF Code", *International Organization* 40 (1986), 815-840. The WHO/UNICEF International Code of Marketing of Breast-milk Substitutes, which was adopted by the World Health Assembly in 1981, bans all promotion of bottle-feeding and sets out requirements for labelling and information on infant feeding. *See* WHA Res. 34/22 (1981), available at http://www.who.int/nutrition/publications/code_english.pdf, last visited 22 September 2006.

2. *Codes of Conduct Illustrated*

a) Sullivan Principles

The so-called "Sullivan Principles"[19] stand for long-running private external efforts to promote socially responsible conduct of multinational corporations. They were introduced in 1977 by Reverend Leon Sullivan, a board member of General Motors and an anti-apartheid activist, to remedy social and economic injustices within the international business community in South Africa, with hopes that corporations would use their influence and channel their resources towards changing the apartheid system from within. Its six principles (amplified in 1978) urged companies to adhere to non-discriminatory labour practices in the areas of wages, housing, health, transportation, and managerial training, aiming at providing a catalyst for the dismantling of discriminatory practices in the larger society. By 1986, up to 150 corporations have taken the pledge to abide by them.[20]

While, in the end, reality failed to live up to the envisaged goals of the Sullivan Principles, they were nevertheless an important contribution to the ultimately successful movement against apartheid, and demonstrated the worth of enlisting companies as agents of change. The specific importance of the Sullivan Principles, then, lies not so much in the historical contingencies, but in shaping the debate if, and to what extent, the business community should be accountable not only to their shareholders, but to the communities in which they operate at large.[21]

---

[19] *See* The Sullivan Statement of Principles (4th amplification), Nov. 8, 1984, 24 ILM 1496 (1985); *see* also Leon H. Sullivan, *Moving Mountains: The Principles and Purposes of Leon Sullivan*, 1998, 193-96.

[20] While the Principles did not single-handedly end apartheid, they did aid in desegregating many companies. Of the 150 signatories, approximately 95% ended segregation within their workplaces. These signatories also accounted for 95% of the blacks employed by U.S. corporations in South Africa. In addition, more than two-thirds of the signatories offered scholarships to non-whites and non-white managers increased by thirty percent. *See* Jorge F. Perez-Lopez, "Promoting International Respect for Workers Rights through Business Codes of Conduct", *Fordham International Law Journal* 17 (1993), 1, 42-43.

[21] In that, the Sullivan Principles marked a turning point in societal expectations of corporate behaviour, *see* Prakash Sethi/Oliver F. Williams, "Creating and Implementing Global Codes of Conduct: An Assessment of the Sullivan Principles as a Role Model for Developing International Codes of Conduct – Lessons Learned and Unlearned", *Business and Society Review* 105 (2000), 169-200.

Since the 1970s, several other privately initiated codes of conduct have been created to set standards for corporations' behaviour when operating in foreign legislative environments that do not uphold the same labour practices as the host state. For instance, the MacBride Principles, introduced in 1984, apply to U.S. corporations conducting business in Northern Ireland with the goal of providing non-discrimination protections for the Catholic workers in the Protestant-dominated society.[22]

The initial Sullivan Principles[23] spawned a more general code in 1999, known as the Global Sullivan Principles of Social Responsibility,[24] which purport to be "a catalyst and compass for corporate responsibility and accountability."[25]

b) UN Draft Code on Transnational Corporations

On the international stage, the United Nations, or its specialized agencies, has been a principal actor in the creation of codes of conduct. After an initial period in the 1960s, when developing countries welcomed foreign direct investment, concerns over the social and economic impact, not least political interventionism of transnational corporations, increasingly mounted. Sparked by the "ITTC"-case,[26] concerns for TNC

---

[22] Other examples are the Slepak Principles, the Miller Principles, and the Maquiladora Standards of Conduct. Although labour standards were instrumental to these codes, they dealt with broader sets of issues. *See,* e.g., Lance Compa/Tashia Hinchliffe-Darricare, "Private Labour Rights Enforcement Through Corporate Codes of Conduct", in: Lance Compa/Stephen Diamond (eds.), *Human Rights, Labour Rights, and International Trade*, 1996, 181-198.

[23] For an analysis of the Sullivan Principles and their success, see Prakash Sethi, *Setting Global Standards. Guidelines for Creating Codes of Conduct in Multinational Corporations*, 2003, 95-109; Sethi/Williams, note 21.

[24] Global Sullivan Principles of Social Responsibility (1999), available at http://www.globalsullivanprinciples.org/principles.htm, last visited 22 September 2006.

[25] Quoted from http://www.thesullivanfoundation.org/gsp, last visited 22 September 2006.

[26] At the 1972 meeting of the United Nations Economic and Social Council (ECOSOC), Mr. Santa Cruz, the representative of Chile, formally denounced the US International Telephone and Telegraph Company (ITTC) for its interference in Chilean internal politics and called for a study of TNCs' activities. Subsequently, the ECOSOC passed a resolution directing the Secretary-General to appoint a group of eminent persons to study the impact of TNCs. The group recommended that ECOSOC establish an institution to study

regulation were taken up at the United Nations in the early 1970s, leading to the establishment of a UN commission and a UN centre on transnational corporations, which were mandated with drafting a comprehensive code of conduct for TNCs. Over the course of nearly two decades, considerable time and resources were expended on efforts to develop a broad code of conduct for TNCs, with the latest draft produced in 1990.[27] The latter aimed at being an essential element in the strengthening of international economic and social cooperation"[28] and an instrument "to maximize the contributions of transnational corporations to economic development and growth and to minimize the negative effects of the activities of these corporations".[29]

Under the 1990 Draft Code, TNCs are required to respect local laws and cultural traditions, to respect human rights and to avoid corruption. It further imposes broad duties relating to ownership and control, compliance with national economic and developmental objectives, restrictive business practices, taxation, and transfer pricing.[30] In addition, TNCs must disclose corporate information, including financial data, to the public of the host country.[31]

Notwithstanding the great investment made into it, the draft process was eventually discontinued in 1993 due to failure to produce agreement on an acceptable code. In the end, while it did not itself achieve a UN imprimatur, the draft code resulted in a "springboard effect", providing a template for codes that followed.

c) ILO Tripartite Declaration

Given the failure of the UN efforts to promulgate a *broad* code of conduct for TNCs, other codes that pursued standards in specific fields contrastingly met with more success, such as with respect to interna-

---

TNCs. In 1974, ECOSOC adopted resolutions to establish both a UN intergovernmental commission and a UN centre on transnational corporations, with a mandate to negotiate a code of conduct for TNCs.

[27] Proposed Text of the Draft Code of Conduct on Transnational Corporations, U.N. E.C.O.S.O.C., 2d Sess., Annex, U.N. Doc. E/1990/94 (1990) [hereinafter UN Draft Code of Conduct].

[28] Id.

[29] Id.

[30] Id., § 14, 21-34.

[31] Id., at 44-46.

tional human rights law, international health law and international labour law. A prime role in promoting good social business practice with regard to labour issues is played by the International Labour Organization (ILO). The ILO has undertaken extensive standard setting, primarily in the form of binding conventions. Some of them touch upon basic labour rights and are thus termed fundamental: Freedom of Association and Protection of the Right to Organise (C87);[32] Right to Organise and Collective Bargaining (C98);[33] Elimination of Forced Labour (C29/105);[34] Abolition of Child Labour (C138/182);[35] and Elimination of Discrimination in respect of Employment and Occupation (C100/111).[36]

In 1977, however, the Governing Body of the ILO adopted a code of conduct, entitled "Tripartite Declaration of Principles concerning Multinational Enterprises and Social Policy".[37] In his preface to the first edition, the Director-General of the ILO stated that: "The Guidelines should serve to enhance the positive contribution which multinational enterprises can make to economic and social progress to reducing or resolving the difficulties to which their operations may give rise." The

---

[32] ILO Convention (No. 87) concerning the Freedom of Association and Protection of the Right to Organise, 1948, 68 U.N.T.S. 17 (1950), entered into force July 4, 1950.

[33] ILO Convention (No. 98) concerning the Right to Organise and Collective Bargaining, 1949, 96 U.N.T.S. 257 (1951), entered into force July 18, 1951.

[34] ILO Convention (No. 29) concerning Forced or Compulsory Labour, 1930, 39 U.N.T.S. 55 (2000), entered into force May 1, 2000; ILO Convention (No. 105) concerning the Abolition of Forced Labour, 1957, 320 U.N.T.S. 291 (1959), entered into force January 17, 1959.

[35] ILO Convention (No. 138) concerning Minimum Age for Admission to Employment, 1973, 1015 U.N.T.S. 297 (1976), entered into force June 19, 1976; ILO Convention (No. 182) concerning the Prohibition and Immediate Action for the Elimination of the Worst Forms of Child Labour, 38 I.L.M. 1207 (1999), entered into force November 19, 2000.

[36] ILO Convention (No. 100) concerning Equal Remuneration for Men and Women Workers for Equal Value, 165 U.N.T.S. 303 (1953), entered into force May 23, 1953; ILO Convention (No. 111) concerning Discrimination in Respect of Employment and Occupation, 362 U.N.T.S. 31 (1960), entered into force June 15, 1960.

[37] ILO Tripartite Declaration of Principles Concerning Multinational Enterprises and Social Policy, Nov. 16, 1977, 17 I.L.M. 422 (1978) [hereinafter ILO Tripartite Declaration], available at http://www.ilo.org/public/english/employment/multi/download/english.pdf.

Declaration is the combined work of governments, labour organizations and employers' groups and draws its strength from this tripartite partnership. It contains extensive regulations in the field of social policy, covering such areas as employment, training, conditions of work and life, and industrial relations. It calls for TNCs to pursue policies that promote equal opportunity, security, collective bargaining in employment, and policies that preclude arbitrary dismissal, strikebreaking, and other unfair practices.

The Declaration stipulates respect not only for national laws and local practices, but also for the International Bill of Rights and, particularly, the ILO Constitution[38] and a wide variety of ILO Conventions and Recommendations.[39] Importantly, it extends its reach to transnational parent companies, affiliates and business partners.

While the Declaration is not subject to the reporting and monitoring systems of ILO Conventions and Recommendations, there is a procedure requiring governments to reply to queries regarding implementation of the Declaration. A summary and an analysis of the replies are submitted to the ILO Governing Body. In the event of disagreement over the application of the Declaration, the parties may submit a request to the ILO for an interpretation of its provisions.

d) OECD Guidelines for MNEs[40]

The Organization for Economic Co-operation and Development (OECD) is the major economic policy-formulating body for the developed nations. Early on in 1976 it became involved in the development of a code of conduct for TNCs, that is to say, with the adoption of a declaration on international investment and multinational enterprises (MNEs), which contained a set of guidelines for MNEs.[41] These Guide-

---

38 Constitution of the ILO, Oct. 9, 1946, 62 Stat. 3485, 15 U.N.T.S. 35.

39 A list of such conventions and recommendations is appended to the Declaration.

40 For a brief outline of the OECD Guidelines *see* Sean Murphy, "Taking Multinational Corporate Codes of Conduct to the Next Level", *Columbia Journal of Transnational Law* 43 (2005), 389, 408-411.

41 OECD, Guidelines for Multinational Enterprises, 15 *I.L.M.* 969 (1976); for the 2000 revision of the Guidelines, see OECD, The OECD Guidelines for Multinational Enterprises: Review 2000 [hereinafter OECD Guidelines], available at http://www.oecd.org/dataoecd/56/36/1922428.pdf, last visited 22 September 2006; see also Cornelia Heydenreich, *Die OECD-Leitsätze für Multi-*

lines "basically establish recommended standards for good practice for all MNEs operating in or from OECD countries."[42] As a general policy, MNEs should take full account of countries' general objectives, co-operate with local community and business interests and refrain from bribery and improper political activities. The specific guideline chapters cover the range of corporate activities, including practices relating to taxation, financing, and information disclosure. The chapter on "employment and industrial relations", among other protections, prohibits discrimination in the employment or promotion of personnel, establishing a general standard that MNEs should "respect the right of their employees to be represented by trade unions". With respect to environmental protection, the guidelines state that MNEs should "take due account of the need to protect the environment and avoid creating environmentally related health problems". The most recent revision of the Guidelines, adopted in 2000, further includes a new general policy stating that MNEs should "[r]espect the human rights of those affected by their activities consistent with the host government's international obligations and commitments." Furthermore, the 2000 guidelines address the problem of corporate structure by calling on MNEs to "[e]ncourage, where practicable, business partners, including suppliers and subcontractors, to apply principles of corporate conduct compatible with the guidelines." Moreover, new recommendations have been added relating to the elimination of child labour and forced labour and to improving internal environmental management and contingency planning for environmental impacts, and the sections on disclosure and transparency have been updated in line with enhanced social and environmental accountability.[43] Finally, new sections on combating corruption and on consumer protection have also been incorporated into the 2000 Guidelines.

As stressed in the introduction, the Guidelines are voluntary and, consequently, not legally enforceable. However, they carry the weight of a joint political commitment on the part of the OECD governments that represents their firm expectation of good corporate conduct, reflecting the values and aspirations of OECD members.

---

nationale Unternehmen – Ein wirksames Instrument zur Unternehmensregulierung?, Germanwatch, 2005, available at http://www.germanwatch.org/tw/kw05ls.pdf, last visited 22 September 2006.

[42] Murphy, note 40, at 409.

[43] Murphy, note 40, at 409.

II. Private Voluntary Codes

1. Corporate Self-Regulation

There was an astounding upsurge of private codes of conduct in the field of corporate responsibility in the late 1980s and particularly the 1990s. The emergence of these codes is reflective of the economic developments in the 1980s that saw a major shift in state policy attitudes toward TNCs – away from so-called state-led "command and control" regulation of TNCs to an emphasis on deregulatory, market-driven policies as dictated by the new ideological wave of neoliberalism.[44] As a result of *deregulation* and the more general challenges of the globalisation of economic activity, states have arguably been weakened both in their will and capacity to perform regulatory functions in the pursuit of common or public goods.[45] Against this structural background, along with the limited effectiveness of earlier international regulatory initiatives,[46] the notion of improving corporate responsibility through *private* voluntary initiatives gained ground as a possible means to fill the emerging *regulatory void*.[47] Particularly, multinational companies were urged to assume regulatory responsibilities on their own behalf, and corporations have had an instrumental interest in voluntarily adopting codes of conduct as a way to ease concerns regarding industry practices and pre-empt external regulation.

The ethical background accounting for this development was provided by the global discourse on corporate social responsibility[48] and citizen-

---

[44] "The emphasis on monetarist policies and increased integration of international markets [...] and the shift in developing countries to trade liberalization and export promotion [...] served to redefine the economic role of the state" whose governmental policies towards TNCs "shifted dramatically from regulation of their activities to intense competition to attract FDI." (Rhys Jenkins/Ruth Pearson/Gill Seyfang, "Introduction. The Rise of Voluntary Codes of Conduct", in: id. (eds.), *Corporate Responsibility and Labor Rights: Codes of Conduct in the Global Economy*, 2002, 1, 2).

[45] Cragg, note 3, at 221.

[46] See OECD Guidelines, note 41, and ILO Tripartite Declaration, note 37.

[47] Cragg, note 3, at 213.

[48] Corporate social responsibility can be broadly defined as the notion that companies are not just responsible to their shareholders, but also bear ethical responsibilities towards a broader set of stakeholders and society at large. It recognizes that, beyond the shareholder community, multiple stakeholders too have a legitimate "stake" in the activities and performance of business which,

ship[49] in the context of economic globalisation. A crucial factor has been the growth of global "value chains" through which Northern-based corporations control a web of suppliers in the South and "which has led to calls for the latter to take responsibility not only for commodity aspects such as quality standards and delivery dates", but also for the conditions under which subcontractors operate.[50] At the same time, as corporate reputation became increasingly important in influencing company sales and value, large corporations found themselves particularly vulnerable to negative publicity, thus leading them to take a proactive stance in demonstrating corporate ethics.

Initially, private voluntary initiatives focused on *corporate self-regulation* involving companies unilaterally designing and implementing their own codes of conduct. While the initial focus of the new wave of codes in the early 1990s rested primarily on labour conditions, this was soon juxtaposed against the promotion of the case for sustainable development of business. As with the first wave in the 1970s, the new trend for companies to adopt codes was fuelled by scandals about corporate practices. In addition to company codes of conduct, business or industry associations developed their own industry-wide codes.

Over time, self-regulatory initiatives met with increasing criticism that they were essentially public relations charades. The anxiety voiced by NGOs and trade union communities centred on numerous codes of conduct that sprang up but were not seen to be of significance in improving the environmental and – particularly – the social performance of companies. Rather, company and industry codes were seen to be guided by business interests merely in order to deflect criticism, in a bid

---

hence, needs to be responsive to their concerns, *see*, e.g., Corporate Social Responsibility, Labour Education, Labour Education 2003/1, No. 1 (2003), available at http://www. ilo.org/public/english/dialogue/actrav/publ/130/130.pdf.

[49] The notion of "corporate citizenship" provides the philosophical underpinning of the corporate social responsibility movement, connoting as it does an analogy to the domestic social contract theory between individuals and the state in which each had certain rights and responsibilities. It holds that the increasing freedoms enjoyed by business in the context of liberalization need to be countervailed by increasing responsibility for the social and environmental impacts of business activities.

[50] Rhys Jenkins, "Corporate Codes of Conduct. Self-Regulation in a Global Economy", *Technology, Business and Society Programme Paper* no. 2, United Nations Research Institute on Social Development, 2001, available at http://www.unrisd.org, last visited 22 September 2006, at iii.

to protect brand image and/or pre-empt governmental regulation. Codes thus became an "attempt to deceive the public into believing in the responsibility of an irresponsible industry"[51] – a cynicism for which in environmental respects the term "greenwash"[52] was coined. With regard to the criticism levelled against the discrepancies between what companies and business or industry associations preached, and what was in fact practised, a central concern focused on the lack of independent monitoring and verification procedures.

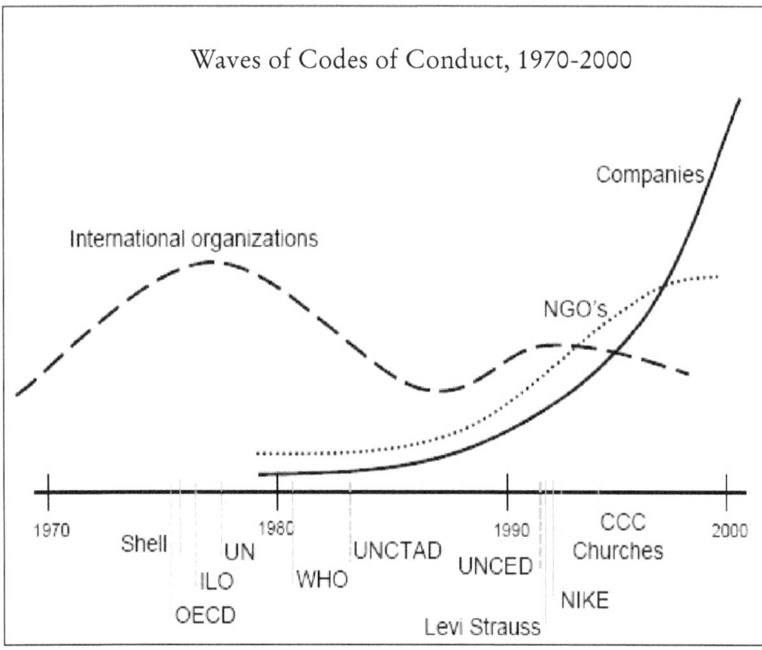

Source: Ans Kolk & Rob van Tulder, International Codes of Conduct. Trends, Sectors, Issues and Effectiveness, 2002, 2.

---

[51] John Braithwaite, "Responsive Regulation in Australia", in: Grabowsky/Braithwaite (eds.), *Business Regulation and Australia's Future*, 1993, available at http://www.aic.gov.au/publications/lcj/business/chap06.pdf, last visited 22 September 2006, 91.

[52] The Oxford English Dictionary defines it as "disinformation disseminated by an organization so as to present an environmentally responsible image." (The Concise Oxford English Dictionary, 1999).

2. *Multistakeholder Initiatives*[53]

With mounting NGO and consumer pressure on business during the 1990s, the perceived limitations of self-regulatory initiatives led to a conceptual rethinking of how to more effectively design and implement social and environmental regulatory norms. This involved a redirection of the regulatory process from corporate self-regulation towards civil regulation, a development that is essentially linked to the rebalance of social forces associated with the growth of transnational civil society organizations and networks. Moreover, notions of 'good governance' that stress the importance of multi-stakeholder collaboration and dialogue and the merits of 'social learning' gained in popularity.[54]

Civil society and business groups – with or without some governmental input – have attempted to design more coordinated mechanisms to respond more sensibly to the challenges of promoting socially and environmentally responsible corporate conduct across borders. By the late 1990s, then, new regulatory approaches – so-called *multi-stakeholder initiatives* (MSIs) – became the "plat du jour".[55] These draw on the participation of multiple stakeholders – including companies or industry associations, NGOs, trade unions and, on occasion, governmental bodies – and involve standard-setting, stakeholder dialogue, social and environmental management systems, and, significantly, certification and monitoring mechanisms related to social and environmental issues. MSIs mark an attempt to overcome the limitations of unilaterally designed company codes and respond more sensibly to advancing the social responsibility cause. Importantly, the inclusion of often-divergent interests in the drafting process "leads to a level of credibility not necessarily found in other codes."[56] Here the third party participation goes beyond simple advisory services, resulting in a joint responsibility for the actual drawing up and conclusion of the codes; those civil society

---

53 For a comprehensive study of 'multistakeholder initiatives', *see* Peter Utting, "Regulating Business via Multistakeholder Initiatives: A Preliminary Assessment", in: *Voluntary Approaches to Corporate Responsibility: Readings and Resource Guide*, NGLS/UNRISD, Geneva 2002, available at http://www.unsystem.org/ngls/Section%20II.pdf, last visited 22 September 2006, 61-130.

54 Id., at 62.

55 Désirée Abrahams, *Regulating Corporations. A Resource Guide*, 2004, available at http://www.unrisd.org, last visited 22 September 2006, at 3.

56 Ivanka Mamic, *Implementing Codes of Conduct. How Businesses Manage Social Performance in Global Supply Chains*, 2004, at 43.

organizations see themselves in the role of a custodian of public interest, which in their eyes gives them legitimacy.

Two noteworthy examples of MSI are the Ethical Trading Initiative (ETI) and Social Accountability 8000 (SA8000). Others include the Clean Clothes Campaign, the Ethical Trading Initiative, the Fair Labor Association, the Forest Stewardship Council, the Global Alliance, the Global Sullivan Principles, the Global Compact,[57] the Global Reporting Initiative, ISO 14001, SA8000, WRAP, and the Workers Rights Consortium.

The multitude of existing voluntary codes and initiatives has contributed to a bewildering pluralism of approaches that differ significantly in terms of their origin, degree of institutionalization, scope, purpose, underlying incentives, and monitoring mechanisms. With such a broad array of approaches, a crucial question is raised as to the effectiveness and legitimacy of codes of conduct.

3. UN Sub-Commission Draft Norms on Human Rights

The untempered actuality of human rights issues related to corporate activity prompted the UN Sub-Commission on the Promotion and Protection of Human Rights to further standard-setting efforts in this regard, resulting in the 2003 adoption of a code on the human rights obligations and responsibilities of TNCs.[58]

---

[57] It is worth noting that the Global Compact carries the cachet of the United Nations and is therefore a voluntary *public* initiative that brings together corporations, UN agencies and civil society organizations in support of good corporate practices set out in ten general principles (*see* page 277 f. of this paper).

[58] UN Office of the High Commissioner for Human Rights, Sub-Commission on the Promotion and Protection of Human Rights, Norms on the Responsibilities of Transnational Corporations and Other Business Enterprises with Regard to Human Rights, U.N. Doc. E/CN.4/Sub.2/2003/12 (2003) [hereinafter Sub-Commission Draft Norms on Human Rights]; *see* Karsten Nowrot, "Die UN-Norms on the Responsibility of Transnational Corporations and Other Business Enterprises with Regard to Human Rights. Gelungener Beitrag zur transnationalen Rechtsverwirklichung oder das Ende des Global Compact?", *Beiträge zum Transnationalen Wirtschaftsrecht* 21 (2003), 1-37; David Weissbrodt/Maria Kruger, "Norms on the Responsibilities of Transnational Corporations and Other Business Enterprises with Regard to Human Rights", *AJIL* 97 (2003), 901-922; Detlev Vagts, "The UN Norms for Transnational Corporations", *Leiden Journal of International Law* 16 (2003), 795-802.

While recognizing that states maintain the primary responsibility for the promotion and protection of human rights, the Norms also assert the obligation of TNCs (and other business enterprises), as organs of society, to ensure the respect for and the promotion of human rights within their sphere of influence and activities.[59] Importantly, the enormous economic potential of TNCs translates into a positive duty to "use their influence to help promote and ensure respect for human rights."[60] Next to stating the general obligations of TNCs with regard to human rights, the code sets out more specific types of rights or obligations that TNCs must observe, relating to: the right to equal opportunity and non-discriminatory treatment; the right to security of persons; the rights of workers (rights against forced or child labour, to a safe and healthy working environment, to remuneration that ensures an adequate standard of living, and to collective bargaining); respect for national sovereignty and human rights; obligations with regard to consumer protection; and obligations with regard to environmental protection (i.e. complying with relevant national and international laws).

The code extends beyond pure voluntarism to include mechanisms for implementation: TNCs "shall adopt [...] internal rules of operation in compliance with the Norms", shall periodically report on implementation, and shall incorporate the code in their contracts and dealings with contractors, suppliers, distributors, licensees, and others.[61] The code continues to state that TNCs shall be subject to transparent and independent monitoring and verification by the United Nations and "other international [...] and national mechanisms already in existence or yet to be created,"[62] and that states "should" establish the legal framework necessary for implementing the code.[63] Further, TNCs "shall provide

---

[59] Sub-Commission Draft Norms on Human Rights, pt. A.

[60] *See* Commentary on the Norms on the Responsibilities of Transnational Corporations and Other Business Enterprises with Regard to Human Rights, UN Doc E/CN.4/Sub.2/2003/38/Rev.2 (2003), para. 1; *see also* Sub-Commission Draft Norms on Human Rights, para. 12 ("Transnational corporations and other business enterprises shall respect economic, social and cultural rights as well as civil and political rights *and contribute to their realization*, [...].") (emphasis added).

[61] Sub-Commission Draft Norms on Human Rights, pt. H, para. 15.

[62] Id., para. 16.

[63] Id., para. 17.

prompt, effective and adequate reparation to those persons, entities, and communities" adversely affected by failure to comply with the norms.[64]

Initial enthusiasm among supporters of the code,[65] who had hailed it as a "landmark step" and even as the "first nonvoluntary initiative accepted at the international level,"[66] were muted, inter alia, by major business organizations criticizing the code as an "inappropriate effort to 'privatize' vague human rights standards in a manner that will invite 'highly subjective, politicized claims."[67] In a joint statement, the International Organization of Employers (IOE) and the International Chamber of Commerce (ICC) declare: "The IOE and the ICC remain convinced that the overall approach taken by the Working Group would not constitute a positive contribution to either the encouragement of responsible business conduct or to the promotion and protection of human rights."[68]

Most importantly, however, the Commission on Human Rights, to which the Sub-Commission Draft Norms on Human Rights were referred for final adoption, affirmed in its recommendation to the UN Economic and Social Council that the code "has not been requested by the Commission and, as a draft proposal, has no legal standing, and that the Sub-Commission should not perform any monitoring function in this regard."[69]

---

64 Id., para. 18.

65 *See* Rodrigo Osorio, *The 60th Commission on Human Rights: Norms on the Responsibilities of Transnational Corporations and Other Business Enterprises with Regard to Human Rights*, Geneva, 15 March - 23 April 2004, available at http://www.casin.ch/web/pdf/normstncshumanrights.pdf, last visited 22 September 2006, 1 ("[T]he Norms constitute a useful legal instrument, providing clarity, legitimacy (as a product of a formal and wide consultation process within the United Nations), and effectiveness to the field of international corporate accountability.").

66 Weissbrodt/Kruger, note 58, at 903.

67 *See* Murphy, *supra* note 40, 408 (citing International Chamber of Commerce, Joint Views of the IOE and ICC on the Draft Norms on the Responsibilities of Transnational Corporations and Other Business Enterprises with Regard to Human Rights, UN Doc E/CN.4/Sub.2/2003/NGO/44 (2003) [hereinafter Joint Views of the IOE and ICC]).

68 Joint Views of the IOE and ICC, note 67.

69 Responsibilities of transnational corporations and related business enterprises with regard to human rights, Office of the High Commissioner for Human Rights, 60th Sess., 56th mtg., UN Doc. E/CN.4/DEC/2004/116 (2004).

D. Typology of Codes of Conduct

I. Relevant Parameters

1. Actors

There is great variance among codes of corporate conduct in form and origin, involving a wide range of actors at the global, regional and national levels. A categorization of voluntary codes may depart from a preliminary distinction between public and private codes. Public codes are drafted under the auspices of governments or by government representatives working through international organizations. The great range of corporate responsibility initiatives, however, has been developed by private actors. While in some cases codes have been developed at the initiative of individuals, codes of conduct have traditionally proliferated within the corporate sector; in addition, a growing number of codes are being developed by interest groups, including trade unions as well as labour, environmental and human rights organizations.

The vast majority of codes can be divided into the following categories:

Company codes refer to those voluntary codes adopted unilaterally by individual corporations. Typically developed without any outside participation, they either relate to the companies' own operations or are applied specifically to their suppliers. Codes have also been drawn up by business associations representing particular industries (i.e. for a class of companies in a particular field) or as joint undertakings by corporate entities. An example of an *industry code* is the international chemical industry's 'Responsible Care' programme. Such an industry-wide code bears the advantage of being competitively neutral, as all the enterprises that are otherwise competitors are subject to the same standards of conduct. In addition, sometimes the relevant association is entrusted with certain control functions. The latest developments involve the emergence of the above-mentioned *multi-stakeholder initiatives*, which have the advantage of wider public credibility.

An OECD survey of 246 codes of conduct has shown a clear preponderance of codes issued by individual firms (118 codes) and by business/industry associations (92 codes), compared to multi-stakeholder initiatives (32 codes) and intergovernmental codes (4).[70]

---

[70] OECD, Codes of Corporate Conduct – Expanded Review of their Contents, Directorate for Financial, Fiscal and Enterprise Affairs, Working Papers On International Investment, No. 2001/6, Paris (May 2001), 5, available at

2. Addressees

Codes of conduct have arisen essentially in response to public outcry against socially irresponsible behaviour of TNCs. Functionally, thus, codes purport to be instruments of accountability for TNCs. A key question in the codes debate, therefore, is to what extent the codes do in fact serve this function in relation to the various stakeholders involved. Taking this wider view into account, "'a code of conduct should address the corporation's functional relationship and responsibilities toward outside constituency groups', not just the narrow focus of internal employees."[71]

The primary audience for many codes, however, remains the company itself, namely its business units, managers, employees, and shareholders. Some companies may adopt a code to signal sound business practices to current or potential host governments, thereby maintaining or enhancing the company's licence to operate. In other cases, codes may aim to broadcast a company's involvement with the communities in which it operates. Importantly, codes are also targeted at a corporation's customers or suppliers, with a view to enhancing brand image and being applied along the supply chain.

To be sure, codes must account for the complexities prevalent in a global economy, where the tangled web of TNC activity draws workers – especially those from the developing world – into the intricate process of cross-border production.[72] Much labour-intensive export production is located in developing countries, where labour is relatively cheaper than in the North and regulation of employment is usually less stringent. The challenge is to ensure that corporate codes also apply to distant suppliers and subcontractors. That challenge is increased by the fact that the consumer community has only a certain amount of commercial leverage.

---

http://www.oecd.org/dataoecd/57/24/1922656.pdf, last visited 22 September 2006.

[71] Jill Murray, Corporate Codes of Conduct and Labour Standards, International Labour Organization Bureau for Workers' Activities, 16 (referring to Kline), available at http://www.itcilo.it/english/actrav/telearn/global/ilo/guide/jill.htm, last visited 22 September 2006.

[72] Adelle Blackett, "Global Governance, Legal Pluralism and the Decentered State: A Labor Law Critique of Codes of Corporate Conduct", *Indiana Journal of Global Legal Studies* 8 (2000/2001), 401.

On the international level, the 2000 revision of the OECD Guidelines extends beyond the individual companies to include a company's suppliers and sub-contractors. Many codes adopted by northern-based companies have been developed to apply along their value chains. According to the OECD research, over 40% of the codes surveyed covering labour issues placed obligations on suppliers, particularly in the clothing industry, where 26 out of 32 company codes surveyed were addressed to suppliers and contractors.

The value chains through which codes apply can be quite complex, with many suppliers applying codes at different points of the chain. Conversely, "a single supplier could be producing for a number of global buyers, and be subject to a range of codes. The extent to which and how suppliers implement and comply with different codes will depend on a wide range of factors, including their location, size and employment conditions, but a crucial factor is also their position within the value chain."[73]

3. *Substance*

a) General Information

Codes of conduct vary significantly in terms of the breadth and detail of their content. Reflective of the underlying diversity of the issuing organizations, partnerships and the differing motivational underpinnings, code content may be wide and aspirational or detailed and operational.[74]

Some codes, such as the International Code of Ethics for Canadian Business and the OECD Guidelines for Multinational Enterprises, set out principles that are comprehensive in nature and designed to cover commercial activities across a broad range of issues. Some focus on the

---

[73] Stephanie Barrientos, "Mapping Codes Through the Value Chain: From Researcher to Detective", in: Rhys Jenkins/Ruth Pearson/Gill Seyfang (eds.), *Corporate Responsibility and Labor Rights: Codes of Conduct in the Global Economy*, 2002, 61-76.

[74] Some codes incorporate specific action statements. The codes of Reebok and Levi Strauss alike, e.g., direct the respective MNE to withdraw operations in countries that violate human rights. Levi Strauss took this course of action with respect to China and Burma, *see* John Christopher Anderson, "Respecting Human Rights: Multinational Corporations Strike Out", *University of Pennsylvania Journal of Labor and Employment Law* 2 (2000), 463, 485-486.

environment (the CERES Principles, the UNEP Financial Statement) or labour (SA8000, ICFTU Code of Labour Practice, the ILO Tripartite Declaration on Multinational Enterprises, the Fair Labour Association Workplace Code of Conduct, the Ethical Trading Initiative Base Code), while others cover a variety of issues (e.g. the United States Model Business Principles, the UN Global Compact).[75]

Codes are innovative instruments that address a wide range of regulatory issues, notably in relation to human and labour rights and environmental standards. According to an OECD report based on a survey of 246 codes, environmental stewardship (145 codes) and labour standards (148 codes) have been most commonly referred to among the variable code commitments,[76] and in many cases either issue area may be the exclusive focus of so-called "single issue" codes.[77] The report mentions that the codes that have been developed within the clothing industry evidence a consensus that has been formed around a narrow range of labour issues, such as child labour, bonded labour, working environment and compensation. In addition to labour standards and environmental stewardship, 'social accountability' concerns may also extend beyond labour and environmental issues to the enhancement of the economic and social well-being of the host country and local population (corporate citizenship).

While aspects of social responsibility figure most prominently among codes, they may address a number of other issues related to corporate governance, such as fair business practices, questions of internal financial control and protection of shareholder value,[78] and litigation risks.

---

[75] *See*, e.g., Michael Hopkins, "Corporate Social Responsibility: an Issues Paper", *Working Paper No. 27, Policy Integration Department. World Commission on the Social Dimension of Globalization. International Labour Office, Geneva* (2004), available at http://www.ilo.org/public/english/bureau/integration/download/publicat/4_3_285_wcsdg-wp-27.pdf, last visited 22 September 2006, 13-14.

[76] Kathryn Gordon/Maiko Miyake, "Deciphering Codes of Corporate Conduct: A Review of their Contents", *OECD Working Papers on International Investment* (1999/2) [hereinafter Gordon/Miyake, Deciphering Codes of Corporate Conduct], available at http://www.oecd.org/dataoecd/23/19/2508552.pdf, last visited 22 September 2006, 12.

[77] Of the 246 codes surveyed, 24 codes are dedicated exclusively to environmental issues and 36 to labour standards.

[78] E.g. no insider trading, the need to safeguard proprietary information, the importance of maintaining accurate financial accounts.

There is "widespread agreement on the values and principles that should guide corporations beyond social and environmental aspects in dealing with their shareholders, consumers, suppliers and other stakeholders."[79] Typically, the principles stipulate respect for the values of honesty, fairness, due diligence and observance of the law.[80] Consumer protection and avoidance of bribery and corruption, to be sure, have received particular attention from codes, in addition to labour and environmental standards.[81]

b) Labour Standards

Labour standards have been set out in international conventions drafted by the ILO and were extensively explored in the ILO Tripartite Declaration of Principles concerning Multinational Enterprises and Social Policy (ILO 1977). As regards the substantive content of voluntary codes of conduct relating to labour, there is general agreement among NGOs, unions and human rights groups on the importance for codes to incorporate, at a minimum, provisions based on core labour standards that ought to serve as benchmarks for the legitimacy of the code in question. Core labour standards have been defined in a number of ILO conventions relating to child[82] and forced labour,[83] freedom of association[84] and collective bargaining[85] and discrimination issues;[86] the

---

79 Cragg, note 3, at 216.

80 Id.

81 Gordon/Miyake, Deciphering Codes of Corporate Conduct, note 76, at 12.

82 ILO Convention (No. 138) concerning Minimum Age for Admission to Employment and ILO Convention (No. 182) concerning Worst Forms of Child Labour Convention, note 35.

83 ILO Convention (No. 29) concerning Forced or Compulsory Labour and ILO Convention (No. 105) concerning the Abolition of Forced Labour, note 34.

84 ILO Convention (No. 87) concerning the Freedom of Association Convention and Protection of the Right to Organize, note 32.

85 ILO Convention (No. 98) concerning the Application of the Principles of the Right to Organise and to Bargain Collectively, note 33.

86 ILO Convention (No. 100) concerning Equal Remuneration for Men and Women Workers for Equal Value and ILO Convention (No. 111) concerning Discrimination in Respect of Employment and Occupation, note 36.

ILO Declaration on Fundamental Principles and Rights at Work (adopted 1998) incorporates the core labour standards in a single normative framework that is binding on all ILO member countries (to date: 178). The ILO conventions convey a high degree of legitimacy, as they are directly derived from the founding principles of the ILO that bind all members.

Qualitatively, the nature of codes can be assessed by the extent to which they incorporate or even surpass the ILO's core labour standards. While the data of the OECD survey on the coverage of core labour issues does not differentiate between the various types of codes, such a compilation has been undertaken by Jenkins (reproduced in the table below) on the basis of 153 codes relating to labour relations. From it we see that a far higher percentage of multi-stakeholder initiatives than company and business association codes incorporate the ILO's core labour standards. As far as freedom of association and collective bargaining is concerned, these are the most frequently mentioned core labour standards in multi-stakeholder codes (95%), while least frequently cited in both company and business association codes.[87] This finding reflects the importance that non-corporate stakeholders attribute to the function of codes as a basis for workers' self-organization. As can be inferred from the table below, company codes are much more likely (roughly at a proportion of 2:1) to include core labour standards as compared to business association codes[88] – a finding that may be accounted for by the consideration that business association codes tend to be weaker than company codes because they need to be acceptable to most companies within the respective organization, and hence must accommodate the interests of smaller companies, which are less exposed to public scrutiny and pressure.

[87] *See* Rhys Jenkins, "The Political Economy of Codes of Conduct", in: Rhys Jenkins/Ruth Pearson/Gill Seyfang (eds.), *Corporate Responsibility and Labour Rights: Codes of Conduct in the Global Economy*, 2002, 13, 19.

[88] Id., at 20.

Proportion of codes referring to core labour standards

Attribute	Company codes (%)	Business associations (%)	Multistakeholder codes (%)	Total* (%)
No forced labour	41.6	20.0	65.0	39.9
No child labour	46.5	23.3	70.0	44.4
No discrimination/ harassment	67.3	30.0	75.0	61.4
Freedom of association and collective bargaining	23.8	13.3	95.0	32.0
ILO codes mentioned	3.0	6.7	60.0	11.8
Total number of codes	101	30	20	153

* Includes two inter-governmental codes

Source: Rhys Jenkins, The Political Economy of Codes of Conduct, in: Rhys Jenkins/Ruth Pearson/Gill Seyfang (eds.), *Corporate Responsibility and Labour Rights: Codes of Conduct in the Global Economy*, 2002, 19 [Table 2.1].

In addition to core Labour standards, a code may include a number of other aspects of labour conditions, e.g. provisions on health and safety, maximum hours of work, wages/compensation, compliance with local laws and human rights. From the compilation of non-core labour standards covered in the different code types (see below), it follows that the most heavily cited non-core labour standards relate to reasonable working environment, compliance with local laws and compensation.

Proportion of non-core labour standards covered in codes

Attribute	Company codes (%)	Business associations (%)	Multistakeholder codes (%)	Total* (%)
Reasonable working environment	76.2	80.0	75.0	76.5
Compliance with laws	69.3	53.3	70.0	66.7
Compensation	51.5	16.7	70.0	47.1
Working hours	35.6	13.3	60.0	34.0
Provision of training	29.7	30.0	40.0	32.0
Human rights	22.8	26.7	30.0	24.8

* Includes two inter-governmental codes

Source: Rhys Jenkins, The Political Economy of Codes of Conduct, in: Jenkins, Rhys/Pearson, Ruth/Seyfang, Gill (eds.), Corporate Responsibility and Labour Rights: Codes of Conduct in the Global Economy (2002), 21 [Table 2.2].

4. Compliance Mechanism

Central to the debate around voluntary codes of conduct is the compliance issue. The effectiveness of voluntary codes hinges on their capacity to translate into practice, i.e. the extent to which they are taken seriously as shown through compliance. If a code is to be worth more than the paper it is printed on, it is crucial that effective compliance mechanisms are in place.

Questions such as who performs the monitoring task, whether the workforce is involved, if monitoring extends to the supply chains, how the monitoring exercise is conducted and the transparency of the findings, are of crucial importance for judging the value of the relevant compliance mechanisms. A key issue relates to the independence of the individual or entity undertaking verification of a corporation's code compliance.

Monitoring mechanisms can take various forms.[89] An inherent conflict of interest is involved when the corporation itself does the monitoring. In contrast to such *internal monitoring*, the credibility of the monitoring exercise, and hence the legitimacy of the code, will be heightened by external mechanisms. *External monitoring* involves the on-site inspection by a third party, i.e. an external auditing firm hired by the corporation, to which the auditor reports. In contrast, *independent monitoring* is done by monitors who enjoy financial independence from the company in question.[90] Of these three types, independent monitoring is best suited to providing public credibility on code compliance. The trend now is to verify code compliance altogether externally through auditing firms.

According to the OECD survey (2001), only 32% of all the company codes discussed implementation issues,[91] and only a quarter of all the codes sampled specifically addressed labour monitoring at all.[92] Monitoring issues are far more likely to be discussed with multi-stakeholder codes, while they receive the least attention in the case of business associations. The most common form of labour monitoring among the company codes involves the monitoring of suppliers, rather than the company's own activities. Other studies also observed very loose compliance mechanisms. A survey of 132 codes by Kolk, for instance, found that 41% of the codes did not specifically mention monitoring, and that where monitoring systems indeed had been in place, in 44% they relied on internal monitoring.[93] As for cases of non-compliance,

---

89 *See* Ruth Rosenbaum, "In Whose Interest? A Global Code of Conduct for Corporations", in: Oliver Williams (ed.), *Global Codes of Conduct. An Idea Whose Time Has Come*, 2000, 211-220.

90 David Schilling, "Making Codes of Conduct Credible. The Role of Independent Monitoring", in: Williams (ed.), note 89, 221, 227-231.

91 OECD, Corporate Responsibility: Results of a Fact Finding Mission on Private Initiatives, Directorate for Financial, Fiscal and Enterprise Affairs, no. 2, 2001, available at http://www.oecd.org/dataoecd/45/28/1922698.pdf, last visited 22 September 2006, at 10.

92 OECD, Codes of Corporate Conduct – Expanded Review of their Contents, Directorate for Financial, Fiscal and Enterprise Affairs, Working Papers On International Investment, No. 2001/6, Paris (2001) [hereinafter OECD, Expanded Review], 10; *see* also Jenkins, note 87, at 22.

93 Ans Kolk, Rob van Tulder & Carlijn Welters, "International Codes of Conduct and Corporate Social Responsibility: Can Transnational Corporations Regulate Themselves?", *Transnational Corporations* 8 (1999), 143, 168.

often no clear sanctions are defined. Approximately 60% of the company and business association codes in the OECD inventory do not specify any penalties for non-compliance.

II. Codes of Conduct and Soft Law

In the traditional view, states are both the architects and addressees of international law. Codes of conduct, however, are neither exclusively produced by nor addressed to states as the primary subjects of international rule making. In fact, a distinguishing feature of codes is their development and implementation by private, i.e. non-state actors. In addition, codes are not designed to be legally binding, but rather rely on voluntary compliance. Because of these features, codes do not fit into the traditional sources of international law as listed in Art. 38 of the Statute of the International Court of Justice.[94] While codes of conduct do not qualify as 'hard law', a promising attempt at their normative categorization is to depart from the binary view of international law as of necessity either falling into the realm of binding law or, otherwise, that of non-binding 'soft law'.

Soft law is a generic term referring to a category of social norms that are not legally binding per se as a matter of 'law' but which nevertheless have a certain legal relevance in influencing the conduct and decisions of state and non-state actors.[95] Soft law has long existed in international public life, yet it is in the context of new global governance challenges that soft law arrangements have gained specific salience and flourished across the international stage. Acting in their own right or through intergovernmental organizations, national governments have turned to soft law solutions, yet a prominent feature of soft law instruments is the involvement of non-state actors. Today, the international system is no longer determined only by states but also influenced by a number of non-state actors. Departing from the traditional state-centred approach

---

[94] For a treatment on the rigidity of the traditional sources triad in international law, *see, e.g.,* Eibe Riedel, "Standards and Sources. Farewell to the Exclusivity of the Sources Triad in International Law?", *EJIL* 2 (1991), 58-84.

[95] *See* Thürer, note 5, 452-453; on the concept of soft law in general and on its various meanings: Richard Baxter, "International Law in "Her Infinite Variety"," *International and Comparative Law Quarterly* 29 (1980), 549-566; for a terse review of soft law *see* Christine Chinkin, "Normative Development in the International Legal System", in: Shelton (ed.), note 5, at 21-22.

to public international law, soft law is not to be understood as being developed exclusively by states. Importantly, soft law accords a role to non-state actors, particularly NGOs, that is only rarely possible in traditional law-making processes.[96] However, do normative arrangements that are exclusively developed by private actors still qualify as soft law?

'Soft law' is a very vague concept, rooted in international law theory. Drawing on the conceptual dichotomy between hard and soft law, one might conceive soft law as a normative realm encompassing everything that is not hard law, or apply it with a more bounded degree of definitional freedom. For many codes of conduct soft law is a fitting concept. The most straightforward examples in this regard are provided by the codes issued by international organizations. However, what is one to make of the Sullivan Principles,[97] and what of the company/industry code and multi-stakeholder initiatives? Where are the definitional boundaries to be drawn?

For the sake of simplicity and to avoid semantic hair splitting, it is reasonable to employ 'soft law' as an inclusive, expansive and flexible category. However, it is clear that not all instruments that do not belong to the formal sources of international law[98] can be subsumed under soft law, for the contrary would mean an overstretching of the ways in which the term 'soft law' has been traditionally understood. Therefore, one is arguably to exclude from the definitional scope of 'soft law' the codes that are drawn up by *corporate actors*. Soft law, in many ways, is an appropriate notion in the context of codes of conduct, yet it falls short of encompassing the phenomenon of the codes of conduct in its entirety.

---

[96] Dinah Shelton, "Introduction", in: Shelton (ed.), note 5; *see* also Juliane Kokott, "Soft Law Standards under Public International Law", in: Peter Nobel (ed.), *International Standards and the Law*, 2005, 15, 21.

[97] *See* Christopher McCrudden, "Human Rights Codes for Transnational Corporations: The McBride and Sullivan Principles", in: Shelton (ed.), note 5, 418-449.

[98] In this regard, the concept of soft law as used by Fastenrath appears too wide, i.e. all-encompassing, *see* Ulrich Fastenrath, "Relative Normativity in International Law", *EJIL* 4 (1993), 305, at ftn 2 ("The concept of "soft law", as employed in the following, denotes instruments which do *not* belong to the formal sources of international law." [emphasis added]).

III. Variety of Codes of Conduct: Illustrative Examples

1. Intergovernmental Codes of Conduct

The need for standard setting to regulate TNC conduct has given rise to code creation driven by international organizations, which notably has led to the adoption of the OECD Guidelines and the ILO Tripartite Declaration. Within the UN family, the UN General Assembly endorsed a code on restrictive business practices, whereas efforts concerning the adoption of the UN Code of Conduct for TNCs and an International Code of Conduct on Transfer of Technology were unsuccessful.

Over the last few years, voluntary environmental codes of conduct have come to the fore as new and promising tools to raise awareness of environmental issues and improve behaviour and practices. UNEP has been a principal agent in the development of environmental codes of conduct. To implement Agenda 21,[99] UNEP has not only become increasingly involved in strengthening voluntary environmental initiatives through developing guidelines[100] and cooperation with stakeholders, but has also been active in the development of global voluntary initiatives by industry sector.[101] UNEP has also developed cross-sector voluntary initiatives to promote cleaner production and ozone protection.

The latest example of an international code of conduct constitutes the UN Sub-Commission's "Draft Norms on the Responsibilities of TNCs and other Business Enterprises with regard to Human Rights".[102]

---

[99] Chapter 30 of Agenda 21 encourages business and industry "to adopt and report on the implementation of codes of conduct promoting best environmental practice".

[100] UNEP has developed guidelines for voluntary initiatives in general, and, more specifically, for the tourism industry and for reducing greenhouse gases.

[101] Starting with finance and insurance sectors (1992/1995), tourism in 1999 and more recently, gold mining, telecommunications, automotive and advertising industries.

[102] *See supra* C II 3.

2. *Private Sector Codes*

a) Industry/Business Associations' Codes

Responsible Care (RC) is an initiative of the global chemical industry, a voluntary programme that helps to raise industry standards and win greater trust from the public. It constitutes one of the most encompassing and globally accepted codes for an industrial sector. It was first conceived in 1985 by the Canadian chemical industry to address and deflect growing public concerns relating to its environmental performance, with a view to forestalling public regulation. It demonstrates the commitment of chemical companies, represented by their respective national associations, to work together to continuously improve their environmental, health, and safety performance in a manner that is responsive to public concerns, and so to contribute to the sustainable development of local communities and of society as a whole.

Member companies are obliged to comply with a base code of ten "Guiding Principles" that calls on companies to prioritize environmental, health and safety concerns, work towards the diminution of environmental impact, show responsiveness to citizens' concerns and to report swiftly on health and environmental hazards. The RC Guiding Principles are backboned by a set of six codes of management practices establishing detailed obligations in relation to issues such as: pollution prevention, process safety, the distribution of chemicals, employee health and safety, product stewardship and the fostering of community awareness and the establishment of an emergency response programme.

While the Guiding Principles and the management practices apply in the same manner for each country, the national chemical associations differ greatly in how they go about the monitoring and enforcement of the RC standards. In general, RC brings accountability through its requirement that national associations develop credible processes to verify that member companies are meeting RC expectations (http://www.chemicalguide.com).[103]

Caux Principles for Business: The Caux Round Table is an international network of "principled business leaders working to promote a moral capitalism".[104] The Caux Round Table promotes the application of Caux Round Table Principles for Business at the company level as the

---

[103] Last visited 22 September 2006.

[104] http://www.cauxroundtable.org/about.html (last visited 22 September 2006).

cornerstone of "principled business leadership".[105] The objective of the principles is to establish ethical standards against which business behaviour can be measured. Participating companies can make use of a specially designed process (consisting of a Self-Assessment and Improvement Process) intended to incorporate the CRT principles into the company culture. The principles aim to bring together the ethical ideal of *kyosei*, a Japanese term for the concept of working together for the common good, and human dignity which stresses the value of each person as an end in him- or herself (http://www.cauxroundtable.org).

CERES Principles: CERES (the Coalition for Environmentally Responsible Economies) announced the creation of the Principles (initially named Valdez Principles, later renamed CERES principles) in 1989. They constitute a ten-point code of corporate environmental conduct to be publicly endorsed by companies as an environmental mission statement or ethic. Today, over 65 companies have endorsed the principles and committed to a concurrent process of continuous learning and systematic public reporting. Endorsing companies can benefit from having access to a diverse array of experts in the network, covering a wide range of organizational and environmental issues (http:// www.ceres.org).[106]

b) Multi-stakeholder Initiatives[107]

Accountability 1000 (AA1000) was established in 1999 by the UK-based Institute of Social and Ethical Accountability. It is an accountability standard committed to enhancing the social responsibility and ethical behaviour of the business community and NGOs through promoting best practice in social and ethical accounting, auditing and reporting. At the heart of AA1000 lie stakeholder engagement and the improvement of the overall performance through organizational learning.

The AA1000 Framework was extended in 2002 to include additional components and is now known as the AA1000 Series (http://www.accountability21.net).[108]

---

105 http://www.cauxroundtable.org/principles.html (last visited 22 September 2006).

106 Last visited 22 September 2006.

107 The following illustration of multistakeholder initiatives draws in part on the overview provided by Peter Utting (Utting, note 53, at 75-80).

108 Last visited 22 September 2006.

Clean Clothes Campaign (CCC) is an international campaign comprising a network of NGOs, trade unions, solidarity groups and activists with the aim of improving working conditions in the global garment and sportswear industries, and which provides for independent verification to ensure compliance with the CCC Code of Labour Practices (http://www.cleanclothes.org).[109]

ETI (Ethical Trading Initiative), established in 1998, is an alliance comprising companies, NGOs and trade unions working to identify and promote good corporate practices in the global supply chains that produce goods for the UK market. A key dimension of this initiative is securing implementation of the labour standards set out in the ETI Base Code. ETI does not certify performance or conduct audits itself; rather, it focuses on information exchange and related learning processes concerning the experiences of companies in promoting socially responsible corporate conduct along the diverse supply chains (http://www.ethicaltrade.org).[110]

Fair Labour Association (FLA) was established in the United States in 1998 as a successor body to the White House Apparel Industry Partnership. It is a non-profit-making organization based in the USA, combining the efforts of industry, non-governmental organizations (NGOs), colleges and universities to promote adherence to international labour standards and improve working conditions worldwide. The FLA conducts independent monitoring and verification to ensure that the FLA's Workplace Standards are upheld where FLA company products are produced. Through public reporting, the FLA provides consumers and shareholders with credible information to make responsible buying decisions. Its Code of Conduct condemns forced labour, child labour, harassment and abuse, and calls for non-discrimination, health and safety procedures, and freedom of association among other rights (http:// www.fairlabor.org).[111]

Global Reporting Initiative (GRI) is an independent multi-stakeholder institution whose mission is to develop and disseminate globally applicable Sustainability Reporting Guidelines. These Guidelines are for voluntary use by organizations to report on the economic, environmental, and social dimensions of their activities, products, and services. The GRI incorporates the active participation of representatives from

---

109 Last visited 22 September 2006.

110 Last visited 22 September 2006.

111 Last visited 22 September 2006.

business, accountancy, investment, environmental, human rights, research and labour organizations from around the world. Started in 1997, GRI became independent in 2002, and is an official collaborating centre of the United Nations Environment Programme (UNEP), and works in cooperation with UN Secretary-General Kofi Annan's Global Compact (http://www.globalreporting. org).

Social Accountability 8000 (SA8000), established in 1997 by the US-based Council on Economic Priorities and Accreditation Agency (CEPAA), now known as Social Accountability International (SAI), represents one of the most rigorous voluntary codes of conduct yet crafted. It is a cross-industry standard for workplace conditions and a verification and certification system, which draws heavily on the ILO Conventions and other key human rights instruments. SAI accredits monitors to audit factories and certify their compliance with the SA8000 standard (http://www.sa-intl.org).[112]

Worker Rights Consortium (WRC) was established in 2000 on the initiative of the United Students Against Sweatshops (USAS). It aims to improve labour standards in the factories that form part of the supply chain of companies that produce clothing and other goods under licence for US colleges and universities. Independent verification of compliance with the WRC Code of Conduct is performed by the WRC in response to specific complaints (http://www.workersrights.org).[113]

E. The Legitimacy Dilemma

'Legitimacy' is an elusive concept. As a study object, one might – in some ways – term it holographic, since, depending on the perspective from which one approaches it, it shines in different colours. The variance in theoretical stances corresponds to different epistemological premises that underlie the many probings of issues of legitimacy. One may understand legitimacy as an *empirical*, social-scientific concept, or employ it in a *normative* sense. Political theory and sociology have long recognized legitimacy as a cardinal element in national political and governance regimes, focusing, respectively, "on societal acceptance of

---

[112] Last visited 22 September 2006.

[113] Last visited 22 September 2006.

regimes and institutions and their ability to exercise power and authority effectively".[114]

Legitimacy, however, is hard to measure, since – domestically at least – it regularly appears fused with coercive power. From an empirical viewpoint, then, the international system presents a formidable laboratory for examining the legitimacy issue, precisely because of the absence of a central political enforcement agency.[115] Normative political and legal theory, however, likewise claims its share in the international legitimacy debate. The only common denominator is that of exploring the normative conditions of the exercise of authority beyond the state, in prescriptive or descriptive terms respectively.

While Franck seemed to ask fundamental questions about legitimacy in the international system in 1990, recent years have seen a remarkable increase in academic interest in this issue.[116] With regard to international legitimacy, the following approaches can be distinguished. A first strand of theory seeks to answer the question under which conditions governance (global/transnational governance) deserves to be called legitimate, employing a concept of legitimacy that draws on normative theories of democracy.[117]

Other literature is more empirically oriented and falls into the domains of both international relations[118] and international law.[119]

---

[114] Derick Brinkerhoff, "Organisational Legitimacy, Capacity and Capacity Development, Discussion Paper No. 58A", *European Centre for Development Policy Management*, 2005, available at http://www.ecdpm.org, last visited 22 September 2006, 1.

[115] Thomas Franck, *The Power of Legitimacy Among Nations*, 1990, at 20; Michael Zürn, "Global Governance and Legitimacy Problems", *Government and Opposition* 39 (2004), 260-287.

[116] "Currently there is hardly an essay on international or global governance that does not at least mention the issue of legitimacy." (Jens Steffek, "Why IR Need Legitimacy: A Rejoinder", *European Journal of International Relations* 10 (2004), 485-490.

[117] David Held, "The Transformation of Political Community: Rethinking Democracy in the Context of Globalisation", in: Ian Shapiro/Casiano Hacker-Cordon (eds.), *Democracy's Edges*, 1999, 84-111.

[118] Harold Koh, "Review Essay: Why Do Nations Obey International Law?", *Yale Law Journal* 106:8 (1997), 2599-2659; Ian Hurd, "Legitimacy and Authority in International Politics", *International Organization* 53 (1999), 379-408; Jens Steffek, "The Legitimation of International Governance: A Discourse Approach", *EJIL* 9 (1998), 249-275; Ian Clark, "Legitimacy in Global

As an object of scientific study, 'legitimacy' has long left behind its traditional domain of political science and philosophy to transcend to the realm of international law. This chapter intends to give an outline of the common legitimacy theory in international law with a view to conceptualizing the legitimacy of codes of conduct.

I. Legitimacy in International Law in a Nutshell

The Westphalian conception of international law was succinctly put forward by the Permanent Court of Justice in the Lotus case, holding that "[I]nternational law governs the relations between independent States. The rules binding upon States emanate from their own free will as expressed in conventions or by usages [...] in order to regulate the relations between these co-existing independent communities or with a view to the achievement of common aims."[120] State sovereignty, in this view, serves as the defining organizational principle of the international system. In keeping with this principle, states may accordingly incur international obligations only to the extent that they submit to them by virtue of consent. From the finding that the international legal order is premised on state consent, which in turn is a sovereign act, it follows that state sovereignty constitutes the traditional basis of international legitimacy.

This depiction of international law as based purely on state consent, however, no longer adequately portrays the actuality of contemporary international law.[121] The expanding global agenda of common aims in the course of globalisation, i.e. the need for instruments to address the pressing challenges of the world, has seen the proliferation of international institutions and regimes, paralleled by an increasing role of non-state actors on the international legal plane. The global governance debate has drawn public attention to the fact that states are ceding more

---

Order", *Review of International Studies* 29 (2003), 75-95; Id., *Legitimacy in International Society*, 2005.

[119] Franck, note 115; Daniel Bodansky, "The Legitimacy of International Governance: A Coming Challenge for International Environmental Law?", *AJIL* 93 (1999), 596-624.

[120] The SS. 'Lotus' (Fr. v. Tur.), 1927 PCIJ, (ser. A) No. 10, 18.

[121] Mattias Kumm, "The Legitimacy of International Law: A Constitutionalist Framework of Analysis", *EJIL* 15 (2004), 907-931.

and more competences to international organizations, and in turn have become dependent upon their rules and decisions. Importantly, however, the gravitation of decision-making authority from the national to the international level has been followed by a gradual erosion of the consensual underpinnings of international institutions.[122] The decoupling of state consent from international legal processes has given rise to questions of legitimacy that particularly hover about the so-called democratic deficit[123] of international institutions. The resulting strain on national political authority has been referred to as a crisis of governance, or a legitimacy crisis.[124] It appears that "the system of legitimation at the international level has not kept pace with perceived changes in the operation or location of political authority."[125]

Proposed solutions to enhance the perceived lack of international legitimacy draw heavily on domestic notions of democratic legitimacy.

1. The Unitarian Model of Legitimation[126]

In essence, international law continues to be a system of rules that rest on the consent of the very states to which they apply. To the extent that international law is founded on state consent, then, the latter legitimizes the former. With regard to democratically organized states, a conceptual shift in the location of legitimacy may be assumed. As in these states all public acts ought to be retraceable to the democratic will of the people ("chain of democratic legitimation"[127]), a two-level consent for interna-

122 Bodansky, note 119, at 596-597.

123 Acknowledged democratic deficits include the inscrutability of international decision-making, lack of stakeholder participation and accountability.

124 *See e.g.* Jürgen Habermas, *Legitimationsprobleme im Spätkapitalismus*, 1973 and William Connolly, "Introduction: Legitimacy and Modernity", in: id. (ed.), *Legitimacy and the State*, 1984, 1-19.

125 Steven Bernstein, "The Elusive Basis of Legitimacy in Global Governance: Three Conceptions", in: *The Institute on Globalisation and the Human Condition, Working Paper Series*, GHC 04/2 (2004), available at http://globalization.mcmaster.ca/wps/Bernstein.pdf, last visited 22 September 2006, 1.

126 Armin von Bogdandy, "Globalisation and Europe: How to Square Democracy, Globalisation, and International Law", *EJIL* 15 (2004), 885, 902.

127 Ernst-Wolfgang Böckenförde, "Mittelbare/repräsentative Demokratie als eigentliche Form der Demokratie", in: G. Müller et al. (eds), *Staatsorganisation und Staatsfunktionen im Wandel. Festschrift für Kurt Eichenberger zum 60. Geburtstag*, 1982, 301-328.

tional norms can be pictured: directly, through the role of states in the context of international norm creation (international legitimacy); indirectly, through the legitimizing effect of the state's popular will as warranted by the democratic principle (domestic legitimacy).

In this way, a correlation between state sovereignty and domestic legitimacy is established. Whereas states remain at the basis of the international system, the notion of democratic will, it has been claimed, is now the basis for legitimacy in international law.[128] In this view, the democratic legitimacy of international law can be enhanced by improving domestic democratic accountability – through better parliamentary control over the executive or referenda.

On the international level, democratic accountability may be enhanced through the establishment of international institutions of a parliamentary nature. However, as Franck notes, "[...] global forums and institutions, despite [the] evident 'democratic deficit', remain almost exclusively the domain of states attest to the continuing potency of the Vattelian idea. [...] A textbook solution to this would be world governance through directly elected representatives. Since this is not to happen, a second best approach is to ensure that those who speak in global discourse themselves represent democratically elected governments."[129]

The above solutions depart from the notion that international law is ultimately legitimized by the democratic will of the national electorate; accordingly, international legitimacy may be enhanced through a 'chain of democratic legitimation' that may transcend the domestic to reach the international level. The emphasis lies on the institutional realization of the democratic principle through elected bodies, and bestowing an "aura of legitimacy"[130] on public decision-making through lines of accountability.

---

128 Thomas Franck, "The Emerging Right to Democratic Governance", *AJIL* 86 (1992), 46-49.

129 Thomas Franck, *The Empowered Self: Law and Society in the Age of Individualism*, 1999.

130 David Held, *Democracy and the Global Order: From the Modern State to Cosmopolitan Governance*, 1995, 1.

2. *The Pluralist Model of Legitimation*[131]

In contrast with an understanding that ultimately credits the national *demos* with legitimizing international law, another way of enhancing international democratic legitimacy is to focus on the direct participation of those affected or of other civil actors in international law- or decision-making processes. Such borrowing of notions of public participation in democratic states, going beyond elections and referenda, responds both to the realization of the democratic principle and the detachment of international processes from national parliamentary control. Public participation, it is posited, can contribute to international legitimacy by giving stakeholders a sense of ownership in international legal and decision-making processes, and thereby prove a measure of accountability. In this view, the participation of NGOs, as exponents of international civil society represents a prime strategy for furthering the democratic principle on the international level.

3. *Deliberative Democracy*[132]

The legitimacy of international decision-making processes depends not only on their inclusiveness, but also on the quality of the mode by which decisions are achieved among the various actors. Rather than relying on bargaining and coercive means, reaching a reasoned consensus through deliberation ("discursive rationality") takes centre stage with proponents of deliberative democracy. The central concept of this theory is about involving the various stakeholders in a deliberative process

---

[131] von Bogdandy, note 126, at 903.

[132] A leading proponent of generating procedural legitimacy through deliberation based on "discursive rationality" is Habermas, according to whose discourse theory legitimacy rests on institutionalized procedures for open communication and collective reflection. In his view, the "procedures and presuppositions of justification are themselves now the legitimating grounds on which the validity of legitimation is based. The idea of an agreement that comes to pass among all parties, as free and equal, determines the procedural type of legitimacy in modern times." (Jürgen Habermas, *Communication and the Evolution of Society*, 1979, 185); *see* Held, note 130; James Bohman/William Regh, *Deliberative Democracy. Essays on Reason and Politics*, 1997; Jon Elster, *Deliberative Democracy*, 1998; Klaus Dieter Wolf, *Die neue Staatsräson – Zwischenstaatliche Kooperation als Demokratieproblem in der Weltgesellschaft*, 2000; Thomas Risse, "Global Governance and Communicative Action", *Government and Opposition* 39 (2004), 288-313.

of arguing and mutual persuasion about the normative validity of particular norms and standards. Importing notions of deliberative democracy to the international level, it is argued, constitutes a significant instrument for enhancing the democratic legitimacy of international decision-making processes.

4. Right Process

A somewhat different approach in defining legitimacy in terms of procedures is adopted by Franck's notion of right process in his influential book "The Power of Legitimacy Among Nations".[133] In his definition, legitimacy is "the property of a rule or rule-making institution which itself exerts a pull towards compliance on those addressed normatively because those addressed believe that the rule or institution has come into being and operates in accordance with generally accepted principles of *right process*."[134] Franck has identified four factors that combine together to influence a rule's perceived legitimacy: determinacy, symbolic validation, coherence and adherence of a rule to right process, i.e. its relation to a hierarchy of validating secondary rules governing the creation, interpretation and application of primary rules.[135]

II. Deficiencies of the Common Legitimacy Theory for Codes of Conduct

In their function as arbiters of standards, codes of conduct represent social steering mechanisms and thus purportedly fulfil a governance function. Legitimacy is a necessity for the viability of any governance scheme. Traditional forms of international governance are state-based, relying on hard law regimes and multilateral institutions. These regimes and institutions depend on the political authority of the consenting member states for their legitimacy. Codes of conduct, however, are non-binding instruments developed outside formal, state-centric pro-

---

[133] Franck, note 115 (emphasis in the original).

[134] Id., at 24.

[135] Id., at 183-194. Bodansky criticizes Franck's approach, arguing that "[d]espite initially defining legitimacy in terms of "right process", virtually none of his analysis focuses on such procedural issues such as transparency, deliberation, elections, voting and so forth." (Daniel Bodansky, see note 119, 601).

cesses of international rule-making and thus do not fall within the traditionally accepted sources in international law doctrine.

Both international public and private codes are established in the absence of democratic mechanisms of parliamentary consent. They are decoupled from direct state authority and thus lack the legitimacy offered by hard law. Intergovernmental codes like the OECD Guidelines and the ILO Tripartite Declaration, while voluntary and non-binding, nonetheless assume a measure of political authority derived from the indirect endorsement of the governments of the respective international organization's member states in the drafting process – thus reflecting the latter's expectations and values. The particular authority of the ILO Tripartite Declaration stems not only from the near universality of ILO state membership, but also from the fact of its tripartite elaboration, combining the interests of the governments, labour and employer organizations.

The legitimacy question gains particular salience with private codes of conduct, where governmental involvement is virtually non-existent. In the absence of state-based consensual underpinnings, notions of political legitimacy rooted in democratic theory, as elaborated above in the context of the *unitarian model of legitimation*, are of little use when attempting to legitimatize private codes of conduct. Other sources of legitimation hence need to be explored.

F. Specific Legitimacy Approach for Codes of Conduct

I. Governance Beyond the State

1. The Governance Challenge

"Governance", as we may understand it very broadly, relates to any form of creating and maintaining political order and providing common goods to a particular constituency.[136] The proper design of such governance within the framework of the nation-state, i.e. the establishment of a legitimate political order within a community, falls into the classic domain of political philosophy. With the rise of the nation-state, gov-

[136] Thomas Risse, *Transnational Governance and Legitimacy*, 2004, available at http://www.atasp.de/downloads/tn_governance_benz.pdf, last visited 22 September 2006, at 2 (referencing Oliver Williamson, *Markets and Hierarchies: Analysis and Anti-Trust*, 1975).

ernance has traditionally been viewed as the vested right and responsibility of the constituted political authority within the relevant territorial confines. Contrastingly, the regulation of matters within the political space *beyond* the state was thought of as falling within the incumbency of international law, the traditional conception of which was that of a body of rules primarily designed to guide the conduct of states *inter se.*

This construction of international law, however, gradually proved too narrow to infuse a modicum of order into the increasing complexities of modern life, but it was not until the second half of the last century, propelled by a profoundly changed political landscape after World War II and the forces of globalisation, that it underwent an extraordinary evolutionary process. The emergence of new regulatory issues led to an expansion in the functional scope of international law, which, in turn, meant a broadening of its original conception to encompass successively international institutions and even individuals. The evolution of the international human rights regime is a notable example of the expanded functional role of international law; more specifically, it stands as an early revelation *pars pro toto* of the invigorated role of international law as a governance device called upon against the background of the limitations of national regulation. The limitation of domestic regulatory power became all the more evident as the agenda of global challenges grew, owing in large part to the proliferation of interdependencies with the onset of modern globalisation.[137] From the environment to terrorism, from financial risk to local conflict, the 'global agenda' raises a vital question: how can the "authority of governance"[138] be brought to bear on these challenges? In particular, the integration of the values of

---

[137] The regulatory problematic faced by states amid a globalizing world is captured in what is commonly referred to as "denationalisation", a term meant to denote the emergence of an increasing incongruence between the transnational nature of regulatory problems and the limited reach of national governmental authority; see Michael Zürn, *Regieren jenseits des Nationalstaates. Globalisierung und Denationalisierung als Chance*, 1998, and Marianne Beisheim/ Sabine Dreher/Gregor Walter/Bernhard Zangl/Michael Zürn, *Im Zeitalter der Globalisierung? Thesen und Daten zur gesellschaftlichen und politischen Denationalisierung*, 1999; Oscar Schachter, "The Decline of the Nation-State and its Implications for International Law", *Columbia Journal of Transnational Law* 36 (1998), 7-23.

[138] James Rosenau, "Governance in a New Global Order", in: David Held/Anthony McGrew (eds.), *Governing Globalisation. Power, Authority and Global Governance*, 2002, 70.

economic growth, environmental stewardship and the protection of the social realms has become ever more pressing.

2. Codes of Conduct as a New Governance Mode

The need for accommodating regulatory exigencies, therefore, has led to much dynamism on the intergovernmental level, resulting in the establishment of international institutions and a sharp increase in the number of international regimes,[139] i.e. "social institutions consisting of agreed upon principles, norms, rules, procedures and programs that govern the interactions of actors in specific issue areas".[140] *Global governance,*[141] the generic term used to describe the governance of global affairs, thus refers to institutional and normative arrangements that reach beyond the state as the traditional regulating structure into the international arena. In this sense, it is "governance beyond the state"; in reference to the specific characteristics of the international structure it operates in, that is, the absence of a central political authority/government with a legitimate power monopoly, it may be termed "governance without government".[142]

Speaking of 'global governance' usually readily conveys the image of "large and arguably powerful intergovernmental institutions such as the World Trade Organization (WTO), the International Monetary Fund (IMF) and the United Nations and its affiliated agencies."[143] These insti-

---

[139] *See* Robert Keohane, *International Institutions and State Power: Essays in International Relations Theory*, 1989.

[140] Marc Levy/Oran Young/Michael Zürn, "The Study of International Regimes", *European Journal of International Relations* 1 (1995), 267-330.

[141] General treatments include: James Rosenau, "Governance in the Twenty-First Century", *Global Governance* 1 (1995), 13-43; Ernst-Otto Czempiel/ James Rosenau (eds.), *Governance Without Government: Order and Change in World Politics*, 1992; Craig Murphy, "Global Governance: Poorly Done and Poorly Understood", *International Affairs* 76 (2000), 789-803; Franz Nuscheler, "Global Governance, Development, and Peace", in: Paul Kennedy/ Dirk Messner/Franz Nuscheler (eds.), *Global Trends and Global Governance*, 2002, 156-183; *see also* Robert Keohane/Joseph Nye, "Governance in a Globalizing World", in: Robert Keohane (ed.), *Power and Governance in a Partially Globalized World*, 2002, 193-218; Rosenau, note 138, at 70-86.

[142] Czempiel/Rosenau, note 141.

[143] Steven Bernstein/Benjamin Cashore, "Non-State Global Governance: Is Forest Certification a Legitimate Alternative to a Global Forest Convention?",

tutions and their attendant regimes are established by states to solve collective action problems and manage interdependence, and for the most part rely ultimately on the authority of their state members.[144] Other regimes partaking in global governance include the Nuclear Non-Proliferation regime, the regime to prevent global climate change, and the various treaties of the international human rights architecture. They all form part of global "governance without government".

Significant objections, however, may be raised against this traditional mode of ordering global affairs. On the one hand, an often-voiced critique is aimed at the perceived lack of democratic legitimacy of international institutions and inter-state agreements. On the other hand, one might challenge the capacity of heavily legalised, intergovernmental institutions and hard law interstate agreements to effectively address global problems.[145] Indeed, the inherited intergovernmental regime, normatively rigid and substantively fragmented, seems improperly designed to produce sustainable solutions to cope with the pressing needs of today's fast-paced, increasingly complex world – a world that is shaped not only by states, but also by non-state actors.

In view of the shortcomings of hard law regulations, new forms of rule setting have emerged that seek to more appropriately address the social and environmental challenges posed by economic globalisation. The issue of TNC regulation serves as an illustration. Given the fact that TNCs lack international personality and thus are a priori excluded from being direct rule addressees by international law, in the 1970s governments 'discovered' a new type of international instrument: voluntary codes of conduct setting out ethical standards of corporate practices, which, in a departure from traditional state-centric soft law, shifted the

---

in: John Kirton/Michael Trebilcock (eds.), *Hard Choices, Soft Law*, 2004, 33, 35.

144 Id.

145 David Held, "Cosmopolitanism: Ideas, Realities and Deficits", in: David Held/Anthony McGrew (eds.), *Governing Globalisation. Power, Authority and Global Governance*, 2002, 305-324; James Caporaso, "Democracy, Accountability, and Rights in Supranational Governance", in: Miles Kahler/David Lake (eds.), *Governance in a Global Economy. Political Authority in Transition*, 2003, 361-385; Robert Keohane/Joseph Nye, "Redefining Accountability for Global Governance", in: Miles Kahler/David Lake (eds.), *Governance in a Global Economy. Political Authority in Transition*, 2003, 386-411; Joseph S. Nye, "Globalisation's Democratic Deficit: How to Make International Institutions More Accountable", *Foreign Affairs* 80 (2001), 2-6.

spotlight of attention from the state to the international business community.

The international codes of conduct that were developed, i.e. the OECD Guidelines[146] and the ILO Tripartite Declaration,[147] however, met with only partial success. On the national level as well, the regulation of national and international commercial activity is fraught with difficulties. Policies of deregulation and non-intervention, regulatory competition and the impact of international agreements designed to ensure the free flow of goods and services, not least the transnational nature of commercial activity itself, have seemingly worked to diminish the capacity and willingness of national governments to regulate commercial activity, nationally and internationally, in the pursuit of the public good.

With the difficulty in effective regulation in the international arena, and the shift in the regulatory role of the public sector, *private* codes of conduct, taking the form of corporate self-regulation and more recently of multi-stakeholder initiatives, have emerged as *transnational regulatory norms*. Though of an informal, private nature, they perform a public function and thus can be classified as hybrid norms. The introduction of codes of conduct can be perceived of as a new, informal rule-setting phenomenon that, potentially, may provide meaningful contributions to *transnational governance*.

3. Specifics of Governance Beyond the State

In the international arena there is no supranational type of a "shadow of hierarchy" comparable to that within the nation-state. There is no global sovereign in the sense of a (world) state or other political institution above the state "with a legitimate monopoly over the use of force and the capacity of authoritative rule enforcement."[148] This implies that in the context of governance beyond the state, governance must primarily rely on non-hierarchical forms of steering.[149] Global governance can thus be characterized by the "*horizontal* mode of political consensus-seeking negotiation and deliberation instead of hierarchical subordina-

146 Note 41.

147 Note 37.

148 Risse, note 136, at 1.

149 Id., at 5.

tion."[150] Given the weakness of the enforcement mechanisms of public international law, in the international context the distinction between binding and non-binding norms is considerably attenuated. Besides, there is no world constituency, that is a global *demos,* in the name of which governance could take place. At best, "governance beyond the state relies on a rather "thin" layer of collective cosmopolitan identity of "world citizens"."[151] Rather, what we observe in the international sphere are primarily *functional* constituencies, the composition of which varies according to how affected their members are by specific issues.

From the above it follows that the non-bindingness of codes of conduct, in so far as they form part of trans-national governance, loses importance in the trans-national context; in any case, both global governance arrangements and codes of conduct depend on their acceptance by the addressees and constituencies concerned.

II. Legitimacy of Private Actor Arrangements

As has been elaborated, the issue concerning the regulation of international business conduct is spearheaded by voluntary codes of conduct developed by non-state actors and thus outside the conventional realm of international state relations. Private and non-binding as they are, these codes nevertheless perform a public function in putting forth ethical claims of good corporate practices. Normatively, codes make a claim to authority. This raises the question of legitimacy, as according to the traditional argument of political theory every claim to authority needs to be justified as legitimate. But what are the normative criteria for the legitimation of private self-regulation?

A natural starting point for exploring these normative criteria is to examine the legitimacy question on the traditional terrain of political science. It should be noted at the outset that legitimacy has a dual dimen-

---

150 Klaus Dieter Wolf, "Contextualizing Normative Standards for Legitimate Governance beyond the State", in: Jürgen Grote/Bernard Gbikpi (eds.), *Participatory Governance. Political and Societal Implications*, 2002, 35, 37; Renate Mayntz, "Common Goods and Governance", in: Adrienne Heartier (ed.), *Common Goods. Reinventing European and International Governance*, 2002, 15-27.

151 Risse, note 136, at 1.

sion. In a socio-empirical sense, legitimacy concerns the relationship between a regime's or institution's authority and those – individuals or states – subject to it, questioning whether the latter accepts the former. As a normative concept, legitimacy relates to the justifications of regime or institutional governance authority. The latter is of present interest.

At the national level, democratically constituted governments may lend legitimacy to private actors by authorizing them and their actions.[152] In the case of (private) transnational governance, the central role of the state is asserted in the argument that private authority exists only in so far as private sector actors are "empowered either explicitly or implicitly by governments and international organizations with the right to make decisions for others."[153] Public-policy scholars likewise uphold the centrality of the state in legitimating private authority.[154] According to Michael Howlett, "[T]ruly voluntary instruments are totally devoid of state involvement"[155] and are seen by him as "the product of negative public-policy decisions by which governments consciously choose to 'rely' on these measures."[156] In any case, besides aspects of political feasibility, delegating authority to private actors at the international level is a questionable undertaking, in view of the fact that international agreements themselves suffer from a democratic deficit. Further, there exists "no supranational authority that could delegate some of its power to private actors and oversee the functioning of private self-regulation."[157]

---

[152] Thomas Conzelmann, "The Potential and Limits of Governance by Private Codes of Conduct", Paper for Presentation at the ISA Annual Convention, Hawaii, 1-5 March 2005, at 6.

[153] Benjamin Cashore, "Legitimacy and the Privatization of Environmental Governance: How Non-State Market-Driven (NSMD) Governance Systems Gain Rule-Making Authority", *Governance: An International Journal of Policy, Administration, and Institution* 15 (2002), 503, 514 (quoting Claire Cutler/Virginia Haufler/Tony Porter, "Private Authority and International Affairs", in: C. Cutler/V. Haufler/T. Porter (eds.), *Private Authority and International Affairs*, 1999, 3, 19).

[154] Cashore, note 153, at 514.

[155] Id. (quoting Michael Howlett, "Complex Network Management and the Paradox of Modern Governance: A Taxonomy and Model of Procedural Policy Instrument Choice." Paper read at annual meeting of the Canadian Political Science Association, 6 June, University of Sheerbrooke, Sheerbrooke, PQ).

[156] Id.

[157] Conzelmann, note 152, at 6.

Rather than adamantly relying on state authority, a shift in perspective is useful, in the sense that self-governance is not "a favour handed down by public authorities", but instead "an inherent societal quality that greatly contributes to the governability of modern societies".[158] While formal authorization by way of delegation of competencies by the state or by interstate agreements is not feasible or is at least cast into serious doubt, what other normative criteria exist for the legitimation of private self-regulatory regimes?

One way of conceptualizing the legitimacy of private self-regulation is to focus on certain qualifications of the involved private actors themselves.[159] In this regard, drawing on the legitimacy theory propounded by organizational legitimacy is helpful. According to a much-cited definition by Suchman, organizational legitimacy "is a generalised perception or assumption that the actions of an entity are desirable, proper, or appropriate within some socially constructed system of norms, values, beliefs, and definitions."[160] In this view, legitimacy is socially constructed in that it reflects a congruence between the social values associated with or implied by organizational activities and the shared (or assumedly shared) normative beliefs of some collective audience. Underlying organizational legitimacy is a "process, legitimation, by which an organization seeks approval (or avoidance of sanction) from groups in society."[161] Legitimacy, in this respect, is an "operational resource [...] that organizations extract – often competitively – from their cultural environments and that they employ in pursuit of their goals."[162]

Moral legitimacy, or substantial authority, is accorded to an organization (e.g. corporation, NGO) by external audiences when its behaviour reflects socially acceptable norms, standards and values.[163] In so far as a

---

[158] Id. (citing Jan Kooiman, "Governance. A Social-Political Perspective", in: Jürgen Grote/Bernard Gbikpi (eds.), *Participatory Governance. Political and Societal Implications*, 2002, 71, 83).

[159] Claire Cutler/Virginia Haufler/Tony Porter, "Private Authority and International Affairs", in: id. (eds.), *Private Authority and International Affairs*, 1999, 18.

[160] Mark Suchman, "Managing Legitimacy: Strategic and Institutional Approaches", *Academy of Management Review* 20 (1995), 571, 574.

[161] Steve Kaplan/Robert Ruland, "Positive Theory, Rationality and Accounting Regulation", *Critical Perspectives on Accounting* 2 (1991), 361-374.

[162] Suchman, note 160, at 576.

[163] Id., at 579-582.

participant in private self-governance shows a credible commitment to generally accepted norms, its moral authority serves as a source of legitimation for the latter. The adoption of a (private) code of conduct, in this respect, signals a prima facie commitment of a company to adhere to commonly shared norms and values of ethical business conduct in the larger social environment in which it operates; from a managerial perspective, thus, codes of conduct contribute to a corporation's strategic quest for societal legitimation. The legitimacy of private self-governance may also result from the recognition of the expertise and problem-solving capacity of a private actor.

On the normative level, the legitimacy of private governance may be considered to rest on two pillars: 'input' and 'output' legitimacy.[164] Input legitimacy, for present purposes, we may generally define as the participatory quality of private governance. It implies that those concerned, i.e. the stakeholders, ought to have an input in the drafting processes leading to the adoption of a code of conduct. Output legitimacy refers to questions of effectiveness and efficiency.

But how can private transnational governance arrangements solve the dual problems of ensuring "input legitimacy" through participation of those concerned by the governance arrangements and of "output legitimacy" through effective and enhanced problem solving?

This debate has a long history, "starting with the first liberal thinkers on trans-national relations for whom trans-border interactions were an unproblematic ingredient of liberal democracy and a guarantee for peaceful international relations."[165] Insofar, however, as transnational governance structures involve private, i.e. non-state actors, this poses a problem in terms of democratic accountability: claims by these actors to act on behalf of the "common good" are to be taken with a "grain of salt" when it comes to democratic accountability and participation.[166]

The quest for remedies concerning the "democratic deficit" diagnosis with respect to the involvement of private actors, i.e. TNCs and stakeholders, in trans-national governance may draw on the positions put forward in the debate about the legitimacy problem in global governance. Increasing democratic participation ("input legitimacy) in international governance faces the problem that in the international realm there is no transnational "demos", no international public sphere as known

---

164 *See* Fritz Scharpf, *Regieren in Europa*, 1999.

165 Risse, note 6, at 269.

166 Id.

from the nation-state. Thus, it is postulated, a deficit in "input legitimacy" has to be counterbalanced by an increase in "output legitimacy", that is the effectiveness and problem-solving capacity of governance arrangements. But there are practical limits to this approach.

An alternative position focuses on the concept of "deliberative democracy" as a remedy to overcome the problems of democratic accountability (democratic deficit) of private governance mechanisms. It rests on the assumption that the legitimacy of private actor arrangements can be increased through the open exchange of arguments and deliberation with the stakeholder community. The deliberative approach might also, in turn, increase the problem-solving capacity of transnational governance schemes ("output legitimacy"). The concept of deliberative democracy offers a way to tackle the legitimacy problems of "governance beyond the state" since it does not rely on a collective identity in terms of a "global demos".

In the end, from a sociological view, the viability of codes depends on whether the relevant audiences, i.e. the stakeholders accept them as *appropriate* instruments of corporate responsibility. Procedures and structures that ensure stakeholder access and accountability to those affected by corporate activities are crucial in this regard, because norms of access and accountability increasingly reflect shared understandings of "right process" transnationally.[167]

III. Corporate Motives Behind Voluntary Codes of Conduct

Are voluntary codes of corporate conduct mere public relations tactics or do they have a genuine governance potential? The governance potential of codes depends on whether they are indeed observed in practice. Compliance issues are thus at the heart of the debate revolving around codes of conduct. This draws attention to the importance of understanding the conditions that motivate business actors to comply with the codes.

The starting point for studying corporate compliance behaviour is the company itself. It would be futile, however, to concentrate solely on the actor level since business operations are embedded in a specific milieu and thus are contingent on the relevant environmental conditions.[168]

---

[167] Bernstein/Cashore, note 143, at 41.

[168] Conzelmann, note 152, at 12.

Both the actor level and the level of structural business action are thus relevant.

Potentially, three generic motives might account for the compliance behaviour of an actor:[169] first, an actor may comply with a rule out of fear of a threatened sanction, i.e. rule enforcement through coercive action; second, rule compliance may be guided by a rational calculus in pursuit of self-interest; finally, rule compliance may be elicited by the power of truth or validity inherent in a norm, that is: by virtue of a normative belief of rectitude on the part of the actor concerned that a rule ought to be obeyed. In short, this latter steering mode operates by means of the norm's perceived 'legitimacy'.[170] From the above, thus, the three keywords for motivating an actor to obey a norm may be seen as: coercion, self-interest, and legitimacy.

As has been seen above, international and transnational governance alike operate in realms marked by the absence of traditional enforcement capacities associated with the state. To be sure, no modern state relies solely on hierarchical modes of social control backboned by the power monopoly, for domestic governance notably presupposes, as an "a priori" element, a basic (democratic) consent of the people. The main difference between governance beyond the state and domestic governance, however, is that the former has to rely *solely* on voluntary compliance through non-hierarchical steering modes.[171]

Barring the coercive element for rule enforcement, voluntary compliance in the context of transnational governance thus essentially draws on the two other motives of the aforementioned matrix: self-interest and legitimacy. These two sources of compliance form the conceptual framework for studying the compliance behaviour of private actors with voluntary standards as set out by codes of conduct. A crucial focus of attention, therefore, is the question of how these steering modes can be operationalized.

1. Economic Rationalism

If self-interest is the defining criterion influencing an actor's conduct, this means that an actor's choice of action can be manipulated towards code compliance by a certain configuration of incentives and disincen-

---

[169] *See* Hurd, note 118, at 379.

[170] *See* Hurd, note 118, at 381.

[171] Risse, note 136, at 5.

tives. Such manoeuvring rests on extrinsic factors that influence an actor's cost-benefit calculations. In other words, this mode of steering follows a logic of instrumental rationality as theorized by rational choice. In short: actors are seen as egoistic utility maximizers who conform to norms because compliance is perceived to be in their own interest.

As regards the general conduct of business actor orientation, traditional understandings of the modern investor-owned corporation have been dominated by the view that its primary purpose and social responsibility are simply to maximise profits. One would expect companies endorsing this management paradigm to define their social and ethical responsibilities narrowly, i.e. only within the boundaries of legal requirements.[172] One would expect, as Cragg writes, "that when companies with this management orientation went beyond their legal obligations, it would be for clearly defined public relations purposes governed by self-interest."[173]

The findings from studies of codes of conduct suggest that this is in fact the dominant attitude. Evidence is provided by statements like that of Francois Vincke, Secretary General of Pero Fina, who says in a recent discussion of the International Chamber of Commerce's campaign against bribery that "until recently, [...] corporate responsibility was dictated by the law, or to put in even simpler terms: the ethical code of a company was the criminal code".[174] A recent OECD report states that "[M]ost industrialized societies recognize that generating long-term economic profit is the corporation's primary objective. In the long run, the generation of economic profit to enhance shareholder value, through the pursuit of sustained competitive advantage, is necessary to attract the capital required for prudent growth and perpetuation."[175] The authors of the group acknowledge that ethics and ethics codes have a clear place in corporate governance the goal of which is profit maximization. They propose, however, that ethical values endorsed by a corporation must connect directly or indirectly to enhancing the bot-

---

[172] Wesley Cragg, "Ethics Codes: The Regulatory Norms of a Globalized Society?", in: Arend Soeteman (ed.), *Pluralism and Law*, 2001, 191, 200.

[173] Id.

[174] Cragg, note 172, at 201 (citing François Vincke/Fritz Heimann/Ron Katz, *Fighting Bribery: A Corporate Practices Manual, International Chamber of Commerce*, 1999, 15).

[175] Ira Millstein (Chairman), *Corporate Governance: Improving Competitiveness and Access to Capital in Global Markets, A Report to the OECD by the Business Advisory Group on Corporate Governance*, 1998, 27.

tom line. Nonetheless, almost all the codes developed over the past decade acknowledge either explicitly or implicitly an obligation to contribute to common public interests beyond simply maximizing shareholder wealth. How, then, does economic rationality relate to ethical commitments enshrined in voluntary codes?

One would easily be prone to argue that there is an inherent contradiction between economic rationality and the principle of corporate social responsibility: so far as voluntary self-regulation is subordinated to profit maximization, this would entail that business actors approach voluntary standards advancing the common good from a purely instrumental perspective. If this were generally the case, discussing the merits of voluntary codes as regulatory schemes would be futile. Being mere window dressing, they would be incapable of setting bounds to corporate conduct.

It can be argued, however, that this line of reasoning is too simplistic, for the national and transnational context in which businesses operate is too complex to be reduced to a pure market constellation in which only the avoidance of costs and the outwitting of competitors count. Corporations operate in a space populated by public actors, shareholders, consumers, and other stakeholders, civil society groups, and, last but not least, by other companies. All of these actors heed certain normative expectations relating to business conduct. Amid conditions of a normatively enriched environment, the argument goes, the very concept of "economic rationality" is changing its definitional scope. A more differentiated view of the rational logic guiding business actors is therefore needed.

Both public and private actors can incur costs that need to be taken into account.[176] The risks associated with binding national regulation, for example, count among the considerations that motivate business actors to adopt voluntary codes. While national regulations are founded on the principle of territoriality and thus are of limited effect on the global scale, they may well complicate the conditions for doing business in some markets and lead "to a complex and unwieldy regulatory situation at the global level."[177] In the context of increased consumer awareness and sensibility, the opportunities associated with making profits by producing for ecologically and socially "aware" consumers can be attractive incentives for ethically oriented investors. Most importantly,

---

[176] Conzelmann, note 152, at 13-14.

[177] Id., at 14.

however, corporations have to take into account the normative expectations of the consumer community and of civil society in general. Aired through the media or adverse campaigning of civil society groups, negative publicity in the wake of disclosed labour rights abuses or environmentally irresponsible corporate performance may result in a backlash of consumer demands and adversely affect a company's reputation. Given that a company's "good name" is an invaluable asset for its competitiveness, its protection is a major motive for the adoption of codes of conduct by the business sector.[178] The importance of civil society and consumer expectations has been stressed by the finding of a cross-sector study by OECD researchers that of the 246 codes surveyed a large number were installed in response to the concerns of the general public and were "designed to reassure the public that the company is acting responsibly in areas such as environment and labour relations."[179] Codes of conduct, therefore, are often seen as an instrument used by companies to forestall (and deflect) the attention of a critical public, and, in turn, to vitiate or even decrease calls for public regulation. Hence, it becomes understandable that the major trigger for companies or associations to enter into codes of conduct is the aim to ease and accommodate civil society stakeholders' demands.[180]

---

[178] The OECD survey of 246 codes found that the single most competitive advantage of the codes reviewed was to protect the company's reputation, see OECD, Expanded Review, *supra* note 92, 17 [Figure 14]; similarly, an Arthur Andersen survey (Arthur Andersen, *Ethical Concerns and Reputation Risk Management: A Study of Leading UK companies,* 2000) has shown that desire to protect or enhance business reputation is "the most common factor influencing the development of business ethics activities among major UK companies", particularly among "heavily branded" companies" (Kathryn Gordon,, "Rules for the Global Economy: Synergies between Voluntary and Binding Approaches", *Working Papers on International Investment* 1999/3 (last revised 2000), available at http://www.oecd.org/dataoecd/57/25/1922674.pdf, last visited 22 September 2006, 6).

[179] Gordon/Miyake, note 76, at 6.

[180] Economic considerations may also be served, albeit indirectly, by a code's potential effect of increasing the commitment of company staff, *see* OECD Expanded Review, note 178, at 20; employees, in fact, are not neutral actors, but "bring their own values and ethics to work with them (Gordon (2000), note 178, at 6) – codes, according to the Andersen survey (Andersen, note 178), can thus serve as an effective way of raising employee morale and loyalty. However, there exists also a range of other, more specific codes that are directed to employees and address questions of internal financial control and protection of shareholder value; while such codes are designed to ensure shareholder protec-

Reputational concerns may not be limited to an individual company, but extend to the whole of an industry and thus account for the rise in popularity of industry-wide codes of conduct. Often, criticism first levelled at an individual company may extend to the entire business sector, which in turn becomes subject to public pressure. If a single corporation fails to comply with certain normative expectations of the public regarding corporate performance, this may cast a shadow on the whole industry's performance, which, in turn, makes a strong case for developing a sector-wide standard that has the potential to evade the risks associated with adverse campaigning and public regulation. Since industry codes measure all members against a common benchmark, this also procures greater transparency regarding the industry performance. In addition, by creating a "level playing field", sector codes seek to tackle the "free rider"-problem.

2. *Acting out of a Normative Belief*

a) Concept

Another type of non-hierarchical social steering relies on the compliance pull that is elicited by an actor's perceived legitimacy of a norm. Legitimacy in this sense refers to the intrinsic authoritative quality of a norm as perceived by those normatively addressed. Such legitimacy may be the function of the substance of a norm or derive from beliefs in the validity of the procedure by which the norm was constituted. As Ian Hurd put it, "[w]hen an actor believes a rule is legitimate, compliance is no longer motivated by the simple fear of retribution, or by a calculation of self-interest, but instead by an internal sense of moral obligation [...]".[181] Voluntary compliance in this sense is based on a particular "logic of appropriateness".[182]

As seen previously, corporations are guided in their adoption of voluntary codes primarily by enlightened self-interest. How then do business actors come to accept a new logic of appropriateness?

---

tion and compliance with securities and company law, other codes respond to litigation risks related to non-compliance with competition and environmental law (Gordon/Miyake (1999), note 76, at 6).

181 Hurd, note 118, at 387.

182 Conzelmann, note 152, at 16 (referring to James March/Johan Olsen, "The New Institutionalism. Organizational Factors in Political Life", *The American Political Science Review* 78 (1984), 734-749).

b) The "Deliberative" Approach[183]

The answer to that question relies on challenging the different actors' value perceptions by involving the actors in a process of deliberation about the validity of particular norms and standards. The underlying mechanism at work here involves learning and persuasion based on arguing. This, however, presupposes a disposition on the part of the discourse participants to be persuaded by the better argument. Where such argumentative rationality prevails, actors are not in pursuit of attaining their fixed preferences, but aim to challenge and justify their inherent claims to validity, and are indeed prepared to modify their set of interests in light of the better argument.

As corporations operate in a dynamic environment that is characterized by a web of interactive relations, learning processes through dialogue and deliberation are expected to take place. Through the sharing of experiences and of "best practice" within the business community itself and in the course of interaction between corporations and the stakeholder community, business actors may come to reflect their own practices and, eventually, be persuaded to change their preferences. While interactive relations are a general characteristic of the business environment itself, dialogue and learning can be specifically institutionalized – such as is the case with some multi-stakeholder initiatives.

To sum up: companies may embrace voluntary initiatives out of a "rationalist" logic, but this rationale may be supplanted in the course of events by another rationale relying on the inherent validity, i.e. the "legitimacy", of the code content. Where a corporation acts out of such normative persuasion, corporate ethics standards become important to it not because of related risk management, but because these standards *per se* become a point of orientation for corporate conduct. Compliance issues, then, are no longer subordinated to cost-benefit consideration, but are dealt with as a matter of course.

Companies may enter into a discourse over good corporate behaviour both with actors from the business community and with the larger set of stakeholders (employees, unions, environmental, human rights, labour advocacy groups). Where stakeholders are given a share in a company's decision-making processes regarding its external accountability, this at least partially responds to the principle of congruence between those who shape corporate governance and those who are affected by it.

---

[183] For references *see* note 132.

At the same time, stakeholder participation serves to enhance the 'input' legitimacy of corporate actors.

Deliberation and arguing between the business and stakeholder communities thus fulfil the two-fold function of increasing voluntary corporate compliance with codes of conduct and enhancing the input legitimacy of corporate governance.

c) Illustrations

In what follows, the deliberative approach will be illustrated by two examples of voluntary initiatives: the Global Compact and Accountability 1000. Both arrangements rely on learning processes by means of stakeholder dialogue.

aa) Global Compact

The Global Compact is a United Nations initiative called into life at the instigation of United Nations Secretary-General Kofi Annan. In an address to the World Economic Forum on 31 January 1999[184] Annan challenged the business sector to engage in partnership with international labour and NGOs, with a voluntary international initiative – the Global Compact – to promote good corporate practices by adhering to universal environmental and social principles;[185] these are drawn from the Universal Declaration on Human Rights,[186] the ILO 1998 Declaration

---

184 Secretary-General Kofi Annan, Address at the World Economic Forum in Davos, Switzerland (Jan. 31, 1999), U.N. Doc. SG/SM/6881 (1999).

185 The principles and other information about the Global compact may be found at http://www.unglobalcompact.org: Principles 1 and 2 deal with the protection of international human rights by requiring corporations to ensure that they are not complicit in human rights abuses. Principles 3 to 6 concern labour rights, calling for the elimination of child labour practices and discrimination in the workplace, as well as guaranteeing the freedom of association. Principles 7 to 9 encourage measures aimed at protecting the environment, such as developing environmentally friendly technologies. While there were initially only nine principles, at the Global Compact Leaders Summit in New York (June 2004) the tenth principle on working against corruption was added

186 Universal Declaration of Human Rights, G.A. Res. 217A (III), U.N. Doc A/810 at 71 (1948).

on Fundamental Principles and Rights at Work,[187] the Rio Declaration on Environment and Development,[188] and the UN Convention Against Corruption.[189] With 2,900 participants and other stakeholders from 90 countries, the Global Compact is the world's largest voluntary corporate citizenship initiative.

The Global Compact seeks to advance responsible corporate citizenship so that the business sector – in partnership with other social actors – can be part of the solution to the challenges of globalisation and further the vision of a more sustainable and inclusive global economy. A company initiates participation by having its chief executive officer send a letter to the UN Secretary-General expressing support for the Global Compact, whereupon that company is expected to implement its principles so that they become part of its culture and day-to-day operations. Further, a company is expected to publicly advocate the Global Compact and to publish in its annual report (or similar public venues) a description of the ways in which it is supporting the Global Compact.[190] The progress of participating companies is reported on annually on the Global Compact website.[191]

The Global Compact is not a regulatory instrument – it does not provide for the monitoring and enforcement of company compliance. Rather, to achieve its ends, it relies on *policy dialogues and learning processes* triggered among the various participants through the open sharing of company submissions whereby peer review and other stakeholder comment is invited. The Global Compact thus provides a learning forum in which good corporate practices are identified, dissemi-

---

[187] ILO, Declaration on Fundamental Principles and Rights at Work, June 18, 1998, 37 I.L.M. 1233 (1998).

[188] Rio Declaration on Environment and Development, June 14, 1992, U.N. Conference on Environment and Development, Doc. A/CONF.151/5/Rev. 1, 31 I.L.M. 874 (1992).

[189] United Nations Convention against Corruption, October 31, 2003, available at http://www.unodc.org/pdf/crime/convention_corruption/signing/Convention-e.pdf.

[190] This "Communication on Progress" is an important tool to demonstrate implementation through public accountability.

[191] *See* UN Global Compact, Frequently Asked Questions ('How Do Companies Participate in the Global Compact?'), available at http://www.unglobalcompact.org/About TheGC/faq.html, last visited 22 September 2006.

nated and promoted through the exchange of information, dialogue and deliberation.[192]

The design of the Global Compact thus purports to induce corporate change through a "logic of appropriateness" by means of deliberative processes. In that, the Global Compact represents a good example of a deliberative approach to governance.

bb) Accountability 1000

Accountability1000 (AA1000)[193] is an accountability standard that was established in 1999 by the UK-based Institute of Social and Ethical Accountability to provide guidance to an organization – a company or an NGO – on what constitutes good practice in accountability and performance management. It aims at improving the accountability and overall performance of organizations by increasing the quality of social and ethical accounting, auditing and reporting. Through training and stakeholder dialogue, companies are encouraged to define goals, measure progress made against these targets, audit and report on performance and develop feedback mechanisms. The process of engagement with stakeholders is at the heart of AA1000. Through stakeholder dialogue, AA1000 aims to support organizational learning and "overall performance (social and ethical, and indirectly environmental and economic) in progress towards sustainable development." Benefiting from stakeholder participation through learning processes is the underlying motif of AA1000.[194]

---

[192] John Gerard Ruggie, "The Global Compact as Learning Network", *Global Governance* 7 (2001), 371-378.

[193] Extensive information on the AA1000 Framework is available at http://www.accountability.org.uk. Particularly, an overview on the AA1000 Framework is provided at http://www.accountability21.net, last visited 22 September 2006.

[194] http://www.ashridge.org.uk/Ashridge/anonymousTailoredPortals.nsf/Al l/1FCD404BB014F5AE80256F470032C74B/$file/Aa1000.pdf#search=%22Ac countability%201000%22 (last visited 22/09/2006).

G. Monitoring Codes

So long as business actors approach the principle of corporate social responsibility from an instrumental, economically defined perspective, compliance with adopted codes of conduct is on a loose footing. Thus, especially in relation to a company's social and environmental performance, the establishment of effective systems for monitoring labour conditions in factories around the world is at the very heart of questions directed at the value and legitimacy of codes of conduct as instruments of corporate accountability.[195]

I. Internal Monitoring

The great number of monitoring systems in place are internal.[196] By definition, self-monitoring entrusts the monitoring task to the very company whose compliance behaviour ought to be verified; in other words, self-monitoring involves the paradox of entitling those to be monitored to monitor themselves. Nonetheless, a good argument can be made that a thorough internal monitoring process could actually make a difference to a company's ethical performance, if only it were willing to carry it through. Reliance on a company's good intentions, however, is precisely the problem, which relates to the fact that self-monitored results are hardly ever made public, thus providing little incentive for code compliance. Often, therefore, outside observers (in fact, shareholders as well) do not know whether company claims to code observance are genuine or mere public relations gestures. Troubling questions about the company's intention genuinely to address the compliance issue thus arise. In so far, the notion of allowing the "fox to

---

[195] Monitoring contributes significantly to determining whether or not factories/plants are in compliance with codes of conduct. In a 1996 study of garment shops in Los Angeles, the U.S. Department of Labour found that a shop is three times more likely to be in compliance with wage/hour laws if it is monitored. 27 % of monitored shops had some violations, while 64 % of non-monitored shops had violations (U.S. Department of Labour Study, September, 1996).

[196] *See* Michelle Leighton/Naomi Roht-Arriaza/Lyuba Zarsky, *Beyond Good Deeds: Case Studies and A New Policy Agenda for Corporate Accountability*, 2002, 50.

guard the hen-house"[197] acquires particular immediacy and invites criticisms emphasizing the disingenuity of voluntary codes, i.e. that such compliance systems allow business to "greenwash" themselves, but otherwise are of little significance in improving the environmental and social performance of corporations.[198]

A good illustration of this is the following case: in 1992, Guess Inc became the first American clothing manufacturer to enter into an agreement with the Department of Labor (DOL) whereby contractors would be monitored for compliance with labour standards, a fact that was hailed as a blueprint for corporate responsibility. However, the Guess monitoring programme proved a blatant failure, as in 1996 widespread continuing labour rights violations, including child labour, illegal industrial homework, unpaid overtime and sub-minimum wages in Guess contract shops were exposed.[199]

As illustrated, self-monitoring bears an inherent risk of conflict of interest and is thus prone to be conducted in a disingenuous way, if at all. As Dubinsky writes, it is "risky to allow manufacturers, who profit from lower labour costs, to control the policing of working conditions in their contractors."[200] The validity of internal monitoring, therefore, is cast into serious doubt.

---

[197] Internal monitoring is criticized because it "smells of the fox minding the chicken coop, and serious question arise regarding the extent to which code violations will be disclosed." (Sarah Cleveland, "Global Labour Rights and the Alien Tort Claims Act", *Texas Law Journal* 76 (1998), 1533); *see also* Mark Baker, "Private Codes of Corporate Conduct: Should the Fox Guard the Hen-house?", *University of Miami Inter-American Law Review* 24 (1993), 399-433; Laura Dubinsky, "The Fox Guarding the Chicken Coop: Garment Industry Monitoring in Los Angeles", in: Rhys Jenkins/Ruth Pearson/Gill Seyfang (eds.), *Corporate Responsibility and Labour Rights: Codes of Conduct in the Global Economy*, 2002, 160-171.

[198] "The most remarkable effect of internal monitoring may be to provide MNCs with a useful public relations device, enabling them to divert attention from any existing gap between what they say and what they do." (Emeka Duruigbo, *Multinational Corporations and International Law. Accountability and Compliance Issues in the Petroleum Industry*, 2003, 132, citing Robert Liubicic, "Corporate Codes of Conduct and Product Labelling Schemes: The Limits and Possibilities of Promoting International Labour Rights Through Private Initiatives", *Law and Policy in International Business* 30 (1998), 111, 157).

[199] *See* Dubinsky, note 197, at 160.

[200] Id., at 161.

II. Third-Party Monitoring

There is general agreement among labour rights advocates and increasingly within the business community itself that internal monitoring of company (and notably supplier) compliance with codes of conduct is inadequate; for codes to claim any legitimacy, therefore, it is deemed necessary to resort to some form of third-party external monitoring or verification. While increasingly efforts are being made to circumvent the shortcomings of internal monitoring by mandating third-party monitors to conduct audits and compliance verification, disagreement persists as to the appropriate form of such third-party monitoring.

1. External Monitoring

While the external monitoring of codes does – prima facie – confer a higher measure of credibility by removing the monitoring function from the discretion of the company itself, here too empirical evidence points to serious credibility problems, which are associated with the rapid expansion of a social auditing industry led by large private sector auditing firms. First, doubts may be raised about the competence of these firms engaging in social auditing services, which require special skills and expertise. Second, there may be an inherent conflict of interest if the auditing firm is paid by their own clients to monitor their social and environmental performance. As Mamic stresses, "research has revealed that auditors may hesitate to present truly damaging information, based on a desire to maintain good business relations and receive future work from the client. Further, the question of competence and qualification of the auditor is a critical issue."[201] Accordingly, even some of the more respected initiatives, such as SA8000 and FLA, under which the companies themselves choose and hire the external social auditors from among a list of accredited certification bodies, are faced with criticism relating to the deficiencies of their monitoring systems.

As the world's largest private monitor of labour and environmental practices, PricewaterhouseCoopers (PwC) has taken the lead in this emergent non-financial auditing industry. In view of the fact that PwC is leading the development of corporate monitoring systems, one would expect its auditing procedures to reflect a high standard of professionalism. A strong critique of PwC's monitoring practices – with regard to

---

[201] Ivanka Mamic, see note 56, at 59.

two instances of factory audits[202] – however, has been delivered by O'Rourke.[203] In her analysis, she highlights a wide range of flaws related to the PwC's auditing process:

workers' voices had not received due regard – rather, instead of adequately involving the workforce as a crucial non-management source of information, there was a general bias towards management. Thus, as O'Rourke noted, the PwC monitoring "failed to protect against the major challenge of evaluating factory conditions", i.e. access to reliable information on normal, everyday conditions.[204] Information, for instance, was gathered on site primarily from managers rather than workers,[205] and no pre-visit information had been collected from workers. Worker interviews were also problematic. Significantly, the PwC audits failed to seriously address the challenge of obtaining accurate information from worker interviews: poor implementation of the questionnaire[206] was compounded by the failure to establish a context in which sensitive issues could be discussed. Other insufficiencies include PwC's failure to adequately assess restraints on freedom of association.

This illustration serves to show that external monitoring through auditing firms is, at the least, not without its flaws. While in other cases external audits of this type may in fact produce valuable information on whether or not a company or its supplier is in compliance with a code, they largely rely on infrequent on-site inspections and may be flawed by a lack of human rights expertise or commitment to workers' rights and lack of information. Detractors go so far as to assert that the "service industry is driven by the logic of global corporate rule" and that ultimately codes and certifications of code conformance are not only inefficient, but detrimental to more truly responsible corporate behaviour.

---

202 The two factory sites were based in Shanghai, China and Seoul, Korea.

203 Dara O'Rourke, "Monitoring the Monitors: A Critique of Corporate Third-Party Labour Monitoring", in: Rhys Jenkins et al. (eds.), note 197, 196-208.

204 Id., at 202.

205 In one instance, the managers were actually asked to enter the data on wages and hours into the PwC spreadsheet.

206 According to O'Rourke, many questions were skipped during the interviews. In one instance, the auditor omitted the sections on freedom of association and collective bargaining, and often skipped questions on discrimination, forced labour and child labour.

2. *Independent Monitoring*

The credibility of a monitoring exercise can be enhanced by the direct involvement of workers, and if the monitoring task is carried out by local organizations familiar with the living and working conditions in the country in question. Such an approach has been the object of several alternative monitoring models that have emerged in recent years in Central America. Companies such as Gap and Liz Claiborne are contracting local independent monitoring groups in countries like El Salvador and Guatemala.[207] The Independent Monitoring Group of El Salvador (IMGES), for instance, consists of respected local religious, human rights and labour rights organizations: representatives of the Secretariat of the Archdiocese of San Salvador, Tutela Legal (the Human Rights Office of the Archdiocese of San Salvador), the Human Rights Institute of the University of Central America and the Center for Labour Studies, a labour research organization.

The IMGES provides credibility to the monitoring process, and, conversely, to the Gap's code of conduct: on the one hand, its members are rooted in the communities where the factories are located and they are accountable to those communities, not to the company. On the other hand, the IMGES consists of respected non-governmental organizations with specific expertise on human and labour rights; significantly, they are familiar with the local social, cultural and legal context, and enjoy the trust of the workers.

Monitor independence is crucial for the validity of the compliance report. From a stakeholder's perspective, the results of verification procedures of a company's code compliance are simply more credible when coming from a source independent of the company's control. To this extent, independent monitoring adds legitimacy to the relevant company code.

---

[207] Marina Prieto/Angela Hadjipaternas/Jane Turner, "The Potential of Codes as Part of Women's Organizations' Strategies for Promoting the Rights of Women Workers: A Central America Perspective", in: Jenkins et al (eds.), note 197, 146, 155.

III. Monitoring System Profiles of Multi-stakeholder Initiatives

1. Social Accountability 8000 (SA8000)

A fairly thorough attempt at improving labour conditions is marked by the "Social Accountability 8000" (SA8000) standard. Modelled on business certification standards developed through the International Organization for Standardization, particularly the quality control standard ISO 9000, it was established in 1997 by the Council on Economic Priorities Accreditation Agency (CEPAA) with the aim of providing a cross-industry standard for workplace conditions and a verification and certification system. In 2000, CEPAA was renamed Social Accountability International (SAI). It is a global system that helps manage the process of attaining and verifying facility-level conformance to the SA8000 standard through independent, accredited auditing and public reporting.

SAI convenes multiple stakeholders – companies, NGOs, and trade unions – to promote understanding and implementation of SA8000 standards worldwide. The SA8000 is based on the ILO Conventions and key human rights instruments. Its standards cover child labour, forced labour, occupational health and safety, compensation, working hours, discrimination, disciplinary practices, freedom of association and the right to bargain collectively, and "management systems".

At the heart of the SAI system is the SA8000 certification of compliance at the facility level and assistance for companies seeking to improve the social performance of their operations and those of their supply chains. The SA8000 implementation options are as follows:

Certification. For credible verification of SA8000 implementation, SAI places a premium on third party monitoring through accredited certification bodies.[208] Companies may seek certification of individual manufacturing facilities by these external auditors. As certification of SA8000 conformance is not issued to the company as such, but at the facility level, compliance guarantees apply locally.[209]

---

[208] For relevant information, *see* the SAI homepage at http://www.sa-intl.org. So far, there are 12 SAI-accredited certification auditors: ALGI, BSI, BVQI, CISE, CSCC, DNV, Intertek, SGS-ICS, TUV Asia Pacific, TÜV Rheinland Hong Kong, UL.

[209] As of December 2005, a total of 881 factories and facilities had obtained SA8000 certification, *see* http://www.sa-intl.org.

Corporate Involvement Programme (CIP). Retailers and companies combining production and selling that commit to steering their facilities and those of their suppliers towards an SA8000 standard may join SAI's Corporate Involvement Programme (CIP) as "Signatories". Those simply wishing to investigate SA8000 may join the programme as "Explorers". The CIP includes training courses for managers, suppliers and workers, technical assistance for managing audits, and SAI-verified reports. SA8000 Signatories promote SA8000 certification in some or all of their supply chain facilities.[210]

Over time, the SA8000 standard has been extended to include not only manufacturing industries, but also agriculture and extractive industries. In that, it is a cross-industry standard. Although there are provisions for and recommendations to subcontractors, these do not constitute an enforced or enforceable part of a company's agreement with SAI.

The accredited auditors prepare a report and issue a statement of "conformance" or "non-conformance" with a view to certification. The audit reports go to the companies and to SAI. Other parties can receive them only after signing a confidentiality agreement with the company management and the external auditor.

The SAI issues a public list of certified facilities.[211] Signatories are required to disclose annually the number of their certified suppliers and applicants for certification as well as the approximate number of their suppliers.

2. *Ethical Trading Initiative (ETI)*

The Ethical Trading Initiative (ETI) is an alliance of companies, NGOs and trade unions working to improve labour conditions in the global supply chains that produce goods for the UK market. The ETI approach is premised on the notion that understanding how to overcome the difficulties in implementing internationally agreed-upon labour standards along supply chains can be achieved through a collaborative approach involving business and civil society.

---

[210] As of April 2006, signatory members of the CIP are: Four-D Mgmt Consulting, Charles Vögele, Cutter & Buck, Dole Food, Eileen Fisher, Otto Versand, Solidaridad, Synergies Worldwide, Tex Line and Toys "R" Us.

[211] The SAI issues a public list of certified facilities. As of December 2005, 881 facilities had obtained SA800 certification, *see* http://www.sa-intl.org.

The ETI functions on the principle of incorporating internationally accepted labour standards into codes of labour practice as set out in the ETI Base Code. Corporate members agree to promote and observe the terms of the Base Code in their supply chains and are expected to collaborate with NGOs and trade unions as well as their suppliers with a view to identifying the most effective approaches to making codes of conduct a credible social accountability tool, particularly with regard to monitoring and verification.

Unlike the approach adopted by SAI, ETI does not certify good performance or offer consulting services. Rather, the ETI approach follows the principle of continuous improvement, portraying itself as a learning forum promoting good practice, sharing learning with members and the public, as well as measuring the impact on the lives of the workers of implementing the ETI Base Code.

Although supply chain monitoring is part of a member company's commitment to ETI, this does not constitute an "enforced and enforceable part of the agreement" between the company and the supplier. Though monitoring remains imperfect, the increasing number of auditing programmes is cause for optimism. While individual members are following their own approaches (ranging from in-house monitoring by technical advisors to the use of independent auditors), ETI conducts its own pilot projects designed to test monitoring and verification systems based on information exchange and related learning. The pilot projects are the main instruments for learning how to monitor supply chains, and they require the three caucuses of the tripartite alliance (companies, NGOs and trade unions) to work together.

One such example is the South Africa project (1998-2001), which aimed at inspecting labour practices in the wine industry of the Western Cape. The ETI members built relationships with wine producers, labour unions, NGOs and the Department of Labour in South Africa. The three rounds of inspections of six wine co-operatives and their farms were followed by improvements of labour conditions. As a result, the South African stakeholders decided to establish a local monitoring initiative ("Wine Industry Ethical Trade Association" (WIETA)).

Companies are expected to report progress to the ETI. Although they are not required to make their reports publicly available, most companies share them with the other ETI members of the stakeholder alliance.

3. Fair Labour Association (FLA)

The Fair Labour Association (FLA) is a multi-stakeholder coalition of companies, NGOs and colleges and universities established in 1998 as a successor body to the White House Apparel Industry Partnership, which had been initiated by the White House in 1996 to promote labour rights standards in the US and worldwide clothing industries.

The FLA Charter Agreement outlines an industry-wide code of conduct and monitoring system. Member companies must submit to regular internal monitoring; internal company monitoring must cover half of all applicable facilities in the first year and all of them in the second year. In addition, the FLA accredits third-party monitors to conduct independent external verification of code conformance in member companies' facilities as well as along the supply chains. After 2-3 years of satisfactory external monitoring results, the FLA accredits member companies' compliance programmes, which must be reviewed every two years.

The FLA's third-party complaint procedures enable third parties to report serious labour problems or patterns of non-compliance with the FLA code of conduct. The FLA provides for a subsequent process of remediation, after which the third party will be informed of the results.

All internal and external monitoring reports are provided to the FLA, which publishes annual overviews of the global compliance record of its participating companies on its website. The companies are required to provide a complete list of its applicable facilities to the FLA.

4. Worker Rights Consortium (WRC)

Established in 2000 on the initiative of the "United States Against Sweatshops" (USAS), the Worker Rights Consortium (WRC) aims to assist colleges and universities with the effective enforcement of their manufacturing codes of conduct; these are designed to ensure that factories that form part of the supply chain of companies producing goods under licence for US colleges and universities adhere to internationally accepted labour standards.

The WRC Code has been designed as a model code that is juxtaposed with the codes of conduct of the member universities. The WRC does not certify a company's conformance with the WRC code or a member university's code of conduct, nor does it establish a comprehensive independent verification system. In contrast to other monitoring approaches, the WRC does not resort to accrediting a third-party monitor to carry out factory investigations, but independent verification is conducted by the WRC itself. This verification is conducted in response to worker and third-party complaints, as well as on a proactive basis. Reports of factory investigations are made public on the WRC website and distributed to affiliate colleges and universities.

H. Beyond Legitimacy – A More Pragmatic Approach: Potential and Limits of Self-Regulatory Initiatives

I. Limitations

Management theories that emerged in the sixties and seventies forcefully argued that a corporation's sole obligation was to generate economic profit for the benefit of its owners or shareholders. As Milton Friedman put it: "The business of business is business". With the advance of globalisation and heightened concerns about the negative impacts of MNE activity, this managerial view has come to be increasingly challenged by global demands for corporate responsibility.[212]

The idea that corporations do in fact have responsibilities that go well beyond the simple maximisation of profit has found expression in a wealth of codes of conduct that define ethical standards of corporate practice. The hallmark of private codes is that they are *voluntary*, and for this, codes have been widely attacked as lacking in teeth to translate into practice. The voluntary and non-binding character of a code, however, does not *a priori* anticipate its ineffectiveness. In so far as the regulatory capacity of voluntary codes is cast into doubt by the argument that they cannot fall back on the enforcement capacities of the state, two preliminary caveats seem warranted.

First, in the context of "governance beyond the state", there is no "shadow of hierarchy" available either on which state actors can rely if they wish to influence the behaviour of other state or non-state actors, at least on a legal basis. Second, while it is true that in the context of the nation-state the enforcement of legal norms ultimately rests on the sanctioning power prerogative of the state, no modern legal and politi-

[212] "[C]orporations, because they are the dominant institution of the planet, must squarely face and address the social and environmental problems that afflict mankind." (Paul Hawken/William McDonough, "Seven Steps to Doing Good Business", in: Inc. (1993), 79, 80).

cal system, to be effective, can solely rely on coercion and the "shadow of hierarchy", for "the most stable support will derive from the conviction on the part of the member [of a political system] that it is *right and proper* for him"[213] (emphasis added) to obey the law. In the international arena, likewise, acceptance of and consent to norms by those subject to them are more important than enforceability.[214] In other words, norm effectiveness hinges on the perceived *legitimacy* by those subject to a particular norm.

It can be argued that norms are more likely to be honoured in compliance when those that are subject to them can claim involvement in the norm-creation process, which, in turn, may facilitate their *internalization*. However, problems arise when the adoption of codes of conduct does not lead to internalization and compliance, and enforcement mechanisms such as are characteristic of national hard law do not exist. In practice, this precisely is a major weakness of voluntary codes. In view of the great variety of codes of conduct, assessments of the real achievements are not without ambiguity. Generally, however, it is fair to say that despite the considerable publicity surrounding codes of conduct, their record of achievement, to date, has been relatively limited.

The 1990s have seen a remarkable explosion of company codes, many of which are little more than general statements of business ethics lacking specificity and any indication of the way in which they are to be implemented. Despite the great popularity of company codes, they generally appear to be of strictly limited influence on corporate behaviour and thus are often criticized as public relations instruments. In addition, many of the codes drawn up by NGOs (SA8000, ETI, FLA) have been adopted by a relatively small number of firms.

One category of practical shortcomings that limits the regulatory potential of corporate codes of conduct relates to the problem of *determinacy*. The language chosen in drafting a code may suggest the degree of likelihood that a firm will comply with the standards. Code language may be detailed and precise and suggest a high level of commitment to the standard, or general and vague and indicate a low level of commitment. Many codes, however, are marked by vague and non-operational standards. The lack of clarity and specificity leaves room for interpretation and entails that rules can easily be evaded. The blurring of the lines between "what is required and what is recommended, and between that

---

213 David Easton, *A Systems Analysis of Political Life*, 1965, 278.

214 *See* Kokott, note 96, at 34.

which employees are prohibited from doing and that which is merely discouraged, portends a scenario in which everything is acceptable."[215] Significantly, vague stipulations also make monitoring difficult. Detractors maintain that codes "tend to be limited to what the corporation already does well and ignore the problematic issues."[216] Codes issued by non-profit-making actors, namely the notable multi-stakeholder codes, have emerged precisely to address this weakness of corporate codes – however, the vast bulk of codes are issued by corporations themselves (48%[217]) or by business associations (37%[218]).

Another major limitation of codes relates to the lack or ineffectiveness of compliance mechanisms. Independent monitoring is crucial to ensure that codes do not simply remain rhetoric, but translate into practice in relation to a company's operations and those of its subcontractors. Of the 246 codes covered in the OECD inventory, however, a total of only 52 codes provided for independent (external) monitoring, and only 4 of 118 company codes included such provisions.[219] Similarly, a survey of 132 codes by Kolk et al. found that in 41% of the cases there was no specific mention of monitoring, and in a further 44% the monitoring systems provided for were internal.[220] A study by Ferguson in the United Kingdom found that none of the company codes surveyed made a clear commitment to systematic monitoring and independent verification. The reluctance of many firms to include independent monitoring to verify code compliance invites suspicion that they may be used more for public relations purposes than to constitute a genuine attempt at improving corporate performance. The growth of a social and environmental auditing and certification industry seems promising. How-

---

[215] Emeka Duruigbo, *Multinational Corporations and International Law. Accountability and Compliance Issues in the Petroleum Industry*, 2003, 133 (citing Rubin Seymour, "Trans-national Corporations and International Codes of Conduct", *American Journal of International Law and Policy* 10 (1995), 1286).

[216] Alain Lapointe/Corinne Gendron, "The Regulatory Limits of Corporate Codes of Conduct", *Les Cahiers de la Chaire, Working Paper* 19 (2003), 5, available at http://www.crsdd.uqam.ca/pdf/pdfCahiersRecherche/19-2003.pdf, last visited 22 September 2006.

[217] Codes of Corporate Conduct – Expanded Review of their Contents, Directorate for Financial, Fiscal and Enterprise Affairs, Working Papers On International Investment, No. 2001/6 (2001), 5.

[218] Id.

[219] OECD, Expanded Review, note 92, at 35 [Table 6].

[220] Kolk et al., "International Codes of Conduct", note 93, at 68.

ever, as seen above, a report by Dara O'Rourke on factory inspections in Asia by PricewaterhouseCoopers, the world's largest private monitor of labour and environmental practices, gives rise to serious concerns regarding the utility and credibility of external monitoring processes. With the exception of the Global Compact, most MSIs stress the need for independent monitoring.

Other limitations relate to the scope and extent of the codes. Many codes, as noted above, fail to cover even the ILO core labour standards, particularly in relation to freedom of association and collective bargaining, let alone to go beyond these core standards to include other aspects of labour conditions. The notable multi-stakeholder codes covered in this paper provide a more promising picture. The SA8000, the Ethical Trading Initiative, the Clean Clothes Campaign, the Global Compact and the Worker Rights Consortium all incorporate the ILO core labour standards related to prohibitions on child labour, discrimination in the workplace, the use of forced labour as well as the right to collective bargaining and freedom of association. Apart from the Global Compact, these initiatives also include explicit references to minimum or "living wages".

Many codes include provisions that apply to suppliers and subcontractors along the supply chain; they usually extend to immediate suppliers but do not always reach further down the supply chain. While some MSI schemes, especially in the clothing and sportswear sector, focus explicitly on standards and independent monitoring related to suppliers, others, including SA8000 and ETI, contain provisions and recommendations relating to suppliers and subcontractors which, however, do not constitute an enforced or enforceable part of a company's agreement to submit to a MSI code. As regards certification, suppliers and subcontractors are certified only at their request.

The relatively narrow sectoral focus of codes of conduct is also an issue. One of the striking characteristics of the recent growth of codes of conduct is their tendency to be concentrated in certain industry sectors where brand names and corporate image play an important role. Codes addressing labour issues are concentrated around the clothing, sportswear and toy sectors, whereas environmental codes focus on the chemical, forestry and mining industries; these are sectors that have particularly been the focus of northern NGO campaigns and the media spotlight. With regard to SA8000, it understands itself as a global standard to be applied to any industry sector, yet firms from only a limited number of sectors have pledged to adhere to it. As of December 2005, the greater number of SA8000 certified facilities belonged to either the toy or clothing sector.

Multi-stakeholder initiatives more sensibly address the challenges of making regulatory norms of corporate conduct work, as opposed to self-regulatory initiatives. In some respects, however, MSIs seem to follow a similar path as company codes, as the proliferation of the former has led to several competing base codes and monitoring systems being developed by different NGOs and multi-stakeholder groups. This is particularly so in the clothing and sportswear sectors; largely in response to northern consumer concerns about and civil society campaigns against sweatshops, various US initiatives have emerged, including: the Fair Labour Association (FLA), the Worker Rights Consortium (WRC), the Worldwide Responsible Apparel Production (WRAP) and SA8000, along with European schemes, notably the Ethical Trading Initiative (ETI) and Clean Clothes Campaign (CCC). The struggle between competing standards is thus cause for uncertainty.

II. Dangers

Codes are often aspirational in character. Owing to this, they may be conditioned on initial stakeholder goodwill and trust, i.e., that despite diverging rhetoric and deeds, a good-faith effort is made toward progress. If such trust is rewarded, it will often be extended further. If, however, business efforts are disingenuous, the disillusionment may result in a backlash. Many codes, especially those developed unilaterally by corporate actors, in fact have been seen simply as window-dressing exercises.

Critics of voluntary initiatives voice concern that these may take the pressure off government control of corporations or even supplant government regulation. While private codes are partially the result of the reduction in the regulatory role of the nation-state, one commentator notes "the codes as such have not led to the reduced role of the state."[221] To be sure, codes often refer to the observation of local legal standards as a code element. However, the very fact that the private code phe-

---

[221] Rhys Jenkins, "Corporate Codes of Conduct. Self-Regulation in a Global Economy", *Technology, Business and Society Programme Paper* no. 2, UNRISD, 2001, see note 50, available at http:// www.unrisd.org, last visited 22 September 2006, 30.

nomenon is a manifestation of the diminished role of the nation-state implies a shift in regulatory competences from the public to the private. In this respect, a significant concern is what one might consider the privatization of regulatory functions traditionally perceived to be performed by national and international public policy makers.

III. Potential

The regulation of international economic activity and that of its adversarial impacts on labour and the environment developed mostly on separate tracks. Given the flexibility of codes in terms of issue area coverage and their ability to provide a negotiating platform for the various stakeholders, they could become a useful tool for breaking down the historically conditioned but artificial separation between the regulation of economic, social and environmental interests.

With respect to the potential beneficial effects of private codes, one could argue in their favour by stressing that their non-binding nature may serve to lower the hurdles for code accession and bring companies to commit to ethical standards. Upon accession to a code, there is the potential that – through stakeholder dialogue and the psychological entrenchment of the corporate social responsibility debate – both an internal process of value change and an external process of peer and public (civil society, government) pressure is set in motion.

Despite their limitations, private codes do have the potential to provide positive benefits for stakeholders, and in fact have been causal in improving corporate responsibility. Through the introduction of codes of conduct, labour conditions for workers at the Mandarin factory in El Salvador were improved. Dismissed workers were reinstated and allowed to re-establish their union. Similar results were also witnessed at the Kimi garment factory in Honduras, where workers were also reinstated and allowed to unionize. Concrete benefits resulting from code adoption have also been reported in Nike's factories in Vietnam.

MSIs have arisen largely in response to the perceived weaknesses of corporate self-regulation, notably in relation to the incorporation of labour rights, the responsibilities of suppliers and provisions for independent monitoring. The inclusion of stakeholders lends the code added legitimacy. Beyond increasing the input legitimacy of the code, stakeholder participation may initiate learning processes that serve to enhance a company's compliance performance. MSIs have the potential for providing a platform for *dialogue* between the business sector and civil society organizations from which internationally shared values may emerge (Global Compact, Accountability 1000).

Voluntary codes of conduct could lay the foundation for future public initiatives at domestic and international levels. Where codes of conduct are seen to be followed in practice, the exhibition of good business practices may not just inspire other companies to follow suit, but codes may also serve as a catalyst for legally creative action. Domestic and international courts may enhance the power of codes of conduct by referring to them. Over time, codes of conduct may transform from soft law into hard law, on both the national and international levels. To that extent, they may be seen as stepping stones in the crystallization of law.

I. Conclusion

A vital question in our globalising times is how to bring the authority of governance to bear on the agenda of world affairs. International law exists to bring regulation to the life of international society, with states being the pristine entities of international rule making. With growing complexity of the state of international affairs as well as of the international system itself, as evidenced by the rise of a multiplicity of actors, the regulatory enterprise of state-centric international law, structured upon its traditional sources triad, was frequently perceived to be inadequate to cope with the modern problems of international relations and new global challenges. As a result, new forms of norm creation emerged that sought to respond more flexibly to the challenges of ordering international and trans-national relations.

This article focused on one feature of an emerging trans-national regime: codes of conduct – voluntary, non-binding instruments setting out standards and principles of behaviour. Typically, they relate to social and/or environmental issues and aim at improving the accountability of TNCs and their suppliers. Whereas earlier initiatives were driven by intergovernmental organizations, a plethora of non-state actor codes emerged from the 1990s on, created by corporations and NGOs.

While private codes of conduct have enjoyed remarkable popularity and continue to be a prominent part of the business landscape, ever since their inception they have been accompanied by criticism of their effectiveness, begging the question of how *in fact* they do contribute to *shaping* the business landscape in more ethical ways. Rule setting within the international arena has proved more difficult than within the state, and it has always been difficult to enforce agreed-upon rules. Nonetheless, the establishment of codes of conduct contributes to filling some of the international regulatory voids.

The pivotal point in the debate on codes of conduct concerns the issue of compliance mechanisms. Monitoring and sanctions, in fact, "remain the most important test for the seriousness of the codes' implementation."[222] For codes to be meaningful and credible, *independent monitoring*[223] of a company's compliance record is imperative. A large number of firms, however, are reluctant to submit to independent monitoring, and instead self-monitoring is prevalent, a fact that invokes the image of "the fox minding the chicken coop."

The initiation of private codes can be perceived as a contribution to transnational governance. However, due to the extant diverse multiplicity of codes, critics warn against placing too much faith in a fragmented system that yet remains in a developmental stage. However, codes of conduct do have a potential for governance provided that effective compliance mechanisms are in place. While many codes may be lacking in teeth, they nevertheless form part of the new rules of the game and contribute to the setting up of new regulatory institutions amid "an era of uncertainty regarding the shape of national and international regulatory regimes."[224]

Studies of codes indicate that they are most likely to be responsive to the real concerns of workers when they are designed as multi-stakeholder codes rather than developed unilaterally by companies or business associations. Codes should not be seen as carved into stone; rather, they should be conceived as a "process which facilitates stakeholder engagement, and which provides a platform for further advances in terms of improving the impact of big business on social and environmental conditions."[225] Codes open up a space for dialogue and learning and should rather be seen as a platform for political disputation

---

[222] Kolk et al., International Codes of Conduct, note 93, at 175.

[223] In a broad sense, 'independence' may simply be understood as an incongruence between the monitoring entity and the organization to be monitored (through external auditing firms); more specifically, the requirement of 'independence' may also be understood to signify financial independence between the external monitor and the corporation (or facility) in question.

[224] Kolk/van Tulder, note 9, at 19.

[225] Jenkins, note 9, at 29.

than as a solution to the governance challenge posed by economic globalisation. The limitations of codes are real, but they do have regulatory potential.

In the end, private voluntary codes rely on the goodwill of the adopting companies for effective implementation. The bottom line, Klein asserts, "is that corporate codes of conduct [...] are not democratically controlled laws. Not even the toughest self-imposed code can put the multinationals in the position of submitting to collective outside authority."[226]

Codes are hybrid norms; while private in nature, they fulfil a public function that raises the question of their legitimacy. In the normative sense, the question of legitimacy relates to the justification of their authority, as compared to the acceptance of this authority by those affected. The legitimacy concerns need to be seen against the background of the continuing debate over the reconfiguration of authority beyond the state. With respect to compliance, the legitimacy of voluntary codes gains added importance, precisely because codes of conduct "lack the traditional enforcement capacities associated with the sovereign state."[227]

Sourcing the legitimacy of private codes, however, implies a departure from the traditional legitimacy models of international law; as private codes are disconnected from state authority, invoking domestic notions of political legitimacy and looking at democratic processes within states or at the authority of states as a source of legitimacy is misleading. Generally, the legitimacy of governance rests on the two pillars of input and output legitimacy. Avenues relating to the enhancement of input legitimacy of private codes of conduct focus on expertise, stakeholder participation and deliberative democracy models. In a sociological sense, legitimacy rests on the shared acceptance by affected audiences, i.e. stakeholders, and on justificatory norms accepted by the latter.

Legitimacy of codes of conduct, in this connection, at its most basic means acceptance as appropriate by relevant audiences, i.e. the stakeholders. The perception of appropriateness, in turn, correlates with the participatory quality ('input legitimacy') and the perceived effectiveness ('output legitimacy') of the codes. However, a strict sociological notion of legitimacy "moves directly to addressing the empirical issue of the requirements for the acceptance of particular norms of governance (de-

---

226 Naomi Klein, *No Logo*, 2002, 437.

227 Bernstein/Cashore, note 143, at 33.

scriptive stance), while bypassing thorny philosophical questions of what non-state governance should ideally consist of" (normative stance), "or whether permitted at all."[228]

Enterprises operate in, and need acceptance by, society. To provide "the necessary framework conditions for the fundamental principles of social justice is the duty of political leadership"[229], i.e. the state. It is for the corporate sector to take the increased societal sensitivity for fundamental principles of social justice into account in their "own sphere of activities which they have the freedom of shaping directly."[230] Codes of conduct may serve to signal a congruence between corporate activities and societal values and expectations. In the final analysis, what is crucial is not the code, but the conduct.

[228] Id., at 41.

[229] Codes of Conduct. Position Paper of the International Organization of Employers, adopted by the IOE General Council, Geneva, 11 June 1999, available at http://www.ioe-emp.org, last visited 22 September 2006, 15.

[230] Id.

Codes of Conduct and the Legitimacy of International Law

Armin von Bogdandy

Fully agreeing with Helen Keller's paper[1] on codes of conduct this comment will develop a further argument in support of its conclusions. It will show that the legitimacy of such codes affects the legitimacy of international law. For that purpose it will address the legitimacy of international law in the light of its lacunae. At issue is whether a legitimate code of conduct can justify a gap in international law and the relevant omission by the international community. A gap in the broad meaning of this contribution exists either because the relevant international law does not apply, or because existing international law is not respected, or because there is no adequate regulation in international law.[2]

1. The legitimacy perspective on codes of conduct

Before addressing how the legitimacy of a code of conduct affects that of international law, the legitimacy perspective on codes of conduct needs to be deepened. Of all topics of this conference that on the legitimacy of codes of conduct is the most difficult. The difficulty results from the fact that legitimacy is genetically a public law issue and codes do not form part of public law. The legitimacy issue arises because an

---

1 H. Keller, "Codes of Conduct and their Implementation: the Question of Legitimacy", in this volume, 219 et seq.

2 On the issue of gaps in detail U. Fastenrath, *Lücken im Völkerrecht*, 1991, 15 *et seq*.

act is unilaterally binding; its bindingness does not require the consent of the addressee.[3] In fact, one can construe much of public law in liberal democracies as an exercise in legitimacy: by providing good reasons to accept the unilateral infringement of an individual's freedom. Accordingly, legitimacy appears to be a non-issue for any free exercise of one's own will: *volenti non fit iniuria.*[4] This is true for contracts (which may explain why it took so long for international law to discover the issue of legitimacy),[5] and even more so for non-binding self-commitments.[6]

This raises the question why this topic made it into this conference. A short answer is that this conference is a follow-up from the last one which dealt with developments in law-making beyond the state.[7] As Helen Keller rightly points out, codes are regulatory instruments beyond the state since they address transboundary activity. Moreover, codes can be effective tools for holding corporations accountable for their transboundary activities that affect human rights, labour rights and the environment.[8] For that reason, they need to be dealt with, although neither of an international nature nor binding.

---

3 See in detail on this issue the contributions by Rüdiger Wolfrum, p. 1 et seq., Robert Keohane, p. 25 et seq.

4 I. Kant, *Metaphysik der Sitten*, 1870, ed by J. H. von Kirchmann, § 46, 152.

5 The third world approach to international law has always questioned this understanding, B. S. Chimni, "An outline of a Marxist course on public international law", *Leiden Journal of International Law* 17 (2004), 1.

6 In that respect one can even doubt that codes are to be considered soft law. One should reserve that category for measures enacted by public institutions after a legally defined procedure; for a fitting concept of law see F. von Alemann, "Die Notwendigkeit eines formalen Rechtsbegriffes der Unionsrechtsordnung", *Der Staat* 3 (2006), 35.

7 R. Wolfrum/V. Röben (eds), *Developments of international law in treaty making*, 2005.

8 That corporate activity can severely affect such rights is shown by the cases brought under the US-American Alien Tort Statute which provides for federal jurisdiction over violations of international law. Examples of cases with corporate defendants are: *Wiwa v. Royal Dutch Petroleum Co.*, 226 F.3d 88, 105 (2nd Cir. 2000) (allegations of human rights violations); *Estate of Rodriguez v. Drummond Co.*, 256 F.Supp.2d 1250 (D.C.N.D. Alabama 2003) (allegations of labor rights violations); and *Flores v. Southern Peru Copper Co.*, 343 F.3d 140 (2nd. Cir. 2003) (allegations of environmental destruction).

At this point Helen might have given a short answer: codes are – to a limited extent – a functional equivalent to international law. This functional equivalent, however, raises no issues of legitimacy as long as it represents the free exercise of an enterprise's will. Helen, however, apart from providing a magnificent survey and systematization of codes, develops a genuine legitimacy perspective. She construes it by arguing – convincingly along the lines of Thomas Franck – that a legitimate code has a stronger "compliance pull". Accordingly, the issue of the legitimacy of codes is mainly presented as a way to increase their normativity.

I share that approach. Yet, the legitimacy issue of codes has a further dimension under which an additional argument to Helen's conclusions can be developed. My core argument is that the criteria she develops for legitimate codes – deliberative development, involvement of stakeholders, determinacy and effective compliance mechanisms – can serve as criteria to determine when it is legitimate, or perhaps even legal, to refrain from regulation through international law.

2. The legitimacy of international law in view of gaps and of international inaction

a. The legitimacy of codes of conduct and of international law

This argument draws on the discussion of the legitimacy of private law and individual behaviour under a municipal legal order. A strategy to develop a legitimacy perspective on the private exercise of freedom is to conceive of this freedom as provided for by the municipal legal order. The freedom of an individual or an enterprise is not a fact of nature, but depends on rules that provide for that autonomy, i.e. the private law of a society (or 'state', 'political collective' or 'legal community'); that is at least the public law view of private law.[9] If the exercise of that freedom

---

[9] This derived legitimacy of private law and contracts is contested; some construe freedom of contract as a fundamental right no public power can interfere with. Be that as it may, very few constitutions protect international economic activity, and those who do give public authorities much more leeway to curtail it than with respect to purely domestic activity; see in detail on the constitutional protection of transnational economic activity H. Hohmann, *Angemessene Außenhandelsfreiheit im Vergleich. Die Rechtspraxis der USA,*

impinges heavily on rights or interests of others, the legitimacy of those rules of the municipal legal order on which that freedom is based comes into question. In that light, a legitimacy perspective on private action unfolds: a society needs good arguments for why it allows a certain type of private action, why it empowers private actors to act freely. If such empowerment is conceived as illegitimate, the political institutions and eventually the people are called upon to change that, to curtail that freedom.

This type of request is to a large extent political, but there is a legal dimension, too. Most important is the understanding of fundamental rights as not only prohibiting direct infringement, but also requiring adequate protective legislation. If human rights, labour rights or even important environmental principles are seriously endangered by private action, there is a constitutional duty to regulate.[10]

At this point, a code of conduct, i.e. the voluntary, non-binding commitment of a powerful private actor not to endanger such positions, can provide the responsible political institutions with a political and even a legal justification to refrain from action, i.e. for the legitimacy or even the legality of inaction.[11] However, not just any code of conduct lends itself to such an argument. The code itself needs to be legitimate. The relevant criteria are those developed by Helen Keller.

Can the argument that there is a legal duty to protect individuals and that inaction needs to be justified be transposed to international law, international institutions and eventually the international community?[12] At first glance, that looks like silly utopian thinking in the way some

---

Deutschlands (inklusive der EG) und Japans zum Außenhandel und ihre Konstitutionalisierung, 2002; V. Epping, *Die Außenwirtschaftsfreiheit*, 1989.

[10] This dimension is well developed in many constitutional orders, but not in the US. For a reconstruction in the German tradition see T. Giegerich, *Privatwirkung der Grundrechte in den USA. Die State Action Doctrine des US Supreme Court und die Bürgerrechtsgesetzgebung des Bundes*, 1992.

[11] In the German legal order there are important examples of private schemes (though not strictly Codes of Conduct) by which public regulation is avoided, see M. Burgi, *Funktionale Privatisierung und Verwaltungshilfe*, 1999.

[12] There is another possibility for transposing this argument to the transnational plane: one can also ask whether the people of the home country of an enterprise have a responsibility towards individuals under other legal orders. Since this is an issue of comparative constitutional law and not international law, I leave this aspect aside.

scholars like to present global constitutionalism. But perhaps that thinking is not so silly after all.

If we start with international law, on a legal level a fundamental difference comes to the fore. As Helen Keller rightly points out, the contractual relations by which enterprises exercise their freedom are not part of international law. They are stipulated under municipal legal orders: their corporate law, labour law or contract law. So it appears that whatever transnational enterprises do, it is not within the ambit of responsibility of international law.

Yet, international law cannot wash its hands of this. Transboundary economic activity is hardly protected by domestic constitutional law.[13] The current freedom of enterprises to engage in transnational activity is to a large extent premised on international law: in particular the law of the WTO, the law of the international financial institutions, the law of investment protection, the law of the European Union and myriad free-trade agreements. In fact, for the major part of the world population, these are the visible parts of international law. To a considerable extent the municipal legal orders allow private transnational activity in order to live up to international obligations.[14] Consequently, challenging the legitimacy of a national provision which allows private activity which endangers other individuals' interests affects the international law which lies behind the domestic rule.

This challenge to the legitimacy of international law can be considered external. Yet, a further and internal challenge to the legitimacy of international law can be discerned at this point. Here, the issue of legal coherence, derided by some when applied to international law, shows its progressive potential. If one part of international law provides the legal framework for economic activity which endangers individuals, this is at odds with those parts of international law which aim at the protection of such interests, and which lay down duties to protect them.[15] Moreover, it is a common feature of legal systems that a legal order is not meant to protect activities which undercut its basic tenets: Art. 17

[13] See references in footnote 9.

[14] Put in other words, we are dealing here with the issue of legitimacy in multilevel systems.

[15] I. Winkelmann, "Responsibility to protect", in: R. Wolfrum et al. (eds), *Max-Planck Encyclopedia of Public International Law* (forthcoming); CESCR General comment 3, The nature of States parties obligations (Art. 2, par.1), 1990.

European Convention on Human Rights, Art. 5 ICCPR and Art. 18 German Constitution express this principle. If we conceive of international law as a whole which needs to live up to some requirements of coherence,[16] the issue needs to be addressed that some parts of the international legal order require domestic laws to provide for freedom the exercise of which might imperil fundamental principles of this international legal order.

The conclusion is that corporate transnational activity impinging on human or labour rights or the environment affects the legitimacy of international law. A lack of adequate international regulation can, however, be justified by the existence of legitimate codes. Helen Keller's standards therefore provide criteria not only for the legitimacy of codes, but also for the legitimacy of international law.

b. The legitimacy of codes of conduct and of international institutions and the international community

This line of argument is also of relevance for the legitimacy of international institutions and thinking about the international community. With respect to international institutions one has to ask whether they are adequate addressees of political, and perhaps even legal, claims based on the above-developed arguments. Put in other words: is it possible to construe the UN Secretary General's Global Compact initiative as a response to a duty incumbent upon him, and should he be concerned with Helen Keller's standards of legitimacy?

An affirmative answer to this question is not straightforward. Duties to respect human rights and labour rights as well as environmental duties are addressed to states. Yet, there are good reasons for assuming that international institutions are bound by them, too.[17] More tricky is the issue of competence: *ultra posse nemo obligatur*. International institutions

---

[16] The question whether this is the most appropriate reconstruction of international law will not be deepened at this point. In my understanding some coherence is an indispensable requirement of justice. On coherence see V. Bruns, "Völkerrecht als Rechtsordnung", *Zeitschrift für ausländisches öffentliches Recht und Völkerrecht*, 1 (1929), 1.

[17] See the contributions of W. E. Holder, G. Hafner and K. Wellens on the topic "Can International Organizations be Controlled? Accountability and Responsibility", in: American Society of International Law, *Proceedings of the 97th annual meeting* 97 (2003), 231.

are not in control of international law, as are domestic institutions of municipal law. There is no general regulatory power vested in international institutions to determine how transnational corporations treat their employees, their contractors or the environment. The only exception is the European Union, whose law, consequently, provides for an action for failure to act, Art. 232 EC.

And yet, many international institutions have some leeway in reacting to gaps in international law threatening its legitimacy. They may initiate a process leading to international instruments, they may spur a political initiative, such as the Global Compact, they may react by correspondingly interpreting the law, for example Art. XX GATT. The legitimacy of a body of law is an accepted element of its teleological interpretation. It is therefore incumbent on international institutions to consider the legitimacy of a code whenever they are confronted with a gap in international law and a code purporting to fill that regulatory gap. Helen Keller's standards should guide them.

Yet, those in control of international regulation are mostly the states. Since that control is exercised in the main not individually, but collectively, they are often conceived for that purpose as the 'international community of states'. Often, and in particular when it comes to requests for international action, such requests do not address the international community of states, but the international community *tout court*. Should the international community have an interest in legitimate codes?

Some might say that this is sloppy talk. This reproach, however, would be sloppy scholarship: it would show ignorance of the considerable scholarly effort that has gone into a reconstruction of international law as a common law of mankind, based on shared values enshrined in the principles of international law. There are political and even legal discourses where the international community is conceived of as a political collective with its own institutions, quite similar to a national government which provides the institutions for a 'people'. There are narratives of international law in which the states assume a *role* in a *play* written and directed by the international community, in which they are conceived of as agents of the international community.[18] At this point, we

[18] H. Kelsen, *Reine Rechtslehre*, 1934, 115 *et seq.*, 328; G. Scelle, *Le Pacte des Nations et sa liaison avec Le Traité de Paix*, 1919, 101 *et seq.*, 105 et seq.; id., 1 *Précis de droit des gens*, 1932, 188 *et seq.*; W. Schücking, "Die Organisation der Welt", in: W. van Calker (ed.), *Festschrift für Paul Laband*, 1908, 533; A. Verdross, *Die Verfassung der Völkerrechtsgemeinschaft*, 1926; C. W. Jenks,

can discuss to what extent it is meaningful to conceive of the international community as a political collective to which claims concerning gaps in international law can be addressed. Some will see this as a fake dreamt up by a few thousand individuals who make their living in international law. Others will argue that this perspective is the only one to save mankind.

In any event, one can hardly deny that the international community appears in a considerable number of discourses as an addressee of political and legal requests. And it is also hard to deny that some, although not all, countries want to present themselves as good citizens of that international community.[19] For such countries, the issue of the legitimacy of codes of conduct can reach a domestic and even a constitutional dimension because the legitimacy of international law is a domestic concern. In that light, a domestic government may lend support to such codes which support the legitimacy of international law. In order to find out how such codes should be construed, they should turn to Helen Keller's criteria.

3. Conclusion: Adding arguments to Helen Keller's requests

Summing up: corporate transnational activity which endangers human rights, labour rights or the environment affects the legitimacy of international law because international law is part of the legal framework which allows for such activity. A gap in adequate international regulation can be justified by legitimate codes of conduct supporting the legitimacy of international law. For that reason the issue is also of importance to international institutions as well as to states who wish to be good members, 'citizens', of the international community. Helen's stan-

---

The Common Law of Mankind, 1958; C. Tomuschat, "International Law: Ensuring the Survival of Mankind on the Eve of a New Century, General Course on Public International Law", *Recueil des cours* 281 (1999), 2001, 95, 161 *et seq.*

19 The relevant developments in Europe are synthesized in Art. I-3 para. 4 Treaty establishing a Constitution for Europe: "In its relations with the wider world, the Union shall (...) contribute to peace, security, the sustainable development of the Earth, solidarity and mutual respect among peoples, free and fair trade, eradication of poverty and the protection of human rights, in particular the rights of the child, as well as to the strict observance and the development of international law, including respect for the principles of the United Nations Charter."

dards therefore provide criteria not only for the legitimacy of a code, but also for judging the legitimacy of international law and international inaction.

The Concept of Legitimacy in International Law

Daniel Bodansky

The paper that I circulated for today's meeting built on an article that I wrote in the American Journal of International Law back in 1999. At that time, relatively little had been written about the issue of legitimacy by international lawyers, except for Tom Frank's pioneering book[1] and some more topical papers such as David Caron's paper analysing the legitimacy of the Security Council.[2] In the last decade, there has been an explosion of interest in the problem of international legitimacy – what one writer has called a veritable renaissance in international legitimacy talk.[3] This, I think, reflects the growing authority and importance of international institutions. When international institutions were relatively weak, legitimacy was not a pressing issue. But as they have become more influential, and as the need has grown for international institutions with greater authority to address collective problems such as climate change, this has prompted more questions about what will make such institutions legitimate.

Now, in my talk today, I will depart from my written paper, since much of what I said there is similar to what others have already said. In particular, I want to associate myself with the remarks yesterday by Rüdiger Wolfrum in opening the conference and also by Professor Keohane. Instead, in my remarks, I will try to react to some of the discussion that has occurred thus far and to raise some more general questions about legitimacy.

---

1 Thomas M. Franck, *The Power of Legitimacy among Nations,* 1990.

2 David D. Caron, "The Legitimacy of the Collective Authority of the Security Council," 87 *American Journal of International Law* 552 (1993).

3 Ian Clark, *Legitimacy in International Society,* 2005, at 12.

Now, to begin with, when I speak of legitimacy, I'm using the term in essentially the same way that Professors Wolfrum and Keohane did yesterday, namely, as relating to the justification and acceptance of political authority. This brings me to the first issue that I would like to discuss, the relationship between legitimacy and legality, which has been a subject of considerable discussion both yesterday and today. In my paper, I tried to explicate the concept of legitimacy by contrasting it with two other bases of governance: rational persuasion on the one hand and power on the other. I started by asking the question: Why might someone follow another's directive? – a decision of the WTO Appellate Body for example; or a decision by the Security Council pursuant to Chapter VII of the U.N. Charter; or a decision by the Montreal Protocol meeting of the parties to increase the stringency of the control measures for a particular ozone-depleting substance? One possible answer to this question is that the addressee of a decision is rationally persuaded that the decision is correct, based on whatever standard of correctness he or she chooses to apply. The losing side in a WTO dispute, for example, might be persuaded by the Appellate Body's reasoning about what the GATT requires. Or a country might be persuaded by the arguments made by other countries in the Security Council that sanctions are appropriate in a particular case. At the opposite end of the explanatory spectrum, an individual or state might comply with a directive not because it believes the directive is correct but because of some kind of pressure – because it fears the adverse consequences of not complying. In domestic litigation, for example, the losing side might comply with a court decision, even when it thinks it should have won the case, because it would be imprisoned or fined if it disobeys. Similarly, in a WTO dispute, even if the losing side thinks that the decision was incorrectly decided, it might comply with a WTO ruling because, if it doesn't, the other side can impose trade measures in response. In the 1980s, for example, Japan accepted the International Whaling Commission's moratorium on commercial whaling, not because it was persuaded that the moratorium was correct, but because the US threatened to impose trade sanctions against Japan if it did not go along.

Now, legitimacy, in my view, represents a third basis of compliance. An individual or state might comply with a directive, not because of the fear of sanctions or because it is rationally persuaded that the decision is correct, but rather because it accepts the decision-making process as legitimate. In contrast to rational persuasion, legitimacy involves the idea of deference. If an institution has the right to rule, then people should defer to its decisions even when they disagree with the substance of those decisions. But in contrast to compulsion (which also involves the notion of obedience), legitimacy has a normative quality. It represents not merely a reason for action, but a justification.

Now I continue to believe that understanding legitimacy as a basis of compliance in these terms is illuminating. But the discussion over the last couple of days has made me realize that it can also give rise to a misimpression that legitimacy is the same thing as legality, since both represent content-neutral bases of compliance. So it is worth exploring in more detail the relationship of legitimacy and legality. Now of course, law and legitimacy have a long and close relationship. Indeed, the Latin root of legitimacy means lawful, and the Oxford English Dictionary continues to define legitimacy as "the condition of being in accordance with law or principle". This connection is particularly apparent in the emphasis of several speakers yesterday that international institutions need to stay within their mandates. Legality plays a vital role in ensuring that the exercise of authority by an international institution can be linked back to its treaty basis – its basis, that is, in state consent. And, of course, if we take a sufficiently expansive view of law, much of the conceptual work that legitimacy does might be incorporated into the concept of law itself. This is the approach that was suggested by Jutta Brunnée in her comment earlier today. For her, the very concept of law incorporates many of the factors that we think help provide legitimacy.

But if we take a narrow or more positivist view of law, then legitimacy is a much broader concept than legality, in at least three ways:

First, although legality provides one possible justification for the exercise of authority, it is by no means the only criteria that we apply in assessing how institutions exercise their authority. That is why it is a meaningful statement to say that Kosovo was illegal but still legitimate – because the criteria of legitimacy and legality are not exactly the same.

Second, the exercise of authority can exist outside of a legal system. And these non-legal exercises of authority can also raise issues of legitimacy. When I tell my six-year-old daughter, for example, to brush her teeth or to stop yelling, she often replies: That's just what you say; that's not the law. Obviously, she is already a lawyer in training. And clearly she is right, brushing your teeth is not the law. But I am not trying to exercise legal authority, I'm exercising what might be called parental authority, which, even though non-legal, also raises issues of legitimacy. In this connection, let me mention one very small quibble I would have with Professor Rüdiger Wolfrum's excellent elaboration of the idea of legitimacy yesterday. Although I generally agree with his approach, I think that his emphasis on binding rules is too limited, a point to which I will return a little bit later in my talk. Authority can be exercised in many different ways, to different degrees. Although the UN Human Rights Commission for example lacks the authority to promulgate binding rules, its resolutions still exert some softer form of authority. Hence I think it makes sense to analyse the transition from the Human Rights Committee to the Human Rights Council at least partly in legitimacy terms. And as Professor Keller's very interesting presentation just now indicates, codes of conducts, although formally non-binding, nevertheless exercise de facto authority in a variety of ways and hence also raise issues of legitimacy.

Finally, legitimacy relates not simply to compliance, but to the justification of authority more generally. In establishing a new international institution or reforming an existing one, an important question is: How should institutions be designed in order to enhance their legitimacy? What should be the rules, for example, regarding participation, transparency and so forth? These questions cannot be answered in terms of legality because when we are creating a new institution, no legal rules yet exist. The issue of legitimacy must be addressed in other terms, for example in terms of the kinds of source-based, process-based or output-based factors that Professors Wolfrum and Keohane discussed yesterday.

This brings me to my second general point, which has to do with the relationship of legitimacy, not to legality, but to self-interest, an issue that Curt Bradley raised yesterday in one of his comments. Legitimacy is sometimes contrasted with self-interest as a basis of action. But in my paper, I argue that self-interest cross-cuts the distinction I am drawing between rational persuasion, power, and legitimacy. As Professor Keohane noted, one of the reasons why states might agree to subject themselves to the authority of an international institution, and consider its authority legitimate, is that they think that such institutions are in their self-interest. In fact I tend to agree with both Professors Keohane and Bradley that self-interest is not simply one among many reasons for the creation of international governance institutions, it is the principal reason. So in these cases, self-interest and legitimacy work in tandem. Indeed, one way of understanding the kind of legitimacy factors that both Professors Wolfrum and Keohane elaborated yesterday is that they help to ensure that institutions will exercise their authority in a manner that serves the interest of their creators and of their subjects.

But in my view, self-interest does not represent a complete account of legitimacy. The fact that, based on self-interest, we may need global governance institutions does not mean that any such institutions will necessarily be legitimate – unless we take a Hobbesean perspective, where the need for order is so over-riding that one should be willing to accept any kind of Leviathan, no matter what rules it applies.

My third point has to do with the distinction between social and normative legitimacy. It has often been observed, including by many here, that we can consider legitimacy from two perspectives: that of philosophy or political theory and that of sociology. One way to study legitimacy is from the perspective of philosophy – to think of legitimacy in normative terms. Here the issue is: what gives some institution or individuals the right to rule? Why does the WTO Dispute Settlement Body, for example, or the International Court of Justice, have the right to decide cases? Or why should the Security Council get to decide when the use of force is appropriate? But legitimacy, of course, also has a social dimension. Here, the question is, what do the relevant actors think about legitimacy? On what basis do they think that an institution or person has the right to rule? That was the issue with which Max Weber was concerned in his work on legitimacy and it is an issue that many contemporary writers continue to address. In contrast to normative legitimacy, which is an issue of philosophy and political theory, social legitimacy is a factual issue, an issue of social psychology and politics. And in principle, it can be studied empirically, for example through interviews and public opinion surveys, or by studying the claims that public authorities make in trying to justify their authority. In the international arena, a particular issue arises as to whether, in studying social legitimacy, we should focus on the views of states or of individuals or of the public more generally. When we speak of the legitimacy of the Security Council and the ICC for example, usually we are thinking about acceptance by states. But as the demonstrations against the WTO and the G-8 in places like Seattle illustrate, issues about the legitimacy of international institutions are now being raised by NGOs and individuals as well. And this illustrates one of the very important points that Professor Keohane made yesterday, namely that in considering social legitimacy we need to consider the social contract under which international institutions operate. As he notes, this social contact changes over time, leading to changes in the bases of social legitimacy.

Although the normative and the sociological perspectives on legitimacy are fundamentally different, much of the writing on legitimacy blends the two. Indeed, often it is difficult to distinguish which approach a particular author is taking. And this, I think, is also true of many of the comments that we have heard over the last couple of days here. I think this is exemplified by Professor Keohane's very interesting paper. On the one hand, the complex standard of legitimacy that he elaborates is heavily normative in orientation. At the same time, he thinks that it is grounded in social reality and that if it were operationalized, it would in fact enhance the effectiveness of international institutions. This blending of the normative and the sociological perspectives is characteristic of any theory that aims to be prescriptive. Prescription aims at a particular normative goal, but it must take into account present reality in order to achieve that goal. Now I think that Professor Keohane would be the first to agree that his paper is not empirical in nature – it does not try to show, empirically that his complex standard of legitimacy reflects the actual views of relevant actors. In my view, it is not self-evident that it does reflect social reality, that government officials or individuals in fact assess the legitimacy of international institutions in terms of the complex standard that he elaborates. Although Professor Keohane believes that his complex standard of legitimacy makes concessions to reality, rather than representing his normative ideal, his theory may still be far more ideal than the views held by relevant actors.

Let me make two very tentative observations in this regard about social legitimacy: The first is that the bases of social legitimacy may not be universal. They may differ between actors along a number of different lines. Governmental actors, for example, may have different views about legitimacy than members of civil society. They may put a much greater premium on sovereignty and consent, while civil society organizations may place much greater emphasis on participation and transparency. As a result, factors that may help to legitimise an institution in the eyes of non-state actors may help to delegitimise it in the eyes of state-actors. Attitudes about legitimacy may also differ along cultural grounds. For example, there may be differences between people (and government officials) in developing and developed countries in terms of their attitudes about legitimacy. So I think it is an open question whether a single standard of legitimacy, even a very complex and sophisticated one such as that proposed by Professor Keohane, will capture the different views about legitimacy of different audiences.

This bring me to a second point about social legitimacy, which I want to advance here in a very tentative way, namely, that the bases of normative and sociological legitimacy may be very different in nature. Normative theories such as the one elaborated by Professor Keohane generally take an *ex ante* perspective. They focus on the procedural requirements for legitimate authority – factors such as transparency and accountability. To the extent that they care about outputs, this is manifested not by looking at the actual outputs themselves, but rather by trying to elaborate procedures that will help produce good outcomes, factors such as expertise or participation or getting good information. But I think it is at least plausible to think that people's views on legitimacy tend to be much more *ex post* and *ad hoc* in nature. In assessing the legitimacy of an institution, people focus on its actual outputs: Does it produce just results? Does it produce greater economic welfare? And so forth. To the extent that an institution or decision-maker is producing good results, we tend to defer to its decisions. To the extent that it produces bad results, this tends to call into question whether the institution is entitled to deference. This may be one of the reasons why building the legitimacy of an institution is a slow and incremental process. Legitimacy cannot be created at once, it takes time to develop, because it takes time to develop a body of experience to evaluate whether an institution is producing good results. Deference to an institution develops gradually as the institution proves itself worthy of support.

My fourth general point is that legitimacy is among that class of concepts that we can define with more confidence negatively than positively. It is a little like the role of falsification in science. According to positivist theories of scientific method, we cannot verify theories, we can only falsify them. And I think the same may be true of legitimacy. It is difficult to establish that something is legitimate, but it is much easier to show that it is illegitimate. The kinds of factors that are bases of illegitimacy are widely agreed: bias, grossly unjust results, results for example that violate fundamental human rights. In several recent articles, Benedict Kingsbury, Nico Krisch,[4] and Dan Esty[5] have attempted to ground international legitimacy in various administrative law values. To a significant degree, these administrative law values can be understood as intended to protect against decisions being made for the wrong types of reasons. They are intended essentially to protect against illegitimacy. Understood in this way, these administrative law rules, in essence, represent necessary rather than sufficient conditions for legitimacy. They are necessary to ensure that a decision is not illegitimate, but they are not sufficient to ensure that it is legitimate.

My final point is that, in going forward, we need to think about the problem of legitimacy in a much more differentiated, contextual way.

---

[4] Benedict Kingsbury/Nico Krisch, "Global Governance and Global Administrative Law in the International Legal Order," 17 *EJIL* 1 (2006).

[5] Daniel C. Esty, "Good Governance at the Supranational Scale: Globalizing Administrative Law," 115 *Yale L.J.* 1490 (2006).

Much of the writing about legitimacy tries to elaborate some general theory of legitimacy. But not every exercise of authority requires the same degree of justification. What is required in order to legitimise an institution may vary depending on how much authority it is exercising, the kind of authority it is exercising, and the kinds of issues it is exercising authority over. And I think this is probably true from both the normative and the sociological perspectives. The greater the authority an institution exercises, for example, the greater the legitimacy concerns. The more one cedes control to an institution to make decisions, the greater the legitimacy that will be demanded of it. The extent of an institution's authority is a function of several factors. First, how binding are its decisions? An institution that can make binding rules obviously poses a greater issue of legitimacy than those that can only adopt resolutions or make recommendations. Second, how broad is its decision-making authority? Institutions with broad competence raise greater issues of legitimacy than those with narrowly specified competences. Finally, how removed is the decision-maker from those subjects to its authority? The greater the distance between ruler and governed, the greater the legitimacy concerns.

How we think about the issue of legitimacy also depends on the type of authority an institution is exercising. Institutions exercising different types of authority may need different bases of legitimacy; we may need different theories of legitimacy for legislation, adjudication and administration. In liberal democracies, legislation is legitimated on democratic grounds through voting rules that aggregate preferences. In contrast, adjudication is largely legitimated in process terms. Finally, administrative authority was originally legitimated in terms of the idea of delegation, which links administrative rule-making back to some kind of democratic basis. The demise, at least in the US, of the non-delegation doctrine has required the development of alternative theories of administrative legitimacy that focus on process or on expertise. So our discussions over the last few days have shown that we may need different theories of legitimacy for adjudicative bodies such as the ICJ and the WTO Appellate Body, and for quasi-judicial legislative bodies such as the conferences of the parties of multilateral environmental treaties. The basis of legitimacy of the Security Council may similarly vary depending on whether it is making a decision in an individual case or acting in a quasi-legislative capacity by promulgating more general rules.

Finally, different types of issue areas pose different problems of legitimacy. For example, issues involving a choice among values may require a different basis of legitimacy than issues that are more technical in nature, which might be addressed by institutions with the appropriate technical expertise. There may also be a difference, as Professor Ulfstein indicated in a comment earlier today, between issues involving coexistence and cooperation. So while I am sympathetic with efforts to elaborate general typologies of the different factors that promote legitimacy, such as the one we opened with by Professor Wolfrum, which distinguishes between source-based, process-based and output-based approaches to legitimacy, I think going forward we also may need a much more differentiated theory, which focuses on the different characteristics of different institutions and tries to develop an appropriate legitimacy theory for each. Thank you very much.

Discussion Following Presentations by Helen Keller, Armin von Bogdandy and Daniel Bodansky

R. Keohane: This was a wonderful series of presentations. I am just going to focus on one issue which Daniel Bodansky raised and try to clarify at least my view on it. This is the relationship between normative and sociological legitimacy. They are fundamentally different conceptually and if we can fuse the two, we're making a mistake. But they're linked empirically because legitimacy is a threshold concept, i.e. it's in the realm of what the philosophers call non-ideal theory. And therefore, to ascertain what the appropriate standards for legitimacy are at any given point in time, one needs to know the conditions of civil society and values and beliefs. Daniel is quite right. The Buchanan-Keohane paper does not demonstrate our view about the sociological conditions. To do so one would need to develop a theory that links the *ex ante* procedures with *ex post* results. For example, the theory of democracy does that. It makes the claim that if you follow democratic procedures you will in the long run get better results, even if in any given situation, a dictator might have given you a better policy. So, the theory is that there is a link between the *ex ante* and the *ex post*, which connects normative with sociological legitimacy. The objective is to promote a set of standards that are somewhat above current levels. I'm not claiming that people actually follow these standards. But the standards are not so far above the level of behaviour that they're utopian or unattainable. So the idea is to promote an institutionalised process of learning. Thank you.

R. Müller: Thank you for giving the floor to an illegitimate media law maker, who is not accountable, of course. And by the way, the Frankfurter Allgemeine Zeitung never frowns. Anyway, obviously everybody who talks about legitimacy and law means that there is something wrong with the law, that it's law in transition or there's a gap within the law or the law making body, or that an institution is wrongfully composed. Furthermore I had at first sight difficulties in detecting what's wrong with codes of conduct and international law. It was said it's a challenge for international law, ok, I can agree with that. Finally to

Armin von Bogdandy: You said states were acting as agents of the international community. Do you really think that states see themselves as actors of an imaginary international community? Don't you think that states primarily see themselves as agents of their own interests or as their own agents?

E. Riedel: First of all, I would like to congratulate the speakers this afternoon for their truly inspiring contributions. I think they really raised a highly interesting and innovative topic for this symposium. Not because codes of conduct are innovative and new. They have been with us since the 60s and I thought the debate was nearly dead at the end of the 70s. But to link it up with the question of legitimacy or justification for governmental behaviour, that I thought was particularly interesting and entitles us to take a new look at it. But to start with: why do we talk about codes of conduct? In the typology that was presented to us in the excellent slides, we saw there were three or four types of actors, state actors, and non-state actors in their various denominations. We might have spent a little more time on multinational enterprises that are increasingly using in-house codes of conduct and the exogenous side of it teeming up with other multinational enterprises to pre-empt positive action by other international actors, NGOs and states. So that could be elaborated, but that is not my point. My point is: why do states resort and why does the international community of states resort to codes of conduct when really and truly problems are huge, particularly in the economic sphere? Armin von Bogdandy raised the issue of the global compact, and others have done so in the economic sphere, that there are problems in the areas of human rights, in the areas of environmental law, in the areas of international economic cooperation and in the areas of international development law because states that should be acting there for various reasons are not doing so or cannot do so. And so, if we take a look at states themselves we can find that they resort to codes of conduct for various reasons. As Helen Keller said, they are flexible, they have the advantage of being attractive because the outcome is non-binding, at the end of diplomatic discussion on the elaboration of such codes of conduct, if they are produced in the intergovernmental sphere. They provide new platforms for dialogue and create a learning process and, ultimately, they can serve as stepping stones in the development and future elaboration of how hard law might develop. As such, no matter whether you call them codes of conduct, guidelines or common core document in relation to human rights or just recommendations, they can serve this preparatory function.

Why do states resort to such codes of conduct? Because it is in their interest to do so because consensus may not be had, and I will give you one example which illustrates this. Two years ago in November, in the context of the Food and Agriculture Organization, voluntary guidelines on the human right to food and food security at the national level were juxtaposed in a code of conduct type guideline. And the interesting thing was: 190 states by consensus, not consensus minus 1, by consensus agreed on these voluntary guidelines. But 154 states, that were party to the International Covenant on Economic, Social and Cultural Rights, for whom the human right to food is part of their binding legal obligations, why should they agree to voluntary guidelines? Is this not a lessening of the standard? And if you look at the code of conduct that was the outcome, there was agreement that you need all actors in the vote. The states that are bound by hard law, the states that are not bound at all, but for whom the recommendatory function is an additional step and the NGO community that can put pressure on non-state actors in order to achieve the aims which for 154 states are fully binding and to get this done in a joint effort. And states are resorting to this. Why? Because they say: it is much cheaper to have an intergovernmental conference without going through the motions of a multilateral treaty conference, which might take many years and is a very expensive thing and also involves a lot of internal domestic law, when you can get it much cheaper and when you can rely on the progressive development component of development of new rules of international law. So the legitimacy issue raised by Armin von Bogdandy in response to Helen Keller's presentation to my mind highlighted very clearly that these codes of conduct have an excellent complementary function to play in the legitimacy sphere. At the end, when I asked people in Rome from the Food and Agriculture Organisation: how on earth did you manage to get the United States to agree to these voluntary guidelines when they were so totally against economic, social and cultural rights as such? Because as you know they have not ratified the Social Covenant. It was explained to me that the United States felt that they had to participate and see to it that the worst effects are kept out of those voluntary guidelines, because otherwise customary international law might develop against their wish, which in the long run would even work against the United States. I thought that was a perfectly valid argument to be against it and to argue that, as a non-signatory state to the Social Covenant, but in the end not to prevent the adoption of the voluntary guidelines by consensus. They can rely on the word "voluntary", but of course the intention is not voluntary. And this is the new quality in international relations: very many activities in international organizations, particularly in the specialized agencies, are policies and strategy-oriented, not law-oriented. We lawyers place too strong an emphasis on the law side. Where you have hard law, by all means use it and do not give that up. But the other utterances of the new developments of international law and codes of conduct as part of that I really think have to be taken much more seriously by international lawyers. Thank you very much.

D. Vagts: I was very interested in Professor Keller's talk. I taught both corporations and international law for 45 years, which is sort of a recipe for schizophrenia since there are such different fields and corporation law is so intent on specificity and determinacy. I can be a much more cynical person than the last speaker and I'm impressed by the tremendous power of shareholder wealth maximization as a driving force. And it's more and more so because laws in the United States and elsewhere give shareholders more power. Institutions hold more shares and exert pressure on management. And management is more and more paid according to how much they get on the bottom line. So that the pressures to do what is profit maximizing, not what is noble, are tremendous. Now sometimes you can tie up with voluntary guidelines at very little cost. I think American firms that followed the Sullivan principles discovered that they had done well by doing good. Because, particularly after Mandela came to power, what they had done was symbolic and it gave them an advantage over the Japanese and Europeans who hadn't done that sort of thing.

Another note: you refer to an international chamber of commerce initiative on bribery. If there is anything going to reduce bribery it has been the United States' Foreign Corrupt Practices Act and now the OECD Convention. That's something where you need state practice and state intervention, and it isn't going to happen without that. And remember that in a lot of cases if the firms have any advantage, it is because they in effect have an agreement, which should otherwise violate the anti-trust laws, not to try and take on certain competitive practices in the field that would otherwise maximize profits. So I have a rather grim sense of what lies ahead on this road.

M. Bothe: A question to the chair: is time a common heritage or a shared resource? I have a little critical remark about something which is lacking in this symposium: This is the historical dimension. There are no historians here. But legitimacy is to a large extent a historic concept.

It is about perceptions of relevant actors at any given time. Let me explain by taking as an example the question of the legitimacy of governments in the age of enlightenment. The absolute monarchs were perfectly lawful governors. But the grace of God no longer provided enough legitimation. A new concept of legitimation was developed, mainly compact or contract theories. What was the result? History changed. A few revolutions happened. Law changed as a consequence. This is a continuous problem. It is still with us today, and these are questions which are behind the legitimacy discourse: to maintain the law as it is because it is legitimate or to change the law because it is not legitimate. This brings me to the question of the legitimacy of the gap or the hole. In this respect, the crucial point is that there is a perceived need of regulation which is not fulfilled. The ensuing question is whether this problem can be styled in terms of legitimacy. Is the fact that there is this gap, a non-fulfilment of a need to regulate, "illegitimate"? Is the question of legitimacy the right way to phrase the problem?

It leads us to another question that is very much debated: the question of fragmentation or the fact that international law develops in regimes. There are two possible conflicts between regimes, a positive and a negative one. The most debated conflict is the positive one where two regimes impose on the same actor different and contradicting requirements. But there is, of course, also the other type of conflict, the negative one, where certain things which should be regulated are not regulated by any of the treaty regimes in question. If you ask that question in terms of legitimacy, you presuppose that international law or the international legal order, although we can observe this fragmentation, has to be seen as a whole, that it is a function of the entire international legal order to fulfil certain regulatory tasks, to heed certain expectations by providing security, welfare and justice. In this framework, I think, styling the question as one of legitimacy is correct.

A very short remark on the codes of conduct. This is part of a more general discussion on new regulatory instruments. It is the recognition that the command and control approaches do not do an efficient job. So codes of conduct may be a more efficient way of dealing with a gap. Thank you.

F. Morrison: Michael Bothe has already said some of what I was going to say, but I will put it another way.

I will start with a short question: when was the Code of Justinian repealed? When was divine right repealed? They weren't. They simply became irrelevant. That is the same question that Professor Bothe was raising. Imperial authority and divine right were once the standards by which the legitimacy of rules and actions were judged at one time, but they are no longer relevant in our view of the world. The rules of a system of sovereign states may be equally irrelevant at a future time.

What I want to suggest is that we need to split the question of the two legitimacies that Dan Bodansky has identified. One is a legitimacy in terms of the validating norms of the current world. That is an Austinian legitimacy that looks backwards to the rules of recognition that have been given us in the past. The other is a legitimacy in terms of the norms of the emerging international system that most of us in this room believe that we see emerging. That is an aspirational legitimacy that looks forward to the rules that we see emerging to govern our relations in the future.

International law presents particular problems in separating these two questions, because we do not have explicit institutional decisions recording the changes that take place. The Treaty of Westphalia did not create the nation state system; it recorded an evolution that had already been taking place for a century or more. The United Nations Charter did not create the modern international legal order; it recorded developments that had been emerging for half a century or more. Both of them reflected the culmination and confirmation of developments and were not simply constitutive acts.

So we may need to ask the two questions separately, but then relate them in our response. First we ask whether an action is consistent with the existing set of rules (and rules of recognition). Then we ask whether an action is consistent with the emerging set of rules for developing international relations, and also whether the existing set of rules of recognition are consistent with those developing principles. Those are different questions, but closely interrelated. Unless we bridge the gap between them, our responses run the risk of becoming as irrelevant to the emerging world as the concepts of imperial authority and divine right are to the law of today. But, to bridge the gap, we must make clear whether we are talking about legitimacy in terms of what was, or of what is to be.

W. Benedek: I would like to thank the panellists for their very informative and inspiring presentations. As a veteran of the UNCTAD Conference on the Code on the Transfer of Technology, which failed, I can say that if you do not involve all the stakeholders – in that case, in particular the transnational corporations – you will hardly be successful. And therefore, we have only a few codes of conduct in the public sphere, like the OECD Code, which has been mentioned. And for them, I think, it is obvious that legitimacy will increase the compliance factor.

What I found even more challenging was the comment of Armin von Bogdandy regarding the private codes. I think that it is really a big challenge to link the legitimacy of the private codes with the legitimacy of international law. There are a few thoughts that I would like to contribute. One is that private codes obviously are no longer philanthropy these days. This is being done for business interests. And there is a constituency out there, let us say: an international public, including international civil society organizations and international consumers at large, who observe the actions of these companies. If Adidas is suspected of producing footballs with child labour, it can lose its reputation and its market share very easily. Therefore, in their own interest, companies have to elaborate such codes and to stick to them.

But how do we get from the private codes with private legal obligations – if these are legal obligations at all – into a public legal sphere? One could argue that such private codes create legitimate legal expectations. Because they are often based on international standards in the field of human rights, labour law and the environment they enter and use the public space for their interests. Therefore, it is also legitimate to expect compliance. If not, there will be a delegitimizing effect, not only for the company but for codes of conduct in general. So, there is a common interest. I also think that there is an international community, which has an interest in the functioning of private codes. Yet the question remains: does this mean that those who adopt such codes, who commit themselves to such codes, that they also get some status under international law? Would it be a logical consequence also in order to make them more easily accountable to understand them as functional international legal subjects?

E. Hey: I would like to add two perspectives to the discussion. The first concerns the North-South dimension of legitimacy; the second regards legitimacy discourse. When discussing issues of legitimacy, both yesterday and today, we seem to focus on issues that affect developed countries and developing countries more or less equally. However, if we take into account formally legally non-binding rules and regulations adopted by international institutions such as the World Bank and the IMF the following picture emerges: the South is being subjected to rules and regulations adopted through decision-making procedures in which the North has a dominant voice and vote. That is, the South only to a limited extent participates in making the rules of the game that are applied to it. I suggest that there concerns of legitimacy are at stake in this context and that these should be of concern to international lawyers. I add that the fact that a developing state signs on to an agreement that gets made before a project is implemented or the restructuring of its economy takes place does little to mitigate this concern. I come to my second point regarding legitimacy discourse. In considering legitimacy in international law, and I refer to the concept of legitimacy as introduced by Jutta Brunnée earlier on, I am astonished by the distaste that some exhibit at the use of the term, suggesting that the term should not be used; instead they seem to prefer to discuss matters in terms of democracy. I find this confusing in relation to international law because there is no democracy and democracy is unlikely to emerge anywhere in the near future at the international level of decision-making. I make two remarks. First, I fail to see the problem with the use of the term legitimacy as employed by Thomas Franck, i.e. in the sense of procedural fairness. Procedural fairness, according to Franck, is one of the determinants of fairness in international law, the other determinant being distributive justice. Secondly, I suggest that we have an adequate legal vocabulary available to us to discuss issues of legitimacy. That is the vocabulary of national public law and administrative law, in particular. While relevant notions such as those regarding accountability or the delegation of powers, familiar from national public law, cannot be translated to the international level of decision-making without further ado, I do suggest they offer a useful lens through which to analyse ongoing decision-making processes and procedures at the international level, such as within the World Bank or the Security Council. Discussions regarding the legitimacy of the internal rules and standards developed by institutions such as the World Bank are reminiscent of discussions that took place in the Netherlands when national administrative law was emerging during the 1950s. Moreover, the role of the Netherlands Council of State, now the highest administrative court in the country, in its original dispute settlement function, was rather similar to that of the World Bank Inspection Panel today: that of an advisory body very close to the executive branch of government. The same goes for the French Conseil d'Etat. I suggest that the legal language of public law and administrative law, in particular, can help us in analysing and characterizing ongoing developments at the international level, also in terms of legitimacy, and even if the character of the international legal order is very different from the national legal order. Thank you.

W. Heintschel v. Heinegg: Thank you very much. I understand Helen Keller had to concentrate on private codes of conduct. I am aware of the fact that public codes of conduct or inter-states codes of conduct were the subject of a former conference. Still, I think there is much more about those public codes of conduct than just filling gaps. Look at the other codes of conduct, like in arms control regimes or in environmental law, which lead us to different kinds of categories of such codes of conduct: hard codes of conduct, hard-soft ones and soft ones, depending on whether and to what extent they are specifying existing legal rules or whether they are really meant to just fill a gap that is felt necessary to be filled. In view of that, I wonder, Helen, whether and to what extent the criteria you have elaborated with regard to those private codes of conduct could help us in grasping the legitimacy problem or paradigm with regard to those public codes of conduct. Finally, Mr. von Bogdandy, I congratulate you on the logical stringency of your model. I think that nobody can really find an argument against it, if anybody looks at the model as you presented it today. I only have one little problem, and I cannot refrain from articulating it. It is your premise I cannot agree with, i.e. the perfect world, the perfect legal order and the perfect international legal order. And I am sorry to say that the international legal order is far from having reached that status. Thank you very much.

S. Vöneky: I would like to support the statement of Mr. Bodansky that there is no *necessary* connection between legality and legitimacy: if you look at a legal order which is unjust and unfair nobody, I think, presumes that just lawfulness makes an action legitimate. Therefore one has to say: there is no necessary connection between legality and legitimacy. However it is the question if there are different normative standards – different normative standards from the legal ones – where can we derive these standards from? Where do they stem from? Can we deduce them from something? And is not there the problem, or rather the danger, of stating a *petitio principii* in saying: we have some action which needs a certain outcome, so we are saying it is legitimate if we get this outcome. Therefore the core question, in my opinion is, and we have not concentrated enough on this question, yet: what is a "good" standard for legitimacy? I would argue: even if there is no *necessary* connection between legality and legitimacy if a legal order exists, like the international one, which has certain principles which are seen generally as fair and just we can and we have to use, first of all, these standards as standards of *legitimacy* and we have to test other actions in regard to these standards, even if there is no *legal* need to do so. Perhaps you could elaborate on this. Thank you very much.

A. D'Amato: Professor Keller has talked about a certain discourse within the private sphere of codes of conduct. Because these codes are not connected to the legal sphere, the ideas of legitimacy and governance within these codes have a specialized meaning that is at best parasitic upon the meaning we attribute to these terms in the international legal system. Thus for Professor Keller, legitimacy *within* the private sphere is a factual question, an empirical question, a question of political science. It may involve norms, but not legal norms.

I suppose that the idea of including private-sphere codes of conduct within a symposium devoted to legitimacy in the international political-legal arena is rooted in the hope that the private-sphere discourse can either throw some light upon, or be illuminated by, the quite separate political-legal discourse that is our current concern. However, I could not detect any cross-fertilization of ideas between the two discourses. Instead, my tentative conclusion, after hearing the well-researched paper, is that bringing the two discourses together does not do any useful work.

The world contains many discourses. On my way here I wondered what kind of discourse taxicab drivers have. When is it legitimate, for example, for them to avoid seeing a pedestrian who is signalling for a cab? Interesting though this question may be, it can hardly be said to throw any light upon the legitimacy of international organizations – unless, perhaps, the pedestrian happens to be an international diplomat.

Perhaps Professor von Bogdandy is just trying to extend the reach of public international law – to expand the empire so as to bring in private spheres and private discourses. As you can tell, I am somewhat sceptical about this initiative.

M. Böckenförde: Professor Keller, if I understood you correctly, you described the codes of conduct quite generally as a type of soft law. And for me, in the international context, the term soft law, in contrast to hard law, focuses on some kind of activities in the international arena, taken by the classical international actors. And as Professor Riedel pointed out, there are good reasons for applying and using the tool of soft law in this respect. Hence, I felt quite uncomfortable when you transferred the notion of soft law to activities of private entities. And so, that's my question: have they really become soft law makers or are the commitments of those private entities not something qualitatively different?

D. Bodansky: Thank you, I think relatively few of the comments were directed at my remarks. But I'd like to pick up on three that I think relate to what I was talking about.

The first is Professor Keohane's clarification of the relationship between normative and sociological perspectives on legitimacy. I take his point that the two are linked. As I mentioned in my talk, one needs to blend the two when one engages in prescription, where one aims to develop institutions that satisfy certain normative standards of legitimacy, but in doing that, one needs to take into account social realities. So I accept his comment.

Now, one other point he made was that the *ex ante* approach, which focuses on the procedures necessary for legitimate institutions, in part focuses on what the outputs of an institution are going to be. In establishing an institution, one tries to design procedures that will result in outputs that are desirable by whatever standard of desirable one is applying. I think his point here is true as well. But I would note two qualifications: the first is that, to the extent that relevant actors view the legitimacy of institutions in terms of their outputs, then it's not enough that there is consensus about procedures. One also needs consensus about what the appropriate standards are for evaluating the outputs. So that suggests that the arena where the concept of legitimacy can operate may be a limited one. It may not operate over all areas of international relations, only those areas where there can be some agreement among the relevant actors as to what the standards are for evaluating outputs. And then you can try to establish procedures that are going to be likely to produce those outputs or substantive results. My other comment is that there is a bit of a chicken and egg issue here. If the relevant actors evaluate the legitimacy of institutions by their outputs, how do you get institutions up and running in the first place? How do you get agreement on what kind of procedures to use for those institutions? And I think this is why it's useful to think about legitimacy not in static terms but in dynamic terms, as a process over time. How do you build the legitimacy of institutions? It is an incremental process – and here I would refer back to Curt Bradley's comment about the building of legitimacy of adjudicative bodies. To the extent that actors view institutions in terms of their outputs, then institutions need to develop in an incremental way. An institution cannot go too fast, because it's only over time, after actors become comfortable with an institution and develop trust in its outputs, that they're willing to accept the exercise of greater authority by it.

Ellen Hey mentioned the perspective of developing countries, in particular in relation to the legitimacy of the IMF. My perception is that the IMF operates not so much on a model of legitimacy as on a model of pressure or coercion. In most cases, developing countries accept the dictates of the IMF, not because they accept the IMF process as legitimate, but because they have little choice but to accept IMF requirements.

The final point I'd like to take up is the point by Ms. Vöneky about the relationship of legality and legitimacy. It seems to me that the notion of the rule of law does encompass some important values associated with legitimacy. So the two are not unrelated. There is a concept of legal legitimacy reflecting rule of law values, so legality can provide some of the different criteria by which we evaluate the legitimacy of institutions. But to the extent that the two concepts are not coextensive – to the extent that an institution, although legal, may be seen as illegitimate because, for example, it produces unjust results – where, Ms. Vöneky asks, do those additional standards of legitimacy come from? In my view, they flow from more general notions of political theory, which say that institutions need to meet certain requirements in order to be legitimate and, if a legal order fails to meet those requirements, then even though there may be legality there may still be illegitimacy. Thanks.

A. v. Bogdandy: Thank you very much for your questions.

First, Reinhard Müller, you're asking whether I really think of states as being agents of the international community. No, I don't think that that is the case. But, first I have to say that type of thinking has already been developed in the 1920s by people such as Kelsen. So those who see it that way – are in very good company. And I think that today, those who have that position have stronger arguments than in the 1920s. I think it's a possible, scholarly possible, reconstruction. These people are trying to provide for a paradigm shift, just how people see the world. And if that type of teaching continues, the coming elites who will run the foreign offices in 20 years' time have that vision of the world, we will live in another world. So I think to teach international law in that way is something one can be proud of. And, last but not least, there are a number of states and societies who really see multilateralism as a supreme constitutional value. They say: multilateralism is a high constitutional value. So that would be my answer to your position.

The next question is Professor Riedel's. I am very grateful that you stress the necessity that international legal scholarship also deals with instruments which are not part of international law but which are functional equivalents, such as codes of conduct. And why is that important? I can give many reasons; one is that that type of legal scholarly reconstruction provides legitimacy. If we think of Max Weber, he said there are three types of legitimacy: there is traditional legitimacy, there is charismatic legitimacy and there is rational legitimacy. One core element of rational legitimacy is a construction of the law according to the principles of legal positivism. Now if we see that in the international sphere we have norms which are functional equivalents to law, the little that we can provide to make the world more rational is applying our way of construing that normative world according to the premises of our scholarship. So I think that it is important that we research these topics.

The next question came from Michael Bothe. Where is the problem of legitimacy of the gaps? Can they be styled as an issue of legitimacy? I think that is quite easily possible. First of all, because it's a fact of life. Many people in the third world say that the current situation they are living in is to a large extent due to international law. No, we can accept it or not, but it is a fact of life. So we have that kind of argument in the political arena. Now the question is: is it possible from a legal point of view to reconstruct that type of argument? And I think it is possible. It's the argument that I have presented to you. I think we can present it as a legal argument because there is a link of causation and that link of causation leads to a link of responsibility.

With respect to Ellen Hey, you say that many of the issues on legitimacy we can more adequately phrase in the terms of administrative law. I think you are absolutely right. We have a lot of knowledge in domestic public law and we should use that knowledge in order first of all to discover and define the problems in the international sphere. The issue is not to apply a blueprint of domestic public law to international issues. But we have sound experience of domestic constitutional and administrative issues. It sharpens your sensibility to see the problems and also sharpens your ideas about how you might solve them. So I think that the public law perspective is in fact the right perspective on international issues, and that is the very essence of the idea of my institute which studies domestic public law and international public law. So it's not very new; it was born in the 1920s.

Heintschel von Heinegg: is my premise a perfect world? That really makes me think what for me a perfect world is. So my answer: What is a perfect world? I would say there are only moments of perfection. So I don't think that really my construction of international law is premised on the idea that the world is perfect. My argument is premised, and that is very much the response to Michael Bothe, on the fact that international law lies behind many private laws in many countries, that private law allows for certain activities and, since international law sits behind, there is a link of causation and a link of responsibility. That is premise no. 1, and premise no. 2 is that there is to some limited extent a duty to protect and an issue of coherence.

The last issue is with respect to Professor D'Amato. Am I expanding the empire? Is it still meaningful to distinguish between international law and domestic law. Is that a meaningful distinction? Ellen Hey has mentioned the issue of global administrative law. Those who argue in favour of global administrative law are trying to do away with that distinction. I think for the very topic of our conference, we should maintain the distinction between international law and domestic law. And why is that? Because the sources of legitimacy are so different. And since the sources of legitimacy are so important to the entire construction of international law, it is meaningful to keep these bodies of law apart. Thank you very much.

H. Keller: I will touch first upon the easy questions, starting with Mr. Böckenförde. I completely understand that you feel unease with the view regarding private codes of conduct as part of soft law. I have just had a discussion on this issue with a member of the institute. To be sure, if you understand the notion of 'soft law' in the traditional sense, then private codes of conduct fall outside the definition. In so far, they are neither hard law nor soft law, but something else. However, the contemporary inflationary talk of soft law seems to be indicating a blurring of the traditional definitional boundaries of soft law, and if you think of it as a flexible, more inclusive category, anything that is not 'hard law' is – in differing forms – 'soft' in its obligatory character; in this broader sense, one might even subsume private codes of conduct under the label of 'soft law'.[1]

Mr. Müller, what is wrong with codes of conduct? On the face of it, I am perfectly happy with codes of conduct, that is: as long as they are not disguised as mere public relations tactics. If codes of conduct in fact turn out to be no more than window dressing, a red light should flash in our minds, and it is there where suspicions are warranted.

I completely agree with Professor Riedel and Professor Vagts that the transaction costs of having a new code of conduct are minimal in comparison to new hard law. That, arguably, is one of the major advantages of a code of conduct. I made this point in referring to 'flexibility'. Let me now turn to public codes of conduct, and the different questions referring to them. Well, we should have time for a separate speech on public codes because here we're talking about a fundamentally different category of codes.

Are the criteria I described at the end of my talk also relevant for public codes of conduct? Yes, I think so. As regards the determinacy of code language, public codes more often than not contain rather detailed statements covering specific aspects of a company's social policy or environmental responsibility. The point made in connection with a clear distinction between hard and soft law – you might in some ways term it 'transparency' – is also applicable to public codes. There shall be no fallback behind the normative yardstick set by international hard law. And as far as 'compliance' is concerned: yes, this is a relevant criterion as well. It is important to bear in mind that no public code is equal to another and that the effectiveness of a code essentially hinges on the institution's capacity for compliance monitoring. The OECD Guidelines, for instance, are relatively successful because they are backboned by a powerful institution that boasts the necessary financial resources. Not every international organization has this power and these financial means. So, if we look into public codes, we really have to differentiate between them.

1 *See*, e.g., the definition of 'hard' and 'soft' law in: John Kirton/Michael Trebilcock, "Introduction", in: John Kirton/Michael Trebilcock (eds.): *Hard Choices, Soft Law*, Burlington (2004), 8–9 ("For some purposes, it may indeed be useful to conceive of the hard law-soft law duality as a continuum rather than a dichotomy [...]."; Kenneth Abbott/Duncan Snidal, "Hard and Soft Law in International Governance", *International Organization* 54:3 (2000), 422 ("The realm of "soft law" begins once legal arrangements are weakened along one or more of the dimensions of obligation, precision, and delegation.").

With respect to Mr. Benedek: is it a logical consequence that we have to widen the circle of international legal subjects? Yes, that would be the case indeed, but we all know for sure that it is quite a revolutionary idea in international law. I do not think that we are very close to this stage although, in national law, there are some developments pushing in that direction. I think of national criminal law, for instance, where firms are now held responsible for breaching environmental law, or bribery law. But these developments are by far outshone by what you are suggesting.

I completely agree with Michael Bothe that the subject of codes of conduct is a small sub-subject of the broader subject of new regulatory instruments. I have nothing to add to that.

I think I am all done.

Legitimacy: A Problem in International Law and for International Lawyers?

Hanspeter Neuhold

1. Legitimacy: *faux problème* or legally relevant issue?

As was almost to be expected, the papers presented and the discussions that followed at our symposium have not reduced, but rather added to, the confusion which characterises the debate on the place and relevance of legitimacy in international law. Some participants rejected the concept out of hand and insisted that the only notion which counted was that of legality; or that they were at best willing to accept that problems could arise if the rules of international law conflicted with the dictates of justice. *Alain Pellet* preferred the term "fairness" and eventually equated legitimacy with *opinio juris*, the elusive psychological element necessary for the emergence of customary international law.[1] Other words which are used in the debate or come to one's mind in order to designate the controversial concept are "authority",[2] "rectitude"[3] or "acceptance".[4]

---

1 Alain Pellet, "Legitimacy of Legislative and Executive Actions of International Institutions", in this volume, pp. 63 et seq. It is suggested, however, that *opinio juris* should rather be understood as the conviction of the competent decision makers that a behaviour pattern is required or permitted by international law, a conviction to which the perception of the practice concerned as legitimate may make a major contribution. Cf. also the somewhat tortuous definition by the International Court of Justice in the North Sea Continental Shelf Cases: "The States concerned must therefore *feel* that they are conforming to *what amounts to a legal obligation.*" (italics added). ICJ Reports 1969, pp. 3 et seq. (para. 77). See also infra or below, p. 337 et seq.

2 Defined as compliance with a demand because the behaviour concerned is regarded as reasonable according to the values of the actor who complies, as

Despite the terminological controversy and confusion, it cannot be denied that the underlying problem does exist and is of critical importance to the smooth functioning of any legal system.[5] Moreover, it hardly needs to be emphasised that it is particularly relevant to the effectiveness of international law.

There may be more than one reason why the subjects of a legal order reject certain rules of their normative system or, in extreme cases, the entire order itself. A variant of this attitude is to defend acts contrary to law as morally justified, in other words as legitimate and therefore acceptable. As *Rüdiger Wolfrum* states in his introductory chapter, the perception of illegitimacy may be due to three factors: firstly, the authority of the law-creating body may be contested; secondly, the procedure and process of norm-creation could be flawed; thirdly, the resulting legal rules may be considered unsatisfactory and the solutions provided by them inadequate by the subjects in terms of their interests or

---

stated by Peter Bachrach/Morton Baratz, "Decisions and Nondecisions: An Analytical Framework", *American Political Science Review* 57 (1963), pp. 632 et seq. (p. 638).

[3] One of the "base values" in Harold Lasswell's conceptual framework which Myres S. McDougal applied to international law, meaning a "sense of rightness of cause and of responsibility shared, integration of community purpose that transcends all factionalism." Cf. Myres S. McDougal, "International Law, Power, and Policy: A Contemporary Conception", *RCADI* 82 (1953 I), pp. 137 et seq. (p. 199).

[4] Allen Buchanan und Robert O. Keohane have added to the conceptual complexity (or confusion) of the debate by their distinction between justice and legitimacy. The former concept is defined as an ideal standard, the latter as a threshold value, in a non-ideal world, for the conditions under which an institution has the right to rule. See Allen Buchanan and Robert O. Keohane, "The Legitimacy of Global Governance Institutions", in this volume, pp. 25, at 34.

[5] Particularly important conceptual contributions to the debate on legitimacy have been made by Thomas M. Franck, "Legitimacy in the International System", *AJIL* 82 (1988), pp. 705 et seq.; *Fairness in International Law and Institutions*, 1995; "The Power of Legitimacy and the Legitimacy of Power: International Law in the Age of Power Disequilibrium", *AJIL* 100 (2006), pp. 88 et seq. Franck emphasises another aspect of legitimacy, understood as the capacity of a rule to pull those to whom it is addressed toward consensual compliance. This "compliance pull" also exerts its influence in cases where behaviour in accordance with a rule is detrimental to short-term national interests of the state concerned, even of a superpower. Compliance in such a situation is due to the fact that states have an interest in the law as such. See Franck, op. cit. (2006), p. 93.

values or both.[6] If law is felt to be illegitimate in this sense, voluntary compliance with it will probably decline, and enforcement by coercive means is likely to become increasingly necessary.

Or to approach the problem from a different angle: the socialisation of human beings early on in their lives includes the internalisation of rules, be they moral, religious, social or legal norms. We are taught as children to obey rules without questioning the reasons. However, if the above-mentioned factors lead to an awareness of the negative effects of those rules, "automatic" obedience by the persons subjected to them will be eroded as a result.

One way out of this dilemma would of course be to change the law, but such transformation may take time or may prove altogether impossible. This is particularly true of international law, above all of treaties. For those rules that are objected to as illegitimate, as unjust, or as dysfunctional by one side may well be regarded as more advantageous than before by the other, so that the necessary consent to adaptation will be withheld. Such conflicting positions can be caused by a change of circumstances which upsets the balance of mutual concessions reflected in the treaty. However, invoking a fundamental change of circumstances, provided the conditions listed in Article 62 of the 1969 Vienna Convention on the Law of Treaties are met, may be a legal remedy which could prove too radical, if it results in the termination or suspension of the entire treaty, including provisions which are still acceptable to all contracting parties.

However, it cannot be denied that the notion of legitimacy or rather illegitimacy is a driving force behind the transformation of the law. If a legal rule is widely regarded as illegitimate by those to whom it is addressed, it is likely to be disregarded with increasing frequency, even if such violations continue to entail sanctions provided by law. Lack of legitimacy may indeed go a long way to explaining a fundamental legal paradox: widespread and repeated breaches of a norm may lead to the "qualitative jump" from previously unlawful behaviour to a new rule of law. Such a radical change may be brought about either by formal

---

[6] Rüdiger Wolfrum, "Legitimacy of International Law from a Legal Perspective: Some Introductory Considerations", in this volume, p. 1 at 6 et seq.; idem, "Legitimacy in International Law", in: August Reinisch/Ursula Kriebaum (eds.), *The law of international relations – liber amicorum Hanspeter Neuhold*, 2007, pp. 471 et seq.

means, the enactment of new law in domestic law[7] or the revision of an existing or the conclusion of a new treaty in international law. It may also result from *desuetudo*, i.e. legalisation through the process of customary law, with shared perceptions of the legitimacy of an illegal practice leading to the eventual emergence of the necessary *opinio juris*, i.e. the conviction that this custom has become lawful and legally binding or permissible.[8]

2. Legitimacy: the historical dimension

The debate on legitimacy in the area of international law has come to the fore in recent years in the wake of "Operation Allied Force" in 1999. It will be recalled that member states of NATO conducted an air campaign in order to stop atrocities by Serbian forces against the Albanian majority in Kosovo. In the debate on the lawfulness of this military operation some writers, including this author, concluded that while humanitarian intervention,[9] the main justification advanced for NATO's air strikes without authorisation by the UN Security Council, was illegal it could be considered morally justified, in other words legitimate.[10] More recently, the focus of the debate has shifted to the democratic legitimacy and accountability of international institutions.

The current debate on the "legitimacy deficit" of international law ought to be placed in its proper historical perspective. The international legal order confronted more radical challenges in the course of the 20th century when its very foundations were put into question. Firstly, after the October Revolution of 1917, the Soviet Union rejected the entire

---

[7] The debates on the legalisation of abortion or, more recently, of euthanasia in many countries are cases in point.

[8] See above, footnote 1.

[9] Humanitarian intervention may be defined as the use of armed force in order to protect persons in another state, above all the nationals of that state, against large-scale atrocities committed by the authorities of the target state.

[10] Hanspeter Neuhold, "Die „Operation Allied Force" der NATO: rechtmäßige humanitäre Intervention oder politisch vertretbarer Rechtsbruch?", in: Erich Reiter (ed.), *Der Krieg um das Kosovo 1998/99*, 2000, pp. 193 et seq.; the same conclusion was reached by the Independent International Commission on Kosovo, The Kosovo Report: Conflict, International Response, Lessons Learned (2000), http://www.reliefweb.int/library/documents/thekosovoreport.htm.

body of international law created by the "capitalist", "imperialist" states. Together with the other "socialist" states, the USSR later developed an uneasy relationship characterised by conflict and cooperation with the opposite camp until the communist regimes collapsed and the Soviet bloc began to implode in 1989. In contrast, the young developing countries in the Third World which emerged in the process of decolonisation after World War II did not roundly oppose the then existing international law in the creation of which they had not participated; instead, they opted for a "pick-and-choose approach", accepting those norms which corresponded to their political preferences and economic interests but refusing to be bound by those that did not.

Today's legitimacy crises are less fundamental and comprehensive in scope, but serious enough. This is due to the fact that after the end of the East-West conflict Western values which are also reflected in international law, above all individual-oriented human rights and multiparty democracy,[11] are more widely embraced than ever before, first and foremost by the nations of the former Soviet camp. Although capitalism, which leads to an increasingly unequal distribution of wealth, is challenged by the populist leaders of some developing countries, notably in Latin America, the Third World is not radical, powerful and united enough to mount an attack on the global neo-liberal system similar to the demands for a New Economic Order in the 1970s in the wake of the successful resort to the oil weapon in 1973/74. However, some key institutions have come under widespread criticism, at both the universal and regional levels. The effects of the rejection of Western liberal values by Islamic states on the international legal order remain to be seen.

3. Legitimacy problems of the UN

A major example of a "legitimacy" deficit is provided by the dissatisfaction with the UN Security Council.[12] The crisis is due to criticisms con-

---

[11] For a discussion of the legitimacy of international law against the backdrop of the principles of constitutional democracy, see Mattias Kumm, "The Legitimacy of International Law: A Constitutionalist Framework of Analysis", *EJIL* 15 (2004), pp. 907 et seq.

[12] However, this is by no means a new problem. See, for instance, David D. Caron, "The Legitimacy of the Collective Authority of the Security Council", *AJIL* 87 (1993), pp. 552 et seq.

cerning its authority in terms of representativeness and structure, as well as the unsatisfactory performance of its duties.[13] Although membership of the world organisation has increased from 51, when it was founded more than 60 years ago, to 192 with the recent admission of Montenegro, the number of Council members has been increased only once, from 11 to 15 in 1965. However, what is even more strongly resented than the small number of members, making the Security Council a rather "exclusive club", is the privileged position of the five permanent member states. Not only do they enjoy the advantages of uninterrupted representation. What is more, they may prevent any non-procedural decision by a negative vote.[14]

---

[13] Secretary-General Kofi Annan put the problem in a nutshell in para. 168 of his report of 2005 to be discussed below: "... a change in the Council's composition is needed to make it more broadly representative of the international community as a whole, as well as of the geopolitical realities of today, and thereby *more legitimate* in the eyes of the world. Its working methods also need to be made more efficient and transparent. The Council must not only be *more representative* but also *more able and willing to take action* when action is needed." (italics added).

[14] The five permanent members of the Security Council enjoy a similar privileged position in the context of the Non-Proliferation Treaty (NPT) as nuclear-weapon states. Their obligation under Article I of the treaty not to transfer nuclear weapons to any recipient or to assist non-nuclear weapon states to manufacture or otherwise acquire such weapons corresponds to their common interest not to enlarge their "exclusive club". With regard to the topic under discussion, their failure of the "*beati possidentes*" to comply with their disarmament obligations under Article VI of the NPT in exchange for the renunciation of nuclear weapons by the other contracting parties has eroded the legitimacy of their privileges and of the treaty.

It will be recalled that India, Pakistan and North Korea have meanwhile successfully tested nuclear devices; Israel, with its "no show, no tell" policy is believed to possess nuclear weapons; and Iran, despite its denials, is widely suspected of pursuing a nuclear weapons programme. At the same time, it should also be borne in mind that these weapons are less decisive than before, since nuclear deterrence fails to impress terrorists willing to commit suicide and possibly "rogue" states. The mild response of the United States to the provocations by North Korea, one of the "rogue" states on the "axis of evil" according to the terminology of the present Bush administration, may only encourage other governments, especially those that are not on good terms with the West and have to fear sanctions from the latter, to follow the example of the regime in Pyongyang.

This special role could be justified by the special responsibility of the five main victorious powers for world peace due to their dominant position at the end of World War II. Yet, while in the meantime the United States has risen to the status of the world's only "hyperpower",[15] the strength of France and the United Kingdom has clearly declined. After the fall of the former Soviet Union from the rank of one of the two Cold War superpowers as a result of its disintegration, Russia is now benefiting from its energy assets but still has a long way to go to hold a position comparable to its Soviet predecessor. China is also on the rise but continues to lag behind the main industrial powers in terms of its economic development. Other states like Japan, Germany and India have advanced to the ranks of major powers. None of these countries, however, is in a position to challenge the United States as the hegemon in today's world.

Most importantly, the Security Council has not met the expectations that it would better live up to its responsibility for the maintenance of international peace and security after the Cold War. This is particularly true of its failure to take effective action in order to prevent or quickly put an end to humanitarian disasters with international repercussions, for instance in Bosnia-Herzegovina, Rwanda or Kosovo, and more recently Darfur. The main blame for this disappointing record obviously lies with the permanent members; for if they could agree among themselves on measures to deal with critical situations, they should have no difficulty persuading at least four other non-permanent members to support their initiative and thus obtain the necessary quorum of nine votes.

After earlier calls for Security Council reform various proposals were made in the context of the meeting of the UN General Assembly at the summit level in September 2005. In particular, the 16 eminent members of the "High-level Panel on Threats, Challenges and Change" appointed by Secretary-General *Kofi Annan* elaborated two models in their report entitled "A more secure world: Our shared responsibility," which they submitted in December 2004.[16] Both provided for an enlargement of the Council to 24 members, with six seats for each of the four major regional areas, Africa, Asia and the Pacific, Europe and the Americas, and did not extend the "veto" beyond the circle of the

---

[15] The term « *hyperpuissance* » is attributed to the former French Foreign Minister Hubert Védrine.

[16] UN document A/59/565; http://www.vmpeace.org/pages/hllp_report.htm.

five original permanent members. The Panel urged that those member states which contributed most financially (to development assistance), militarily (to peacekeeping operations), and diplomatically should also be involved more in the decision-making of the Security Council. One model introduced six additional permanent seats, the other eight four-year renewable seats. The Secretary-General endorsed these proposals in his own report "In larger freedom: towards development, security and human rights for all" in March 2005.[17]

Four major powers, Brazil, Germany, India and Japan, joined forces and called for a permanent seat; they were promptly opposed by their respective regional rivals led by Argentina, Italy, Mexico and Pakistan. Since the five permanent members, whose ratification is required for any amendment or revision of the Charter,[18] also showed little enthusiasm for sharing their privileged position with newcomers, the concluding document of the General Assembly summit is restricted to a few general sentences and falls short of any concrete reforms of the Security Council.[19] The appeal by the High-level Panel, not reiterated by *Kofi Annan* in his report, that the veto[20] should be limited to matters where vital interests are genuinely at stake, and not be used in cases of genocide and large-scale human rights abuses, was also ignored in the World Summit Outcome.[21]

---

[17] UN document A/59/2005; http://www.un.org/largerfreedom/contents.htm.

[18] In accordance with Articles 108 and 109 (2) of the Charter.

[19] "153. We support early reform of the Security Council as an essential element of our overall effort to reform the United Nations to make it more broadly representative, efficient and transparent and thus to further enhance its effectiveness and the *legitimacy* (italics added) and implementation of its decisions. We commit ourselves to continuing our efforts to achieve a decision to this end and request the General Assembly to review progress on the reform set out above by the end of 2005.

154. We recommend that the Security Council continue to adapt its working methods so as to increase the involvement of States not members of the Council in its work, as appropriate, enhance its accountability to the membership and increase the transparency of its work." UN document A/60/1.

[20] Qualified by the Panel as anachronistic and unsuitable for the institution in an increasingly democratic age.

[21] Para. 256. However, the reform of the Security Council has not been shelved but continues. A statement by the Acting President of the UN General Assembly, Cheick Sidi Diarra (Mali), at the end of the debate on the issue in

A UN organ which had discredited itself even more than the Security Council was the Commission on Human Rights. It included member states with a record of large-scale human rights abuses which saw to it that the Commission did not condemn them and other culprits. In this case, the World Summit followed a recommendation of Secretary-General *Annan,* who had criticised the Commission's declining credibility and professionalism,[22] and decided to create a Human Rights Council.[23] The new institution, replacing the Commission, was then established by General Assembly Resolution 60/251. It consists of 47 member states which are elected directly and individually by secret ballot by the majority of the members of the General Assembly. In addition to equitable geographical distribution,[24] criteria for election are the contribution of candidates to the promotion and protection of human rights and their voluntary pledges and commitments made thereto. Moreover, the General Assembly, by a two-thirds majority of the members present and voting, may suspend membership rights in the Council of a state that commits gross and systematic violations of human rights.[25] It remains to be seen whether the new institution will justify the hopes some optimists are placing on it.

4. Legitimacy problems of the EU

The EU is equally in the throes of a legitimacy crisis which is due to the above-mentioned factors. The crisis came to a head in 2005 when a majority of the voters who participated in the referenda in France and the

---

July 2006 is worth quoting in this context. He pointed to an almost unanimous position that the status quo was not viable and that reforming the Security Council in a way that addressed both its expansion and working methods was vital to that body's increased *authority and legitimacy* (italics added), and to the credibility of the United Nations as a whole.

22 Paras. 182-183 of his report. The High-level Panel had recommended an upgrading of the Commission to become a "Human Rights Council" no longer subsidiary to the Economic and Social Council but a Charter body standing alongside it and the Security Council. Para. 291 of the Panel's report.

23 Paras. 157-160 of the World Summit Outcome.

24 13 African and 13 Asian states; 6 East European states; 8 Latin American and Caribbean states; 7 Western European and other states (para. 7 of the resolution).

25 Para. 8 of the resolution.

Netherlands rejected the Treaty establishing a Constitution for Europe.[26] An in-depth analysis of the problem is beyond the scope of this essay, but its main aspects can be summed up as follows.

All three causes that can undermine legitimacy are relevant in this context.[27] Firstly, the authority of the main EU organs has increasingly been eroded. The European Council and the Council are widely perceived as undemocratic institutions, although their members belong to national governments which are based on the support of parliaments whose composition is in turn determined by free and fair elections. Many citizens of the Union also criticise the Commission as a heavy-handed, bureaucratic institution in far-away Brussels without any democratic legitimation. The visibility of the European Parliament still leaves a great deal to be desired, so that its actual role as a major player in the norm-creating process is still often underrated. Its unique features, above all the direct election of its members by EU citizens and its co-decision powers, which make it a "genuine" parliament, do not make a real difference in the eyes of its critics. Recently, the European Court of Justice has also come under attack for its tendency to make new and not just state existing law.

Secondly, the political and legal processes and procedures lack transparency and frequently take place behind closed doors. Furthermore, they are so complex that not only the average European citizen but also legal and political experts find them difficult to understand, even if more serious efforts were made to explain them.

Thirdly, there is widespread dissatisfaction with the results of these processes, including EU legislation. In particular, the Commission is accused of overregulation, unnecessarily interfering in the citizens' daily lives. Europeans do not today accept a legal and political regime similar to that of enlightened absolutism in bygone centuries,[28] in which decisions are handed down by the authorities in a remote capital many of them have never visited.

---

[26] Those who support a strong Union can only hope that the 2007 "Reform Treaty", which contains the substance of the ill-fated "Constitutional Treaty" without the provisions on elements of statehood like the EU's flag and anthem, will be ratified by all 27 member states and enter into force.

[27] See above, p. 336.

[28] I owe this analogy to Ambassador Emil Brix from the Austrian Federal Ministry for European and International Affairs.

Another major factor responsible for the low esteem in which the Union is held in many member countries, documented in the Eurobarometer opinion polls, are its over-ambitious aims, above all the Lisbon Goal, according to which the EU should become the most competitive and dynamic knowledge-based economy in the world by the year 2010. Yet, instead of shrinking, the gap between the economic performance of Europe and the United States keeps growing. Because of the perfidious policy of national governments which claim credit for the benefits of integration for themselves and blame the Union for the costs and setbacks, the EU is also held responsible for problems about which it can do little, such as the principal concern of Europeans today, namely unemployment. This continued emphasis on the individual national level of member states prevents in turn the emergence and strengthening of European loyalty and a common European identity, two concepts closely related to legitimacy.

5. Legitimacy and the use of force

Against the backdrop of the debate on the legality of "Operation Allied Force",[29] the Canadian government, together with some foundations, responded to a plea by UN Secretary-General *Kofi Annan* and established the International Commission on Intervention and State Sovereignty (ICISS) in 2000.[30] In its lengthy report entitled "The Responsibility to Protect" published in December 2001,[31] the Commission uses this new term instead of "humanitarian intervention".[32] This choice not only marks a semantic change, which should enhance the legitimacy of

---

[29] Also the failure of the international community adequately to deal with the humanitarian disasters in Somalia in 1992/1993, in Rwanda in 1994 and in Bosnia-Herzegovina in the first half of the 1990s.

[30] The Commission was composed of twelve prominent members with rather diverse backgrounds and headed by the former Australian foreign minister, Gareth Evans, and the Special Advisor to Secretary-General Annan, Mohamed Sahnoun, a former senior Algerian diplomat.

[31] http://www.dfait-maeci.gc.ca/iciis-ciise/report2-en.asp.

[32] For more details on this issue, see Hanspeter Neuhold, "Human Rights and the Use of Force", in: Stephan Breitenmoser et alii (eds.), *Human Rights, Democracy and the Rule of Law. Menschenrechte, Demokratie und Rechtsstaat. Droits de l'homme, démocratie et Etat de droit: Liber Amicorum Luzius Wildhaber*, 2007, pp. 479 et seq.

the use of force in order to prevent states from committing atrocities against human beings, above all their own citizens, since the notion of "humanitarian intervention" is associated with controversial practices of colonial powers in the past;[33] more fundamentally, the new term reflects a different understanding of the cornerstone of the international legal order, state sovereignty, as well. In line with the increasing political and legal importance attached to the individual also at the international level, the concept developed by the ICISS emphasises the duty of states to ensure the well-being of their citizens rather than insist on their rights and privileges.

The Commission then defined the principles for military intervention as an instrument of the responsibility to protect:[34]

Firstly, the resort to force must be based on a just cause: either large-scale loss of life or large-scale "ethnic cleansing" has to be occurring or imminently likely to occur.

Secondly, four precautionary principles must be observed:

1) right intention: the primary purpose must be to halt or avert human suffering;

---

[33] In the same vein, the traditional term "reprisal", which has a similar negative ring to it since in the past it also implied the use of armed force, has been replaced by the more "neutral" expression "countermeasure" by the ILC in the context of the codification of the law of state responsibility. Like "humanitarian intervention", the new concept of "countermeasures", which is subject to far-reaching restrictions including the prohibition of the threat or use of force, is gaining growing acceptance. Semantic changes implying different contents may indeed increase legitimacy and should be welcomed. However, they ought to be distinguished from the "newspeak" practised, in particular, by politicians, who use euphemisms in order to conceal unpopular messages, like "negative growth" instead of the "ugly" word "recession".

[34] The ICISS proposed that these guidelines be adopted in declaratory resolutions by the UN Security Council and General Assembly. Similar criteria had already been formulated in the discussion about the legal aspects of "Operation Allied Force" by Antonio Cassese, "*Ex iniuria ius oritur*: Are We Moving towards International Legitimation of Forcible Humanitarian Countermeasures in the World Community?", *EJIL* 10 (1999), pp. 23 et seq., and Daniel Thürer, "Die Nato-Einsätze in Kosovo und das Völkerrecht. Spannungsfeld zwischen Gewaltverbot und Menschenrechten." *Neue Zürcher Zeitung* of 3/4 April 1999; idem, "Der Kosovo-Konflikt im Lichte des Völkerrechts: Von drei – echten und scheinbaren – Dilemmata", *ArchVR* 36 (2000), pp. 1 et seq.

2) last resort: every non-military option for the prevention or peaceful resolution of the crisis must have been explored, with reasonable grounds for believing that lesser measures would not have succeeded;

3) proportional means: the scale, duration and intensity of the planned military action has to be the minimum necessary to ensure the defined human protection objective;

4) reasonable prospects: the planned military intervention must have a reasonable chance of success, with the consequences of action not likely to be worse than those of inaction.

Thirdly, right authority is required. The most appropriate body is the UN Security Council, whose authorisation should in all cases be sought prior to any resort to armed force.[35]

---

[35] Should the Security Council reject a proposal or fail to deal with it in a reasonable time, the ICISS suggests as alternative options:

1) to have an Emergency Special Session of the UN General Assembly deal with the matter under the "Uniting for Peace" procedure;

2) action by regional or sub-regional organisations under Chapter VIII of the Charter, subject to their seeking subsequent authorisation from the Security Council.

Furthermore, in the somewhat tortuous wording of the Commission, "The Security Council should take into account in all its deliberations that, if it fails to discharge its responsibility to protect in conscience-shocking situations crying out for action, concerned states may not rule out other means to meet the gravity and urgency of that situation – and that the stature and credibility of the United Nations may suffer thereby."

As regards the key issue raised by the NATO air campaign in the Kosovo crisis of 1998/1999, the ICISS concludes that it would be impossible to find consensus on the legality of using military means for humanitarian purposes by an individual state or ad hoc coalitions of states without the authorisation of the Security Council, even in a conscience-shocking situation crying out for action. The Commission poses the relevant political and moral question which arises in this case: whether the damage to international order if the Security Council is bypassed outweighs the damage to that order caused by atrocities inflicted on human beings; however, this does not solve the legal dilemma.

As regards the place of recourse to armed force for human protection purposes in international law, in the opinion of the ICISS there is not yet a sufficiently strong basis for the emergence of a new principle of customary international law, but growing state and regional organisation practice as well as Security Council precedent suggest an "emerging guiding principle," without a definition of the exact legal meaning of this term. Para. 2.24 of the report.

The above-mentioned High-level Panel on Threats, Challenges and Change explicitly addressed the issue of strengthening the legitimacy of the lawful resort to force. To this end, it proposed five criteria which (even) the UN Security Council should take into account when authorising or endorsing the use of force; not surprisingly, they closely follow those stressed by the ICISS:

1) seriousness and clarity of the threat;

2) proper purpose: the primary purpose ought to be to halt or avert the threat in question, whatever other motives may also be involved;

3) last resort: every non-military option must have been explored; there has to be a reasonable belief that other measures will not succeed;

4) proportional means: with regard to the scale, duration and intensity of military action, only the necessary minimum ought to be applied;

5) balance of consequences: there must be a reasonable chance of meeting the threat, and consequences of action likely not to be worse than those of inaction.[36]

These five principles were in turn taken up by Secretary-General *Annan* in his report.[37] While the World Summit also endorsed the concept of the responsibility to protect, it did not retain those criteria it its watered-down concluding document in September 2005.

What is of interest to the topic of this volume is the widespread awareness that especially in the age of weapons of mass destruction the exceptional resort to armed force must not solely be lawful but should also be guided by considerations of legitimacy to make it more acceptable in the eyes of public opinion. Further restrictions not required by law ought also to be observed by the UN Security Council despite its broad powers under Chapter VII of the Charter.

On recent legal developments in Africa concerning the legality of the use of force for humanitarian purposes, see Neuhold, op. cit. (footnote 32).

[36] Para. 207. The Panel also reiterated the proposal of the ICISS that these guidelines should be embodied in declaratory resolutions of the UN Security Council and General Assembly. See above, footnote 34.

[37] Para. 126.

6. Conclusions

On the one hand, the controversy over legitimacy in international law is merely semantic, since some scholars prefer to use a different term for essentially the same concept. On the other hand, however, there are those who disagree more fundamentally with the advocates of including legitimacy on the agenda of international law. Those who reject the notion raise the issue of the limits of the discipline. According to these international lawyers, societal acceptance of or objection to legal norms should be explored by the social sciences. In the objectors' opinion, lawyers ought to confine their efforts to answering the question of whether the subjects of a legal order act in accordance with or contrary to the law in a given situation, a question which is more often than not complex and difficult enough. There are others, including this author, who are not content to determine whether legal rules are complied with or not, but who are also curious to know why legal rules are observed or violated. They feel that this dimension is too important to be left entirely to others, to sociologists, political scientists, philosophers or psychologists. After all, law is not an a-social science, since it regulates human behaviour; lawyers should therefore participate in a dialogue, to which they can contribute the important normative dimension, with the representatives of other disciplines who look at the same reality.

In this context, it is also worth mentioning that the problem of phenomena on the borderlines of international law is not restricted to the dichotomy between legality and legitimacy. A similar debate divides those lawyers who insist that "soft law" has no place in international law, since a norm is either legally binding or legally irrelevant, and those of their colleagues who include the "grey area" between these two extremes in their research.

Those in favour of the broader approach can point out, *inter alia,* that in practice a "soft law" instrument may be more effective than "genuine" law, as illustrated, for example, by the Helsinki Final Act in the controversy over human rights during the Cold War period. In this ideological confrontation the concluding document of the CSCE proved more relevant than the two UN Covenants.[38] In addition to reciprocity, publicity and the mobilisation of public opinion, which is

---

[38] On the possible advantages of "soft law", see Hanspeter Neuhold, "The Inadequacy of Law-Making by International Treaties: "Soft Law" as an Alternative?", in: Rüdiger Wolfrum/Volker Röben (eds.), *Developments of International Law in Treaty Making*, 2005, pp. 39 et seq.

usually unaware of the "soft-law" character of the document invoked, may indeed result in a stronger "compliance pull" than the prospect of a possible resort to the exclusive remedies that are only available in the event of a breach of "hard law".[39]

Furthermore, "hard" methods for the settlement of international disputes are not necessarily more effective than "soft" procedures. Arbitration and adjudication which fall into the former category result in third-party decisions; arbitral awards and judgments of international courts are based on international law and binding on the conflicting parties. However, the typical "winner-take-all" outcome may be perceived as unjust by the losing side. Moreover, the obligatory character of the rulings of arbitral tribunals and international courts does not mean that compliance can be taken for granted, given the lack of effective centralised enforcement mechanisms in the international legal order. In contrast, a non-binding compromise proposal submitted by a mediator, which may go beyond the law binding on the parties, may be regarded as fair, as legitimate by all of them and therefore implemented in practice.

The same is true of merely "unfriendly" retorsions as compared with the above-mentioned "harder" countermeasures. The latter are inherently unlawful responses which are exceptionally justified by the previous breach of international law by the other party. As already pointed out, countermeasures are subject to a number of restrictions, above all the principle of proportionality between the initial violation of international law and the reaction to it. Consequently, a retorsion may hurt the perpetrator of an illegal act more than a countermeasure.

Moreover, some international judicial bodies, above all the ICJ, may not only hand down "hard" judgments but also give "soft" advisory opin-

---

[39] Reprisals or countermeasures, as they are increasingly called (see above, footnote 33), have become more and more toothless, with the obligation not to violate *jus cogens*, which, *inter alia*, prohibits the use of armed force, in addition to the inherent threshold of proportionality, which must be respected. The option of challenging an allegedly unlawful act before an international court or arbitral tribunal remains theoretical in most cases, since the accused perpetrator has not given its consent, which is required for adjudication or arbitration. And even if it has done so, the problem of enforcing a judgment or arbitral award may remain.

ions. The practical impact of the latter may be greater, however, than that of legally binding decisions.[40]

To return the to issue of legitimacy, which could also be understood as "soft legality", law should ideally not only be regarded as binding but also appreciated as reasonable and not just by those to whom its norms are addressed. Lawyers should pay attention to divergences between these two perceptions. If the differences are small, jurists could help to maintain congruence between these two dimensions by using the room for legal manœuvre offered by the possibilities of interpretation. Otherwise they should come up with timely proposals for corrections of the law so that compliance can also be ensured in the future with a minimum of coercion.[41] This goal is particularly relevant to international law, which cannot rely on effective central enforcement mechanisms. Furthermore, a legal order in which resort to coercion for the implementation of its norms is not the exception but the rule is neither politically desirable, nor likely to be durable; for increasing repression will in all probability lead to growing resistance by its subjects, until the system either accepts far-reaching changes or is overthrown by the use of violent means.

---

[40] For instance, compatibility with the object and purpose as criterion for the admissibility of reservations to treaties. Reservations to the Convention on the Prevention and Punishment of the Crime of Genocide, ICJ Reports 1951, pp. 15 et seq. This criterion was later included in the Vienna Conventions on the Law of Treaties of 1969 and 1986 not only in Article 19 (c) on the formulation of reservations, but also in the obligation not to defeat the object and purpose of a treaty prior to its entry into force in Article 18, the definition of teleological interpretation in Article 31 (1) and for the distinction between "material" and minor breaches in Article 60 (3).

A similar "landmark" contributed by the ICJ is the taking into account of the implied powers of an international organisation when interpreting its constituent treaty in its advisory opinion on Reparation for Injuries Suffered in the Service of the United Nations, ICJ Reports 1949, pp. 174 et seq.

[41] A stronger role for international parliamentary assemblies and judicial control by international courts has been proposed as a strategy to enhance the legitimacy of international law. However, it remains to be seen whether states will accept this solution, which would weaken their own position.

What About Hobbes? Legitimacy as a Matter of Inclusion in the Functional and Rational Exercise of International Public Power

Volker Röben

Inspired by Professor Bodansky's powerful analysis of legitimacy and its discussion at this conference and reciprocating his compliment, I should like to address his brilliant ad hoc contribution to the conference. The starting point of the following brief remarks will be Professor Bodansky's intriguing insight that the heart of the matter of legitimacy and our worrying about it is the question why should I obey (public) power? This very question points to the paradox of making collectively binding decisions of the political or the legal variety, in the words of the late Niklas Luhmann. My remarks are thus concerned with the positive theory of legitimacy.

I. Introduction

The term legitimacy is not a specifically and maybe even not a primarily legal term, but it is clearly a concept that law needs to concern itself with. It makes sense, indeed, to approach the question in the cloak of positive theory that is one step removed from the legal discourse in its strictly technical-professional sense. In a second step, results may be transferred into the specifically legal discourse.

The question that has troubled speakers at this conference, whether there is anything more to legitimacy of international law than legality, has a sound reason. Positive theory teaches that the prime concern with regard to legitimacy is for public power, law being a secondary addressee. This is so because law likes to assume the position of a secondary decider who applies primary decisions taken elsewhere, and consequently is less in need of legitimacy than is the primary decider. The legal system is less so, at least if it refrains from autocratic decision-making, preferring instead to base itself on prior decisions, be they laws or precedents.[1] Even enforcement of law is not primarily under the remit of the legal system proper, although the procedure may be legally regulated.

Therefore, the enquiry should start out with the legitimacy of public power, in this case international public power, or we may also speak of governance.[2] Since most public power is expressed through law,[3] law will play an important role in this enquiry, however. It will also be law that enshrines the fundamental principles on the legitimacy of public power that I wish to identify.

Public power in the international realm is aggregate States' power. That is States cooperating and coordinating.[4] States – this is a basic tenet of international law as any student of it will learn – are the (sole) comprehensively competent makers of international law to the exclusion of other entities.[5] The exclusion operates through the use of the legal concept "sovereignty". In the international context that is states imbued with sovereign equality. The sources of international law laid down in

---

1 The wish to respect this bright line explains the emphasis placed by the International Court of Justice on state consent as the indispensable basis of its jurisdiction. See, recently, ICJ, Case Concerning Armed Activities On The Territory Of The Congo (Democratic Republic Of The Congo v. Rwanda), Judgment of 3 Feb. 2006. Lack of such consent indicates the view of states (or at least one state) that the issue remains in the realm of the political, or, in reverse, that law does not govern the issue.

2 See Joseph H.H. Weiler, "The Geology of International Law – Governance, Democracy and Legitimacy", *ZaöRV* 64 (2004), 547. Weiler rightly emphasizes that governance emerging as a thick and critical layer towards the end of 20th Century international law legitimizes the search for an altogether new discourse of legitimacy in the first place (at 553).

3 Infra IV.

4 It is a merit of Goldsmith and Posner's *The Limits of International Law*, 2005, to highlight that constituent nature of public power in the international realm, which will then drive the development of international law.

5 By virtue of the central dogma that states make international law and states are its addressees. But Andreas Fischer-Lescano, "Die Emergenz der Globalverfassung", *ZaöRV* 63 (2003), 717, proposes a states-less model of structural interconnection of international law and international politics.

Art. 3 ICJ Statute bear testimony to: international treaties and international customary law. This is the essence of the Westphalian system still with us today in fact and not least in UN Charter law.[6] The state is the form of the political system since early modernity. The sovereign state mediates other actors and thus excludes them from exercising power both internally and internationally.

II. Functions

Essentially, one can distinguish three rationales for justifying public power:[7] functional, teleological, and inclusion-based. Functionality posits, put simply, that public power is indispensable for security, public order, economic growth, other public goods.[8] The teleological justification additionally attributes certain (moral) purposes, such as justice or fairness or *Sittlichkeit,* to the public power. Thirdly, public power should be based on the consent of the governed; this is about inclusion. Most convincingly, legitimacy of public power calls for a combination of function and inclusion. International public power should meet certain central functions and it should be based on the consent of the governed, i.e. the states.

The functions of the international public power that states cooperating and coordinating exercise remain hitherto largely undefined, although the term international community (of states) may mark the truly crucial functions that international cooperation ought to fulfill in the eyes of

---

6 See Philip Bobbitt, *The Shield of Achilles*, 2002, on the correlation between the internal constitutional order of the states (not an individual state!) over their historical development and the external – international – constitutional order of states at that time.

7 Of course, this discussion is traditionally about the public power of a state. But recourse may be had to it when thinking about aggregate states' public power.

8 Thomas Hobbes may be claimed as the original source of all functional legitimacy theories, see Udo Di Fabio, *Das Recht offener Staaten*, 1998, at 18. Hobbes' argument that the Leviathan will provide security is powerful while, in the context of the modern state, containing a retarding element. Hobbes proposes a construction based on assumed anarchy and a social contract that is not confined to a particular reality. It thus may well be extended to the international context.

states and international organisations alike.[9] A truly convincing legal theory of the objectives and functions embodied in the term international community remains lacking, however, and the search for it could well prove elusive as the history of *Staatszwecklehre* may teach.

At another level of abstraction, however, the fact that cooperation of states is driven by legally operable functions is quite visible: Consciousness of the importance of defined objectives of international public power is most clearly reflected in Arts. 1 and 2 of the UN Charter, which, in this respect, is the model of almost all international institutions, including the European Union.[10]

III. Primary Legitimacy in the International System: The Working of the Inclusion Mechanism

The paradox of the beginning leads to the perspective of those expected to obey the rule in question. In the case of international law, these are states. Whether states can be expected to obey international law depends in essence on their being included in the exercise of this power.

In the state, the central mechanism for reaching inclusion is representation of the people in certain central institutions such as parliaments. In the international sphere inclusion in principle is ensured because sovereign equality requires that states need to consent to any exercise of public power binding them. Inclusion is thus the flipside of the exclusion. If states are the subjects of that very international law then they, and only they, need to be included in the lawmaking process. That is what we mean when we refer to state consent as the basis of legitimacy in international law. Such inclusion refers not to the individual state, which

---

[9] This is not the place for an in-depth study of this issue. But clearly, the international community cares much about security, at least if one goes by the pronouncements of the UN Security Council as one of the central institutional manifestations of the international community. The Council invokes the "international community" when it addresses particularly grave risks such as the proliferation of nuclear weapons of mass destruction. See S/RES 1718 (2006) warning North Korea that the international community will not tolerate its having such weapons.

[10] The recent efforts to re-launch the process of EU treaty reform have been based on reaching consensus on the objectives and function of future European integration. Berlin Declaration (2007) (http://www.eu2007.de/de/About_the_EU/Constitutional_Treaty/BerlinerErklaerung.html).

cannot make international law, but to states cooperating or at least acting in a coordinated fashion in order to make international law.

The issue of representation arises, however, as a consequence of the institutionalization of international relations. Representation in this sense has at least two elements: the membership of all states, representation in the decision-making organs and unanimity as the default voting procedure.[11] Institutions deviate from both elements in the name of effectiveness, of course, and this deviation presents challenges for the legitimacy of these institutions. The challenges for the future growth in international institutionalism lie here and it is worth looking more closely at the problem:

1. International Organisations: Majority Voting

Organisations that provide for substantial majority voting profoundly modify the basic principle of unanimous decision-making in the name of effectiveness. However, even here, the essential mechanism of inclusion can be made to work, e.g., by reserving certain strategic decisions to unanimous decision-making. The EU is an illustration of this strategy:

The trend towards qualified majority voting in the Council of Ministers is counter-balanced by the ever-increasing role of the European Council, which is composed of the heads of State or Government of the member states (and the Commission president) and where unanimity is required. As will be recalled, the European Council was not part of the original scheme of the treaties of Paris and Rome, which established the Coal and Steel, the Economic and the Atomic Energy Communities, yet it has become the central player in the decision-making process of the Union. The European Council physically embodies the crucial advantages of highly visible policy making. Most western democracies vest this specific function of overall (comprehensive) political leadership in a monolithic, ideally one-person, office, be it a prime minister or

---

[11] For conferences of the parties as the preferred institutional set-up in international environmental law see Geir Ulfstein, "Reweaving the Fabric of International Law?", in: Wolfrum/Röben, *Developments of International Law in Treaty Making*, 2005, 145, id., "Treaty Bodies", in: id. et al. eds., *Handbook of International Environmental Law*, 2007, 877; Volker Röben, "Institutional Developments under Modern International Environmental Agreements", *Max Planck UNYB* 4 (2000), 363.

a president. The importance of the European Council is thus closely linked to another dominant structural change in the working of all of the European democracies that follow the Westminster model, i.e. presidentialism within the parliamentary democracy. The European Council draws on the constitutional process in the Member States by involving the person identified by the broadest national constituencies as embodying the national leadership, thus legitimizing both the European polity and re-legitimizing the national polities. Public opinion is focused on these meetings of the heads of State and governments, which enjoy extensive media coverage. Decisions are made by those members of the national governments who are directly accountable either to the people or to the national parliaments: the heads of State or government. The participants detail their objectives to their parliaments prior to a Council meeting and report back after its conclusion. And the unanimity decision mode ensures that each member of the European Council can be effectively held accountable by the relevant national constituency.

As the European Council has gained stature, its revolving presidency has taken to setting out a political agenda of things that it wants to accomplish during its six-month tenure. These Presidency programmes reflect the distinct priorities of the Member State holding the Presidency. In response to increased political weight of the European Council, the European decision-making process has become a dynamic circular process. Its decision-making takes on the form of a four-step approach: a programme of action is developed by the Commission, submitted for approval to the European Council, implemented through manageable pieces of legislation, usually a framework directive to be adopted by the Council of Ministers and implementing legislation to be taken by the Commission in accordance with Arts. 202 and 211 EC pursuant to the regulatory committee procedure. The regulatory committee procedure allows for input by Member States' administrations, through which the national political systems feed their preferences. In the fourth step, the European Council controls steps two and three, in that it may take up any controversies arising during the implementation phase.

The power of the Presidency and the European Council to set the long-term planning of Union action creates a fundamental tension vis-à-vis attempts by the Commission to set the overall agenda for the European Union. This indicates one of the constitutional fault lines of EU constitutionalism.

The European Union illustrates a second avenue for bringing state consent to bear on an international organization with prevalent majority voting. Member States retain control of the treaties, and thus of the highest authority in the Union legal order. Unanimity prevails, in that any amendment requires the constitutionally valid consent of each member state to enter into force. Amending the treaties is a well-established way either to expand or to limit the competences of the Union.[12] Such changes require ratification according to the respective procedures of the Member States but not by the European Parliament. All Member States vest the ratification power in their national parliaments; the federal or decentralized Member States also involve the intra-federal level.

National parliaments have also been directly involved in the process of drafting such treaty amendments. Both the 'Charter of Fundamental Rights of the European Union' and the Constitutional Treaty featured a so-called convention as the body responsible for drafting the provisions of both instruments.

Finally, national parliaments are becoming involved in the process of making so-called secondary EU law, i.e. infra-treaty legislation directly applicable in the member states. The Constitutional Treaty gives the parliaments a role in monitoring that the EU complies with the so-called principle of subsidiarity pertaining to the exercise of its competences. As a matter of autonomous evolution of national constitutional law, parliaments may parallel the decision-making process in the Council of Ministers. Thus, e.g., under the revised Art. 23(3) of the *Grundgesetz* or Basic Law, the German government now has to consult the German Parliament before taking a position on a proposal submitted by the Commission to the Council of Ministers. The German government must act faithfully on the Parliament's opinion during the different phases of decision-making in the EU Council of Ministers. Furthermore, Parliament can enforce the discharge of this obligation in the Federal Constitutional Court.

---

[12] The fact that since 1992 (Treaty of Maastricht) there have been full-blown amendments in 1997 (Treaty of Amsterdam) and 2000 (Treaty of Nice) suggests that engaging in an intergovernmental conference with the aim of treaty revision is not prohibitively costly for member states. On more specific points, Member States establish their views as a matter of treaty law by means of the protocols and declarations that are a regular feature of the final acts concluding the intergovernmental conferences. Such instruments stipulate the agreed understanding of a certain provision of treaty law.

2. Limited Membership (Selection): the Case of the UN Security Council

The most important case of only a selection of states making international law is, of course, the UN Security Council that the UN Charter entrusts with the primary responsibility for the maintenance of international peace and security and that enjoys exclusive powers to take legally binding decisions under Chapter VII and Art. 25 UN Charter, binding on all member states of the organisation. This seems squarely to put the issue of inclusion. And it was perceived as such by the famous High level Panel on Challenges. However, the Panel report went much further in respect of UN Security Council reform. In fact, it recommended institutional reform. Such institutional reform was meant to broaden the Council's membership in an effort to make it more inclusive and thereby strengthen both its effectiveness and its legitimacy. However, the Heads of State and Government demurred. It may also be said that the problem would not have gone away, but merely be mitigated. However, other avenues may be open to address the inclusion matter at least partially.

To a certain extent, however, the Security Council in fact has taken up the core ideas of the Panel's recommendations. It has done so by involving States which are non-members of the Council in its crisis management on an ad hoc basis. More broadly, the legitimacy of the Council's action hinges on inclusiveness. This is not formal inclusiveness but functional inclusiveness, or meritorious inclusiveness. States ready to take on an increased responsibility for the management of international crises may do so on their own initiative by forming or joining an informal group. In other words: if the self-selected informal group effectively comes up with a plan to solve the crisis, it will receive support from the Security Council.[13] States making up the contact group while not being members of the Security Council are indirectly involved in the Council's decision-making. For that body's decisions relate to and are based on the grouping's prior actions. By the same token, the issue of formal membership loses some, if not all, of its practical significance for the Council's representativeness.

---

[13] Cf. World Summit Outcome resolving on the SC (A/RES/60/1, para. 154): "We recommend that the Security Council continue to adapt its working methods so as to increase the involvement of States not members of the Council in its work, as appropriate, enhance its accountability to the membership and increase the transparency of its work."

Decentralization refers first of all to internal processes of a State. Alternatively or mostly complementarily to such state-internal processes, relevant negotiations are conducted through informal groups of States.[14] Special interests and capabilities represented by such groups are of relevance at the negotiation stage and at the – potential – enforcement stage through sanctions which, in turn, will shore up the negotiating power of the group. The range of actors to be considered is not limited to States but includes the UN itself and other international organizations. The Council relies heavily on such informal groups in its recent practice on risks presented by the proliferation of nuclear weapons of mass destruction and by precarious states marred by instability and domestic violence. Space for negotiations conducted by informal groups was recently allocated in the cases of North Korea – the so-called Six-Party Talks –, Iran. Sudan – among others the African Union – and Lebanon – the quartet. The effectiveness of this firmly "bottom-up" approach is evident: Whenever possible the SC makes use of the superior knowledge of the parties close to the crisis. The Council seeks to assume an enabling rather than a prescriptive position. In modern parlance, this is public power reducing transaction costs. By virtue of this self-positioning, the Council itself stays one step removed from the crisis and thereby broadens the options available to it.

3. Multilateralism

An intriguing problem is that international law as it stands today employs many a restricted circle of states, if not to make law, then to provide guidance for its future development. Beyond the obvious candidate – the Security Council – there is the G8, there are the Bretton Woods institutions, there is Antarctica and there is customary international law, where the participation of the most interested states is needed to

---

[14] See UN SG Boutros-Ghali, "The increasing complexity of operations has led, on the political side to the intensification of peacemaking efforts. Thus, a new concept, that of 'Friends of the Secretary General', International Conferences', or 'Contact Groups' means that, while the UN peacekeepers are on the ground, intense diplomatic efforts continue with many parties to a conflict in order to reach a political settlement", SG/SM/5624, 1 May 1995. See Jochen Prantl, *The UN Security Council and Informal Groups of States, Complementing or Competing for Governance*, 2006, analyzing the role of such groups in the cases of Namibia, El Salvador and Kosovo.

form new law.[15] In principle, this squares with the exclusion/inclusion paradigm. For it ensures that those subject to the rules will also participate in their making. At the margin, of course, this creates problems, which necessitate certain adaptations of which the persistent objector doctrine is one. The experience of the EU teaches that a few precautions need to be taken to ensure that flexibility – i.e. a smaller number of states cooperating more closely – does not impair parallel institutionalized forms of cooperation of states. Probably the most difficult issue is multilateralism, i.e. the postulate that the legitimacy of an international regime is a function of the number of states participating. Here I part with Professor D'Amato: multilateralism finding its form in institutions (*Staatenverbünde*) is more likely to reach the inclusivity that it takes legitimately to govern issues that concern mankind, such as climate change.

4. Non-state Actors

Non-state actors – individuals, the private sector and non-governmental organisations – becoming more visible internationally present to a certain extent a most fundamental challenge to the above described legitimacy code characterized by the operation of exclusion and inclusion. This works on several levels.

For one, it is the non-state actors emerging from being mediated by their states. To be sure, there is no reason to exaggerate this point. The instances where significant political influence is exercised by – here mostly – NGOs are still rather few.[16]

Another specific issue is the growth of the global economic system. Transnationally active non-state actors enjoy a large and growing degree of autonomy, which is required by the logic of market economies. To the extent that the economic system is expected to integrate public interest and thus assume functions of the political system, it is in need of legitimacy, as Helen Keller discusses. In as much as it is economically relevant standardisation is entrusted to non-state actors they are directly included in the exercise of international public power. This direct

15 ICJ, North Sea Continental Shelf, ICJ Reports 1969, 1.

16 See Steve Charnovitz, "The Relevance of Non-State Actors to International Law", in: Wolfrum/Röben, note 11, 543; id., "Nongovernmental Organizations and International Law", *AJIL* 100 (2006), 348.

inclusion ensures individual self-determination of these actors. Such individual self-determination complements the collective self-determination of peoples or states (in the sense of sovereignty). However, here, too, the states currently still determine much of the substantive border of that autonomy and the procedural avenues for dispute resolution, as Armin von Bogdandy convincingly argues.

Finally, non-state actors form the public. The public provides public opinion control of public power and those exercising it, hold it accountable in between elections, and thus provides legitimacy. Such a public is an indisputable and indispensable element of all mature democracies. It is also becoming an international reality. This is happening because public discourse moves beyond subjects of national interests to global matters. The several national publics become an international public ensuring accountability of international public power. That, to me, is the core interest of Robert Keohane.

IV. The Rational Exercise of Power

There is nothing inherently rational about (international) public power. Power will be more easily accepted, however, if seen to be rational, not arbitrary. Rational in this specific sense comprises justice and fairness in a positive sense. Rationality is a distinct, complementary source of legitimacy from the processes that ensure inclusion in the exercise of such power. The principal means to ensure such rationality is law, i.e. abstract norms and their concrete application, which is reviewable in a court or tribunal.

It is the job of the international Rule of law to ensure two things: that public power is primarily exercised through law, i.e. making and applying rules, and that the process of making and applying those rules meets certain standards. The first function in this respect is to ensure that the rules of making and applying rules are enshrined in law. Such is the case for the sources of law, the law of treaties, jurisdiction, fundamental rights and obligations of states and so forth. Through the several mechanisms thus open to it – treaty cooperation, unilateral secondary legislation promulgated by international organs and other actors – international public power has pushed for the substantive development of law in three directions: an exchange order for commercial interaction, repressively securing the ethical minimum, and the preventive-prospective action on matters of public interest.

The Rule of law also contains legal standards or directives concerned with the rules themselves and with their application. Rule of law therefore re-enters the form into the form, again borrowing from Luhmann. Such international rule of law has several objects. There are the demands for consistency and coherence within a legal regime and across legal regimes, the central idea being that conflicting and contradictory obligations placed on states will undermine their will and ability to meet either. The fragmentation of international law has been perceived to be a problem in this respect, and the dogma that no international treaty escapes the Vienna Convention on the Law of Treaties has been offered as a solution. The strongest rationalising contribution to rule-making probably lies in the general (substantive) principles located at a medium level of abstraction. Proportionality, the precautionary principle and others are examples in this respect.

The international rule of law, with its power to rationalize public power and to inject substantive justice, is the particular remit of international courts and (arbitral) tribunals, with their professionalism and ability for autonomous doctrinal construction of the law. Witness the ICJ's *La-Grand case* interpreting the Vienna Convention on Consular Relations as international law protecting individuals moving across borders.[17] Judicial review remains a central tenet of the rule also in the more material (justice) sense, in particular as international law branches out into the economic area. The traditional means for this dispute settlement – diplomatic protection and state-to-state dispute before the International Court of Justice – are not sufficient.[18] Hence the growth in international (commercial) arbitration where private non-state actors can bring suits also against states. To a certain extent, courts and (arbitral) tribunals will provide this rationalizing force only if they can be made to work consistently and coherently across their areas of competence. While such coherence is a matter of efficiency only for international organisations as such – witness the explicit demands put on the EU – it is a matter of legitimacy for international courts and tribunals. The understanding of the specific internal logic of public law, on the one hand, and criminal law, on the other, is reflected in the recent ICJ judgment on Genocide in Bosnia, where the Court had to apply the Genocide Con-

---

[17] ICJ Rep. 2001, 466.

[18] This is true even though the ICJ will allow states to bring cases for individuals on the basis of diplomatic protection, as it did in the La Grand case. This still leaves the decision whether to exercise such diplomatic protection within the home state's discretion.

vention as an instrument addressed to states, not to individuals, as is the statute of the International Tribunal for the Former Yugoslavia.[19] While the Court followed the ICTY's practice in assessing the facts of the case, it applied its own standard of proof and it explicitly refuted the ruling of the ICTY on the issue of state control over other actors within the meaning of state responsibility, claiming this issue to be within its (public law) remit.

V. The Limits of International Law

Thirdly, legitimacy of international public power depends on its limits. The states' aggregate power must respect the capacity of individual states to make decisions for themselves. This is a matter of logic: the aggregate cannot substitute its own constituent elements. Also, collective self-determination of a people presupposes that the state they form has reasonably important matters to decide. The traditional means for demarcating the proper reach of the international was the principle of non-intervention (cf. Art. 2(7) UN Charter). However, this has always been a highly flexible concept.[20] At any rate, however, the internal political order of states was off limits to the international during much of the post-post war period.

That is changing, however, with possibly far-reaching consequences. For states increasingly have to meet standards concerning their internal political order. A state has to meet these standards to belong among the states that regularly cooperate, that, in other words, form the international community. Aside from traditional human rights such standards comprise the rule of law and good governance.[21] The international thus piggybacks on the legitimacy inherent in constitutional nation states.

---

19 Application of the Convention on the Prevention and Punishment of the Crime of Genocide (Bosnia and Herzegovina v. Serbia and Montenegro) – Judgment of 26 Feb. 2007.

20 Even the PCIJ stated that the term internal affairs of a state had no absolute meaning, for states were free to subject any matter to international cooperation. This is, of course, a consistent application of the state consent principle. P.C.I.J. 1927 (ser. A) No. 9 (Sept. 7).

21 And democracy, at least for those post-conflict states that receive strong international attention, see Rüdiger Wolfrum, "International Administration in Post-Conflict Situations by the United Nations and Other International Actors", *Max Planck UNYB* 9 (2005), 649.

As a result, inclusion in the process of making international law is affected. At least in the long run, it may no longer suffice to be sovereign to have the right to inclusion. Instead, the right to be included may come to depend on states meeting some of these standards just mentioned.

However, perhaps paradoxically, these standards also restore limits to the reach of the international. To see this, one needs to look at the way international human rights work. Clearly, at the beginning and as formulated by the UN Charter, they were meant to control states or – in the words of Joseph Weiler – to police the boundaries of the states. And they do this ever more powerfully. However, they have assumed further functions. They now define standards of belonging. And, by the same token, they define the limits of international action vis-à-vis individual states. Not just because a state that does respect international human rights standards is shielded from intervention. But also, as we saw in Erika de Wet's paper, because human rights are emerging as checks on international action reaching deep into a state's domestic affairs. Correspondingly, the European Court of Justice has understood human rights to demarcate the space left to national determination and legislation not falling under the EU remit, and that is also the approach taken by the EU Charter of Fundamental Rights. The actual workings are complex but the functionality can be clearly seen. There is also a fundamental reason here. For human rights are primarily negative rights, i.e. rights of the individual to freedom from public intervention. That this right is addressed as much at a state as it is addressed at international organizations should be evident. The EU Charter of Fundamental Rights draws that conclusion.

VII. Globalization

Globalisation is a fact. In particular, the economy has long left the segmentation imposed by the nation state turning itself into the truly global economy. In the process, the nation state is transforming itself into a market state. As a consequence, the global economy becomes the point of orientation of the truly global political system, represented by *Staatenverbünde* of all shapes and varieties, and variable forms of international lawmaking. If, in the long run, states become truly just segments of a global legal and political system, the weight of legitimacy concerns will shift to specific forms and institutions. Closer cooperation also means more international standards for states' internal structure. Or we may look directly at the several functions exercising international law, which is what Professor Bodansky advises, doing away with state consent *à la limite*.

States used to be the sole or exclusive subjects and makers of international law, which made this a perfectly matched operation. As we all know, this is no longer the case, hence the concerns about the legitimacy of international law. This holds true still today even though other actors have emerged to take a place alongside state on the international scene: Intergovernmental organisations, non-governmental organisations, the individual to a certain extent. For today's international reality, this raises many challenges, both with respect to the manifold new actors and for the internal differentiation of international law itself. The following remarks are not intended to exhaust the matter, simply to raise some salient issues.

Construction of the Discourse on Legitimacy of International Institutions*

*Kong Qingjiang***

Abstract

China used to be one of the few countries which had long avoided most international affairs and shunned most international institutions. Recognition of the legitimacy of the West-dominated international institutions was alien or, more precisely, unacceptable to China in Mao's era. Recently, as China has risen, it has begun to embrace regional and global institutions and take on the responsibilities that come with the status of an emerging superpower. It has embraced much of the current constellation of international institutions, rules, and norms. Does this signal that China has begun to perceive international institutions as legitimate? If so, in what context? Does the new Chinese perception vary from multilateral institutions to regional institutions, as it has demonstrated its enthusiasm for regional integration schemes? The article examines the evolving Chinese approach to the issue of legitimacy of international institutions. A preliminary finding is that China views this issue as a means to promote its national interests. Embracing regional integration schemes evidences its drive to shape the evolution of that system in limited ways.

* International institutions can be defined, in a very stylized fashion, as "rules that govern elements of world politics and the organizations that help implement those rules". See R. Keohane, "International Institutions: Can Interdependence Work?", *Foreign Policy* (Spring 1998), 82.

** Professor at the Faculty of Law, Zhejiang Gongshang University, Hangzhou, China. He wishes to thank Dr. Volker Roeben for encouragement.

I. Introduction

In recent years the general feeling towards multilateral institutions has not been very positive. The fiasco of the WTO Ministerial Conferences every other year has demonstrated how strongly non-governmental organizations (NGOs), such as farmers' advocates, environmentalists, human rights activists, trade unions, and consumer groups, protest against the current multilateral trading system. Other influential international institutions such as the International Monetary Fund (IMF), the World Bank and even the European Union (EU) are also confronting similar criticisms from a similar range of NGOs.

Antipathy towards the international institutions largely emanates from misgivings about their recent eye-catching quantitative and qualitative expansion. The international organization system has expanded its regulatory domains beyond the purported treaty interests to regulate an array of non-treaty ones, which are traditionally the prerogatives of the domestic constituencies of their member states.

In addition to their quantitative expansion, international institutions have transformed themselves into entities beyond typical international organizations. This expansion has been perceived as "constitutionalization" of the international institutions. This gives rise to another dimension of worries that, as massive power is increasingly concentrated in the hands of unelected bureaucrats, international institutions are becoming more and more unaccountable; they are further and further removed from the people who are affected by the decisions of the very bureaucrats who preside over the institutions. This criticism seems particularly strong when, for example, a couple of WTO panelists decide against trade laws, policies and measures that an elected national legislature of a given member deems necessary to protect the interests of its people.

These sentiments underscore a real problem: most international institutions suffer from what is often referred to as a "democratic legitimacy deficit".

Interestingly, unlike the general approach to the issue of legitimacy of international institutions, the Chinese perception of this issue is quite different. In fact, the legitimacy of international institutions has never been singled out for meticulous and systemic study. Rarely can one find literature on this issue. Students of international law in China basically are disinterested in this matter. Instead, it is only touched on in the discourse on the international order, which is hotly debated among students of international relations.[1]

In this context, any discussion of legitimacy in China cannot proceed without an understanding of China's approach to international institutions.

II. An Overview of the Evolving Approach to International Institutions[2]

According to the normative-cognitive approach, the moral search for the legitimacy of international institutions can start within each nation.[3] A nation's behaviour regarding an international institution is very much a result of the cognitive necessity for the nation to behave in a morally sensible way in front of its domestic constituency.

China, in the era of Mao Zedong, rejected the rules of the then international system and was never hesitant to pursue change through revolution instead. Mao's foreign policy was noted for its bombastic language, strong opposition to the superpowers (the United States and the Soviet Union), close association with developing countries, relative isolation from international organizations, and economic autarky.

In contrast, Deng Xiaoping took China in the opposite direction. He promoted engagement with the international community to facilitate economic modernization at home. Consequently, China gradually began to emerge from its Mao-era isolation. China expanded its international profile by significantly increasing its participation in intergov-

---

1 In this regard, serious research works include Ye Jiang et Tan Tan, "On the Legitimacy of International Institutions and its Defects" (in Chinese), *World Economics and Politics*, no. 12 (2006), and Wang Lefu et Li Weiquan, "A Study of the Issue of Legitimacy of Subjects in International Governance in the Context of Globalization" (in Chinese), *Journal of Sun Yat-sen University*, no. 9 (2003).

2 The discussion throughout this Section has benefited from the author's reading of Marc Lanteigne, *China and International Institutions: Alternative Paths to Global Powers*, 2005 and Evan S. Medeiros and M. Taylor Fravel, *China's New Diplomacy*, 2003.

3 For a study of the normative-cognitive approach, see, for example, Chih-Yu Shih, *China's Just World, The Morality of Chinese Foreign Policy*, 1993, pp. 11-25.

ernmental and non-governmental organizations, especially financial ones, i.e. the World Bank and the IMF. Notably, Chinese participation in the international community remained thin during Deng's tenure. It has been suggested that China sought to maximize its interests through minimal involvement, by free riding on the actions of other major powers while staking a claim to the moral high ground, i.e. it sought many of the rights and privileges of a great power without accepting most of the attendant obligations and responsibilities.[4]

Today, by contrast, the world's most populous country largely works within the international system. China is taking a less confrontational, more sophisticated, more confident, and, often, more constructive approach toward regional and global affairs. Evidence of the change abounds. The recent transformation began in the early 1990s, with Beijing's drive to expand its bilateral links. It began to establish various levels of "partnership" to facilitate economic and security coordination. The pinnacle of this process was the Treaty of Good-Neighbourliness and Friendly Cooperation that China signed with Russia in 2001.

During this period, Beijing also began to abandon its previous aversion to international institutions. Chinese leaders began to recognize that some institutions could allow their country to promote its trade and security interests. Thus, starting in the second half of the 1990s, China began to engage with the Association of Southeast Asian Nations (ASEAN). In 1995, Beijing began holding annual meetings with senior ASEAN officials. Soon, China helped initiate the "ASEAN + 3" mechanism, a series of yearly meetings among the ten ASEAN countries plus China, Japan, and South Korea. Next came the Framework Agreement on Comprehensive Economic Co-operation between ASEAN and the People's Republic of China, which was based on the "ASEAN + 1" mechanism. With the Framework Agreement, a China-ASEAN free trade area is set to emerge within 10 years. China even signed, with ASEAN, a declaration on a code of conduct in 2002 primarily for the purpose of settling territorial disputes between China and some ASEAN members. Interestingly, the final document included most of the draft language sought by ASEAN – and little of what was offered by China. China also deepened its participation in the Asia-Pacific Economic Cooperation forum, hosting the ninth leaders' meeting in Shanghai in 2001. While clinging to its claims over the islands,

---

[4] Iain Johston, *An Overview of Studies of American Scholars on the Relationship between China and International Organizations* (in Chinese), Institute of World Economics and Politics, Chinese Academy of Social Sciences, 2004.

China has now repeatedly committed itself to settling the territorial disputes peacefully, based on international law.

In Central Asia, meanwhile, China led the establishment of the region's first multilateral group, the Shanghai Cooperation Organization (SCO). Founded to settle long-standing territorial disputes and to demilitarize borders, the SCO has expanded its mission to counterterrorism cooperation and regional trade.

China also spared no efforts to improve its ties to Europe. In 1996, China was a founding member of the Asia-Europe Meeting, which holds biannual summits for heads of state and yearly ministerial meetings. Soon thereafter, China and the EU also initiated an annual political dialogue.

Meanwhile, China has increased its engagement with the Security Council of the United Nations. Until the mid-1990s, China regularly abstained from Council resolutions that invoked Chapter VII of the Charter of the United Nations, which authorizes the use of force, in order to signal its opposition to the erosion of sovereignty such resolutions implied. In recent years, however, Beijing has begun to back these measures. In November 2002, for example, it voted for Resolution 1441 on weapons inspections in Iraq, one of the few times that China has supported a Chapter VII measure since joining the UN in 1971. Beijing has also increased its participation in peacekeeping operations, supporting contingents in East Timor, Congo (Kinshasa), Haiti, and elsewhere. More prominently, China ratified several major arms control and nonproliferation treaties, including the Treaty on the Nonproliferation of Nuclear Weapons and the Chemical Weapons Convention. China has also agreed to adhere to the basic tenets of the Missile Technology Control Regime. And it signed the Comprehensive Nuclear Test Ban Treaty in 1996.[5]

The changes represent an attempt by China to rebuild its image, protect and promote Chinese economic interests, and enhance its security; they also supposedly demonstrate an attempt to counterbalance American influence around the world. They signal a larger transformation: China's emergence as an active player in the international arena. Although the changes are precipitated by the motivation to protect its own interests, China now accepts many prevailing international rules

[5] In contrast, for much of the 1980s, Beijing viewed arms control and nonproliferation as the responsibility of the United States and the Soviet Union, and as attempts to limit China's influence.

and institutions. It is fair to say that Beijing currently is prepared to work within international rules and norms to pursue its interests.

III. Legitimacy of International Institutions: the Chinese Perception

Legitimacy, Sovereignty and Order in China

Jacques Rousseau believed he could resolve the question of legitimacy.[6] This highlights the centrality of Western modernity. Indeed, the Western view asserts that the problem of legitimacy, *per se*, implies that there is no higher authority to which the individual, or indeed the collectivity, naturally or self-evidently owes allegiance or obedience.[7] In the eyes of Hobbes, for example, the question of legitimacy and its solution have been bound up with the construction of sovereignty, a kind of power that, once legitimated, is supposedly insulated from challenge by competing higher authorities.[8] Based on this, it becomes clear how legitimacy of international institutions rests on the sovereignties of constituent states.

Indeed, sovereignty can be historically understood through two broad movements. The first is the development of a system of sovereign states, culminating in the Peace of Westphalia in 1648. The second movement is the circumscription of the sovereign state, which began in practice after World War II and has since continued through European integration and the growth and strengthening of laws and practices to protect human rights. As a result, the assertion that no legitimate power exists above and beyond the sovereign has become less and less tenable.

---

6 His words read: "Humankind was born free but is everywhere in chains.... How can it be made legitimate? I believe I can resolve this question." See Jacques Rousseau, *Social Contract I*, p. 1.

7 See, for example, Robert Howse, "The legitimacy of the World Trade Organization", in: Jean-Marc Coicaud, Veijo Heiskanen, *Legitimacy of International Organizations*, 2001, p. 355.

8 The remarks that follow on Hobbes, sovereignty throughout this Section have benefited from author's reading of Stanford Encyclopedia of Philosophy, The Metaphysics Research Lab. Stanford University.

However, China seems to be sticking to the traditional understanding.[9] Moreover, China's approach has its base in the Chinese tradition. Confucian teaching, which served the Chinese Empire well for 2,000 years, acknowledged the "natural order of things" and gave great weight in particular to the need to accept the supremacy of family above all other institutions. A typical example in this regard is that during some dynastical periods sons could not be prosecuted for aiding and abetting a criminal father, because it was natural that a family would aid and shelter its own members. Manifested in the social institutions, the Chinese tradition tended to grant some legitimacy to the hierarchy of priorities, and it still has a bearing on the Chinese perception in modern days.[10]

Legitimacy of International Institutions in the Discourse of International Order in China

While China's caution and conservatism are still visible in its dealings with the international order, the Chinese ambition to assume the privileges of superpowerdom in the international institutions, which is expected to display the characteristics of a Chinese perception of the international order, is not new. It is therefore a plausible argument that, as China's power accumulates, it is just a matter of time before it will be rigorously promoting a conceptualization of the international order with Chinese characteristics, unless the nation is assured that more power can be developed through cooperation.[11]

However, the author wishes to argue that frustration associated with the contemporary international order, which is undoubtedly characterized by US supremacy and the unilateralism that the US tends to pursue, helps shape the new Chinese view, i.e. that unilateralism, *per se*, constitutes a real threat to the legitimacy and democratic decision-making processes of international institutions. It is proven that American supremacy is not enough to guarantee the effective action of the

---

9 For a detailed discussion of the People's Republic of China's perception of sovereignty, see Cheng Hu, *Globalization and State Sovereignty* (in Chinese), 2003, pp. 112-122.

10 For an argument that Confucianism still serves as the mode of governance for contemporary China, see Ross Terrill, *The New Chinese Empire: And What It Means for the United States*, 2003.

11 See, for example, Chapter 5: China's institutional openings and shifts in international power, in: Marc Lanteigne, *China and International Institutions: Alternative Paths to Global Powers*, 2005.

United Nations until the US respects other states' proper national interests. Without the collaboration of other big powers, the United Nations may turn out to be paralyzed again. Furthermore, since no power can overreach indefinitely, clinging to unilateralism will definitely do harm in the long run to the country concerned. Multilateralism enjoys greater effectiveness than unilateralism.

It is clear that in the discourse on the international order this issue of legitimacy of international institutions is not separable from unilateralism, multilateralism, and regionalism. Unilateralist action, which is likely to be viewed as an instrument for one's national interests, but not for the collective interests of the international community, will do no more than damage to its legitimacy. In this context, multilateralism promises to be beneficial in that it increases the legitimacy of transnational governance. It provides a chance for the international community to express its ideas and interests; negotiation and decision-making can be accomplished in such a multilateral situation. From the Chinese point of view, multilateralism is the way for the international community to constrain the caprice of a superpower and for international institutions to avoid making mistakes. This is particularly important when more and more developing countries and relatively weak powers prefer to pursue global governance through international institutions, which were often initiated by big powers. After all, transnational democracy – albeit still in an early stage of development – should not be forgotten when democracy is a key word in domestic policy. Faced with an array of international institutions that do not fit China's model of the international order, China – as was said before – has generally shown a preference for cooperation to resolve conflict in dealing with international institutions. China is expected to continue cooperation with other states within the boundaries of international rules and norms of behaviour.

This prognosis of China's future foreign policy does not depend on some quality inherent in the international order that seeks legitimacy or, at least, a symbolic or normative legitimacy; rather, it depends on China's awareness that it is still a developing country, albeit a rising power. This provides an explanation of why China tends to link the legitimacy of an institution with the decision-making process. As a pragmatic choice, China attaches great importance to its own weight in the decision-making process when it evaluates the legitimacy of an international institution. In other words, it equates the legitimacy of an institution with the existence of either a democratic mechanism or a balance of interests of the institution's constituent members in the decision-making process within the institution. In fact, the criteria for judging whether one of these two exists are twofold: firstly, whether the big powers among the institution's members share the power or responsibility, including the presence of a formal or informal consultative mechanism between the big powers, which China considers to be paramount; secondly, whether the interests of developing countries at large are taken into consideration in the decision-making process. In other words, China sees the need for the international order to accommodate the participant nations, whether manifested in a certain degree of coordination of sovereignties or in response to the concerns of the participating nations.

What is also worth mentioning is that multilateral institutions do not necessarily lend support to the legitimacy of international institutions. Instituting genuine multilateralism, or multilateral democratic decision-making processes, is a prerequisite for the legitimacy of international institutions.

IV. Do Regional Institutions Have More Legitimacy Than Multilateral Institutions?

China is in favour of promoting democratic decision-making processes in the international order. As a realist, however, China is aware that with US predominance, the current multilateral institutions cannot deliver the sort of legitimacy that it expects.

The Chinese have, as mentioned above, proposed a blizzard of Asian regional economic arrangements in recent years. China's efforts to promote regional institutions so far have been heeded within its economic greenhouse; this regional bloc of countries is expected to rely primarily on the use of China's "soft power"; they are also frustrated by the fact that multilateralism does not necessarily confer legitimacy on international institutions.

Indeed, China is dissatisfied with some aspects of this system, the US unilateralism in particular. China has never ceased its efforts toward establishing a new international political and economic order that is fair and rational. The trend toward pervasive regional integration provides the nation with an opportunity to test whether regionalism lends support to the legitimacy of international institutions.

Regional institutions are those in which membership consists of geographically proximate states, and they are often a result of regional integration. In this context, the situation seems quite simple as regards the legitimacy of regional institutions, for their legitimacy depends to a large extent on how they perform in the eyes of the governments of those regional countries. Indeed, regional institutions tend to operate with small numbers and higher levels of interaction than global organizations, and they are more likely to involve member states in their decision-making process. It has been observed that international dimensions of democracy seem much clearer in international institutions at a regional level than at the world-wide level. In addition, causal processes such as socialization, binding, monitoring, and enforcement are more likely in the regional economic institutions as the vast majority of agreements are made under the auspices of, or to create, regional institutions.

However, the real picture is far more complicated, because international institutions, multilateral or regional, have also to deal with the other audience: various groups of the public, who, at the same time, also have an opinion about the legitimacy of regional institutions.[12] And there is criticism of the "democratic legitimacy deficit" phenomenon in regional institutions, just as in multilateral institutions. In other words, as for regional institutions, there is also a question of legitimacy in the eyes of the public at large.

V. Some Preliminary Comments on the Chinese Practice

The reason for the Chinese perception of legitimacy and for the practice of institutionalizing legitimacy through regionalism has to do with China's unique national experience as an aggrieved victim of Western imperialism and the sense of desire that has arisen from it, that is, the desire that the reality of its expanding regional role be recognized. China is rapidly emerging as the engine of growth in Asia, which affords it increasing influence and leverage.

The Chinese are to some extent like the Americans; that is, both believe that nation-states must ultimately look out for themselves when it comes to matters of their critical interest. But China is more aware that it is dependent on international institutions and cooperation to manage the global economy from which they benefit enormously.

---

[12] G.C.A. Junne, "International organizations in a period of globalization: New (problems of) legitimacy", in: Jean-Marc Coicaud, Veijo Heiskanen, *Legitimacy of International Organizations*, 2001, pp. 191-192.

As observers have pointed out, over the past decade China has shifted its posture from that of an aggrieved victim of Western imperialism to that of an increasingly responsible member of the international community. Against this backdrop, some might argue that the Chinese are theoretically right, but wrong in the practice of institutionalizing legitimacy through regionalism.

Firstly, legitimacy of international institutions does not always obtain only through multilateralism or unilateralism. International institutions are, after all, not forums for members to share powers. An international institution's legitimacy is at its lowest when it fails to serve the common public good of the international community.[13] Also, institutional deficiency partly accounts for the legitimacy crisis. For example, two principles in the UN Charter, i.e. "non-interference with domestic affairs" and "respect for human rights", are sometimes viewed as contradictory, and this may often give rise to an outcry for an evaluation of the legitimacy of humanitarian intervention in the territory of a member state by certain other member states.

Secondly, the Chinese idea that legitimacy is handed downward from a disembodied international community rather than handed upward from existing democratic institutions (which reflect the public will on a nation-state level) might invite criticism. To the extent that international organizations have legitimacy, it is because duly constituted democratic majorities have handed that legitimacy up to them in a negotiated, contractual process, which they can take back at any time. Having a democratic decision-making process in place is only and should be only part of this general democratic process.

Thirdly, China should not necessarily take for granted the conventional wisdom that, as a matter of principle, the decision-making process of legitimately constituted democracies cannot make grave mistakes. In order to promote the common public good of the international society, a strong leadership is often as necessary in a multilateral institution as in a regional institution.

Fourthly, the issue of legitimacy always lingers wherever a nation-state uses an international institution, a multilateral institution of the American style, or a regional one of the Chinese style as an instrument to pursue its national interests. Indeed there is a risk that weak states under-

---

13 See, for example, Ye Jiang et Tan Tan, "On the Legitimacy of International Institutions and its Defects" (in Chinese), *World Economics and Politics*, No. 12 (2006).

standably want stronger multilateralism constrained by norms and rules, while great powers seek freedom of action. In this regard, China should still recall the risk of being unilateralist as it is nurturing its superpower status via regional integration schemes.

Round Table

Y. Dinstein: I have not taken the floor so far in this Seminar on the central issue of legitimacy. It is perhaps time for me to comment on some of the theses advanced in the various presentations made in the course of a day-and-a-half deliberations.

I regard legitimacy as a bastard term. I mean that both metaphorically and literally. Metaphorically, legitimacy is a bastard term since it is a hybrid expression: sometimes it means legality and on other occasions (as I shall try to explain) it denotes anything but legality. Literally, it is necessary to recall the most critical context in which legitimacy has played a role in the course of history. Legitimate or illegitimate circumstances of birth – in or out of wedlock – have been of pivotal consequence in European annals by affecting the bloodline of the nobility. Bearing in mind that only a legitimate heir could aspire to the throne, the peerage or any other privilege derived from one's ancestors, a determination whether a child – especially, a son – was born in wedlock became a matter of far-reaching ramifications.

When did legitimacy penetrate the discourse in the international arena? Although I have not written a dissertation on the subject, to the best of my knowledge the expression was first introduced by Talleyrand in the celebrated Congress of Vienna of 1814-1815. In the 1814 Paris Conference and in the early part of the Congress of Vienna, France, as the defeated belligerent party, was treated in the same manner as Germany would be in Versailles in 1919: it was excluded from the inner councils of the victorious Allies. Talleyrand was skilfully and methodically seeking access to a seat at the table where the future fate of Europe lay at stake. He came up with a brilliant idea by coining the phrase "légitimité" as a sacred principle of public law. *Cui bono*? Of course, the restored House of Bourbon that Talleyrand represented at the time. The postulate was: better gloss over the previous 25 years of revolution, upheaval and usurpation; Louis XVIII was the legitimate monarch of France and he should therefore be recognized as a co-equal and partner of the Allies. Talleyrand's efforts were crowned with success: Metternich and his colleagues bought the argument; France rejoined the ranks of the Big Powers; legitimacy prevailed. Subsequently, albeit for a limited period, the notion of legitimacy became predominant in the Concert of Europe. For a number of years, there was a readiness – if necessary – to invade any European country where the principle of legitimacy was challenged by revolution. Constitutional legitimacy was thus the historical underpinning of the concept of legitimacy in international law.

However, since Vienna, legitimacy has been used on the international plane in three disparate senses. The simple and straightforward meaning is that of legitimacy as a synonym of legality. For instance, the right of self-defence is rendered in French as "légitime défense". What does "légitime défense" signify? The essence of the phrase is lawful defence, to be set apart from other modes of the use of counter-force that are illicit. One could easily think of multiple additional illustrations of a semantic equivalence between legality and legitimacy.

The second meaning of legitimacy comes into play when the law is not exactly observed but is "stretched". The leading example is that of the Kosovo air campaign, conducted by NATO in 1999. Needless to say, none of the NATO countries has ever challenged the cornerstone of the architecture of the Charter of the United Nations, to wit, the prohibition of the use of force in international relations, subject to only two exceptions of self-defence and enforcement action carried out by virtue of a decision of the Security Council. However, in 1999, believing that they were facing evil incarnate, the NATO countries resorted to what scholars usually call "humanitarian intervention" on behalf of the Kosovars. The NATO countries decided to have recourse to inter-State force against Serbia, notwithstanding the fact that they could invoke neither the right of self-defence nor the seal of approval of the Security Council. As I (and not only I) see it, in the absence of Security Council authorization, the construct of "humanitarian intervention" is not in conformity with the law of the Charter. Yet, given the "ethnic cleansing" policy being implemented in Kosovo, the Governments – fully supported by public opinion – in Western Europe and North America strongly adhered to the view that the law should be stretched beyond the range of the black-letter words of the Charter. The action taken by the NATO countries was not *stricto sensu* lawful, but they felt that it was legitimate. Legitimacy in this instance did not coincide with lawfulness; still, the actors (NATO) sincerely believed that they were not breaching international law. Legitimacy thus occupied a borderline position between lawfulness and unlawfulness, somewhat akin to a yellow traffic light flashing between the green and the red.

These two senses of legitimacy by no means exhaust the field. There is a third, crucially important, meaning of the word that has surprisingly commanded scant attention thus far in the Round Table. I have been sitting here for a day and a half, on German soil, and I have been straining to hear a very specific name. Nobody saw fit even to allude to it. The situation appears to resemble the non-mention of Cyrano's nose in his presence. Everybody thinks about it, but no one dares to articulate the thought lest that may provoke Cyrano with his fearsome sword. The missing name, of course, is that of Carl Schmitt. After all, Schmitt is the one who came up with the idea of a total discord between „Legalität und Legitimität", and he did that as part of a bitter campaign against the democratic institutions of the Weimar Republic. Shortly after the publication of „Legalität und Legitimität", Schmitt became a conspicuous advocate of Nazism (Schmitt's nefarious role under the Nazis is described by Detlev Vagts in his classical article on "International Law in the Third Reich" in the American Journal of International Law). For my part, when I read the debate on the topic that raged in the pre-Nazi era, my instinctive reaction is to side with Hans Kelsen against Carl Schmitt.

There is reason to keep in mind who Schmitt was and what he stood for, because legitimacy for him was the opposite of what legitimacy means to those trying to uphold the law. Schmitt's entire purpose in presenting the dichotomy of legitimacy/legality in the closing days of the Weimar Republic was to conjure up legitimacy in order to delegitimize legality. In other words, legitimacy was recruited in a struggle to subvert the existing legal system: what was lawful was allegedly illegitimate, and consequently it could be disregarded with impunity. When you hear the word legitimacy, I would therefore urge you to be cautious. You must always ask yourselves who is using the term, in what connection and especially why.

Legitimacy is not the sole abstract expression that should put you on your toes. In the course of the discussion, we have repeatedly heard three other buzzwords that are deemed to be the pillars of legitimacy. These three words are democracy, fairness and justice.

The reference to democracy as a measuring rod of the legitimacy of international law astonishes me. Like quite a few other people in the room, I have written an article dealing with the dilemmas of democracy, the cardinal question being whether there is a right to democracy pursuant to international law. The answer, in my opinion, depends on the geographic framework within which the analysis is made. In Europe, the concept of democracy is well-entrenched, thanks to the European Convention of Human Rights. By contrast, there are valid doubts about the status of democracy as a right protected by international law globally. You may agree or disagree with this eclectic approach, but that is not the thrust of my argument today. No matter how you answer the question as stated, at least you look at democracy through the lens of international law (regional or global). But in our Round Table the whole conundrum of democracy has been turned on its head. Instead of the perspective being that of international law, examining whether democracy is vested with the status of a fully-fledged legal right, we are now told that we ought to look at the international legal system from the angle of democracy and ask ourselves whether international law deserves the label law. This is not only wrong: it is ahistorical.

By now, international law has come a long way – incidentally, not 5,000 years, as we have heard, but approximately 400 years from the days of Grotius and the other founding fathers. For centuries, it never occurred to anyone to speak about a "democracy deficit", for democracy was conspicuous by its almost total absence from the scene. Had democracy been applied as a benchmark, international law would have been stillborn in the 17th century. Democracy is a far more recent development than international law, and even today most of the Members of the United Nations scarcely qualify as authentic democracies. If democracy were to trump international law, democracy and international law would remain ascendant in Europe, North America and several other parts of the world; but, as a global normative system, international law would be seriously undermined. My advice to you is to forget about democracy as an acid test of international law.

The two other buzzwords – fairness and justice – seem to be immensely appealing and even impregnable constructs. Except that usually they represent subjective vantage points. Pascal said that what is true on this side of the Pyrenees is not true on the other side of the Pyrenees. The same observation can be made with respect to fairness and justice. What appears to be fair to Indians is often looked upon as unfair by Pakistanis. What is considered just by Israelis is rejected as unjust by Arabs. And so it goes on. At bottom, fairness and justice – just like beauty – are in the eye of the beholder. When the proposition is advanced that justice or fairness clashes with a customary or treaty rule of international law, this should normally be appraised as an unsubstantiated subjective allegation. I still prefer, as a rule, to stick to international law as it stands. Law is much more objective than the alluring notions of fairness and justice.

True, sometimes a particular postulate of justice or fairness evolves *contra legem*, sweeping the entire international community. In such a case, there is every likelihood that a novel customary law will consolidate (thanks to a new general practice of States and a new *opinio juris*) or a new multilateral treaty will be drafted and enter into force. If so, the old *lex lata* will be superseded by a new *lex lata* that reflects the communal perception of justice or fairness. But as long as the old *lex lata* remains unaltered, the perception of justice or fairness continues to be a mere *lex ferenda, i.e.*, desired law (in the view of some), as distinct from positive law. If and when the law does change, and you ask yourselves why the transformation has occurred – what the root cause of recasting the law was – the answer may well be that the international community has reached the conclusion that the previous law was unfair or unjust. But justice and fairness are not the exclusive reasons for a revision of a pre-existing law. An amendment of the law may equally be derived from a sense that it is illogical, impolitic or otherwise obsolete. Progress in the law is happening all the time. The law metamorphoses because it has the built-in capability for growth and because life presupposes change. What counts in the final analysis is not the reason for a legal development but the fact that it has in fact transpired. As long as it has not, I think it a mistake to rely excessively on fairness or justice as an alternative to law.

I fully agree with Professor Doehring that, *au fond*, legitimacy ought to be regarded as interchangeable with legality. That being the case, you may well ask: what is the value added of legitimacy when juxtaposed with legality? Why bring legitimacy into the picture at all? My response is that this may be either a shrewd stratagem or a useful debating tool. A stratagem inasmuch as we, the lawyers, have created – to use computer lingo – a firewall around us. We resent political scientists and other scholars from diverse disciplines who address us in their peculiar jargon, an argot that we often do not fathom properly. If somebody talks to us in that other-discipline language, we may not pay too much heed to what is being said. Reliance on legitimacy is one way for the outsider to penetrate the firewall, because on the face of it the expression is an integral part of our vocabulary. But be careful: the outcome is liable to be that whoever employed that term chose to do so only in order to lower our defences, and that this person wishes to implant a virus – or a Trojan horse – contaminating our mental software.

As for my reference to legitimacy as a debating tool, what I mean is that if I present an argument and I persuade you, fine. But I may look at you, notice that your eyes are glazed and conclude that you are not really listening. So what do I do? I raise my voice. This may still not help. What do I do next? I bang the table. Let me tell you, extrapolating on Alf Ross, resort to the term legitimacy is the equivalent of banging the table.

H. Keller: My discussion input consists of three points: the first point is an observation concerning the development of international legal discourse. The second one concerns the dialogue we have with partners coming from other disciplines. And, lastly, I will talk about the difficulties we have discussing 'legitimacy' in international law.

First: whenever we discuss fundamental issues in international law, we can, generally speaking, distinguish two phases. In the first one, the discussion is mostly dominated by ideas, metaphors or topoi borrowed from the national level. The relationship between national and international law, for instance, is a good illustration of this point. In the first phase, we are prone to devise a hierarchy of norms and draw an analogy between the supremacy of federal over state law on the one hand, and the international law - domestic law duality on the other. The rationale for this reaction is simple. We are all trained lawyers in national, mostly constitutional law. It is our education and socialisation that pre-structure our way of reasoning, and through which we are given our anchorage in national connotations.

The second phase of the discussion is mainly characterized by a differentiation. The usual argument is: the domestic analogy[1] is a dangerous one because the national and international realms are fundamentally different in character. With regard to the legitimacy problem in international law, we are in this second phase of the discussion. The first writings on international legitimacy were clearly dominated by a domestic approach, i.e. in the sense of transposing domestic notions (democratization, state consent, cohesion) into the international arena. Soon after that we entered the second phase admitting that the domestic analogy is too undifferentiated a concept to fit the unique characteristics of the international system. In the international arena, there is no global demos in the name of which governance could take place. State consent is only a very limited instrument to legitimize secondary international law. In this second phase, the discussion becomes more differentiated in character, but also more complex, because we have to argue from a purely

[1] For an excellent review of the domestic analogy debate *see* Asher Alkoby, "Non-State Actors and the Legitimacy of International Environmental Law", in: *Non-State Actors and International Law* 3 (2003), 50–64.

international law point of view where the specifics of the international system form the nodal point of the argumentation.

My second point: since the 1990s, we have been observing a growing interest in international law and therefore an increasing amount of scientific writings about the legitimacy question. Traditionally, the probing of the legitimacy question was the terrain of lawyers and political philosophers. Nowadays, however, we have a much broader scientific interest in this issue. Political scientists, sociological scientists and economists are all dealing with legitimacy. This diversification of the legitimacy analysis eclipses more than it elucidates. Not only does every discipline have its own conception of legitimacy, but also its own methological approach for measuring legitimacy. My perception is that we know little about the methological approaches of the other disciplines. For example, how do we measure the implementation of international law? What are the relevant data that ought to be collected? My impression is, in that I follow Mr. Dinstein, that the dialogue we have with academics from other disciplines is really in a fledgling state. Our discipline has to overcome certain inhibitions and probably we have to approach scientific researchers from other fields more enthusiastically, and more interdisciplinary work has yet to be done.

My third point: as mentioned earlier, we are in the second stage of legitimacy enquiry, in which the argumentation is somehow emancipated from the national law discourse and more differentiated. The programme drafted by Professor Wolfrum clearly shows this growing sensibility and the need for differentiation. The legitimacy question is different for secondary law promulgated by international organizations than for judgments by international courts.

However, even within this narrower categorization of the legitimacy question we still have to take into account even more specifics. And I agree with Robert Keohane who yesterday said: "Legitimacy is the very question of an ecological, environmental run institution" or with Mr. Bothe, who said that "legitimacy has a very historical dimension". I want to illustrate this with the example of *competence-competence*: The *competence-competence* question is clearly linked to the legitimacy question, which can be answered very differently. Take the example of the European Court of Human Rights and the European Court of Justice. For both courts in the European realm, it is clearly accepted that they have *competence-competence*. What may be accepted in Europe, however, is disputed, for example, with the Inter-American Court of Human Rights and is highly disputed with the Committee of the International Covenant of Political and Civil Rights. Thus, even in the context of the narrower category of international tribunals or courts we have to take into account a variety of specifics in answering one legitimacy question.

J.A. Frowein: I'm not surprised that it was Yoram Dinstein who told us a moment ago that the notions of legality on the one hand, legitimacy on the other hand have played a crucial and very destructive role in the late period of the Weimar Constitution in Germany, and he quoted the famous Carl Schmitt sayings. That is something which should warn us and should make it clear that one can easily misuse these terms. On the other hand, I do not believe – and in that respect I part company with Yoram Dinstein – that you can do away with the issue just by showing that dangerous development. And I think in fact Yoram Dinstein proved that he was not really doing away with the issue, because he then came to the procedure by which law is being changed and he somehow admitted that as soon as the partners, who are the important ones, feel that the law is no longer legitimate, it will finally be changed. I think the important issue before us during this conference is: how do you find indications for the law having become illegitimate? And that of course is a very difficult issue.

Now, I think one should make a little distinction – which came about in several of the papers and I think very much in Professor Wolfrum's paper – between two questions of legitimacy, namely on the one hand legitimacy of international law as such and on the other hand legitimacy of specific rules, or rather international law, in specific areas, for instance concerning specific institutions or specific decisions which have been taken. Now the issue of legitimacy of international law as such has been a subject of discussion throughout the centuries, and the difficulty with a valid enforcement procedure of international law has very much to do with that. For a long time, international lawyers could have the feeling that other areas of the social sciences for that reason did not regard international law as something in any way legitimate. And I must say I think we have proof on the table today, in particular with Professor Jürgen Habermas sitting with us and discussing the issue of legitimacy, that this period is over. From what he has written recently, I take it he is not going to try to convince us that international law has no legitimacy whatsoever. When we first discussed these matters about 30 years ago, I had the feeling that he was willing practically to dispute that the law in international disputes or issues really has a role to play.

What can we say concerning the legitimacy of international law? Although it is very difficult to add a few new thoughts to what has been debated over one and a half days, I shall come back to some truisms which are, I assume, not very much debated among us. It has been confirmed that, of course, where you have the consent of all those involved, namely all the subjects of international law either to a treaty or to practice and custom and opinio iuris, as Professor Pellet rightly underlined, you have no difficulty in coming to the conclusion that all those have recognized the outcome as legitimate. Let me remind you that we have a very important notion still valid in international law, and that is the notion of the persistent objector to rules of international law. Remember that when the Federal Republic of Germany had not ratified the first treaty on the continental shelf of 1958 it was argued that the rules of delimitation had already become binding international law. The Federal Republic argued before the International Court of Justice: we have always opposed that and the Court held, rightly, that Germany cannot be bound, even accepting that there could have been a custom otherwise.

This shows that where you have consent of the states, legitimacy of the legal rule can hardly be put into question. There may nevertheless be interesting constitutional issues in the internal order of states. Professor Wolfrum referred to that in his first introduction. He used one of the Constitutional Court decisions, the one concerning the NATO strategy, putting in an indirect manner the question whether the Court decided the matter rightly. Since I defended the case before the Court, I think the Court was right! But what is the important issue that Professor Wolfrum referred to? He said: the question arises: how do you involve parliament in such a developing situation? And did the Court see all the possibilities there? I am not going to go into details, but I think that's a very valid and important point.

I would like to add concerning general international law that we can see here something which is very well known in legal philosophy and legal tradition in internal law: there are many rules of international law which you can deduce on the same basis as the notion of Not- and Verstandesstaat (the state born out of bare necessity and because of reason), the rational argument which was alluded to a moment ago. Let me just mention two very important matters we will all agree on: pacta sunt servanda on the one hand, neminem caedere on the other, namely not to violate the rights of others and in particular to respect the sovereignty of others. Those are intrinsic rules which cannot be put into doubt, and their legitimacy stems from the very idea of a legal system. Now I come to the famous Henkon saying in that context: almost all states respect almost all rules of international law in almost all cases. This is more meaningful than many people think. And it is clear proof that international law as national law plays a very important role in interstate dealings.

Legitimacy of international institutions. The question was put: to what extent can the mandate of an international institution be broadened by practice? I think we all know that this is a continuous procedure and nobody can claim that you could foresee in 1945 what the Security Council would do with the Criminal Tribunals or with the terrorism resolutions. Although, if you look closely, it is quite evident that you had early indications that what the Council could do could go very far. But during a period where it was practically blocked, there was little evidence for it. Where you have all those concerned in a specific international organization involved in the development of the practice, no issue of legitimacy will arise. But where you have the typical insider-outsider problem, which was mentioned concerning the Security Council, the issue becomes very relevant and very important. And there are no easy solutions. I have tried to appeal to the responsibility in particular of the P5 in that area concerning transparency and concerning the overcoming of formulations which from the very beginning gave both sides the possibility of unilaterally interpreting the resolutions and thereby come to the conclusion that what one part of the Security Council sees as a binding resolution is seen by the other side as exactly the opposite in legal terms. I think this is a very great problem for the legitimacy of the system and must be avoided. In the European Union system with a much more institutionalised fabric, you have a clear legitimacy of the outcome and you have judicial control and appeal mechanisms. And I think that is something which must be brought into the procedure of the Security Council in the area where individuals are being directly affected by Security Council decisions. I mentioned the listing procedure this morning. Concerning the listing issue, there is no doubt that judicial protection must exist. If on the international level, you don't have it, national or regional courts must step into that lacuna and must provide the individual with that protection. What the Court of First Instance completely overlooked in its decision in the autumn of last year is what the United States courts during the Rhodesia embargo already decided – and rightly so I submit – that national courts are not automatically bound by decisions of the Security Council. This depends on the link between the international and the national systems.

I skip what I wanted to say on specific rules concerning due process. What I have considered to be a partial constitutionalisation of international law as a phenomenon which you can watch from developments during the last 20 or 30 years is something which can and must be seen as adding to the legitimacy of the international law fabric as a whole. What is being called regime building or global governance is – if developed in the right manner by states and by those concerned – really something which can be of great importance for legitimacy. And in that respect, I refer in particular to the system controlling the use of force, which is not fully operative, but nevertheless plays an important role, to human rights institutions, to institutions sanctioning states which do not comply with fundamental standards of human rights. And in all that what you have now is a common recognition of specific common international law values, and they make international law much more legitimate than it used to be at earlier times. Thank you.

R. Keohane: In view of the controversy that my arguments at this conference here have generated, I am especially grateful to the organizers that I've been invited. And since I agree with the last three speakers and almost everything they said, my comments can be seen as a response to Professor Dinstein and his stimulating talk.

Three preliminary remarks: first, I would bang the table, but after 10 hours of a conference – this is a record for me, and I've been around a long time – 10 hours straight of a conference, I don't have the strength to bang the table, so I will talk about legitimacy instead. Rousseau talked about legitimacy in the 1760s. He asked: what would make authority legitimate? This is the same question that Daniel Bodansky raised today. This is not a concept that comes entirely out of the old regime and it's not a concept of international law that somehow has been hijacked by political theorists, it's a deep concept in political philosophy. It may go back beyond Rousseau, but it certainly goes back to Rousseau, which is almost 250 years ago. And Rousseau is not noted for having used political science jargon. Professor Dinstein sees legitimacy as a bastard term – well, images depend on one's view. I would regard it as a potentially sturdy hybrid.

Now I want to make six general points. But what I want to do is to speak to Professor Dinstein and to those of you who believe that international law should be strengthened. I take that as a premise, probably shared by almost everybody, maybe everybody at this conference. Why should you want to promote and specify the concept of legitimacy in international law? My view is, Professor Dinstein, that it is in your self-interest, broadly conceived, to support the notion of legitimacy. By opposing it you're shooting yourself in the foot. The concepts of legitimacy and especially of sociological legitimacy are needed to keep international law viable and strong in the modern era. The first point is that international law lacks the constitutional status of law in a constitutional democracy. The people have not said: we authorize. We authorize courts to make binding decisions for us. Only states have done this. So the authorization is highly indirect. Second, in democratic theory and practice, authorization needs to be continually repeated. It's not sufficient to have authorization at some point in the past, in the distant past. It needs to be repeated in a regular fashion. In domestic democracies, elections regularly repeat authorization – if only implicitly. But no such process, no overall process, takes place in world politics. Third: as a result, international law not only lacks centralized power, it lacks the reaffirmation of public support. And it may lack such support entirely, especially if governments – far be it from me as a citizen of the United States to suggest the possibility – oppose and undermine international law with their citizens. Fourth: there is no regular political process in which the public participates, by which the content of international law can be changed through legislation. So the primary rules of international law may not change quickly when values or conditions change. There is no regular procedure for doing that. And, as a result, support for international law may decline, not because the law changes, but because it failed to change in response to changes in conditions or values. Two examples: first, globalisation has made an international law of cooperation more essential. The long peace has made international law of coexistence less needed because of declining threats of great power war. So demands are made for an extension of international law, which some people resist, but which is a necessary result of these shifts in conditions. And, secondly, the spread of democracy means that to gain the support of states, international law increasingly needs the support of publics. And to gain public support, international law norms must bear some relationship to democratic principles. Fifth: a demand for legitimacy in international law is therefore a useful indicator, a kind of warning signal of gaps between international law and political values or conditions. If you see controversy about legitimacy, it's probably a danger sign. The analogy is: if the oil light is on in your car, you had better stop and check it. So legitimacy therefore is very valuable or should be valuable to any supporter of international law because it provides this kind of warning indicator before the car stops entirely and blows up in the middle of the road. Now, it's clear that in a democratic era it would be a mistake for democracies to overemphasize democratic principles. That's why I am not in favour of simply relying on the domestic analogy, because we are in a divided world. There are other states that are not democratic; we have to have agreements with those states as well. What this suggests is that John Rawls, a name that has not yet been mentioned at this conference after 15 hours, in the *Law of Peoples* pulls back on what many thought would be his extension of democratic or liberal principles to world, to say: no, we have to be content with other decent peoples following certain more limited principles. Democratic norms are important because, if international law is consistent with them, support for international law in democracies will be enhanced. Support for democratic norms doesn't mean that democratic principles have to be overextended, much less by the use of force elsewhere.

So, if I conclude that if we want to have strong international law in an age which is a democratic age, the concept of legitimacy is essential. Now I recognize that there is indeed a real danger, as the invocation of Carl Schmitt's name suggests, that emphasizing legitimacy could undermine legality. But to me the antidote to this danger cannot be to banish the idea of legitimacy or the word legitimacy from discourse, because issues of fairness, issues of democratic principles will not disappear. The issue would come up in some other word, in some other form. It seems to me that the best antidote to this potential problem, which is a serious problem, is to specify conditions for legitimacy and in as precise a way as possible, so that the concept is more difficult to abuse. The more precisely defined, the harder it will be for those who will indeed try to abuse it to abuse it.

So my conclusion is that specifying the conditions for legitimacy and listening to the demands for greater legitimacy is in the self-interest of those who favour stronger international law. Professor Dinstein, I conclude that in pursuing your enlightened self-interest, you should embrace the concept of legitimacy and not reject it. Thank you.

Y. Dinstein: Let me start with Professor Keohane's comments. What you want is not a stronger international law: what you want is a totally different legal system which may very well exist in a far-away galaxy, but has nothing to do with the realities of Planet Earth. You envisage some sort of a world-wide gathering of people in which they elect their representatives for a world parliament; and that world parliament will enact certain laws that, for reasons that escape me, you call international law. Yet, should this scenario ever unfold – which I doubt, at least in the foreseeable future – the emerging legal system would no longer constitute veritable international law. The world that you dream about will be united into a single global State – perhaps based on a system of world federalism – and that, by definition, will eliminate the need for international law. International law posits the coexistence of several sovereign

States, independent of each other. This is the system that you, political scientists, like to call the Westphalian System.

The Westphalian System obviously has undergone tremendous modifications since 1648. Nevertheless, the foundations of the system have not been shaken. The most fundamental element is that only States (plus clusters of States, namely, Inter-Governmental Organizations) – and not individual human beings – create international law, principally through custom or treaty. Since the State itself is a creature of international law, what this construct denotes is a paradox of sorts: only the creatures of international law create international law; whereas those who are not created by international law (human beings) do not create it. Human beings can be, and are, the subjects of multiple international human rights as well as duties, but they do not participate at all in the process of international law-making. Consequently, the convocation of a rather fantasy-oriented world parliament – elected directly by human beings – is irrelevant to the actual world in which we find ourselves (for better or worse).

As for the self-interest of international law, I always suspect people who tell me that they know best what my self-interest is: I'd rather define my self-interest for myself. Allow me to reiterate what I said earlier: international law has come a long way, and so far it has survived quite successfully by adapting itself to ever-altering circumstances. I am sure that further adaptations will be required, and they will take place in the years ahead. But, whereas I believe in evolution, I do not believe in an utter revolution. I suspect all revolutions, since – like the French Revolution – they ultimately devour their own children.

I want also to respond to Professor Frowein. I was thinking: what illustration should I come up with? I have decided that the most fitting example might relate to the instrument that is probably closest to your heart, *viz.* the European Convention of Human Rights. When the Convention was adopted, it lacked *inter alia* a right of appeal and, moreover, it lacked a complementary European Social Charter. Over the years, European public opinion was aroused: people throughout Europe have come to feel – rightly, in my opinion – that in a fair and just constellation of human rights you need a right of appeal, and a Social Charter is indispensable. The system has in the meantime been revised, to incorporate these and other missing pieces in the European human rights mosaic (such as the principle of *non bis in idem*). The question may be posed: what has engendered these additions? The answer is: the communal sense that, in their absence, the system was unfair or unjust. But it does not follow that, as long as the system endured without the subsequent changes, it was illegitimate. When legitimacy permeates the discourse, there is an invidious – not to say insidious – implication that the pre-existing system deserved to collapse. The Carl Schmitt attack against the Weimar Republic epitomizes this mindset, even if it is a rather extreme case in point.

I am suggesting – and I am convinced that you, Professor Frowein, will completely agree – that, even as long as the pre-existing system lasted unaltered, it still did a lot of good, warts and all. Yes, it had to be rectified, repaired, fixed; and yes, it has been rectified, repaired, fixed. But it does not follow that, until being fixed, the system was tainted with illegitimacy. This is why I'd rather do away altogether with the notion of legitimacy. I do not close my eyes to what lies behind the expression legitimacy. What lies behind it, as I indicated in my presentation, is the notion of what is fair and just. The trouble is that, although we can sometimes all agree on what is fair and just – as happened in Europe in the sphere of human rights – frequently our subjective perceptions collide head-on. When there is no agreement, neither fairness nor justice *in abstracto* provides us with a reliable compass.

R. Keohane: Can I make one factual correction? Those of you who read my paper know that it opposes a world parliament. Indeed, it takes some pains to criticize the notion of a world parliament and argues that there is no global public and, therefore, there can't be in a foreseeable future any such entity.

R. Müllerson: My friend Yoram Dinstein always uses very vivid allegories and comparisons that well emphasise his points, which usually are interesting and inspiring. Today he used the analogy of IT technology in trying to clarify the relationship between legality and legitimacy. I would try to respond to him along the same lines. I don't know, Yoram, what you do when different viruses or spam start to enter your computer, but I have in such situations sometimes increased the level of protection of my computer. This isolates it from undesired outside interferences, Trojan horses included. But do you know what then happens? Isolating your computer from outside interferences you yourself become isolated from the wider world. You can't then reach certain web sites, open certain attachments or download some files. And new updates don't reach your computer because you have isolated it from the many services and benefits of the Internet. I believe something like that happens if international lawyers try to isolate themselves from other disciplines like political science, philosophy and history; retaining the purity and internal coherence of their discipline they at the same time become isolated from the context within which, and even more importantly for which, international law exists. Then international law may find itself in the situation of a computer that has been too well protected from any outside interference. Law becomes self-sufficient, internally coherent and maybe even full of noble ideals, but such international law has very little impact on the real world. There would be two parallel universes – legal and factual – that do not overlap or interact. I believe this, to a certain extent, has happened to international law. One of the reasons why at King's College London, together with the War Studies Department of the College, I initiated a new programme (MA on International Peace and Security) was the sense of the existing wide gap between studies of international law and politics. This is an interdisciplinary programme that tries to combine elements of international law and politics, and through such combination to increase the impact which international law has on international politics. Yoram, you gave a very good comparison but it may well work against the point you were trying to make. Thank you.

W. Heintschel v. Heinegg: First of all, I strongly reject any accusation that those who are characterized as traditionalist or conservative international lawyers refuse a dialogue with international relations or with political sciences. This is certainly not true. Otherwise, we wouldn't be international lawyers. It is only the concept of legitimacy which gives me a little headache. I hope that nobody will be surprised that I am a supporter of Yoram Dinstein, and not of anybody else who has taken the floor so far in favour of legitimacy. I also disagree with what Professor Frowein has concluded from what Yoram Dinstein has said – even though I do not need to defend Yoram Dinstein against anybody in the world. But the point is the following: let us just concentrate on the question of a change in the law. It may happen that one state starts to consider the existing law as inappropriate to its interest, for whatever reasons. It could be that the state considers the existing law illegitimate, it could be also for mere greed that the state in question wants to change the law. We usually do not care about the motives unless it comes to opinio iuris, then we do deal with some subjective element. In all other respects, however, we do not care about motives. Who cares about motives? At least international lawyers should not. It is interesting to understand why states have taken the one choice or the other. This, however, has nothing to do with the law. So let us assume that a state has started deviating from the law and slowly but surely other states follow. So what is the situation which ensues from that development? Well, some of you would say: yes, the reason why an increasing number of states have been deviating from the law is that they consider the existing law illegitimate. So what? What benefit is in that finding? None at all. And it would not even contribute to a clarification of the situation because I would say: let's wait and see where the development ends. It may be that some new norm of international law develops from that deviation, or it may not. Therefore, the question is whether the old law has become derogated by the emergence of a new norm of customary international law. If doubts remain we may be confronted with a non-liquet situation but we may certainly not say that we have a gap that may be filled by reference to legitimacy. I'm sorry. But this is certainly not what international law is about. Thank you very much.

R. Howse: I've been trying to think hard about what is actually producing some of the sharp and even polemically expressed divisions that we've been hearing over the last few hours and even over the last couple of days. And in one view it might be some kind of conflict between disciplines. But I wanted to propose an alternative or perhaps complementary account of what in fact is the issue here. I think that the issue may well be that there are really very different implicit views of our historical situation at play. One view of our historical situation is represented by the ideas of the international human rights movement, and ideas that have been expressed to some extent by Armin von Bogdandy here, which are that there is an emergent, if not universal, political order, a kind of universal political morality that's reflected in the international legal order that's been developing. There genuinely are agreed global values that produce a kind of political morality that can underpin a conception of legitimacy that can be widely agreed. And there are historical accounts of progress that might underpin such a conception. And then there is the view that the world remains fundamentally divided, that actually the sites of normative struggle that produced political moralities remain primarily within closed political communities within states, within nation states. And if one accepts that view or thinks of that as the better account of our current historical situation, then the talk about legitimacy seems in a way question-begging. The problem that legitimacy might need to solve, which is that of normative division or disagreement, is the very problem that prevents the emergence of a global concept of legitimacy. And this is in a way, it seems to me, the fundamental divide that Professor Keohane in his paper tries to finesse by suggesting that there may be a magical equilibrium. In other words, we can split the difference between these historical visions and say: there may be just enough minimal level of agreement to get us the minimum level of legitimacy we need to get international institutions to do what we want them to do and be accepted as doing that. But why should this magical equilibrium actually ever exist? It seems therefore that in fact this is much more of an institutional fantasy than what the lawyers are inventing. I think that unless we address the problem of what our historical situation is and return to the basic question of what a rational account of the trajectory of the human situation is, we will really not address what may be the underlying issue dividing us here or dividing many of you. And, therefore, we will end up, rather than having illumination, getting increasingly irritated with one another.

M. Bothe: Those in the room who know both Yoram Dinstein and myself know that from time to time we have a controversy. However, when I think he is wrong I always have difficulties finding out why, but from time to time I manage – at least I think I do. Now, his thesis is based on at least two assumptions: the first relates to the Westphalian system. Two essential elements of the Westphalian system have been retained: the land surface of the world is still divided into states, territorial states. This is still true. Certainly, the states are not what they were in 1648. And you have yourself said: international law has come a long way. How long a way? The essential difference, I think, is the existence of a number of transnational facts and actors which do not respect these territorial boundaries. This is why, at least sociologically, it is no longer true that only states make the law. International law-making is a much more complex process.

The second assumption is about the role of legal science and of the lawyer. If the lawyer in legal practice just said 'I only find out what the law is', then everything would be simple. That is a kind of self-limitation which is defendable. But it does not take into account the realities of the world. As we all know, it is only after a court hands down a judgment that we really know what the law is. And the parties are bound to abide by the sentence. But we also know that this may or may not happen and it may happen sooner or later. There are, in addition, different circumstances which determine our behaviour. This is the point where the lawyer starts asking questions of legitimacy. Choices about the interpretation of the law are open. So the question is: is any argument which is not a legal one for that reason outside the scope of our consideration as lawyers? Should we lawyers not be interested in it and not argue about it? I think we should.

H. Neuhold: In my opinion, our debate revolves around the limits of our discipline. The key question for international lawyers in this context is: are we satisfied with the diagnosis that the behaviour of a subject of international law is lawful or illegal and leave other aspects of international relations to experts in other fields, in particular to political scientists, economists, historians, sociologists and psychologists, and ignore their findings – or should we try to engage in a dialogue with them and take their conclusions into account? I, for one, would support efforts at an interdisciplinary exchange of views with colleagues like Professor Robert Keohane. We have a lot to learn from them but might also contribute a little to our mutual understanding of complex international phenomena. Political scientists tend to underrate the significance of international law in decision making by foreign policy bureaucracies.

As an international lawyer, I am also interested in the crucial "why" questions. I would like to know more about the reasons for which states and other subjects of international law comply with legal rules. To what extent is compliance voluntary and not motivated by the fear of sanctions? It is here that legitimacy comes into play and accounts for the mid- and long-term effectiveness of the international legal order.

Another question concerns the reasons for changes in international legal norms. One explanation focuses on shifts in the distribution of power or economic and technological developments, yet another on changing value perceptions, in other words considerations of legitimacy.

It is the importance each of us attaches to questions like these and the interdisciplinary perspective which results in the differences in our approach to international law.

T. Treves: I find myself in the situation of agreeing on most points with both Yoram Dinstein and Bob Keohane. How can I perform such a miracle? I simply think that these two participants to our debate adopt different points of departure, move in a different setting. I would say that Yoram Dinstein adopts the internal point of view. He moves within the legal discourse and resents invasions by Trojan horses that belong to another area of language and to another discipline. Bob Keohane's point of view is external to the purely legal approach based on what is obligatory and what is not. He develops a discourse from an external point of view, a discourse that, from that point of view, I share. In my view, the basic idea of legitimacy as proposed by Robert Keohane and synthesized in his image of the red light that puts the driver on the alert that something might be going wrong in the engine is perfectly correct. From the external viewpoint, from a non-normative viewpoint, one can see, for example, defects in the mechanism for the creation and application of rules and perhaps ways and means to mend them. Of course – and I share the point just made by Hanspeter Neuhold – there are and there have always been points of contact between the two worlds, between the two languages. For instance the question: "why does customary law bind states?" is a question that brings us to a kind of point of passage between the internal and the external points of view. And, as you know, different authors from Grotius to Kelsen, among many others, have given different answers. But basically, the two worlds, the two languages are separate. And I think it makes sense to try to keep them separate.

R. Keohane: I'll be very brief. I think the comments from the floor have been extremely interesting. I think, Professor Treves, you're right about the internal-external distinction and it does mean that I'm the driver and not the mechanic. I can't fix the system if I see the light on, but I can perhaps ask you if you might want to fix it because you have the tools to do so. With respect to Professor Howse's point: I agree with the analysis up to a point, but I think there are two different conceptions here, and there is a third conception that Professor Howse mentioned: is there an emergence of a universal political morality? This is one view. Or are there still strong divisions among nation states? Of course the answer is: there are both. And, furthermore, there is what we call globalisation, the emergence of transnational actors, multinational corporations, that is the whole new dimension. So we are in a period of very rapid transition and we have to hold all of these conceptions in our minds. None of them is entirely false and none of them is entirely correct. And the reason that I do not propose a parliament of man is that I don't believe that we have reached the universal political morality which trumps the nation state. But I think these are all elements of the process, and the notion of legitimacy is therefore crucial in making linkages among them.

J.A. Frowein: I would like to make two comments concerning the extremely interesting presentation by Professor Habermas on issues which he sees from a perspective which is not always ours, but which, I think, can enrich us. The first concerns the democratic legitimacy issue. In that respect, I think you did not really address – as far as I could understand it – the difficulties existing in the international system. But here I can just refer to what Professor Keohane has again just stated, namely that you cannot easily transfer the basic system of democratic principles to the international sphere. Nevertheless, concerning transparency or procedure you may be able to pick out some important points from the democratic system. But what I would like to add is something which I find extremely important: with the disintegration of the Soviet Union on the one hand, Yugoslavia on the other, the European Union adopted guidelines for the recognition of new states in areas which were not expected to become part of the European Union and will in fact mostly not become part, particularly the former Soviet Union. Here the rule of law and democracy, and minority protection were seen as conditions for recognition. That is a step in the right direction and is something which international lawyers and political scientists must take into account. My second remark concerns what you called the global governance interference with internal matters, in particular well organized democratic and constitutional states. And you mentioned the case of the Somali citizens who found themselves in Sweden, being deprived of their rights, in fact one of them being a Swedish citizen. Now, my argument was that exactly at that point the internal system must take control of the matter. Swedish courts or regional courts must take control of that. It is a big misunderstanding to say that, because the Security Council has decided that no other control can be possible. We have many examples. I refer to the early American cases on the Rhodesia situation. But we also have the situation that states do not comply with Security Council resolutions under Chapter VII. A much more well organized constitutional democracy should not be willing to comply with Security Council resolutions which are clearly in violation of basic principles of human rights.

Y. Dinstein: A number of questions have been addressed to me. The first – by Professor Müllerson – sounds, to use your terminology, purely allegorical. But I cannot leave that allegory aside. Of course, isolation is not what I am aiming at. Every international lawyer surfs the Internet much of the time, with a view to having extensive communications. However, when I communicate with you, I want to make sure that no hacker will manage to get into the software, contaminate the system and subvert it. I therefore need to create a firewall. But a firewall is not designed to block off communication altogether. There is a trade-off in the firewall: there is less freedom of access – although not a *reductio ad absurdum* – and more protection. One sacrifices some free access for that added protection.

The second is Mr. Howse's comment. Let me again take human rights as a paradigm, this time on a global basis. There is a theory of the evolution of human rights in three successive generations: the first generation is comprised of civil and political rights; the second generation consists of economic, social and cultural rights; and the third generation encompasses the rights to development, to peace, to an unpolluted environment, etc. The first two generations are often linked to two of the three famous slogans of the French Revolution: *liberté* stands for civil and political rights, *égalité* represents social, economic and cultural rights. These two generations of human rights are reflected in the twin International Covenants of 1966 which are in force. The third generation – frequently associated with the third slogan of the French Revolution, *fraternité*, but better expressed in the word *solidarité* – is still in a stage of evolution. The fact that the human rights of the third generation are not yet in place does not delegitimize human rights of the preceding two generations that are part and parcel of the *lex lata*. Even if you think very strongly that there must be a human right to an unpolluted environment, even if you feel that there must be a human right to peace, even if you believe that a human right to sustainable development must be in effect, their non-recognition by positive law does not delegitimize the existing system.

To Professor Neuhold, I say: of course I use language other than lawful and unlawful, and I do that all the time. Whenever I do not like something, I contend that it is unjust, unfair, improper, illogical, socio-economically unsatisfactory, and so on. The sole derogatory adjective that I never use is illegitimate. I do not use it because I find it confusing and misleading.

As for Professor Bothe, my response is that, from the very beginning, international law has dealt with non-State actors. Pirates go back to the dawn of international law. Today we have terrorists. But there is no big conceptual difference, philosophically or intellectually, between pirates and terrorists. And, obviously, we have other non-State actors at the present juncture. But none of them participates in the international law-making process. You have referred to multinational corporations. The point is that multinational corporations – whatever economic weight they throw around – can neither be Contracting Parties to treaties nor can they contribute to the consolidation of customary law. Treaties and customary law are still created exclusively by States and by their progeny: Inter-Governmental Organizations. That has not changed since Westphalia. I know that some scholars would like to modify this state of affairs as part of their vision of *lex ferenda*. You and I have participated in a series of conferences on the subject of sovereignty and we have locked horns on these issues. But I do not believe that we actually disagree on the basics in terms of the *lex lata.*

Finally, with regard to Judge Treves's observation about the red light supposedly flashing in the car of international law. What are we talking about? Since the adoption of the semi-constitutional UN Charter and the prohibition of the use of force in international relations, since the exponential development of human rights, since the tremendous evolution of the Law of the Sea, not to mention other significant recent changes in international law, there has existed a whole new model of car. This new model has replaced countless previous models constructed since 1648. So why would a red light flash? I do not think that the new car is in bad shape, and I certainly do not believe that there is cause for an acute warning signal. Those who complain about the car do not genuinely find too much fault in it, given its specifications. The real question raised is not about the car but about the drivers. The car is being driven today, as previous models have been steered since Westphalia, by States. The course charted by States is often unfortunate, and all of us regret a host of political decisions to go in one direction and not to opt for another. Nevertheless, if you envisage a Brave New World in which individuals are driving the car – instead of States – what you will have is not a new model of the same car, but a totally new device resulting from a quantum leap. Will it be better than our car? Possibly, although nobody knows for sure. For my part, I set my sights lower. I do not gaze at the stars but am addressing the world as it exists around us. I am prepared to take, and live by, international law as I find it. I hope for further improvements, but I do not put my trust in futuristic scenarios.

List of Participants

Abi-Saab, Georges
Institut de Hautes Etudes Internationales, WTO Appellate Body, Clarens, Switzerland

von Achenbach, Jelena
Max Planck Institute for Comparative Public Law and International Law, Heidelberg, Germany

Addison-Agyei, Sange
Max Planck Institute for Comparative Public Law and International Law, Heidelberg, Germany

Afsah, Ebrahim
Max Planck Institute for Comparative Public Law and International Law, Heidelberg, Germany

Anand, Ram
Jawarahal Nehru University, New Delhi, India

Baiyayev, Gochmuhamed
University of Heidelberg, Heidelberg, Germany

Bast, Jürgen
Max Planck Institute for Comparative Public Law and International Law, Heidelberg, Germany

Benedek, Wolfgang
University of Graz, Institute of International Law, Graz, Austria

Benzing, Markus
Max Planck Institute for Comparative Public Law and International Law, Heidelberg, Germany

Bernhardt, Rudolf
Former Director at the Max Planck Institute for Comparative Public Law and International Law, Heidelberg, Germany

Beyerlin, Ulrich
Max Planck Institute for Comparative Public Law and International Law, Heidelberg, Germany

Böckenförde, Markus
Max Planck Institute for Comparative Public Law and International Law, Heidelberg, Germany

Bodansky, Daniel
University of Georgia, School of Law, Athens, GA, USA

von Bogdandy, Armin
Director at the Max Planck Institute for Comparative Public Law and International Law, Heidelberg, Germany

Bothe, Michael
University of Frankfurt (Main), Frankfurt, Germany

Boudass, Ghada
University of Paris V – René Descartes, Paris, France

Bradley, Curtis A.
Duke University, School of Law, Durham, N.C., USA

Braig, Jochen
Max Planck Institute for Comparative Public Law and International Law, Heidelberg, Germany

Brunnée, Jutta
University of Toronto, Faculty of Law, Toronto, Ontario, Canada

Carazo, Pía
Max Planck Institute for Comparative Public Law and International Law, Heidelberg, Germany

Chen, Xiaohua
Peking University, Law School, Peking, China

Clados, Miriam
Max Planck Institute for Comparative Public Law and International Law, Heidelberg, Germany

Cot, Jean-Pierre
Judge at the International Tribunal for the Law of the Sea, Brussels, Belgium

Couzigou, Irène
University Panthéon-Assas (Paris II), Paris, France

Cruz Villalón, Pedro
Universidad Autónoma de Madrid, Faculty of Law, Madrid, Spain

Dagron, Stéphanie
Max Planck Institute for Comparative Public Law and International Law, Heidelberg, Germany

D'Amato, Anthony
Northwestern University School of Law, Chicago, IL, USA

Dann, Philipp
Max Planck Institute for Comparative Public Law and International Law, Heidelberg, Germany

Dellavalle, Sergio
University of Torino; Max Planck Institute for Comparative Public Law and International Law, Heidelberg, Germany

Deutsch, Ulrike
Max Planck Institute for Comparative Public Law and International Law, Heidelberg, Germany

de Wet, Erika
University of Amsterdam, Department of International Law, Amsterdam, The Netherlands

Dinstein, Yoram
Faculty of Law, Tel Aviv University, Tel Aviv, Israel

Doehring, Karl
Former Director at the Max Planck Institute for Comparative Public Law and International Law, Heidelberg, Germany

Edeson, William
Centre for Maritime Policy, University of Wollongong, Wollongong NSW, Australia

Eitel, Tono
Former UN Ambassador, External Member of the Max Planck Institute for Comparative Public Law and International Law, Münster, Germany

Elwan, Omaia
Max Planck Institute for Comparative Public Law and International Law, Heidelberg, Germany

Ernst, Andrea

Max Planck Institute for Comparative Public Law and International Law, Heidelberg, Germany

Feichtner, Isabel

Max Planck Institute for Comparative Public Law and International Law, Heidelberg, Germany

Feinäugle, Clemens

Max Planck Institute for Comparative Public Law and International Law, Heidelberg, Germany

Filos, Altana

Max Planck Institute for Comparative Public Law and International Law, Heidelberg, Germany

Fischer, Andreas

University of Zürich, Faculty of Law, Zürich, Switzerland

Friedrich, Jürgen

Max Planck Institute for Comparative Public Law and International Law, Heidelberg, Germany

Frowein, Jochen Abr.

Former Director at the Max Planck Institute for Comparative Public Law and International Law, Heidelberg, Germany

Gautier, Philippe

Registrar at the International Tribunal for the Law of the Sea, Hamburg, Germany

Goldmann, Matthias

Max Planck Institute for Comparative Public Law and International Law, Heidelberg, Germany

Grote, Rainer
Max Planck Institute for Comparative Public Law and International Law, Heidelberg, Germany

Guder, Leonie
Max Planck Institute for Comparative Public Law and International Law, Heidelberg, Germany

Guhr, Alexandra
Max Planck Institute for Comparative Public Law and International Law, Heidelberg, Germany

Habermas, Jürgen
University of Frankfurt, Former Director at the Max Planck Institute for Social Sciences, Starnberg, Germany

Hachgenei, Susan
Max Planck Society for the Advancement of Science, München, Germany

Hagedorn, Cornelia
Max Planck Institute for Comparative Public Law and International Law, Heidelberg, Germany

Haider, Jan Rumi
Max Planck Institute for Comparative Public Law and International Law, Heidelberg, Germany

Hanschmann, Felix
Max Planck Institute for Comparative Public Law and International Law, Heidelberg, Germany

Hartmann, Benjamin
Max Planck Institute for Comparative Public Law and International Law, Heidelberg, Germany

Hartwig, Matthias
Max Planck Institute for Comparative Public Law and International Law, Heidelberg, Germany

Häußler, Stefan
Max Planck Institute for Comparative Public Law and International Law, Heidelberg, Germany

Hayashi, Mika
Kobe University, GSICS, Kobe, Japan

Heinsch, Robert
International Criminal Court, The Hague, The Netherlands

Heintschel von Heinegg, Wolff
Europa Universität Viadrina, Faculty of Law, Frankfurt (Oder), Germany

Herdegen, Matthias
University of Bonn, Faculty of Law, Bonn, Germany

Hey, Ellen
Erasmus University Rotterdam, School of Law, Rotterdam, The Netherlands

Hilf, Meinhard
Bucerius Law School, Hamburg, Germany

Hinsch, Wilfried
University of Aachen, Institute of Philosophy, Aachen, Germany

Hofmann, Mahulena
Max Planck Institute for Comparative Public Law and International Law, Heidelberg, Germany

Hofmann, Rainer
University of Frankfurt, Faculty of Law, Frankfurt am Main, Germany

Howse, Robert
The University of Michigan Law School, Ann Arbor, Michigan, USA

Intarti, Yuni Reti
Graduate School of the European Studies Programme, University of Indonesia, Jakarta, Indonesia

Jaenicke, Günther
University of Frankfurt, External Member of the Max Planck Institute for Comparative Public Law and International Law, Berlin, Germany

Kaiser, Karen
Max Planck Institute for Comparative Public Law and International Law, Heidelberg, Germany

Keller, Helen
University of Zürich, Faculty of Law, Zürich, Switzerland

Keller, Lucy
University of Zürich, Faculty of Law, Zürich, Switzerland

Kennedy, David
European Law Research Center, Harvard Law School, Cambridge, MA, USA

Keohane, Robert
Princeton University, Woodrow Wilson School of Public and International Affairs, Princeton, NJ, USA

Khan, Rahmatullah
Jawaharlal Nehru University, New Delhi, India

Kirchhof, Paul
University of Heidelberg, Institute for Financial and Tax Law, Heidelberg, Germany

Klein, Daniel
Max Planck Institute for Comparative Public Law and International Law, Heidelberg, Germany

Knust, Mandana
Max Planck Institute for Comparative Public Law and International Law, Heidelberg, Germany

Köbele, Michael
Max Planck Institute for Comparative Public Law and International Law, Heidelberg, Germany

Kokott, Juliane
Advocate General, European Court of Justice, Luxembourg, Luxembourg

Leininger, Julia
Peace Research Institute Frankfurt, Frankfurt am Main, Germany

Less, Steven
Max Planck Institute for Comparative Public Law and International Law, Heidelberg, Germany

Liberti, Lahra
University of Rome "La Sapienza", Roma, Italy

Louth, John
Senior Editor, Law, Oxford University Press, Oxford, United Kingdom

Lutz-Bachmann, Matthias
University of Frankfurt, Frankfurt/Main, Germany

Malanczuk, Peter
City University of Hong Kong, Faculty of Law, Hong Kong, China

Mantlik, Emmanuelle
Max Planck Institute for Comparative Public Law and International Law, Heidelberg, Germany

Guerra Martins, Ana Maria
University of Lisbon, Faculty of Law, Lisbon, Portugal

Matz, Nele
Max Planck Institute for Comparative Public Law and International Law, Research Fellow at the German Federal Constitutional Court, Heidelberg, Germany

Mechlem, Kerstin
Food and Agriculture Organisation – Legal Service, Rome, Italy

Minnerop, Petra
University of Munich, Faculty of Law, München, Germany

Mits, Martins
Riga Graduate School of Law; currently: Max Planck Institute for Comparative Public Law and International Law, Heidelberg, Germany

Mirdha, Ram Niwas
The Indian Society of International Law, New Delhi, India

Morrison, Fred L.
University of Minnesota Law School, Minneapolis, MN, USA

Moschtaghi, Ramin
Max Planck Institute for Comparative Public Law and International Law, Heidelberg, Germany

Müller, Harald
Max Planck Institute for Comparative Public Law and International Law, Heidelberg, Germany

Müller, Reinhard
Frankfurter Allgemeine Zeitung, Frankfurt am Main, Germany

Müllerson, Rein
King's College London, School of Law, London, United Kingdom

Murungi, Jane
North-West University, Faculty of Law, South Africa; currently: Max Planck Institute for Comparative Public Law and International Law, Heidelberg, Germany

Neuhold, Hanspeter
University of Vienna, Institute for International Law and International Relations, Wien, Austria

Nohlen, Nicolas
Max Planck Institute for Comparative Public Law and International Law, Heidelberg, Germany

Oellers-Frahm, Karin
Max Planck Institute for Comparative Public Law and International Law, Heidelberg, Germany

Oeter, Stefan
University of Hamburg, Faculty of Law, Institute for International Affairs, Hamburg, Germany

Pellet, Alain

Université Paris X – Nanterre, Centre de Droit International (CEDIN), Nanterre, France

Pennington, Alison

Max Planck Institute for Comparative Public Law and International Law, Heidelberg, Germany

Petersen, Niels

Max Planck Institute for Comparative Public Law and International Law, Heidelberg, Germany

Philipp, Christiane

Max Planck Institute for Comparative Public Law and International Law, Heidelberg, Germany

Pichon, Jakob

Max Planck Institute for Comparative Public Law and International Law, Heidelberg, Germany

Rao, Geping

Director at the International Law Institute at Beijing University, Peking University, Law School, Peking, China

Rau, Markus

Max Planck Institute for Comparative Public Law and International Law, Heidelberg, Germany

Redman, Andy

Editorial Director, Oxford University Press, Oxford, United Kingdom

Reinold, Theresa S.

Stiftung Wissenschaft und Politik (SWP), German Institute for International Politics and Security, Berlin, Germany

Reuß, Matthias
Max Planck Institute for Comparative Public Law and International Law, Heidelberg, Germany

Riedel, Eibe
University of Mannheim, Faculty of Law, Mannheim, Germany

Röben, Volker
Max Planck Institute for Comparative Public Law and International Law, Heidelberg, Germany

Röder, Tilmann
Max Planck Institute for Comparative Public Law and International Law, Heidelberg, Germany

Roetting, Michael
Max Planck Institute for Comparative Public Law and International Law, Heidelberg, Germany

Rowedder, Heinz
University of Mannheim, Mannheim, Germany

Rudolf, Walter
University of Mainz, Institute of Legal and Economic Sciences, Mainz, Germany

Schlemmer-Schulte, Sabine
University of the Pacific, McGeorge School of Law, Sacramento, California, USA

Schmalenbach, Kirsten
University of Graz, Institute for International Law and International Relations, Graz, Austria

Schweisfurth, Theodor

European University Viadrina, Frankfurt (Oder); Max Planck Institute for Comparative Public Law and International Law, Heidelberg, Germany

Seibert-Fohr, Anja

Max Planck Institute for Comparative Public Law and International Law, Heidelberg, Germany

Steinberger, Helmut

Former Director at the Max Planck Institute for Comparative Public Law and International Law, Heidelberg, Germany; Former Judge of the German Federal Constitutional Court

Steinorth, Charlotte

London School of Economics, London, United Kingdom

Srivastava, Suresh

Indian Federation of UN Associations (IFUNA), New Delhi, India

Stelzer, Robert

Max Planck Institute for Comparative Public Law and International Law, Heidelberg, Germany

Tacconi, Flaminia

Max Planck Institute for Comparative Public Law and International Law, Heidelberg, Germany

Thomas, Eckhart

P. Keppler Verlag, Niederdorfelden, Germany

Thürer, Daniel

University of Zürich, Institute for International Law and Comparative Public Law, Zürich, Switzerland

Tiba, Firew Kebede

University of Hong Kong; currently: Max Planck Institute for Comparative Public Law and International Law, Heidelberg, Germany

Treves, Tullio

Judge at the International Tribunal of the Law of the Sea, Hamburg, Germany; University of Milan, Milano, Italy

Ulfstein, Geir

University of Oslo, Department of Public and International Law, Oslo, Norway

Vagts, Detlev

Harvard Law School, Cambridge, MA, USA

Vitzthum, Wolfgang Graf

University of Tübingen, Faculty of Law, Tübingen, Germany

Vöneky, Silja

Max Planck Institute for Comparative Public Law and International Law, Heidelberg, Germany

Wasum-Rainer, Susanne

Foreign Office, Department of Legal Affairs, Berlin, Germany

Weiler, Petra

Max Planck Institute for Comparative Public Law and International Law, Heidelberg, Germany

Wiesner, Verena

Max Planck Institute for Comparative Public Law and International Law, Heidelberg, Germany

Wolf, Sarah

Max Planck Institute for Comparative Public Law and International Law, Heidelberg, Germany

Wolfrum, Rüdiger

Judge at the International Tribunal for the Law of the Sea, President, Hamburg, Germany; Director at the Max Planck Institute for Comparative Public Law and International Law, Heidelberg, Germany

Wuerth, Ingrid

University of Cincinnati College of Law/Free University, Cincinnati, OH, USA

Zacharias, Diana

Max Planck Institute for Comparative Public Law and International Law, Heidelberg, Germany

Zhang, Qi

World Trade Institute, Switzerland; currently: Max Planck Institute for Comparative Public Law and International Law, Heidelberg, Germany

Zimmermann, Andreas

Walther-Schücking-Institut für Internationales Recht, Christian-Albrechts-Universität zu Kiel, Kiel, Germany

Zobel, Katharina

Max Planck Institute for Comparative Public Law and International Law, Heidelberg, Germany

176 Christiane *Höhn*: **Zwischen Menschenrechten und Konfliktprävention. Der Minderheitenschutz im Rahmen der Organisation für Sicherheit und Zusammenarbeit in Europa (OSZE).** 2005. XX, 418 Seiten. Geb. € 84,95

175 Nele *Matz*: **Wege zur Koordinierung völkerrechtlicher Verträge. Völkervertragsrechtliche und institutionelle Ansätze.** 2005. XXIV, 423 Seiten. Geb. € 84,95

174 Jochen Abr. *Frowein*: **Völkerrecht – Menschenrechte – Verfassungsfragen Deutschlands und Europas. Ausgewählte Schriften.** Hrsg. von Matthias *Hartwig*, Georg *Nolte*, Stefan *Oeter*, Christian *Walter*. 2004. VIII, 732 Seiten. Geb. € 119,95

173 Oliver *Dörr* (Hrsg.): **Ein Rechtslehrer in Berlin. Symposium für Albrecht Randelzhofer.** 2004. VII, 117 Seiten. Geb. € 54,95

172 Lars-Jörgen *Geburtig*: **Konkurrentenrechtsschutz aus Art. 88 Abs. 3 Satz 3 EGV. Am Beispiel von Steuervergünstigungen.** 2004. XVII, 412 Seiten (4 Seiten English Summary). Geb. € 84,95

171 Markus *Böckenförde*: **Grüne Gentechnik und Welthandel. Das Biosafety-Protokoll und seine Auswirkungen auf das Regime der WTO.** 2004. XXIX, 620 Seiten. Geb. € 99,95

170 Anja *v. Hahn*: **Traditionelles Wissen indigener und lokaler Gemeinschaften zwischen geistigen Eigentumsrechten und der public domain.** 2004. XXV, 415 Seiten. Geb. 84,95

169 Christian *Walter*, Silja *Vöneky*, Volker *Röben*, Frank *Schorkopf* (eds.): **Terrorism as a Challenge for National and International Law: Security versus Liberty?** 2004. XI, 1484 Seiten. Geb. € 169,95 zzgl. landesüblicher MwSt.

168 Kathrin *Osteneck*: **Die Umsetzung von UN-Wirtschaftssanktionen durch die Europäische Gemeinschaft.** 2004. XXXIX, 579 Seiten. Geb. € 99,95

167 Stephan *Sina*: **Der völkerrechtliche Status des Westjordanlandes und des Gaza-Streifens nach den Osloer Verträgen.** 2004. XXI, 410 Seiten. Geb. € 84,95

166 Philipp *Dann*: **Parlamente im Exekutivföderalismus.** 2004. XXIII, 474 Seiten. Geb. € 89,95

165 Rüdiger *Wolfrum* (Hrsg.): **Gleichheit und Nichtdiskriminierung im nationalen und internationalen Menschenrechtsschutz.** 2003. VIII, 299 Seiten. Geb. € 74,95

164 Rüdiger *Wolfrum*, Nele *Matz*: **Conflicts in International Environmental Law.** 2003. XI, 213 Seiten. Geb. € 64,95 zzgl. landesüblicher MwSt.

163 Adam *Bodnar*, Michał *Kowalski*, Karen *Raible*, Frank *Schorkopf* (eds.): **The Emerging Constitutional Law of the European Union.** 2003. IX, 595 Seiten. Geb. € 99,95 zzgl. landesüblicher MwSt.

162 Jochen Abr. *Frowein*, Klaus *Schartoth*, Ingo *Winkelmann*, Rüdiger *Wolfrum* (Hrsg.): **Verhandeln für den Frieden/Negotiating for Peace. Liber Amicorum Tono Eitel.** 2003. XIII, 866 Seiten. Geb. € 129,95

161 Michaela *Fries*: **Die Bedeutung von Artikel 5 (f) der Rassendiskriminierungskonvention im deutschen Recht.** 2003. XIX, 429 Seiten. Geb. € 84,95

160 Helen *Keller*: **Rezeption des Völkerrechts.** 2003. XXXV, 855 Seiten. Geb. € 129,95

159 Cordula *Dröge*: **Positive Verpflichtungen der Staaten in der Europäischen Menschenrechtskonvention.** 2003. XX, 432 Seiten. Geb. € 89,95

158 Dagmar *Richter*: **Sprachenordnung und Minderheitenschutz im schweizerischen Bundesstaat.** 2005. LIV, 1315 Seiten. Geb. € 179,95

157 Thomas *Giegerich*: **Europäische Verfassung und deutsche Verfassung im transnationalen Konstitutionalisierungsprozeß: Wechselseitige Rezeption, konstitutionelle Evolution und föderale Verflechtung.** 2003. LXV, 1534 Seiten. Geb. € 199,95

156 Julia *Sommer*: **Verwaltungskooperation am Beispiel administrativer Informationsverfahren im Europäischen Umweltrecht.** 2003. XXX, 891 Seiten. Geb. € 129,95

155 Frank *Schorkopf*: **Die Maßnahmen der XIV EU-Mitgliedstaaten gegen Österreich – Möglichkeiten und Grenzen einer „streitbaren Demokratie" auf europäischer Ebene.** 2002. XIII, 217 Seiten. Geb. € 64,95

SPRINGER NATURE

GPSR Compliance

The European Union's (EU) General Product Safety Regulation (GPSR) is a set of rules that requires consumer products to be safe and our obligations to ensure this.

If you have any concerns about our products, you can contact us on ProductSafety@springernature.com

In case Publisher is established outside the EU, the EU authorized representative is:

Springer Nature Customer Service Center GmbH
Europaplatz 3
69115 Heidelberg, Germany